ONE
STEP
OVER THE
LINE

TOWARD A HISTORY OF WOMEN
IN THE NORTH AMERICAN WESTS

ONE
STEP
OVER THE
LINE

TOWARD A HISTORY OF WOMEN
IN THE NORTH AMERICAN WESTS

ELIZABETH JAMESON & SHEILA McMANUS, EDITORS

Published by

The University of Alberta Press
Ring House 2
Edmonton, Alberta, Canada T6G 2E1

and

AU Press
Athabasca University
1 University Drive
Athabasca, Alberta, Canada T9S 3A3

Printed and bound in Canada by Houghton
Boston Printers, Saskatoon, Saskatchewan.
First edition, first printing, 2008

Index by Adrian Mather.

A volume in The West Unbound: Social and
Cultural Studies series, edited by Alvin Finkel and
Sarah Carter.

LIBRARY AND ARCHIVES CANADA
CATALOGUING IN PUBLICATION

One step over the line : toward a history of
women in the North American Wests / edited by
Elizabeth Jameson and Sheila McManus.

Includes bibliographical references and index.
(West unbound : social and cultural studies)
Includes bibliographical references and index.
print book ISBN 978-0-88864-501-2
e-book ISBN 978-1-89745-20-6

1. Women—West (U.S.)—History.
2. Women—Canada, Western—History.
3. Canada—Boundaries—United States. 4. United
States—Boundaries—Canada. I. Jameson,
Elizabeth II. McManus, Sheila, 1969-

HQ1400.O64 2008   971.20082
C2007-907580-0

The University of Alberta Press is committed to
protecting our natural environment. As part of
our efforts, this book is printed on Enviro Paper:
it contains 100% post-consumer recycled fibres
and is acid- and chlorine-free.

The University of Alberta Press and AU Press
gratefully acknowledge the support received for
their publishing programs from The Canada
Council for the Arts. They also gratefully acknowledge the financial support of the Government of
Canada through the Book Publishing Industry
Development Program (BPIDP) and from the
Alberta Foundation for the Arts for their publishing activities.

Canada Council   Conseil des Arts
for the Arts   du Canada

Canadä   Alberta Foundation for the Arts

*Title page photograph: Women workers were well
represented in a march through the streets of downtown
Medicine Hat on the first day of the Medalta Potteries
strike, 12 August 1947. [Courtesy of Hanna Osborne]*

In memory of my brother David, who pushed the important boundaries, and crossed the final one too soon. —E.J.

For every woman who has ever taken one step over the line. —S.M.

CONTENTS

SECTION THREE: PEOPLE, PLACE, AND STORIES

ACKNOWLEDGEMENTS

THIS BOOK is one product of the "Unsettled Pasts: Reconceiving the West through Women's History" conference, held at the University of Calgary in June 2002. Neither the conference nor the book would have happened without the hard work, support, and enthusiasm of many talented people. We are grateful to all of them. We first thank the diverse group of women—writers, artists, activists, historians, feminists—whose work made the conference possible and ensured its success. We thank the members of the conference organizing committee: Jennifer Bobrovitz, Geertje Boschma, Cristine Bye, Catherine Cavanaugh, Lesley Erickson, Laurel Halladay, Jennifer Hamblin, Sheila Johnston, Nadine Kozak, Margaret McCready, Grit McCreath, Nancy Millar, Patricia Roome, Char Smith, Gayle Thrift, Cora Voyageur, and Anne White. Most of all we thank Sarah Carter, who initiated the conference, provided so much of the energy and inspiration that animated it, and who, with Elizabeth Jameson, co-chaired the conference organizing committee. We also thank Susan Austen, Roland Longpré, Brenda Oslawsky, and Mark White for all their help.

A number of organizations contributed conference funding. For financial support, we thank the Social Sciences and Humanities Research

Council of Canada, the University of Calgary Special Projects Grants Committee, the University of Calgary Research Grants Committee, the Alberta Historical Resources Foundation, and the University of Calgary Planning Initiatives Fund: Office of the President and Vice-Presidents. A number of University of Calgary departments, faculties, institutes, and associations also gave financial assistance. We are grateful to the Faculties of Communication and Culture, Graduate Studies, Humanities, Nursing, and Social Science; the Departments of English, History, Political Science, and Religious Studies; the Graduate Students' Association; Information Resources; Institute for Gender Research; Nursing, Philosophy, and History Group; and the University of Calgary Press. We also thank the following sponsors: Athabasca University; Pat Burke, Remax/Landa; the Calgary Public Library; the Coalition for Western Women's History; Barb Dacks, *Legacy Magazine*; Detselig Press; Dr N.A. Earl, DMD; the Famous Five Foundation; Glenbow Museum and Archives; Historical Society of Alberta; *Historical Studies in Education*; Kris Matthews, The Matthews Group; Scott McCreath, BMO Nesbit Burns; Mount Royal College; University of Oklahoma Press; and University Printing Services. We are grateful to Cheryl Foggo and Detselig Enterprises Ltd. for permission to reprint excerpts from *Pourin' Down Rain*. Elizabeth Jameson acknowledges the support of the Imperial Oil–Lincoln McKay Chair in American Studies, which helped support the editing of this volume. Publication of this volume was funded in part by the Alberta Historical Resources Foundation and by Athabasca University. We are grateful for their support.

Thanks, too, to Walter Hildebrandt, of AU Press, who has shepherded this project from the beginning; to Erna Dominey and Brenda Hennig of AU Press; to Brendan Wild for patient and meticulous copy-editing; and to Michael Luski, Alan Brownoff, Peter Midgley and Linda Cameron of the University of Alberta Press.

Our very special thanks to Amy McKinney, editorial assistant extraordinaire.

We owe our greatest thanks to a wonderful group of authors, whose words animate these pages.

ELIZABETH JAMESON & SHEILA McMANUS

INTRODUCTION

THIS VOLUME is one product of the conference, "Unsettled Pasts: Reconceiving the West through Women's History." Held at the University of Calgary in June 2002, "Unsettled Pasts" was the largest conference yet devoted to the history of women in western Canada, and the first major conference to emphasize comparative and transborder histories of women in the Canadian and U.S. Wests. Ninety-five presenters and seventy-five delegates shared ideas and conversations across boundaries of national citizenship, age, and profession. Participants represented the generations of scholars who developed women's history and women studies beginning in the late 1960s through the most recent generation of feminist historians. The presentations covered a variety of disciplines and combined scholarship with personal experience, art, and activism. It was a multi-national gathering, with participation from the United States, Canada, and Britain. As participants exchanged ideas, perspectives, and e-mail addresses, "Unsettled Pasts" crackled with the energy of new connections.

The conference sparked new comparisons and collaborations, and it generated two anthologies. The first volume, *Unsettled Pasts: Reconceiving the West through Women's History*, edited by Sarah Carter, Lesley Erickson, Patricia Roome, and Char Smith, focuses on the Canadian prairie provinces and British Columbia.¹ That book was inspired, as was the conference, by the desire to represent women's histories during the 2005 centennials of Alberta and Saskatchewan. This volume is inspired by a second goal of the "Unsettled Pasts" conference: to generate conversations that would link and compare the histories of the women of western North America and the women whose journeys crossed the borderlands of the Canadian and American Wests.

In this anthology, sixteen articles are arranged topically to suggest connections and comparisons among the experiences of women in the western United States and Canada. Eight of the authors are American, seven are Canadian, one is British. They include a number of "founding mothers" of western women's history, a number of young scholars in the early stages of their careers, and all the academic generations in between. We carried this cross-generational conversation forward as we collaborated to edit this volume. Sheila McManus represents younger scholars who are forging new transnational approaches to the borderlands of race, gender, and nation. Elizabeth Jameson has studied and taught women's history since the early 1970s and helped organize the first conference on western women's history, the Women's West conference, held in Sun Valley, Idaho, in 1983.² McManus is a Canadian who has lived and researched in the United States. Jameson, a U.S. citizen, has lived in Canada since 1999 and is a permanent resident, a status that illustrates the complexities of nationality and identity that many authors explore in this volume.

Seven of the articles are about women who emigrated from one country to the other, or compare women of the two nations. One aim of the "Unsettled Pasts" conference, and of this volume, has been to stimulate more explicitly comparative and transnational scholarship. Histories that cross national borders are still too rare, largely because most historians have been trained as historians of particular nations. We have sought in this volume to suggest the promise of comparative and transnational approaches both through the essays that explicitly employ these perspectives, and by grouping articles topically to suggest comparisons and the potential of comparative and transnational frameworks. The articles, and the topical pairings, explore the meanings of place and nation in women's histories, adding further depth and complexity to the new scholarship on western women in Canada and the United States.

During the 1970s and 1980s, historians in both countries increasingly researched and wrote women's histories, as more women became professional historians and as the women's liberation movement supported the development of knowledge by and about women. Women's historians wrestled with national histories that marginalized women, and with stories of western settlement that showcased a stock array of male characters. In histories of the U.S. West, these characters might be cowboys, prospectors, mountain men, desperadoes, soldiers, or intrepid explorers. In Canada, they might be explorers, fur traders, voyageurs, or Mounties. Later, the casts would expand to include pioneer farmers, railroad entrepreneurs, and mining magnates. Sometimes a stereotypical woman might flit briefly across the pages: a reluctant, lonely pioneer, dragged west against her will; a bedraggled pioneer helpmate; a whore with a heart of gold; a helpful native woman, who, like Sacagawea or Charlotte Small, guided the newcomers through an unmapped western landscape. Native peoples tended to appear as assistants or as barriers to be overcome. Otherwise, the actors were not only overwhelmingly male, but also overwhelmingly white.[3]

The first western women's histories added women to these all-male casts. Historians of western women, in both countries, emphasized that race, class, and colonial relationships distinguished the historical experiences of women in the North American West. Sylvia Van Kirk's pathbreaking *Many Tender Ties* demonstrated that aboriginal women were essential, economically and socially, to the Canadian fur trade and to the formation of a unique fur-trade society.[4] In the United States, Joan Jensen and Darlis Miller's "The Gentle Tamers Revisited" set the agenda for a multicultural history of women in the American West.[5] As scholars in both countries added women to existing histories, the stories of western settlement became more complex, conflicted, nuanced, and interesting.

The "Unsettled Pasts" conference emphasized a new category to add to these complex contingencies of gender, class, and race: the nation itself. Instead of assuming that a Canadian white settler woman or a native woman in Canada probably had a life that was a lot like that of a white settler woman or native woman in the United States, we asked how comparable the historical experiences of Canadian and American women of similar backgrounds and status really were. How did separate national policies that governed native peoples, property ownership, intimacy, immigration, and citizenship affect women of different races and classes? How did the histories learned in school and the different ways two nations told their national pasts affect the ways we envisioned women's histories and identities and our respective Wests?

Those histories differed in important respects. The United States expanded westward from its birth as a nation. Britain relinquished its land east of the Mississippi River to the new nation after the American Revolution, in 1783. Within seven decades the United States had claimed all the land to the Pacific Ocean, acquiring it through the Louisiana Purchase in 1803, the annexation of Texas in 1845, the Treaty of Oregon with Britain in 1846, the Mexican-American War, which claimed the northern third of Mexico in 1848, and the Gadsden Purchase in 1853. It then purchased Alaska from Russia in 1867, and annexed Hawai'i in 1898. An ideology of "manifest destiny" justified the enormous land grab that indelibly wrote westward expansion into U.S. history and imagination.

The formation of Canada and the process through which it claimed its western provinces was significantly different. The United States became a nation and colonized its West much earlier than Canada. Almost a century separated the U.S. Declaration of Independence from Britain in 1776 and the Confederation that formed the Dominion of Canada in 1867. The colonies that became Canada were often very isolated from one another, did not like each other very much, and did not unite to wage a common revolutionary war. Many late-nineteenth-century Anglo-Canadians embraced and celebrated their British roots and British culture, while American historians sought to explain what, besides a war, made their country different from Europe.

United States history and identity were linked, from the beginning, to westward expansion, and to Americans' encounters with a westward-moving sequence of frontiers. The colonies to the north had much more modest territorial aspirations until well into the nineteenth century, before which European interest in western Canada consisted largely of the economic interests of the fur trade, directed from London by the Hudson's Bay Company (HBC). British, Scottish, French and, later, Canadian and American fur traders operated in the West from the seventeenth century, forging working partnerships with aboriginal peoples. As an opening chapter in the history of European Canadian enterprise, the fur trade started the Canadian narrative in the West, while U.S. history was generally written as starting with the British settlements at Jamestown in 1607 and Plymouth in 1620, and moving west from the Atlantic coast. Yet in U.S. histories, innovation, change, and the national character were all forged on the westward edges of an expanding nation. In the traditional Canadian histories, innovation and development were directed from metropolitan centres and authority rested in "central" Canada (meaning southern Ontario and Quebec, or even more narrowly the quadrangle of Toronto, Ottawa, Montreal, and Quebec City), which was in turn governed by European markets and political allegiances.[6]

The histories of western settlement followed different timelines and trajectories in Canada and the United States. Canada claimed its western territory later, gaining title in 1869 to the huge territory claimed by the Hudson's Bay Company. The new federal government created the province of Manitoba in one corner of this territory in 1870, followed in 1871 by the province of British Columbia. Most of the western U.S. states were established by 1890, when an unbroken line of states lay along the United States-Canada border. Not until 1905, when Alberta and Saskatchewan were formed, was there an unbroken line of western provinces. The last U.S. territories to achieve statehood lay along the southern border and outside the limits of the contiguous forty-eight states: New Mexico and Arizona achieved statehood in 1912; Alaska and Hawai'i in 1959. In Canada, north of the prairie provinces and British Columbia, the Northwest Territories, the Yukon, and Nunavut retain territorial status.[7] The North, and not the West, has often defined the frontiers of Canadian expansion and its limits.

Borders and regions also operate differently in our histories. U.S. historians have paid more attention to the border with Mexico than to the Canadian border, and a whole school of history has explored those borderlands since the 1920s.[8] In popular U.S. imagination, the border between Mexico and the United States separates Americans from darker and poorer people who speak a different language; it appears as a line of cultural and social demarcation that coincides with national sovereignty. In Canada, the U.S. border has marked national identity in similar ways, functioning as a barrier against U.S. cultural and economic hegemony, separating Canada and Canadian culture from the United States.[9]

The border between Canada and the United States was mapped in several different stages, and then established through practice. Thomas Jefferson originally suggested the 49th parallel as a northern boundary of the Louisiana Purchase. In 1818, the United States negotiated with Britain to establish the northern border at 49° north latitude as far west as the crest of the Rocky Mountains. West of there, however, the Oregon Country stretched from the northern border of Spanish/Mexican California to the southern border of Russian Alaska at 54°40′ north latitude.[10] Britain and the United States agreed not to dispute the ownership of this vast territory, but to share "joint occupation" and defer drawing its boundaries. The joint occupation lasted from 1818 to 1846, a unique arrangement in the history of North America.

In a messy stroke of timing, the question of who owned Oregon resurfaced just before the United States entered a war with Mexico in 1846. The question was particularly messy because by the 1840s the Pacific Northwest had become a complicated meeting ground. The joint occupation had seemed a good idea at first because almost no Europeans lived in Oregon Country anyway. But traders, missionaries, and farmers soon eyed the territory. Home to many different native cultures, Oregon Country became the westernmost outpost of the HBC fur trade empire. Rival traders from the United States also moved into the region. The first American missionaries arrived in the 1830s, and then, in the early

1840s, Americans began heading west on the Oregon Trail to claim fertile agricultural land in Oregon.

American expansionists advocated establishing the border at 54°40′ north latitude. Chanting "Fifty-four Forty or Fight," they elected James K. Polk president in 1844, and the new president quickly notified Britain that he would not extend the joint occupation of Oregon country. But despite his supporters' slogans, Polk could not fight a war on two fronts, and so, as he prepared for war with Mexico, he quietly began diplomatic negotiations with Britain. In June 1846, the United States and Britain signed the Treaty of Oregon establishing the border west of the summit of the Rocky Mountains at the 49th parallel, with a jog around the tip of Vancouver Island to place it under British sovereignty.

The border between British North America and the United States remained porous, and was not in fact surveyed, marked, or mapped for many years. The North American Boundary Commission surveyed the border west of the Rockies beginning in 1858. The portion of the border from the Great Lakes to the Rockies was not mapped until 1872–1874.

The lines that divide nations raise questions central to this volume. How do people's individual histories, or the histories of daily social life, connect with the histories of nation states? How do we link the histories of nations to the histories of cross-border migrations, to the people and economies and ecologies that traverse national borders? How do we respect the differences inscribed in national and social boundaries, yet challenge the inequalities of power and privilege they also erect? Crossing the boundaries of the national histories we know, like crossing social or class or racial boundaries, involves entering unfamiliar territory where all sorts of assumptions may be challenged, including unexamined assumptions about gender, history, and the nations to which we offer allegiance. Choosing to step across those lines means giving up the power of the familiar.

The "Unsettled Pasts" conference, and the articles that appear here, build on a generation of scholarship that questioned the categories and assumptions that wrote women out of history. Those assumptions privileged elections and warfare over grassroots activism, public affairs over daily experience, powerful individuals over "ordinary" people. History as a professional discipline developed with the rise of the nation state, and until quite recently historians assumed that nations were the primary and proper subjects of history.[11]

We want to emphasize, then, that all of the categories of analysis used in this volume are historically constructed. Gender, race, class, and nations themselves have been understood and created in specific ways in different times and places. They all involve social relationships, among women and men, people who look different to one another, among citizens of the same country, among people with unequal access to resources and to power. As with all relationships, the behaviors of the participants change what happens, and what it means.

The key analytical concept for women's historians is gender, which is socially constructed depending on how different cultures imagine and interpret differences between men and women. Gender roles are therefore historically and culturally specific, changing and changeable. For example, in some American Indian cultures women were in charge of the agricultural production and it was considered demeaning for men to be involved. By contrast, in the Canadian West in the late nineteenth century the highest form of white masculinity was to be a farmer, clearly distinct from and superior to effete urbanites or "nomadic" Natives, and women's participation in such labour was considered inappropriate except when absolutely necessary. In the American West at the same time, a man who farmed would be considered manly, but perhaps less masculine than a soldier or cowboy, precisely because he was more likely to have a family, and thus to be more "tied down" and less a "rugged individual."

The word "race" is used to denote both a biological construct and a cultural construct, a way of imagining differences in status and capacity based on skin colour and physical appearance. Race operates socially and historically as people assign meaning and construct power relationships based on these perceived differences. First Nations and American Indians, and people of African and Asian descent have, like women, organized to challenge limiting legal and social constraints, and to alter perceptions of the meanings of race, thereby changing relationships of power historically constructed among people of different "races."

Even the physical and cultural inheritances often associated with "race" have changed constantly in new historical circumstances. Nowhere was this more evident than in the North American Wests, where the first European immigrants were often overwhelmingly male. On the resource frontiers that first drew European men in search of furs, gold, or silver, an invasion of male newcomers interacted with native peoples, entering into exchanges with native women that were intimate and sexual as well as economic. Intimacy generated new peoples— métis, mestiza/o, mulatto—for whom race was a messy and complex process of historically defined identities, limits, and possibilities.[12] The complexity of race is illustrated by the acceptance of Métis as a distinct identity in Canada, whereas in the United States, Métis became Indians, Mestizo/as became Mexicans, and Mulattos were considered Black.

These racial terms raise cautionary flags to historians of our respective Wests. Racial and ethnic terminologies, like concepts of race and ethnicity, are historically and culturally specific, and different terms are appropriate for particular times and contexts in Canadian and U.S. history. In Canada, the preferred terms for native peoples are First Nations or Aboriginals; in the United States, they are American Indians or Native Americans. Because the United States did not recognize Métis as a category, Métis who moved to the United States might be assigned a tribal identity, and be considered, for instance, Turtle Mountain Chippewa. In the United States, the terms Hispanic, Mexican, Spanish American, Mexican American, Tejano/a, California/o, Chicana/o, and Mestizo/a may refer to people of similar heritage; the terms have regionally and historically specific connotations. This volume includes a range of terms that are historically and culturally appropriate, and both Canadian and American spellings. We have elected not to edit authors' terminology or spelling preferences because the choices to use *neighbour* or *neighbor*, *labour* or *labor*, *Indian* or *Aboriginal* will alert readers to cultural subtleties and differences.

In contrast to gender and race, class in North America has been more easily imagined as a social and a historical relationship, as many people were drawn here from other continents specifically to improve their economic opportunities, and thus to alter their class status. Yet transplanted class assumptions affected the policies that encouraged western development, including the process of claiming and allocating the land. A British system of class and inheritance that privileged the eldest son in wealthy families sent many younger sons to the Canadian West, to make their fortunes on large cattle ranches. In both countries, land was allocated to homesteaders in 160-acre parcels, in exchange for working the land and improving it for a specific period of time (three years in Canada, five in the United States). But in the United States, women could file for land in their own names if they were single or the heads of families. The situation was much more restricted in Canada, a reality that sparked a southward migration of Canadian women home-steaders.[13] And while 160 acres might promise economic independence for some women, those homesteads represented great losses for native women. For them, the institution of reservations, reserves, and private family homesteads meant the loss of communal gardens, hunting ter-ritories, and of indigenous understandings of property, community, and marriage. As these examples suggest, the processes of class forma-tion throughout North America were always historically connected to processes of national expansion and state formation that established rela-tionships of race and gender as well.

Just as women crossed the 49th parallel to claim homesteads, the pulls and pressures of gender, poverty, or race prompted many other back-and-forth migrations across the border.[14] Many Métis and Cree fled south after the failed rebellion of 1885. Many African Americans fled to Canada to escape slavery and racism. Many people came to western North America fleeing poverty or religious persecution. Germans from Russia, Mennonites, Doukhobors, Hutterites, and Jews all settled in the North American West. They found somewhat different opportunities, depending on when they migrated, what they fled, and where they set-tled. Canada sometimes permitted the formation of a few ethnic colonies called "bloc settlements," while in the United States people could form an ethnic enclave only by filing on adjacent quarter sections of land. The effects were somewhat different. Ethnic colonies preserved customs, languages, and cultures, and deliberately kept their people isolated from other Canadians to a greater or lesser degree. The U.S. policy undermined ethnic cultures and often isolated immigrants from others who shared their background, while supporting greater assimilation. As these few examples illustrate, national policies and the border itself participated in the process of creating specific western communities and possibilities for women and men of different races, classes, religions, and national origins.

The social and cultural complexity of the North American Wests prompts us, too, to voice our regret that this volume does not represent the full diversity of western people and their pasts. No volume could. This book reflects the state of a field in its infancy, and its silences and omissions should be noted as calls for future research and scholarship. No articles follow the histories of First Nations or Indian women much beyond the fur trade. The racial and cultural diversity of neither West is fully represented in these pages. There is no attention to twentieth-century migrations, to the differences in immigration policies and foreign policies that attracted immigrants from the Netherlands, Poland, Germany, India, China, Vietnam, Chile, Mexico, El Salvador, Lebanon, or Iraq—to name some of the origins of recent immigrants—to either the Canadian or U.S. Wests. Nor is there sufficient attention paid to what the West offered women of different sexualities, or about relationships among women of different classes and cultures. There is much more to be done. For starters, we need to incorporate the histories of native women throughout our historical narratives, so that they do not appear as barriers to be overcome by colonial expansion who then fade from the narrative. We need to envision the history of social relationships always from the multiple perspectives of the people who enacted them.

International migrations, differences in local economies, class and race, gender and nationality—all this complexity makes the history of the North American West much richer, much messier, and much more interesting. We have only just begun to consider what regions themselves might mean when constructed from women's particular perspectives, and what national identity meant for all the various women who settled the U.S. and Canadian Wests. Did the West look different viewed from a sod house or earth lodge than it did astride a hunter's horse, or behind a plow? Did it look different from the perspectives of a miner toiling underground and the boarding house keeper who prepared his lunch bucket? What do the West Coast and the Great Plains have in common? What social boundaries, what geographies might map different people's Wests?

These are huge questions and this volume does not pretend to answer them. We do, however, map some of the lines that have distinguished women's lives throughout western North America and some of the territory that some women shared. We chronicle some of the stories of how women helped draw the lines that divide people and nations, and initiated other efforts to bridge them. This volume takes a significant first step toward framing important questions and comparisons.

The articles address a series of topics. We begin with two essays by the editors of this volume, which originated as plenary addresses at the "Unsettled Pasts" conference and that frame some of the challenges and promises of transborder histories. In Section Two, two "founding mothers" of western women's history, Susan Armitage and Sylvia Van Kirk, imagine how the history of one transnational region, encompassing the states of Oregon and Washington and the province of British Columbia, might be written from the perspectives of gender and race. In Section Three, Jean Barman, Molly Rozum, and Joan Jensen address how the stories of individual western women are embedded in particular western places, and how their stories in turn might alter the stories of their Wests. In Section Four, Helen Raptis and Margaret Jacobs explore how women educators worked to push the boundaries of race, using one of the few accepted professions for women as an arena for social activism. In Section Five, Char Smith, Nora Faires, and Cheryl Foggo explore the very different experiences of three very different groups of women who immigrated across the 49th parallel: prostitutes, wealthy American women of Calgary's business elite, and African Canadians.

Next, in Section Six, Laurie Mercier and Cynthia Loch-Drake explore class through the experiences of women who were involved, as workers and as wives, with the International Union of Mine, Mill and Smelter Workers, a union that played a significant role in both Canada and the United States. Finally, in Section Seven, professors Margaret Walsh and Mary Murphy discuss the challenges they have faced and the strategies they have employed in England and the United States to teach the comparative history of women in the Canadian and U.S. Wests. Each section is preceded by a brief introduction that suggests conceptual and comparative issues.

One Step Over the Line is just that: a first step across the line that has divided the histories of women in the Canadian and U.S. Wests. These articles take a giant first step to begin exploring what links and separates our histories, as women of different races, sexualities, classes, and backgrounds; as Canadians and Americans. We are stepping into unfamiliar territory. We cannot build bridges across unmapped divides.

NOTES

1. Sarah Carter, Lesley Erickson, Patricia Roome, and Char Smith, *Unsettled Pasts: Reconceiving the West through Women's History* (Calgary: University of Calgary Press, 2005).

2. See Sheila McManus, *The Line Which Separates: Race, Gender, and the Making of the Alberta-Montana Borderlands* (Lincoln: University of Nebraska Press, 2005); Susan Armitage and Elizabeth Jameson, eds., *The Women's West* (Norman: University of Oklahoma Press, 1987)

3. For the U.S., see Susan Armitage, "Through Women's Eyes: A New View of the West," in *The Women's West*, ed. Armitage and Jameson, 9–18; "Editors' Introduction," in *Writing the Range: Race, Class and Culture in the Women's West*, ed. Elizabeth Jameson and Susan Armitage (Norman: University of Oklahoma Press, 1997), 3–16; Beverly Stoeltje, "A Helpmate for Man Indeed: The Image of the Frontier Woman," *Journal of American Folklore* 88, no. 347 (January-March, 1975): 27–31; Rayna Green, "The Pocahantas Perplex: The Image of Indian Women in American Culture," *Massachusetts Review* 16, no. 4 (1976), 698–714. For Canada, see Sara Brooks Sundberg, "Farm Women on the Canadian Prairie Frontier: The Helpmate Image," in *Rethinking Canada: The Promise of Women's History*, 1st ed., ed. Veronica Strong-Boag and Anita Clair Fellman (Toronto: Copp Clark Pitman, 1986), 95–106; Catherine Cavanaugh and Randi Warne, "Introduction," *Telling Tales: Essays in Western Women's History* (Vancouver and Toronto: UBC Press, 2000), 3–31; Sarah Carter, "Categories and Terrains of Exclusion: Constructing the 'Indian Woman' in the Early Settlement Era," in *Telling Tales: Essays in Western Women's History*, ed. Catherine Cavanaugh and Randi Warne (Vancouver and Toronto: UBC Press, 2000), 60–81; and

Catherine Cavanaugh, "'No Place for a Woman': Engendering Western Canadian Settlement," *Western Historical Quarterly* 28, no. 4 (1997): 493–518.

4. Sylvia Van Kirk, *Many Tender Ties: Women in Fur-Trade Society in Western Canada, 1670–1870* (Winnipeg: Watson & Dwyer; Norman: University of Oklahoma Press, 1980).

5. Joan M. Jensen and Darlis A. Miller, "The Gentle Tamers Revisited: New Approaches to the History of Women in the American West," *Pacific Historical Review* 49, no. 2 (May 1980): 173–213.

6. For two formative works that typified and influenced these distinct interpretations, see Frederick Jackson Turner, "The Significance of the Frontier in American History," and Harold A. Innis, *The Fur Trade in Canada*. Turner first presented "The Significance of the Frontier" at the Historical Congress in Chicago at the World's Columbian Exhibition of 1893, originally printed in *Annual Report of the American Historical Association for the Year 1893* (Washington, D.C.: Government Printing Office, 1894), here referenced from Martin Ridge, ed., *History, Frontier, and Section: Three Essays by Frederick Jackson Turner* (Albuquerque: University of New Mexico Press, 1993), 59–92. Innis's *The Fur-trade of Canada* (Toronto: University of Toronto Press, 1927) is best known in Canada through the revised edition, Harold A. Innis, *The Fur Trade in Canada: An Introduction to Canadian Economic History* (Toronto: University of Toronto Press, 1956) or through the 1999 edition (Toronto: University of Toronto Press, 1999), with a new introduction by Arthur Ray. On metropolitanism, see for instance J. M. S. Careless, *Frontier and Metropolis: Regions, Cities, and Identities in Canada before 1914* (Toronto: University of Toronto Press, 1989).

7. Washington, Montana, North Dakota, and South Dakota all became states in 1889, Idaho and Wyoming in 1890. On the Métis' responses surrounding Manitoba's entry into Confederation, see J. M. Bumsted, *The Red River Rebellion* (Winnipeg, MB: Watson & Dwyer, 1996).

8. The Borderlands school was founded by Herbert Eugene Bolton, a student of Frederick Jackson Turner's. Among Bolton's extensive borderlands scholarship, the formative text was *The Spanish Borderlands: A Chronicle of Old Florida and the Southwest* (New Haven: Yale University Press, 1921). For recent Borderlands histories, see David J. Weber, *The Idea of the Spanish Borderlands* (New York: Garland, 1991), and *The Spanish Frontier in North America* (New Haven: Yale University Press, 1992), and Samuel Truett and Elliott Young, eds., *Continental Crossroads: Remapping U.S.-Mexico Borderlands History* (Durham, NC: Duke University Press, 2004).

9. See Ian Lumsden, ed., *Close the 49th Parallel Etc.* (Toronto: University of Toronto Press, 1973); Richard Gwyn, *The Forty Ninth Paradox: Canada in North America* (Toronto: McClellan and Stewart, 1985); Will Ferguson, *Why I Hate Canadians* (Vancouver: Douglas & McIntyre Ltd., 1997), esp. 96–113.

10. Spanish conquest of Alta California dated from an expedition in 1769 led by military commander Captain Gaspar de Portola and the religious commander, Father Junipero Serra, who founded a chain of Franciscan missions along the California coast. Mexico took possession of Alta California in 1821, when it gained independence from Spain, and claimed the territory through the Mexican-American War, until 1848.

11. See Benedict Anderson, *Imagined Communities: Reflections on the Origin and Spread of Nationalism,* rev. ed. (London: Verso, 1991); Eric Hobsbawm and Terence Ranger, eds.,

The Invention of Tradition (Cambridge: Cambridge University Press, 1983); Geoff Eley
and Ronald Grigor Suny, eds., *Becoming National: A Reader* (New York: Oxford University
Press, 1996); Geoffrey Cubitt, ed., *Imagining Nations* (Manchester: Manchester University
Press, 1998); Ian Angus, *A Border Within: National Identity, Cultural Plurality, and Wilderness*
(Montreal: McGill-Queen's University Press, 1997); Veronica Strong-Boag, Sherrill
Grace, Avigail Eisenberg, and Joan Anderson, eds., *Painting the Maple: Essays on Race,
Gender, and the Construction of Canada* (Vancouver: UBC, 1998); W. H. New, *Borderlands: How
We Talk about Canada* (Vancouver: UBC Press, 1998).

12. See Van Kirk, *Many Tender Ties*, Jennifer S. H. Brown, *Strangers in Blood: Fur Trade Company
Families in Indian Country* (Vancouver: UBC Press, 1980); Ramon A. Gutiérrez, *When Jesus
Came, the Corn Mothers Went Away: Marriage, Sexuality, and Power in New Mexico, 1500–1846*
(Stanford: Standford University Press, 1991); Albert L. Hurtado, *Intimate Frontiers: Sex,
Gender, and Culture in Old California* (Albuquerque: University of New Mexico Press,
1999); James F. Brooks, *Captives and Cousins: Slavery, Kinship, and Community in the Southwest
Borderland* (Chapel Hill: University of North Carolina Press, 2002).

13. See H. Elaine Lindgren, *Land in Her Own Name: Single Women as Homesteaders in North
Dakota* (1991; repr., Norman: University of Oklahoma Press, 1996); Sheryll Patterson-
Black, "Women Homesteaders on the Great Plains Frontier," *Frontiers* 1, no. 2 (Spring
1976): 67–88.

14. See Randy William Widdis, *With Scarcely a Ripple: Anglo-Canadian Migration into the United
States and Western Canada, 1880–1920* (Montreal and Kingston: McGill-Queen's University
Press, 1998); Bruno Ramirez, *Crossing the 49th Parallel: Migration from Canada to the
United States, 1900–1930* (Ithaca: Cornell University Press, 2000); Kenneth Lines, *British
and Canadian Immigration to the United States Since 1920* (San Francisco: R & E Research
Associates, 1978); Marcus Lee Hansen, *The Mingling of the Canadian and American Peoples:
Volume I, Historical* (New Haven: Yale University Press, 1940); Donald George Simpson,
Under the North Star: Black Communities in Upper Canada before Confederation (1876), edited by
Paul E. Lovejoy (Trenton, NJ: African World Press, 2005); Paul F. Sharp, "When Our West
Moved North," *American Historical Review* 55, no. 2 (January 1950): 286–300; Paul F. Sharp,
"Three Frontiers: Some Comparative Studies of Canadian, American, and Australian
Settlements," *Pacific Historical Review* 24, no. 4 (1955): 369–77; John J. Bukowczyk, Nora
Faires, and David R. Smith, eds., *Permeable Borders: The Great Lakes Basin as Transnational
Region, 1650–1990* (Pittsburgh: University of Pittsburgh Press, 2005).

TALKING ACROSS BORDERS

THE ESSAYS IN THIS SECTION identify challenges that historians encounter when they step across the borders of national histories. Women's historians have long pushed another set of historical boundaries, the social boundaries of gender that have made women's options and histories different from men's, and those of race, class, and sexualities that have created inequalities among women who share a common citizenship. National and social boundaries have combined to marginalize most people from history. Histories of nations have often focused on the exploits of public leaders and powerful citizens, thus reinforcing social inequalities by making people with less public power historically invisible—among them poor people, workers, women, gay men, lesbians, bisexuals, transgendered individuals, and colonized peoples. Here, Elizabeth Jameson and Sheila McManus probe a similar process by which people who live outside a known national past become invisible and unconnected.

Both essays originated as plenary addresses at the "Unsettled Pasts" conference. From the different perspectives of Canadian and U.S. history and of two academic generations, they explore the places that women have occupied in the U.S. and Canadian Wests, and in the histories of each nation. Each essay reflects its author's training in national history; each is informed by similar experiences of border crossing.

Elizabeth Jameson opened the conference. A more senior (or at least older) U.S. historian, her essay draws upon her own research, her experience as an American living and teaching in Canada, and a generation of historical scholarship on women in the (mostly U.S.) West. Sheila McManus led off on the second day. A Canadian, McManus has lived in the United States as the first post-doctoral fellow at Yale University's Howard R. Lamar Center for the Study of Frontiers and Borders. Her article speaks from the perspective of a younger generation of historians who have pioneered in comparative and borderlands scholarship; it draws from her own research on gender in the Alberta-Montana borderlands.[1] Both articles explore the challenges and promises of transnational histories and their potential to disrupt inherited histories. The similarities and differences in the authors' perspectives provide an apt introduction to the subtleties, nuances, and textures of women's histories in the Canadian and U.S. Wests.

Jameson and McManus articulated a number of common assumptions: that women have been marginalized in the national and regional histories of both the United States and Canada; that it is important to investigate western women's experiences in both nations comparatively, without assuming commonalities or differences; that both mundane daily experience and state policies shape women's experiences and histories; and that historians' training and personal experiences affect the histories we record. Recognizing the complexities of gender, race, class, sexuality, and other historically constructed identities, each author probes the difference a national border has made for the many women of the Canadian and U.S. Wests.

Comparing how the West and the international border have operated in Canadian and U.S. imagination, and in separate national historical narratives, Jameson examines the assumptions of national and public histories that have marginalized and isolated women. She examines one source, the diary of Mary Dodge Woodward, a relatively privileged white widow who worked on a Dakota bonanza farm in the 1880s, to illustrate how the women of the North American West have been isolated from one another and from "mainstream" histories. Woodward's diary becomes a lens that refracts assumptions about class, race, domesticity, women's roles, about what history is and who makes it, and about western settlement itself. All of these assumptions separated women of different races, classes, and nations, and separated women from the public world of written history. Woodward's diary clarifies, too, how national history and nationalist assumptions erected borders among people who lived on opposite sides of the 49th parallel. The challenge, and the promise, is to reimagine history from the lived experiences of women for whom neither nationality nor gender exhausted the complexities of social networks or personal identity.

McManus takes the power of historical imagination as her starting point. "Women's historians have always unsettled the past," she begins. "It is what we do." History becomes more complex and richer as women are added, and particularly as they are added to narratives of the North American West, a region that has long been seen as "quintessentially male." Acknowledging a generation of scholarship that has emphasized differences of race and class, McManus notes that western women's historians have been more reluctant to cross the line of the nation state and explore national differences.

McManus does not hesitate to take that step. One of the few historians to date who has examined the Canada-U.S. border from a gendered perspective, she probes what the border meant for women of different races and classes, focusing on the aboriginal, black, and white women of the Alberta-Montana borderlands, and on how assumptions about race and gender were embedded in the process of nation building. McManus concludes that borders matter differently for different women, depending on social status, and on whether women are multiply marginalized by virtue of race, religion, or sexuality. Gender and race become powerful tools to unsettle the assumptions of power and privilege that have been fundamental in national histories and national territorial ambitions. The challenge, McManus cautions, is to be aware of our own nationalist assumptions. She warns against assuming similarity in women's experiences across social or national borderlines, and against assuming that the history of any nation is unique, or "normal."

Both authors write from personal experiences of border crossing. McManus, a Canadian, spent the 2001–2002 academic year at Yale University. Jameson ends with a personal postscript from the same period, reflecting on the significance of the international border and of national identity for her, as an American living in Canada, during and immediately after the attacks on the World Trade Center and Pentagon on September 11, 2001. Implicitly and explicitly, both authors' personal experiences of border crossing have informed their historical analyses, and their awareness of the barriers borders have erected. They suggest, too, how powerfully history can transform the meanings of national and social boundaries, and how fragile and contingent those meanings can be.

NOTE

1.   Sheila McManus, "Mapping the Alberta-Montana Borderlands: Race, Ethnicity and Gender in the Late Nineteenth Century," *Journal of American Ethnic History* 20 (2001): 71–87; "'Their Own Country': Race, Gender, Landscape, and Colonization Around the 49th Parallel, 1862–1900," *Agricultural History* 73 (1999): 168–82; *The Line Which Separates: Race, Gender, and the Making of the Alberta-Montana Borderlands* (Lincoln: University of Nebraska Press, 2005).

1

CONNECTING THE WOMEN'S WESTS

ELIZABETH JAMESON

PROLOGUE

FOR OVER A QUARTER OF A CENTURY, I have written, taught, and thought about western women's history. Western women's histories force this question: What on earth do place and gender have to do with one another? Was it different being a woman in the West than in other places? Did women shape or define the West in particular ways? Transnational and comparative histories add the further complication of nationality. Were women's experiences similar throughout the North American Wests? What differences do national borders make?

This article explores some of the challenges of linking different women's histories in two North American Wests, a project that is embedded in a number of broad conceptual questions. What links the histories of western women of different races, classes, and nationalities? What links the histories of daily life and social relationships with the histories of nations? How has the border mattered, historically, in women's lives? How has gender operated in regional and national identities? These are huge questions; they have no easy answers. I try here only to suggest their dimensions.

Historians approach national and social boundaries from our particular national and social perspectives. I write as an American social historian; I study women, class, and gender; I live and teach in Calgary. Soon after I accepted my job at the University of Calgary, I learned a joke that instructed me in the sensitivity required to work across national boundaries:

Question: *What is the difference between a Canadian and an American?*
Answer: *The Canadian knows there is a difference.*

I would not have understood this joke before I moved to Canada. I grew up on the Texas Gulf Coast, lived much of my adult life in Colorado and New Mexico, and understood how concepts of racialized difference operated in popular conceptions of the border between the United States and Mexico and in the social boundaries of race in the U.S. South and Southwest. Until I moved to Calgary in 1999, I did not recognize how significant the differences between Canada and the United States are for Canadian identity. I've begun to understand this, if not always to enjoy, as an American, representing those differences. And I have begun, I hope, to learn a bit of Canadian deference and courtesy. So I try to fulfill what is expected of me. Out of courtesy, I make a special point of trying every day to do something disgustingly American—to be a bit too loud, a bit too self-revealing a bit too soon, to do something rude or disorderly—just to reassure the people around me that the boundaries are still intact. So if I offend Canadian readers, please understand that I am doing so only out of courtesy.

My own experience tells me that nationality and citizenship are only one source of identity and community. My United States citizenship and Canadian residence are both important to me, but so are my sex, race, age, and religion, my profession, the fact that I am a mother, a sister, a daughter. My particular constellation of identities means that my experience and my history are somewhat different from the lives and histories of other women who have lived in the Canadian and U.S. Wests, who built western communities and made their histories.

Even women whose backgrounds and lived experience might seem quite similar appear different through the lenses of national histories. In United States history, the West and western frontiers have been much more important than they have been in Canadian history. Westward movement, codified as "Manifest Destiny," provided both a narrative framework and an ideological justification for a history of U.S. expansion, colonialism, and conquest. The Canadian West has, in contrast, been written as a source of staple resources for economic development directed from the metropolitan centers of Central Canada and Europe, as a region apart from the wild and unruly folk to the south.[1] Because the West "explained" the United States but not Canada, western pioneers have figured more significantly in U.S. histories than they have in Canadian histories. In both countries, men of all regions have been more prominent than women in national and regional histories.

Borders, as well as regions, operate differently in our histories. U.S. historians have paid more attention to the border with Mexico than to the border with Canada. The Mexican border has been constructed in popular imagination and in U.S. immigration policy as a racialized boundary separating darker and poorer Mexicans from whiter, richer Americans. The United States secured that border with a war, whereas it civilly negotiated treaties with Britain and Canada to create, in popular imagination, the longest unpoliced border in the world.[2]

Both of these imagined borders are fictions, of course. The Mexican boundary went straight through Mexican territory, separating people of shared ethnicity and kinship into residents of the United States or Mexico. The Canadian border similarly bisected Native peoples' territories, and has been open only to some people at some times. Yet people cross those border lines, bringing with them personal amalgams of identities, dreams, and desires.

John Sayles explored these boundaries with creativity and insight in his film *Lone Star*, a film that is all about borders, both national and social. The film holds particularly powerful messages for anyone who, like me, had to suffer through Texas history classes in 1950s elementary school classrooms.[3] At one point in *Lone Star*, Sheriff Sam Deeds, played by Chris Cooper, crosses the Texas border into Mexico in search of information. He approaches El Rey de las Siantas [*the King of the Tires*].

"You're the sheriff of Rio County, right?" says El Rey. "Un jefe muy respectado." [*"A very respected leader."*] El Rey leans over and draws a line in the dirt with a Coke bottle. "Step across this line," he says. "Ay, que milagro!" [*"Ay, what a miracle!"*] "You're not the sheriff of nothing anymore. Just some Tejano with a lot of questions I don't have to answer. A bird flying south, you think he sees this line? Rattlesnake, javalina, whatever you got. You think halfway across that line they start thinking different? Why should a man?"

El Rey's perceptions notwithstanding, recent aerial images of the 49th parallel demonstrate that a bird flying *north* can in fact see the U.S.-Canadian border. Unlike the border between Texas and Mexico, which is marked by a river, the border that separates the U.S. and Canadian Wests is a line drawn arbitrarily straight across a continuous landscape. That line has been etched into the land itself through different patterns of land use and property division on either side of the border in only a bit over a century since a Boundary Commission drew the line across the continent. People, not nature, created the differences on either side of that line.

The people I study often cross international borders. I understand El Rey de las Siantas when he insists that the people who cross borders are as important as the states that police them. "I'm talking about people here," he tells the sheriff. "Men."

At this point our perspectives may diverge, or at least our choice of words. I assume that "people" includes both women and men. We are only beginning to explore whether the differences people inscribed on either side of a national border included understandings of gender, whether our Wests and the border that separates them held different meanings for women and men, as they have for Canadians and Americans.

I was first drawn to think about what links and separates our Wests and their borders by the women I studied who inhabited their borderlands, who sometimes crossed those boundaries, and whose lives raised these questions for me. Let me turn, then, to one such woman. I read her diaries in 1988, just over a century after she wrote them.

* * *

THE AFTERNOON OF JANUARY 27, 1885 blew cold and bleak on the eastern Dakota prairies. The thermometer read -28° Fahrenheit [-33° Celsius]. Mary Dodge Woodward, a fifty-eight-year-old widowed mother of five, stood at her kitchen window peering through the spyglass she used to view the outside world. Through it she could see the electric light of Fargo eight miles [13 km] distant, and wondrous mirages telescoped across the snowy prairies. This particular afternoon her son Walter and the hired man John Martin were hauling wheat to the stock yard, bringing loads of hay back to the farm. "They have to go without their dinner or eat frozen 'chuck,'" Woodward wrote, so she had "a good supper ready: boiled beef, vegetables, mince pie, doughnuts—such things as hungry men like." She timed dinner precisely: "I watch with the spyglass...and when they begin to load for the homeward trip, I begin to prepare supper."[4]

Mary Woodward's spyglass evokes the metaphor Susan Armitage used in the early 1980s to suggest the promise of western women's histories: the image of the stereopticon, found in many Victorian parlors. Viewed through the stereopticon, two virtually identical images on a card focused to form a three-dimensional picture. By viewing women's history as well as men's, Armitage suggested, a more-fully dimensional western history might emerge.[5]

Mary Dodge Woodward viewed *her* West from a domestic center. She added her private, interior world to the outdoor world of men's labor she viewed through her spyglass, and to the public events she gleaned from newspapers. Her viewpoint alone could not correct all the distortions of traditional western histories. But she did help me identify them, and to see, as well, the distortions and limits of particular women's Wests.

Woodward accompanied three of her children in 1882 to Dakota Territory, where Walter was to manage a commercial bonanza farm for her cousin, Daniel Dodge. Daniel had traded depreciated Northern

Pacific railroad stock for 1,500 acres of railroad land in the Red River Valley, a much larger spread than the typical 160-acre homestead, but only a minute slice of the twenty-nine million acres the United States government gave railroads to capitalize westward expansion. Woodward's youngest child, Fred, helped with the farm. Her daughter Kate helped with the considerable domestic labor required for the family, hired hands, and the crews of over thirty men who came to plow, seed, harvest, and thresh the "Number 1 hard" wheat bound for the St Paul market.[6]

From 1884 until her cousin sold out in 1888, Mary Woodward did not leave the farm. She recorded in her diaries her daily routine and her observations of an outside world she saw through her kitchen window and through her own assumptions about the proprieties of gender, ethnicity, race, and class. She was particularly concerned about one of her most frequent visitors, Elsie Lessing, and about the gendered division of labor on the neighboring Lessing farm. On October 25, 1885, she wrote, "Elsie is plowing for her father, a stingy old German who makes the women work out of doors. He thinks an hour long enough for them to prepare a meal."[7] In December 1886 she spied Elsie and her sister Lena hauling wood with a four-horse team. "They have done almost all the work on their farm this season: plowing, seeding, and harvesting," she wrote. "I cannot understand how any female can do such work."[8]

Woodward did not, apparently, find her own domestic labor remarkable, though her workload was particularly intensive because of the scale of her cousin's operation. One hot August day during the 1885 harvest season, she baked seventeen loaves of bread, "making seventy-four loaves since last Sunday, not to mention twenty-one pies, and puddings, cakes, and doughnuts."[9] She washed sheets and pillowcases for twelve beds, raised vegetables and chickens, and brought in some cash with eggs and butter. In 1888 she made fourteen pounds of butter a week— not to sell, but to put away to feed the harvest crews.[10]

Threshing season was intense. Serving supper took two to three hours, excluding preparation and clean up. The work got so heavy that other women were hired to help—a succession of Irish, Swedish, French, and Norwegian immigrants, many of whom, to her frustration, spoke little English. The $4 a week they earned was far less than men's wages, but enough to attract a succession of women to the Woodwards' kitchen. Some were married women working to raise money for family home-steads.[11]

For men the heaviest work was over by September. "There is nothing much for the men to do in Dakota in winter," she wrote. For Mrs Woodward, the slack period meant she could sleep in to 6 A.M., rather than rising at 5 o'clock or earlier.[12] Women, she believed, ought naturally to care for the domestic needs of their households. Not until illness confined her to bed at age fifty-seven did Mary Woodward's sons ever get their own breakfast.[13] Her work seemed to her as normal as the Lessing girls' seemed strange.

Mr Lessing may have been every bit as nasty as Mrs Woodward suspected. But perhaps the Lessings simply allocated labor and funds differently than the Woodwards. The women did more field work, but the Lessings hired no farm laborers and did not cook for huge work crews. Mary Woodward's view of gender, like all else in her universe, was particular and rooted in her own sense of domestic propriety.

Woodward penned equally limited glimpses of what linked her world to the Canadian West during that frigid winter of 1885. The day after John and Walter hauled the wheat, she recorded that the family had "been alone all day with the exception of a call from Harry Green who is a Canadian and therefore does not mind the weather. Many Canadians live around here, and they seem to endure the cold much better than we do." Harry called less often when Kate left to visit family in Wisconsin, and Mary Woodward suspected that Harry had designs on her daughter.[14]

Another Canada flashed briefly through her diary. On April 19, 1885, Woodward heard "the melodious sound of the meadow lark." Her domestic peace made it hard to imagine, she wrote, "that there is an army so near us. Riel's half breeds, with the Indians, will give the Canadian soldiers a sorry chase, we think. The half-breeds have so much wild country to fall back into and they think they have right on their side. They have all been down from Winnipeg and bought all the arms and ammunition there are in Fargo."[15]

It is not clear whether Woodward was frightened. She did not fear American Indians. Sitting Bull and One Bull traveled through Fargo to St Paul to make cattle contracts for the Sioux Reservation, and a number of Sioux chiefs from the Standing Rock Agency passed on their way to "pose as attractions at the Minnesota Fair." Woodward assumed that this was progress. The railroad, she said, was "a great civilizer, for besides helping to subjugate the troublesome red man, it has helped build up and make habitable the great Northwest."[16] Her local newspaper viewed the 1885 Rebellion with equal optimism, reporting that "Canada's little war" was a boon for Dakota and Montana: "Horses, hay, oats, and other supplies for the Canadian troops in Saskatchewan are being bought in large quantities on this side of the border.... It's an ill wind that blows no good to somebody in this great Republic."[17]

On November 16, Woodward reported that Walter had been puttying the barn windows, she and Katie had done laundry, they were troubled with mice, Walter had a new suit, new reading material had arrived. She then commented abruptly, "I suppose Louis Riel was hanged today in Canada; but I am afraid that will not end the insurrection."[18]

Woodward's granddaughter, Mary Boynton Cowdrey, edited her grandmother's diaries for publication in 1937. Mary Cowdrey added an historical footnote to this last entry, based on John G. Bourinot's *Canada Under British Rule* and C. P. Mulvaney's *The History of the Northwest Rebellion*. "Riel was tried in Regina in July," Cowdrey wrote, "sentenced to death, and executed on November 16, 1885. For some time after his death other leaders attempted to rouse the half-breeds to further rebellion, but they, as well as the Indians, realized the power of the Canadian Government, and from that day to this, peace has prevailed in that western country."[19]

Woodward's 1885 diary suggests some of the missing connections in western women's histories. North Dakota, like the Prairie provinces, was one of the most ethnically diverse regions of North America, yet she recognized little of the diversity that existed outside her household and neighboring farms. Woodward's spyglass opened only onto her immediate world. Newspapers provided her view of the public world of news and history, a world that was entirely male. The women in between, in the borderlands of her social universe, got lost. She did not mention single women homesteaders, though at various times from 5 to 20 percent of all homesteaders in North Dakota were single women. She did not mention any Canadian women, though 5 percent of all single women homesteaders in North Dakota were Canadians who came to claim homestead land in their own names, as they could not do in Canada.[20]

Her spyglass did not allow her to see into the future, or as far as Grant County, and so she could not see Edith L. Divet, the thirty-two-year-old daughter of an Irish mother and French Canadian father, who filed for land in Grant County in 1906. Edith homesteaded with her widowed sister, Eunice Divet Gilpin, and Eunice's daughter in their eight-room sod home.[21] Woodward's spyglass did not reach the Devils Lake Sioux Reservation, or Rachel Bella Calof who lived near it. Rachel Calof arrived from Russia in 1894 for an arranged marriage and homesteaded until 1917 with her husband, Abe, and their nine children near a North Dakota post office called Benzion. Nor did Woodward witness the departure of Rachel's cousins-in-law, Maier and Doba Calof, as they left to cross the border and settle in Winnipeg.[22]

Woodward assumed that American expansion brought progress and civilization, but she did not apparently ponder her own place in that history or the connection of her private world with the public world of railroad expansion and conquest that had secured her cousin's farm. She did not, evidently, know much about the history of Red River before two nations created Manitoba and Dakota Territory and drew a line between them. She did not consider that Louis Riel might be a husband or a father, or that women might participate in the Rebellion. Canadian troops, she knew, bought ammunition in Fargo, but she did not know that Métis women in Batoche made bullets from lead kettles and the linings of tea tins that they melted in their frying pans. She did not link women's personal concerns with war or know that several of the government employees that the Cree killed during the spring of 1885 were resented for their brutality toward Aboriginal women.[23] She never knew the Métis women who moved south after the Rebellion to the nearby Turtle Mountain Chippewa reservation, nor did she ponder the distinct legal and racial systems that made them Métis in Canada, Chippewa in the United States.

She did not know these things, in part, because of her own class, her racist and nationalist assumptions, *and partly because of the assumptions that separated her firm domestic center from the public world of history.* Woodward's view of Canadian public affairs, like her granddaughter's view of Canadian history, was a "battles, dates, and kings" story, its plot projected from the U.S. history of battles, dates, and presidents that explained the Manifest Destiny of people like her to claim the continent. Mary Dodge Woodward's diary presents some of the challenges of connecting her life with national and western histories; of writing difference, domination, colonization, and conquest into history; of connecting the Canadian and U.S. Wests.

Since the early 1980s, histories of women in the Canadian and U.S. Wests have developed along parallel but critically unconnected lines. Many U.S. historians date the field of western women's history from the Women's West conference in 1983, which generated a book, *The Women's West*; an organization, the Coalition for Western Women's History; and, most importantly, professional networks and collegial exchanges.[24] Like the "Unsettled Pasts" conference, it was an exciting opportunity to share work and insights with other historians and with women who had lived and made western history. Sylvia Van Kirk, the Canadian historian who pioneered the topic of women and gender in the fur trade, spoke at the opening plenary. Her article was published in *The Women's West*, as was Norma Milton's essay on Canadian immigrant domestic workers, based on her University of Calgary M.A. thesis.[25] Canadians Jean Barman, Catherine Cavanaugh and Sarah Carter have won the Jensen-Miller Prize, awarded annually by the Coalition for Western Women's History for the best article in western women's history.[26]

I eagerly devoured these scholars' work, and other histories that introduced me to the women of the Canadian West: *A Harvest Yet to Reap*, *A Flannel Shirt and Liberty*, and Eliane Silverman's collective portrait of Alberta women, *The Last Best West*.[27] But Canadian women's histories did not immediately prompt me to think critically about similarities and differences between the women's Wests of Canada and the United States. In my essay in *The Women's West,* I included material on western suffrage victories in the three Prairie provinces, on women's labor on Canadian farms, and ended with a quote from Nellie McClung, about whom, in truth, I knew very little. But I liked her challenge: "I grew indignant as I read the history and saw how little the people ever counted....When I wrote I would write of the people who do the work of the world and I would write it from their side of the fence." I "included Canadian materials," I wrote, "because western women in the United States and Canada did similar work, received similar messages about domestic roles, and were granted the vote before eastern women."[28] That said, I plowed merrily ahead without taking seriously McClung's challenge to look at her West from her side of the border.

To take that challenge seriously requires collaboration among colleagues whose work illuminates gender on both sides of the border. A generation of historians of women of color have illuminated the complexities of racial and ethnic diversity. Their work has reconceived the women's Wests from more inclusive perspectives, with a more inclusive cast.[29] That scholarly achievement, too, was a collaborative effort.

The beginning points for many of us were the histories we inherited, in which a stock cast of characters—mostly white, mostly young, mostly men—trapped, mined, rode, roped, drank, and shot their way across the West. The mythic American westerners were prospectors, cowboys, desperadoes, vigilantes, lawmen, and soldiers; the mythic Canadian West held more fur traders, stalwart immigrants in sheepskin coats, and Mounties. Both mythic histories erased and marginalized daily acts, private lives, people of color, and women of all races.

That common ground of marginality sometimes obscured significant differences between our western histories and mythic Wests. In the United States, it has been very hard to imagine alternatives to frontier frameworks in western histories, despite the important ways that the new western women's history has reconceptualized frontiers for women. For Native women, frontiers were places where they acted as bridges— economically, diplomatically, socially, sexually, intimately—between colonizers and their own people. For European American women, frontiers were often isolating; their lives improved after the frontier period, when they had neighbors, communities, and the support of other women. The frontier organization of western history texts glorifies a period that was anything but glorious for most women, and it ends the story before some of their most significant community-building activity began. An alternative economic emphasis on the West as a source of staples in Canada, or on extractive industries in the United States, has marginalized women in both nations in histories of national development.

To add women to history will require us to separate the mythic Wests of both countries from history and to analyze how gender has functioned in them. I want to suggest a little of how this might work, which will require me to simplify a bit.

In the mythic American West, defined with frustrating durability by Frederick Jackson Turner in 1893, a succession of trappers, miners, ranchers, and farmers became Americans on a succession of westward-moving frontiers, where European immigrants allegedly merged into a composite nationality. For Turner, the frontier marked the dividing line between "savagery and civilization."[30] As these frontiers became even more mythologized in literature and film, the arrival of women—or at least "good" white women—signaled the arrival of civilization and, with civilization, the end of the frontier.[31] To remain a real guy, the rugged western hero had to ride off alone into the sunset in search of a new frontier.

In Canada, neither frontiers nor the West explained the nation in the same way as in U.S. histories. Harold Innis's West, which furnished staple resources to the metropolitan center, also required miners, ranchers, and farmers, as well as timbermen and fishermen. But these men did not function as mythic heroes to forge the wellspring of Canadian national character.[32] Canadian character, in the mythic Mild West, sprang from English roots and was transported west from central Canada by white men—in this case by Mounties, who brought civilization and order. Because the Canadian western guy *was* a civilizer, he did not have to keep moving in search of new frontiers or escape the stifling influence of white women. To be a western hero, he had only to be more civilized than the U.S. whiskey traders trying to invade Canada from the south.[33]

Comparing our equally distorted myths can help us dissect them. The distinction between the wild and violent U.S. West and the orderly and civilized Canadian West emphasizes that warfare was more commonly used to colonize Native peoples in the United States than in Canada. That is undeniable, but it happened in part because the people of Canada's First Nations sought to avoid the carnage they knew had already happened in the United States. My favorite response comes from Canadian historian Martin Robbins, who quipped that "one cannot excuse a robbery by describing it as orderly."[34]

Women's histories raise the further question of whether Canadian men were less violent toward women than were American men, of whether Mounties were more civilized than the cavalry in their dealings with wives, sex workers, and Native women. For many women, rape and domestic violence mapped a terrain of western masculinity that respected few borders. That frontier awaits comparative analysis.

Multicultural feminist histories stretched our historical vision further yet, and helped us redefine another key category of the U.S. West: the frontier itself. A multi-racial framework reconceived frontiers not as the western edges of white settlement but as places where people of different cultures met, and where women of color were central actors at the cultural crossroads.[35] We then had to look past frontiers to the separate racial and ethnic communities where racial ethnic women maintained families, communities, and cultural identities, as they did at Batoche, Benzion, and Devils Lake.

Sylvia Van Kirk led the way for many of us with *Many Tender Ties*, as she demonstrated how central aboriginal and Métis women were to fur trade society and showed that even filtered sources produced by white men could be used to glean Native women's histories.[36] The old excuse that there were no sources for women's history bit the dust. In 1980 Joan Jensen and Darlis Miller's important article "The Gentle Tamers Revisited" reviewed a huge array of sources for women in the U.S. West and set the agenda for an inclusive, multicultural western women's history, a goal toward which we continue to strive.[37] Multicultural histories have begun to map the ways that race and gender jointly constructed, in Sarah Carter's wonderful phrase, the "categories and terrains of exclusion" in our respective Wests.[38]

Transnational histories can further illuminate that complex terrain as we chart the migrations that brought different people to the Canadian and U.S. Wests—that brought Harry Green and Edith Divet to Dakota, for example, or Kansas farmers disillusioned by the failure of American Populism to Saskatchewan and Alberta. Mining booms and busts drew miners and their families in worldwide migrations, including one of my favorite people, May Wing, whose journeys took her from Leadville to the Cripple Creek District in Colorado; to Rossland, British Columbia; back to Cripple Creek, then Leadville, then Cripple Creek again.[39] Business opportunities and religious communities drew Russian Jews like Maier and Doba Calof from North Dakota to Winnipeg, just as they drew other religious minorities to the Canadian prairies and to larger urban ethnic enclaves on both sides of the border. Colonial and national agendas impelled Native peoples back and forth across the "Medicine Line" long after both nations tried to push them back behind national boundaries that bisected tribal territories.[40]

Cross-border migrations, carefully charted and analyzed, can further illuminate our categories and terrains of exclusion. Canadians are often the most invisible immigrants in the United States, if their native language is English. They "pass," in contrast to Mexicans, who are marked by a different language, who are perceived as poorer and darker, whose border and presence in the United States have historically been more rigorously policed than has the 49th parallel. Harry Green successfully courted Kate Woodward. Mary Dodge Woodward would not have welcomed, with equal equanimity, the attentions of Elsie Lessing's brother, or a thresher, or one of the Sioux Chiefs who passed through on their way to the Minnesota Fair. She grudgingly allowed Irish, Norwegian, and French women into her kitchen, but would not, I suspect, have welcomed the Chinese and Japanese women barred from immigrating to the American and Canadian Wests.[41]

It is a challenging prospect to try to link the histories of women who are thus far still marginal to our respective regional and national histories. Despite the rich harvest of western women's histories on both sides of the border, fur traders' frontiers still dominate hide tanners'; we still have histories of the cattle frontier, but not of the egg or butter frontiers.[42] There are more women in western history texts than there were a quarter century ago, but they are usually slotted into existing plots of frontier and expansion without engaging the challenges to these frameworks that western women's histories have posed.[43] White women are more commonly included than racial ethnic women. Even Mary Dodge Woodward was badly distorted when she appeared in Jon Gjerde's *The Minds of the West* as "a young American woman living in Dakota in the 1880s," in which Woodward functioned as a contrast to Elsie Lessing to demonstrate the different attitudes toward child labor of German immigrants and native-born Americans.[44]

There is a caution in Woodward's tale: to widen the lenses of our own historical spyglasses—to try to approach women as historical actors on their own terms, and to let them help us imagine different plots from their multiple, messy perspectives. It is important to do this for historical accuracy. Mary Dodge Woodward probably saw herself as quite ordinary, but we can recognize that her unpaid labor, and Elsie Lessing's, was as essential a part of the western infrastructure as the railroads, land, and capital that brought her to Dakota. Her daily acts were as much a part of cultural creation as the battles, dates, and soldiers she saw as "history."

Yet if individual lives and daily experience push the nation and public politics out of the centers of history, they do not obliterate the importance of public politics in individual lives, or the significance of national identities. Histories of daily life and private experience lie at the centers of women's histories. Nonetheless, we cannot compare and connect western women's histories without knowing the national and regional histories on both sides of the border in which women's experiences have been located. We cannot, for instance, understand Edith Divet without knowing the differences in Canadian and U.S. homestead laws. And when I equated the suffrage victories in western states and the Prairie provinces, I did not consider the impact of World War I on the Canadian suffrage victories of 1916, though I knew women's wartime contributions had offered many U.S. politicians an acceptable excuse to adopt woman suffrage nationally when they supported the 19th amendment that enfranchised all women in the United States in 1920. It didn't occur to me that World War I was an important context for the first Canadian suffrage victories because, in 1983, I didn't think about the fact that Canada had entered the war in 1914 while the United States did not declare war until 1917, nor did I understand the resonance of that fact for Canadians. A wider historical perspective includes the histories of both nations divided by a common border.

As we widen our historical gaze, we will, I hope, continue to stretch the boundaries and timelines of the pasts we record. Many western historians argue accurately that neither the West nor the Prairies existed as regions before Canada and the United States existed as nations. However, the consequence of making the West or the nation the subject of our histories is that we erase Native peoples, whose histories become a brief prologue to European settlement and fade from the story just as Mary Dodge Woodward expected Sitting Bull and Louis Riel to disappear after she arrived.

It is very hard to bring into common focus the histories of a place and all the people who have called it home. Perhaps no single plot can hold all the women of all our Wests, but that does not mean we should erase some of them. There may be other histories as important as those of states and nations.

This brings me to an important caveat. I have deliberately evaded the question of where we draw the boundaries of our Wests, an issue that seems to obsess historians of the U.S. West, while Canadians have generally followed provincial boundaries to separate the Prairie provinces and British Columbia.[45] The historical constructions of state and region have not yet been mapped from gendered perspectives. For some women, the important geography may not have been the international, state, or provincial boundary lines, but the distance from fuel and water, from letters from kin, from a midwife or another woman's company. Until we map the Wests from women's centers, we cannot know what place meant for western women.

Comparative, transnational, and borderlands histories hold enormous promise to both muddy and clarify the categories of the histories we inherit. I think of Joan Jensen's observation that "change takes place in various ways, often growing from the margins outward."[46] The best of our histories may grow from the lives of people who have been marginal in traditional histories, from the margins of exclusion and inclusion, from the borders between cultures and between nations.

* * *

POSTSCRIPT

I BEGAN WITH A PROLOGUE. I end with a personal postscript about how history shapes borderlands and the significance of borders. I assumed in 1983 that western women were similar in the United States and Canada, that the Canadian and U.S. Wests shared more with one another than they did with Central Canada or the eastern United States. That still seemed true as I drove north in 1999 from Albuquerque to Calgary. The high plains and mountains formed a continuous landscape for the journey, interrupted for only a few hours at the border crossing in Coutts, Alberta, to deal with Immigration Canada. It was only after some time in Canada that the significance of the border and cultural distinctions became clearer. Canada taught me, among much else, how American I am.

Several events immediately before the "Unsettled Pasts" conference brought home the significance of the border and the complexities of identity. The first occurred September 11, 2001. I was madly trying to edit an essay about women in the nineteenth-century West when my American colleague Jewel Spangler called to tell me to turn on my television set. As I watched the World Trade Center crumble, I forgot the article and followed my most urgent instinct—to call my son's school. I babbled something like, "I know this makes no sense, but I'm American, and I just need to know my son is all right." A woman's voice replied, "I am Canadian, I have children and grandchildren, and all I want to do right now is hug them. So if you need to see your son, come on over." As I drove to the school, I noticed an unusual number of airplanes headed for the Calgary airport. And it suddenly dawned on me why they were landing there, and why crossing that line at the border did in fact matter that crisp September morning.

The next day, September 12, I was supposed to lecture on Frederick Jackson Turner and Harold Innis and the ways that the United States racialized and patrolled the border with Mexico but perceived the Canadian border in less racialized and more benign terms. As I reviewed my lecture notes, CNN was already speculating that the terrorist attacks originated in New England because dark-skinned people could sneak across the border from Canada. I winged the lecture, knowing that whatever I thought I knew about borders and national identities was shifting around me as I spoke. I left the classroom more drained than at any time in almost thirty years of teaching, and then I cried.

But I also cried a few months later, this time with excitement and pride, when the Canadian women's hockey team beat the U.S. women's hockey team in the Salt Lake City Olympics. I didn't cry when the Canadian men again beat the U.S. hockey team, but I instinctively rooted for Canada and was taken aback when a colleague offered me condolences at the U.S. loss.

Identity is a slippery business. We all have multiple identities, only some of which are rooted in where we live or the passports we carry. Historical borders mark complex webs of territory, privilege, exclusion, and identity. We all cross some borders; we all police some. Most of us also inhabit *some* borderlands where social territories are redefined and identities are constantly renegotiated. History can be one such borderland, crossing state and social boundaries to re-chart the lines that separate and connect people, to re-map the borders that divide and link our histories.

NOTES

1.   The importance of the frontier in U.S. history dates from Frederick Jackson Turner, "The Significance of the Frontier in American History," first delivered as a paper at the American Historical Association meeting in Chicago, July 12, 1893, coinciding with the World's Columbian Exposition in that city. Reprinted multiple times, references in this article are to the version in Martin Ridge, ed., *History, Frontier, and Section: Three Essays by Frederick Jackson Turner* (Albuquerque: University of New Mexico Press, 1993), 62–71. The staples thesis regarding the significance of western natural resources was authored by Harold A. Innis in *The Fur-trade of Canada* (Toronto: University of Toronto Library, 1927). Innis, too, has been reprinted many times; this work is probably best known in Canada through the edition, *The Fur Trade in Canada: An Introduction to Canadian Economic History* (Toronto: University of Toronto Press, 1956). The interpretation of the Canadian West as milder, less violent, and more orderly than the U.S. West was most famously authored by George F.G. Stanley, "Western Canada and the Frontier Thesis," Canadian Historical Association, *Report of the Annual Meeting*, 1940, 105–14. All of these interpretations generated scholarly debate, elaboration, and revision. The dimensions of these historiographies and of the ways that frontiers and the West have functioned in the two national histories is beyond the scope of this essay, but most historians would recognize the formative influence of these theses. For a comparative review of the historiography of frontiers and the West in Canadian and U.S. history, see Elizabeth Jameson and Jeremy Mouat, "Telling Differences: The Forty-Ninth Parallel and Historiographies of the West and Nation," *Pacific Historical Review* 75, no. 2 (May 2006): 183–230.

2.   The Spanish-Mexican borderlands school of history was founded by Turner's student, Herbert Eugene Bolton, whose borderlands scholarship included *Guide to Materials for the History of the United States in the Principal Archives of Mexico* (Washington, D.C.: Carnegie Institution of Washington, 1913); *Texas in the Middle Eighteenth Century: Studies in Spanish Colonial History and Administration* (Berkeley: Research Services Corp., 1915); and especially *The Spanish Borderlands: A Chronicle of Old Florida and the Southwest* (New Haven: Yale University Press, 1921). For examples of more recent scholarship on the Canada-U.S. borderlands, see Randy William Widdis, *With Scarcely a Ripple: Anglo-Canadian Migration into the United States and Western Canada, 1880–1920* (Montreal and Kingston: McGill-Queen's University Press, 1998); Paul W. Hirt, ed., *Terra Pacifica: People and Place in the Northwest States and Western Canada* (Pullman: Washington State University Press, 1998); Sheila McManus, "Mapping the Alberta-Montana Borderlands: Race, Ethnicity and Gender in the Late Nineteenth Century," *Journal of American Ethnic History* 20, no. 3 (2001): 71–87; "'Their Own Country': Race, Gender, Landscape, and Colonization Around the 49th Parallel, 1862–1900," *Agricultural History* 73, no. 2 (1999): 168–82; and Sheila McManus, *The Line Which Separates: Race, Gender, and the Making of the Alberta-Montana Borderlands* (Lincoln: University of Nebraska Press, 2005); Sterling Evans, ed., *The Borderlands of the American and Canadian Wests: Essays on Regional History of the Forty-ninth Parallel* (Lincoln: University of Nebraska Press, 2006); Beth LaDow, *The Medicine Line: Life and Death on a North American Borderland* (New York: Routledge, 2002); Carol Higham and Robert Thacker, eds., *One West, Two Myths: Essays on Comparisons* (Calgary: University of Calgary Press; Lincoln: University of Nebraska Press, 2005); Jameson and Mouat,

"Telling Differences," and Elizabeth Jameson, "Dancing on the Rim, Tiptoeing through the Minefields: Challenges and Promises of the Borderlands," *Pacific Historical Review* 75, no. 1 (February 2006): 1–24.

3. *Lone Star*, directed by John Sayles (Burbank, CA: Warner Brothers, 1996). See Dennis West and Joan M. West, "Borders and Boundaries: An Interview with John Sayles," *Cineaste* 22, no. 3 (Summer 1996): 14–17.

4. Mary Dodge Woodward, *The Checkered Years: A Bonanza Farm Diary, 1884–88*, ed. Mary Boynton Cowdrey (1937; repr., St Paul: Minnesota Historical Society Press, 1989), 66–67.

5. Susan Armitage, "Through Women's Eyes: A New View of the West," in *The Women's West*, ed. Susan Armitage and Elizabeth Jameson (Norman: University of Oklahoma Press, 1987), 11.

6. For the Woodward family history and the processes of land allocation, see Elizabeth Jameson, "Introduction to the Reprint Edition," Woodward, *Checkered Years*, ix–xxxvii, and Mary Boynton Cowdrey, "Introduction," 11–17.

7. Woodward, *Checkered Years*, 100.

8. Woodward, *Checkered Years*, 151.

9. Woodward, *Checkered Years*, 90.

10. Woodward, *Checkered Years*, 238.

11. Woodward, *Checkered Years*, 41–42, 84–87, 147, 183, 233, 239.

12. Woodward, *Checkered Years*, 151, 169.

13. Woodward, *Checkered Years*, 27.

14. Woodward, *Checkered Years*, 67, 185–86.

15. Woodward, *Checkered Years*, 75–76.

16. Woodward, *Checkered Years*, 34, 71.

17. Woodward, *Checkered Years*, 77.

18. Woodward, *Checkered Years*, 102–03.

19. Woodward, *Checkered Years*, 103. The references Cowdrey used were Sir John George Bourinot, *Canada under British Rule, 1760–1900* (Cambridge: Cambridge University Press, 1900) and Charles Pelham Mulvaney, *The History of the North-west Rebellion of 1885* (Toronto: A.H. Hovey, 1885).

20. H. Elaine Lindgren, *Land in Her Own Name: Single Women as Homesteaders in North Dakota* (1991; repr., Norman: University of Oklahoma Press, 1996), 22, 52, 73–74; Sheryll Patterson-Black, "Women Homesteaders on the Great Plains Frontier," *Frontiers* 1, no. 2 (Spring 1976): 67–88; Paula Nelson, "No Place for Clinging Vines: Women Homesteaders on the South Dakota Frontier," (master's thesis, University of South Dakota, 1978).

21. Lindgren, *Land in Her Own Name*, 106, 186, 246.

22. Rachel Bella Calof, *Rachel Calof's Story: Jewish Homesteader on the Northern Plains*, ed. J. Sanford Rikoon (Bloomington: Indiana University Press, 1995); Maier Calof, *Miracles in the Lives of Maier and Doba Calof* (privately printed, 1941).

23. Diane P. Payment, "La vie en rose? Métis Women at Batoche, 1870 to 1920," in *Women of the First Nations: Power, Wisdom and Strength,* ed. Christine Miller and Patricia Chuchnyk (Winnipeg: University of Manitoba Press, 1996), 19–38, esp. 26–30.

24. The Women's West conference was held in Sun Valley, Idaho, August 10–13, 1983, sponsored by the Center for the American West. A second conference, "Western Women:

Their Land, Their Lives," met in Tucson, Arizona, January 12–15, 1984, sponsored by the Southwest Institute for Research on Women. Anthologies published from these conferences are Armitage and Jameson, eds., *The Women's West* and Lillian Schlissel, Vicki Ruiz, and Janice Monk, eds., *Western Women: Their Land, Their Lives* (Albuquerque: University of New Mexico Press, 1988). The Coalition for Western Women's History was founded at the 1983 Women's West conference, and has sponsored four subsequent conferences.

25. Sylvia Van Kirk, "The Role of Native Women in the Creation of Fur Trade Society in Western Canada, 1670–1830," in *The Women's West*, ed. Armitage and Jameson, 53–62; Norma J. Milton, "Essential Servants: Immigrant Domestics on the Canadian Prairies, 1885–1930," in *The Women's West*, ed. Armitage and Jameson, 207–18.

26. Catherine Cavanaugh won the prize in 1997 for her article "'No Place for a Woman': Engendering Western Canadian Settlement," *Western Historical Quarterly* 28, no. 4 (Winter 1997): 493–518. Jean Barman won in 1998 for "Taming Aboriginal Sexuality: Gender, Power, and Race in British Columbia, 1850–1900," *BC Studies* 115/116 (Autumn/ Winter 1997/98): 237–66; Sarah Carter won in 2006 for "Britishness, Foreignness, Women, and Land in Western Canada, 1880s–1920s," *Humanities Research: The Journal of the Humanities Research Centre for Cross-Cultural Research at the Australian National University*, Vol. 13, No. 1 (2006): 43–60.

27. Linda Rasmussen, Lorna Rasmussen, Candace Savage, and Anne Wheeler, *A Harvest Yet to Reap: A History of Prairie Women* (Toronto: The Women's Press, 1976); Susan A. Jackel, *A Flannel Shirt and Liberty: English Emigrant Gentlewomen in the Canadian West, 1880–1914* (Vancouver: UBC Press, 1982); Eliane Leslau Silverman, *The Last Best West: Women on the Alberta Frontier, 1880–1930* (Montreal: Eden Press, 1984).

28. Elizabeth Jameson, "Women as Workers, Women as Civilizers: True Womanhood in the Canadian West," in *The Women's West*, ed. Armitage and Jameson, 157–58, 161, 148.

29. For reviews of U.S. scholarship, see Elizabeth Jameson, "Toward a Multicultural History of Women in the Western United States," *Signs* 13, no. 4 (1988): 761–91; Catherine Loeb, "La Chicana: A Bibliographic Survey," *Frontiers* 5, no. 2 (Summer 1980): 59–74; Antonia Castañeda, "Gender, Race, and Culture: Spanish-Mexican Women in the Historiography of Frontier California," *Frontiers* 11, no. 1 (1990): 8–20; and Marian Perales, "Empowering 'The Welder': A Historical Survey of Women of Color in the West," in *Writing the Range: Race, Class, and Culture in the Women's West*, ed. Elizabeth Jameson and Susan Armitage (Norman: University of Oklahoma Press, 1997), 21–41. A small sample of this rich and extensive scholarship includes Rosalinda Méndez González, "Distinctions in Western Women's Experience: Ethnicity, Class, and Social Change," in *The Women's West*, ed. Armitage and Jameson, 253–64; Rayna Green, "The Pocahontas Perplex: The Image of Indian Women in American Culture," *Massachusetts Review* 16, no. 4 (1976): 698–714; Cordelia Candelaria, "La Malinche, Feminist Prototype," *Frontiers* 5, no. 2 (Summer 1980): 1–6; Adelaida R. Del Castillo, "Malíntzin Tenépal: A Preliminary Look into a New Perspective," in *Essays on La Mujer*, ed. Rosaura Sanchez and Rosa Martínez Cruz (Los Angeles: UCLA Chicano Studies Center Publications, 1977), 124–49; Peggy Pascoe, "Western Women at the Cultural Crossroads," in *Trails: Toward a New Western History*, ed. Patricia Nelson Limerick, Clyde A. Milner II, and Charles E. Rankin (Lawrence: University Press of Kansas, 1991), 40–58; Judy Yung, *Unbound Feet: A Social History of*

Chinese Women in San Francisco (Berkeley: University of California Press, 1995), 16–24; Antonia I. Castañeda, "Women of Color and the Rewriting of Western History: The Discourse, Politics, and Decolonization of History," *Pacific Historical Review* 61, no. 4 (November 1992): 501–33; Deena J. González, *Refusing the Favor: The Spanish-Mexican Women of Santa Fe, 1820–1880* (New York: Oxford University Press, 1999); Deena J. González, "La Tules of Image and Reality: Euro-American Attitudes and Legend Formation on a Spanish-Mexican Frontier," in *Building with Our Hands: Directions in Chicana Scholarship*, ed. Adela de la Torre and Beatríz M. Mesquera (Berkeley: University of California Press, 1993), reprinted in Vicki L. Ruiz and Ellen Carol DuBois, *Unequal Sisters: A Multicultural Reader in U.S. Women's History,* 2nd ed. (New York: Routledge, 1994), 57–69; Vicki L. Ruiz, *Cannery Women, Cannery Lives: Mexican Women, Unionization, and the California Food Processing Industry, 1930–1950* (Albuquerque: University of New Mexico Press, 1987) and *From Out of the Shadows: Mexican Women in Twentieth-Century America* (New York: Oxford University Press, 1998). Useful anthologies include Rosaura Sanchez and Rosa Martínez Cruz, eds., *Essays on La Mujer* (Los Angeles: UCLA Chicano Studies Center Publications, 1977); Gloria Anzaldua and Cherrie Moraga, eds., *This Bridge Called My Back: Writings by Radical Women of Color* (New York: Kitchen Table/Women of Color Press, 1981); Patricia Albers and Beatrice Medicine, eds., *The Hidden Half: Studies of Plains Indian Women* (Latham, MD.: University Press of America, 1983); Quintard Taylor and Shirley Ann Wilson Moore, *African American Women Confront the West: 1600–2000* (Norman: University of Oklahoma Press, 2003); Ruiz and DuBois, *Unequal Sisters*; and Jameson and Armitage, *Writing the Range*. The latter two volumes contain bibliographies of scholarship about women of color.

30. Turner, "Significance of the Frontier," 62–71.

31. See Beverly Stoeltje, "A Helpmate for Man Indeed: The Image of the Frontier Woman," *Journal of American Folklore* 88, no. 347 (January–March 1975): 27–31; Jameson, "Women as Workers, Women as Civilizers."

32. Innis, *The Fur Trade in Canada.*

33. Stanley, "Western Canada and the Frontier Thesis."

34. Martin Robbins, *The Rush for Spoils: The Company Province, 1871–1933* (Toronto: McClelland and Stewart, 1972), 44.

35. Peggy Pascoe, "Western Women at the Cultural Crossroads." See also Sarah Deutsch, *No Separate Refuge: Culture, Class, and Gender on an Anglo-Hispanic Frontier in the American Southwest, 1880–1940* (New York: Oxford University Press, 1987); Gloria Anzaldua, *Borderlands/La Frontera: The New Mestiza* (San Francisco: Spinster/Aunt Lute, 1987); "Editors' Introduction," in *Writing the Range,* ed. Jameson and Armitage (Norman: University of Oklahoma Press, 1997), 3–16; Elizabeth Jameson, "Bringing It All Back Home: Rethinking Women and the 19th Century West," in *Blackwell Companion to the American West*, ed. William Deverell (Malden, MA, and Oxford, UK: Blackwell Press, 2004), 10:179–99.

36. Sylvia Van Kirk, *Many Tender Ties: Women in Fur-Trade Society in Western Canada, 1670–1870* (Winnipeg: Watson & Dwyer; Norman: University of Oklahoma Press, 1980).

37. Joan M. Jensen and Darlis A. Miller, "The Gentle Tamers Revisited: New Approaches to the History of Women in the American West," *Pacific Historical Review* 49, no. 2 (May 1980): 173–213.

38. Sarah Carter, "Categories and Terrains of Exclusion: Constructing the 'Indian Woman' in the Early Settlement Era in Western Canada," *Great Plains Quarterly* 13, no. 3 (Summer 1993): 147–61.

39. Elizabeth Jameson, *All That Glitters: Class, Conflict, and Community in Cripple Creek* (Urbana: University of Illinois Press, 1998), 27, 33–34.

40. Maier Calof, *Miracles in the Lives*; LaDow, *The Medicine Line*; Theodore Binnema, *Common and Contested Ground: A Human and Environmental History of the Northwestern Plains* (Norman: University of Oklahoma Press, 2001); Michel Hogue, "Disputing the Medicine Line: The Plains Crees and the Canadian-American Border, 1876–1885," *Montana: The Magazine of Western History* 52, no. 4 (Winter 2002): 2–17.

41. Both countries recruited European women to help establish western families and communities, but they discouraged stable families that might encourage Chinese and Japanese workers to settle and stay by means of legislation that severely limited the numbers of Chinese and Japanese women who could legally emigrate. For the United States' restrictive immigration policies see Sucheng Chan, ed., *Entry Denied: Exclusion and the Chinese Community in America, 1882–1943* (Philadelphia: Temple University Press, 1991), esp. chapter 4, Sucheng Chan, "The Exclusion of Chinese Women, 1870–1943," pp. 94–146; and Yuji Ichioka, "*Amerika Nadeshiko*: Japanese Immigrant Women In the United States, 1900–1924," *Pacific Historical Review* 49, no. 2 (1980): 339–57. For Canada, see Erica Lee, "Enforcing the Borders: Chinese Exclusion Along the U.S. Borders with Canada and Mexico, 1882–1924," *Journal of American History* 89, no. 1 (2002): 54–86; Midge Ayukawa, "Good Wives and Wise Mothers: Japanese Picture Brides in Early Twentieth Century British Columbia," in *Rethinking Canada: The Promise of Women's History*, ed. Veronica Strong-Boag and Anita Clair Fellman, 3rd ed. (Toronto: Oxford University Press, 2002), 238–52.

42. William Cronon, Howard R. Lamar, Katherine G. Morrissey, and Jay Gitlin called attention to the ways that male work roles defined American frontiers. Women's work never became the basis for a frontier classification, so we do not speak of a "chicken frontier" as we do of a "cattle frontier," though there is no logical reason not to. See Cronon, et al., "Women and the West: Rethinking the Western History Survey Course," *Western Historical Quarterly* 17, no. 3 (July 1986): 269–90, 272–73.

43. In some recent texts, though the cast of characters is more inclusive, and the definitions of frontiers more nuanced, the frontier narrative itself still provides the basic organizing principle. See for instance Robert V. Hine and John Mack Faragher, *The American West: A New Interpretive History* (New Haven: Yale University Press, 2000). Richard White's important revisionist synthesis, "*It's Your Misfortune and None of My Own": A New History of the American West* (Norman: University of Oklahoma Press, 1991), includes some women actors, but neither women nor gender is central to the narrative. Patricia Nelson Limerick's *The Legacy of Conquest: The Unbroken Past of the American West* (New York: W.W. Norton, 1987) challenged triumphalist interpretations of expansion but included few women; the only women featured were western prostitutes and missionary Narcissa

Whitman. Limerick, *Legacy of Conquest*, 48–54. The New Western History is often defined by its focus on conquest, power, race, and environment. Western women's histories are rarely identified as central texts in the New Western History, nor are new histories of race in the West.

44. Jon Gjerde, *The Minds of the West: Ethnocultural Evolution in the Rural Middle West, 1830–1917* (Chapel Hill: University of North Carolina Press, 1997), 179–80.

45. See, for instance, Robert G. Athearn, *The Mythic West in Twentieth-Century America* (Lawrence: University Press of Kansas, 1966); Walter Nugent, "Where Is the American West?: Report on a Survey," *Montana: The Magazine of Western History* 42, no. 2 (Summer 1992): 2–23; Donald Worster, "New West, True West: Interpreting the Region's History," *Western Historical Quarterly* 18, no. 2 (April 1987): 141–56; David M. Emmons, "Constructed Province: History and the Making of the Last American West," *Western Historical Quarterly* 25, no. 4 (Winter 1994): 437–59, and "A Roundtable of Responses," *Western Historical Quarterly* 25, no. 4 (Winter 1994): 461–86.

46. Joan M. Jensen, *One Foot on the Rockies: Women and Creativity in the Modern American West* (Albuquerque: University of New Mexico Press, 1995), 151.

2

UNSETTLED PASTS, UNSETTLING BORDERS

Women, Wests, Nations

SHEILA McMANUS

WOMEN'S HISTORIANS have always unsettled the past. It is what we do. Narratives of the past that have been written to appear smooth and linear look a lot bumpier, more colourful and complex, after women's historians get their hands on them. This is perhaps most true when we look at the history of the North American West. The region has long been coded as quintessentially and exclusively male. The popular narratives of the American West have been and remain rather more "butch" than those of Canada, with much emphasis placed on famous explorers like Lewis and Clark, doomed soldiers like General Custer, cowboys and Indians, yeomen pioneers, and the violence of western colonization. The popular histories of the Canadian West highlight David Thompson, Louis Riel, the Great March of the North West Mounted Police, and a peaceful, law-and-order settlement.[1] Yet, as historians are beginning to point out, these two Wests have a great deal in common, not the least of which is a primary narrative of white male penetration, exploration, and development. They share, for example, the symbolism of the transcontinental railroads conquering "empty" lands that had been passively waiting to play their part in teleological and nationalist narratives about brave white men. And one way or another, whites quickly assumed the dominant role over the Aboriginal groups of both Wests.

Thanks to three decades of outstanding scholarship in western women's history, the North American West is now seen to contain a wide range of overlapping stories that extend far beyond those about what manly white men were doing on any given day. These historians have established that there was never just one West on either side of the border: there were always multiple Wests, multiple women's Wests, multiple sites of identity, conflict, and community building.[2] Our work has always been about crossing lines and resisting earlier historiographical categories, because the women we write about crossed lines of space, nation, race, ethnicity, gender, and sexuality. Even native women, for whom what non-Aboriginal scholars call "the West" has been home for thousands of years, have had to confront, live through, and challenge the colonizers' categories and demarcations.[3]

Yet the one line we have generally avoided crossing is that of the nation state, particularly the boundary between Canada and the United States. The border between the United States and Mexico has established a place in the historiography of North American women, as much for its racialization as its significance within the past and current political dynamic of the United States. Mexican Americans are recognized as a "visible minority" in the United States, while Canadians in the United States and Americans in Canada are, for the most part, invisible and unacknowledged minorities.[4] We see the U.S.-Mexico border as a border, a border with a contested and artificial past and present, because so much of it is demarcated with razor wire, watch towers, and men with guns. Our eyes are drawn to it, which then makes it easier to look beyond it to the thus-clearly-demarcated Other side. By contrast, the Canada-

U.S. border is nearly three times as long but lacks the razor wire and watch towers, although it does now have the men with guns. Its history has not been racialized, and at the level of popular consciousness it often seems to disappear as a border altogether.

The 49th parallel is a line that western women's historians have taken very seriously; the border has fundamentally shaped the contours of our scholarship, bifurcating it into studies of what women have done in the "Canadian West" and what they have done in the "American West."[5] In particular, we have situated our studies within a region called "the West" without challenging the nationalist category this assumes: one only has a "West" when one also has an "East," and thus a larger nation has to exist for a region called "the West" to exist. We have then proceeded to ask how race, ethnicity, class, and sexuality have intersected with gender within that pre-existing and unexamined spatial category. Historians of the women's West have in fact been historians of either the Canadian women's West or the American women's West, the terrain already shaped by each nation's narratives about its own, supposedly unique, West. One key problem with halting our studies and stories at the 49th parallel is that in doing so we are assuming that the line meant the same thing to the women we write about as it means to us. We know where the borders between the political entities called *Canada* and the *United States* would eventually wind up, we know what those borders have come to mean in today's geopolitical landscape, and so we proceed (quite anachronistically for historians) as if those borders were always there and had always had those meanings. Western historians have always implicitly dealt in borderlands because we pay attention to the places where two or more cultures, races, and classes "edge each other" on the same territory,[6] but we have not yet embraced the national political border as an analytical concept. Borders are malleable, historical constructions that come to shape what happens within their limits.

Most Canadian and American women's historians have paid little attention to national political borders, and most Canadian-American borderlands scholars have paid little attention to gender.[7] This has helped create a surprisingly reactionary reification of borders as gender-less, as something to do with politics and nations and economics and little to do with the kinds of analysis that social historians have been developing for decades. And yet the two kinds of scholarship actually go together quite nicely.[8] As described by Chicana feminist Gloria Anzaldúa in her landmark 1987 book, *Borderlands/La Frontera*, "Borders are set up to define the places that are safe and unsafe, to distinguish us from them. A border is a dividing line, a narrow strip along a steep edge. A borderland is a vague and undetermined place created by the emotional residue of an unnatural boundary. It is in a constant state of transition."[9] Her work specifically addresses the U.S.-Mexico border, but her insights about the nature of borders and how they are expected to work are equally applicable elsewhere. Given the un-settling work women's historians are already experienced with and the historiographical borders our field has erased, the groundlessness of the borderlands ought to feel like familiar territory.

So, say we do step across that line—what do we see? Women's historians already accustomed to the different impact of race, ethnicity, class, and sexuality on women will not be surprised to discover that political borders mean different things to different women depending on the nature of their other relationships with the state. One characteristic of the modern nation state is the way in which it manages the people who live within its borders, categorizing and privileging individuals and groups according to their class, racial and ethnic background, language, gender, and sexuality, as well as where they live and what kinds of work they do. Michel Foucault, for example, has noted that the idea of "population" as a "technique of power" emerged in western Europe in the eighteenth century, coinciding with what Benedict Anderson has called "the dawn of the age of nationalism...."[10] By developing into modern nation states in the nineteenth century, the United States and Canada took for granted their right to manage their populations as a tool for managing their borders. There were (and are) two very different nation-states at work in the North American West, but official assumptions about the intersecting uses of race and gender demonstrate some marked similarities. Western women's historians are well-suited to analyze those differences and similarities.

To the largest and most marginalized group of women in the North American West, the border could make a world of difference at the same time as it meant nothing at all. Across the continent Aboriginal women have shared the experiences of disease, poverty, violence, and a staggering loss of land and resources. The legacy of their dispossession can be seen to this day. For Aboriginal nations, the creation of Euro-North American nations and their artificial borders was one of many proofs of the colonization of the continent, but those borders affected Aboriginal women differently than they did Aboriginal men and other women.

Anzaldúa has called the U.S.-Mexico border a "1,950 mile-long open wound / dividing a *pueblo*, a culture, / running down the length of my body."[11] A similar wound runs through the land from the Lake of the Woods to the Rocky Mountains, through the homelands of the Pikani, Kainai, Cree, and Lakota. Two examples highlight the impact of the 49th parallel on the lives and bodies of Aboriginal women across the northern Great Plains. The most familiar distinction the Canada-U.S. border created is that Canadian Indian legislation specifically defined "Indianness" as male: it excluded women who married non-native men and included non-native women who married native men. An Aboriginal woman who found herself on the north side of the 49th parallel after 1876 discovered that her identity, rights, home, culture, and final resting place depended on her marital status and the racial category of her husband.[12] The United States did not have a clear legal definition of who was an Indian, and it developed a "blood quotient" system instead, so most (although certainly not all) Aboriginal women who married white men south of the line could continue to live on the reservation along with their white husbands. The governments' concerns about the morality of relationships between native women and white men thus played out differently on each side of the line. In Montana, for example, officials worried about the degradation of white manhood and the economic and political consequences that were thought to ensue when white men chose to live with Indian women on what was left of Indian land. Authorities wanted to force these men to marry the women they lived with to salvage some veneer of what the authorities considered respectability.[13] In Alberta the law forced native women to leave their homes and communities if they married white men, yet branded as "prosti-tutes" native women who left the reserve on their own.[14] The Indian Act also unintentionally perpetuated Aboriginal women's older colonial role as intermediaries between their home communities and the white newcomers. For example, during the 1885 Rebellion in Canada's North-West, in which a small group of Métis, First Nations, and whites in what is now Saskatchewan tried to start an uprising against the Canadian government, a Siksika woman named Pokemi, who was living off the reserve with her white husband, informed her white neighbours in southern Alberta of the steps the Canadian government was taking to keep the Blackfoot from getting involved in the hostilities. She thus pro-vided some much-needed reassurance for the frightened whites.[15]

A less familiar example of the impact of the creation of the border is the way it drastically reduced the mobility of Aboriginal women faster and more completely than it did for Aboriginal men. Before there was any such thing as a Canada-U.S. border along the 49th parallel, families and bands of the buffalo-hunting cultures of the northern Great Plains followed a seasonal route from one hunting camp to another. For many bands of the Blackfoot nations, this involved crossing and re-crossing the future line of the border. During the closing decades of the nine-teenth century, as Canada and the United States struggled to make the border into a meaningful demarcation and make Aboriginal commun-ities hold still on their reserves and reservations, Aboriginal women had fewer opportunities to continue to move through their traditional ter-ritories. Unlike young men who continued their horse raids across the line (frustrating white officials in both countries) or who could escape across the line to relatives to avoid charges related to the raids, the real-ity of the border as a barrier was brought home more quickly for women whose mobility, economic activities, and gender roles were more con-strained. Flouting the line became a gender-specific activity.[16]

Women did find ways to resist the localized attempts to limit their mobility, however. For example, Father Lacombe, the Catholic priest who ran the federal government's industrial school near High River, Alberta, spent most of his July 1885 report urging the government to allow the school to forcibly remove children from the reserves and keep them at school because the parents "seem determined not to give up their younger children, unless compelled to do so." Even when the school had managed to take in some children, he wrote, "the squaws—their mothers—came here a month or so afterwards, and demanded their children, pretending they were taken away without their consent."[17] Similar remarks do not appear in the reports from Montana, where the government's schools were deliberately placed close to children's homes to encourage attendance—a stark contrast with the explicit policy of separation pursued by the Canadian government. Aboriginal women were the largest group of women in the West, and the encroachment of the Canadian and American nation states produced a depressingly similar legacy of poverty and marginalization. However, these examples from the Blackfoot demonstrate that there were distinct inflections of race, gender, and sexuality, and distinct opportunities for resistance, on either side of the line.

Black women were one of the smallest groups of women in the West and confronted an official framework of racism and marginalization, but the border seems to have offered them some powerful opportunities. The 1880 census of Choteau County, Montana, counted only two "colored" women, compared to sixteen men, and the Canadian census of 1885 indicated that there were only four people of "African origin" in southern Alberta, but did not specify gender.[18] Black women confronted identical racial slurs and the same menial spaces in the colonial economy no matter what side of the border they were on. May Flanagan remembered a black midwife in early Fort Benton, Montana, whom she called "old Aunt Leah" in her memoirs.[19] Similarly, Mary Inderwick of southern Alberta wrote in an 1884 letter that she had started sending her laundry to an "aristocratic Auntie" in Pincher Creek.[20] Calling these women "Auntie" was a way of reinforcing their menial, racialized status as support staff to white settler communities, and it highlights the way racist stereotypes and labels could and did cross borders: Flanagan's text linked the black woman's presence and usefulness to the birth of one of the first white babies in the area, born to prominent local and cross-border businessman George Baker, while the woman in Pincher Creek saved Inderwick from having to do her own laundry.

Black women did not passively play along with the racial hierarchies of the day any more than Aboriginal women did, and at least one woman attempted to use the border to claim a powerful new identity. The same letter from Inderwick gives another view of the "aristocratic Auntie" in Pincher Creek: Inderwick notes that the woman "boasts that she and the Police Commissioner's wife were the first white ladies to arrive in the country." Inderwick's racialized representation of the woman does not match the representation the woman claims for herself. The woman says she is "white" and a "lady," thus claiming a place in the colonial narrative of southern Alberta; Inderwick says she is "coloured" and calls her "Auntie," thus removing her from that narrative. It is likely that she was American-born and, presumably, had a light skin colour, and consequently seized a chance to redefine her own identity after crossing the border into Canada. Her occupation would have been sufficient evidence for the rest of the town to agree with Inderwick, because a black woman was far more likely than a white woman to take in other people's laundry in the nineteenth-century West. It is equally clear, however, that the woman did not let others' perceptions change her self-identification.

White women were neither the largest nor the smallest group of women in the North American West, but they are certainly the most studied. Although they were highly privileged by virtue of their racial category, their gender meant that they had different relationships with the state than white men, and different relationships with the Canadian and American governments. The familiar example of this difference is that of land policy. The homestead provisions of the 1872 Canadian Dominion Lands Act were initially open to single women, mirroring the 1862 American Homestead Act. In 1876 however, the same year in which the consolidated Indian Act entrenched Indian-ness as male, the Canadian government amended the Dominion Lands Act to specifically bar single women.[21] Whereas in the United States single women made up from 5 to 15 per cent of all homestead entries before 1900 and "proved up" at similar or better rates,[22] single women in Canada had no such access to the west's single biggest resource. Rather paradoxically, at the same time as Canada was limiting women's access to western land, the government was actively trying to recruit white women to settle the West, while the United States gave little thought to white women immigrants as anything other than an administrative problem.[23] Immigration officials in western Canada explicitly stated that white women were needed to help settle the west by marrying white men and having white babies, to forestall the "problems" that arose from the offspring of Aboriginal women and white men. The most explicit statement of this attitude came from Immigration Agent William Grahame in 1879, while he was stationed at Duluth, Minnesota. He noted that Canada needed to be doing more to attract "a good healthy class of domestic servants" to come to the North-West. Not only was it difficult to get a good domestic in the west, and young women could make more money in Winnipeg than in Montreal as a result, but they also would not have to stay in those jobs for very long. Women were guaranteed to find "good comfortable homes in the future" because "so many of our young Canadian farmers are settling alone in the North-West, and are compelled to lead a bachelor's life, or inter-marry with the Indian women, while the introduction of a number of good healthy young women into the Province and North-West, would have a tendency to elevate the morals of our young men, who would be very ready to embrace all the responsibilities of matrimony, were it possible to find good helpmates."[24] But these differences between Canadian and American approaches to white women were at the level of official policies and perceptions. On the ground, only one clear difference is evident in the writing of white women in the Alberta-Montana borderlands in the late nineteenth century: most of the American women, writing in the 1860s to the 1880s, were afraid of local native peoples, and few of the Canadian women, writing in the 1880s, expressed a similar fear. Carolyn Abbott Tyler, for example, was part of the Fisk Expedition that came from Minnesota up the Missouri River and then travelled west of Fort Benton in 1862. She wrote in her diary on September 10 that "every one thankful that Blackfeet had gone to their own country." The whites were told by a local Indian agent not to winter in the valley of the Teton River because "it was claimed by all tribes as neutral ground" as a short-cut to get to the buffalo hunt, and the assumption was that a group of white people would be too much of a target if they were camped in the way.[25] Mary Douglas Gibson wrote of her first trip from Minneapolis to Fort Benton in 1882 that "the river was so low it was impossible to navigate at night, so we were anchored in midstream for greater safety from Indians as well as less danger from running aground." When her group decided to travel the last section overland, she remembered that they "were obliged to travel very slowly for the officers had to remain with their men who were walking, because of possible attacks from the Indians."[26]

This anxiety is absent from the personal papers of the Canadian writers. There was no legacy of so-called "Indian Wars" as there was in the American West, and after the numbered treaties of the 1870s and before the 1885 Rebellion, Canada's national discourse around plains peoples rested on the assumption that they had been contained on their reservations.[27] In 1883 for example, Mary Inderwick passed through Swift Current, Saskatchewan, and wrote in her diary that there were "Indians by the million," but being outnumbered did not seem to worry her. Upon her arrival in Calgary two days later, she wrote that the town was "very nice but it is a village of tents and framed in Indians and squaws in plenty."[28] Even numerous and highly-visible native peoples were merely a backdrop for her own journey.

The North-West Rebellion of 1885 was the only moment when whites in southern Alberta expressed the same kind of general fear of native peoples that was more common among whites in northern Montana. The rebellion was the main topic in twelve-year-old Julia Short's diary in late March and early April of that year. Her family had a ranch south of Calgary on the Highwood River. The three Blackfoot nations (the Siksika, Kainai, and Pikani) did not participate in the uprising, but Short's diary portrays a white community fraught with tension nonetheless. In her reminiscence she wrote that "for a few weeks the settlers all through the West lived in a state of terror. A big Indian Reserve lay to the east of us, two more Reserves were not far south, and there was the chance that at any time they, or scattered bands of unruly young Indian Braves from these tribes, might sweep through the country, spreading death and destruction." The Canadian government increased the food rations to the Blackfoot, and Short wrote that "this did much to calm and discourage any would-be aspirations to regain the territory given over to the white race."[29] It is her reminiscence that mentions the efforts of the Siksika woman Pokemi, discussed earlier, to inform and reassure the whites.

While these different reactions to local Aboriginal people might serve to reinforce the traditional stereotypes of the "wild" American West and the "peaceful" Canadian West, the shared elements in white women's writing, such as their reactions to western landscapes and their efforts to construct familiar communities, are more common. These elements draw attention to the similarities between the American and Canadian colonial processes, and the privileges those processes conferred on Euro-North Americans.

White women north and south of the line often used remarkably similar language when writing about their perceptions of and reactions to the landscape of the borderlands. American and Canadian writers generally admired or were even awestruck by the dramatic landscapes created by the open spaces and Rocky Mountains. For example, in 1878 Alma Coffin Kirkpatrick travelled with her two sisters up the Missouri River to Fort Benton and then overland to the mining camp in south-western Montana where their father worked. She wrote in her diary on August 7, 1878, "I know now why people love the West. The beauty and grandeur of the mountains, rocks and trees, canyons and dashing streams! The vast landscapes revealed in the clear atmosphere are beyond all description." A few years later she "tried to analyze the lure of the far west; its wonderful atmosphere so clear that the distant mountains appear near; the air so keen and invigorating, inspiring one to large undertakings...our valleys surrounded by mountain ranges that never appear twice the same...."[30] In Julia Short Asher's reminiscence of her family's journey from Selkirk, Manitoba, to High River, Alberta, in 1884, she wrote that the views improved considerably once her family made it to the foothills of southern Alberta: "ahead of us were low rolling hills and shallow ravines covered with green grass and quantities of beautiful prairie flowers." The Rocky Mountains seemed "close at hand...a great wall of white peaks with wide masses of dark green at their feet. Streamers of this green ran up in uneven stretches to fill and overflow the ravines, while the higher peaks towered above the timberline in their everlasting snow-crowned glory. Never had we seen such beauty and we thrilled with the joy of it."[31]

A second similarity in the personal writings of white women in the borderlands was their efforts to create new communities for themselves through contact with other local white women. In northern Montana in the 1870s, for example, Lucy Stocking wrote in her diary on June 29, 1871, that prominent Fort Benton merchant Conrad Baker and his daughter had called at her ranch.[32] And no sooner had Alma Coffin Kirkpatrick arrived in Fort Benton in July 1878 than she accompanied a "Captain Haney" on visits to three (presumably white) families. She wrote that "the ladies were at home and very agreeable. Their houses are small, but prettily furnished. One lady played and sang for us, charmingly."[33] Similarly, Mary Inderwick's 1884 diary indicates that, although their numbers were small, she managed to visit other women in her area on a regular basis. For example, during a two-week period she records at least three such visits. On January 24, she and "Mrs. M went to see Mrs. Battles. Think her very nice and nice baby." On January 29 they headed to the Kainai Reserve for dinner with the minister and his wife, Reverend and Mrs Trivett, and had lunch at "Mrs. Bourne's" on the way. And on February 8 she wrote "Mr. & Mrs. Geddes here for coal—stayed about half an hour and I enjoyed it—She is so nice...."[34]

Unlike native women, whose different relationships with the two federal governments meant that the border and its nationalist meanings were enforced more strictly in their daily lives, white women's racial privilege seems to have allowed them to pay infrequent attention to the border and the nationalist identities it was supposed to instil. White women were permitted to cross the border, but if Sadye Wolfe Drew's experiences can be taken as an indication of the relationship white women had with the border, crossing the line had little nationalist meaning. Sadye was ten years old in the summer of 1893 when her family crossed the line twice, first heading to Alberta to homestead and then returning to the United States. They took the train from Shelby, Montana, to Lethbridge, Alberta, and decades later she recalled that "When we came to the line between Canada and the States the customs officers went thru our things. My aunt had twin babies and there naturally was a bag of soiled diapers and when the officials came to that they didn't look any further." The family returned to the States a few months later after the Alberta homestead proved to be a bust, and this time when they arrived at the line the officers "wouldn't let us take our Indian pony across unless dad paid $40. He didn't have much money and besides he paid only $5 for the pony and could buy another for a lot less than $40. We kids were heart broken to have to give her up as we had enjoyed her so much."[35] The Canadian and American governments wanted the border to mean something in nationalist terms, as evidenced by the early presence of customs officers, but for Drew it was remembered as dirty diapers and the loss of a beloved pony.

So when and how do borders matter to women? Do the gender and racial norms of a time and place reinforce or undercut the process of nation-building? Are women's experiences fundamentally shaped by the political boundaries within which those experiences take place? The answer, it seems, is yes and no, and depends on a woman's place within the political and social economies of colonization and citizenship and the historical specificity of her relationship to a particular border. Borders appear to have the biggest impact on a woman's experiences when she occupies an additional category (be it racial or ethnic or religious or sexual) that is already marginalized by the nation state in which she resides or to which she is trying to gain entry. Yet it is clear that in other ways borders matter far less to women than they do to patriarchal nation-states, for which legitimacy through territorial control is a powerful concern. Nations are made and unmade at their borders, not in their heartlands, because a nation begins as a territorial claim. Whatever national identities and values are presumed to rest in the heartland, whatever the heartland can take for granted as the "truth" about itself, must be imagined and defended first and most explicitly at the edges of the nation. It is at a nation's borders that the real or imaginary defence against whatever is on the other side of the line takes place. Heartlands can only become the ideological centre of the nation if national borders are doing their work, because heartlands can only exist when their edges are clearly delineated. And recent scholarship has shown that states rely heavily on gender and race as border-making and nation-making tools.[36] Nations and nationalism have always been and are still about defining who is in and who is out, who belongs and who does not, and the goals and experiences of women and people of colour have little place in that project. Gender and race can therefore also be powerful tools for unmaking those nations and unsettling those borders, by throwing into question the taken-for-granted, essentialized, and normalized meanings ascribed to nations and their borders. This is an important project for feminist borderlands scholars if we want to continue redrawing the past or hope to shape the future with women's diverse experiences at the centre.

But the past three decades of writing in western women's history also makes two cautions appropriate. First, we cannot assume that there will be similarities in women's experiences across a borderline just because they are women. Assuming the existence of an essential category of "women" is as problematic as assuming the existence of an essential category of "nation." We must continue to pay attention, and possibly pay even more attention, to the different effects of race, class, gender, and sexuality on women's lives and experiences on different sides of a border. Women's historians already know, for example, that statements that may be true about white women or heterosexual women may not be true for black or Aboriginal women or lesbians. The same caution needs to be exercised when discussing the experiences of women living on different sides of a national border, particularly a border in a time that is not our own and one that might not yet have the meanings we automatically and unconsciously ascribe to it. It is easy to assume, for example, that white, heterosexual, middle-class women will have a lot in common no matter which side of a border they are living on. A borderlands analysis, however, might reveal that even this highly-privileged combination of race, class, and sexuality will have its own subtle and unique inflections on the other side of a border. Then again, it might not, and either way the questions need to be asked and the answers are worth pondering.

The second caution is that historiographical exceptionalism, the assumption that the history of one country is more unique than the history of another country and yet can, simultaneously, be taken as a norm for other countries, has no place in borderlands scholarship. American historians have grappled for decades with the temptation of "American exceptionalism," and Canadian historians, particularly those who are still invested in the stereotype that the "peaceful, law-abiding" Canadian West was superior to the "wild, violent" American West, need to resist the same temptation. A unique contribution that borderlands scholarship can make to larger national historiographies is to highlight the similarities between different histories and to note more closely actual differences. As the most mythologized region within each national narrative, the history of the North American West stands to gain a significant new depth and nuance from a more careful study of its many borders.

There is no doubt that western women's historians will continue to un-settle the past, even if the past we are writing about deals with the European settlement of the North American West. Just as an inclusive women's history continues to challenge our understanding of the history of the West, so too will these multiple histories challenge what we think we know about the histories of nations and the meanings of nationalism. We should not avoid asking why we think "our" West stops or starts at a national border. We cannot know if, when, how, or why borders matter to women unless we are willing to step across that line. And, as always when one is in the West, watch where you step.

NOTES

1. This stereotypical dichotomy was neatly captured by the title of a comparative course taught at the University of Calgary by Elizabeth Jameson and Sarah Carter in the fall of 2001 called "Mild West, Wild West?" Similarly, it can be seen in the title of *One West Two*

Myths: A Comparative Reader, ed. Carol Higham and Robert Thacker (Calgary: University of Calgary Press, 2004). It is also evident in the amount of attention paid to the Lewis and Clark bicentennial in Montana and North Dakota's tourism advertising, as compared to the "law and order" emphasis at Canadian historic sites like Fort Walsh, Saskatchewan.

2. A very small sampling of this rich scholarship would have to include such American works as Julie Roy Jeffrey, *Frontier Women: The Trans-Mississippi West, 1840–1880* (New York: Hill and Wang, 1979); Lillian Schlissel, Vicki L. Ruiz, and Janice Monk, eds., *Western Women: Their Land, Their Lives* (Albuquerque: University of New Mexico Press, 1988); Joan M. Jensen and Nancy Grey Osterud, eds., *American Rural and Farm Women in Historical Perspective* (Washington, D.C.: The Agricultural History Society, 1994); and Elizabeth Jameson and Susan Armitage, eds., *Writing the Range: Race, Class, and Culture in the Women's West* (Norman: University of Oklahoma Press, 1997); and Canadian studies such as Sylvia Van Kirk, *Many Tender Ties: Women in Fur-Trade Society in Western Canada, 1670–1870* (Winnipeg, MB: Watson & Dwyer Publishing; Norman: University of Oklahoma Press, 1980); Eliane Leslau Silverman, *The Last Best West: Women on the Alberta Frontier, 1880–1930* (Montreal: Eden Press, 1984); Sarah Carter, *Capturing Women: The Manipulation of Cultural Imagery in Canada's Prairie West* (Montreal: McGill-Queen's University Press, 1997); and Catherine A. Cavanaugh and Randi R. Warne, eds., *Telling Tales: Essays in Western Women's History* (Vancouver: UBC Press, 2000).

3. See, for example, Van Kirk, *Many Tender Ties*; Carter, *Capturing Women*; Christine Miller and Patricia Chuchryk, eds., *Women of the First Nations: Power, Wisdom and Strength* (Winnipeg: University of Manitoba Press, 1996); Laura F. Klein and Lillian A. Ackerman, eds., *Women and Power in Native North America* (Norman: University of Oklahoma Press, 1995).

4. For examples of the prominence of Mexican American women in American women's history, see such collections as Schlissel, Ruiz, and Monk, eds. *Western Women: Their Land, Their Lives*; Jameson and Armitage, eds., *Writing the Range*; Linda K. Kerber and Jane Sherron De Hart, eds., *Women's America: Refocusing the Past*, 5th ed. (New York: Oxford University Press, 2000). The limited scholarship on Canadians in the United States and on Americans in Canada includes such works as Marcus L. Hansen and John Bartlett Brebner, *The Mingling of the Canadian and American Peoples* (New Haven, CT: Yale University Press, 1940); Karel D. Bicha, *The American Farmer and the Canadian West, 1896–1914* (Lawrence, KS: Coronado Press, 1968); Harold Martin Troper, *Only Farmers Need Apply: Canadian Government Encouragement of Immigration from the U.S., 1896–1911* (Toronto: Griffen, 1972); Randy W. Widdis, *With Scarcely a Ripple: Anglo-Canadian Migration into the United States and Western Canada, 1880–1920* (Montreal and Kingston: McGill-Queen's University Press, 1998); Bruno Ramirez, *Crossing the 49th Parallel: Migration from Canada to the United States, 1900–1930* (Ithaca, NY: Cornell University Press, 2001); John M. Findlay and Ken S. Coates, eds., *Parallel Destinies: Canadian-American Relations West of the Rockies* (Seattle: Center for the Study of the Pacific Northwest in association with University of Washington Press; Montreal: McGill-Queen's University Press, 2002).

5. For example, the two standard anthologies, Jameson and Armitage's *Writing the Range* and Cavanaugh and Warne's *Telling Tales*, contain no articles that cross the Canada-U.S.

border. The same is true of the classic monographs, from Carter to Jeffrey. Only Sylvia Van Kirk's *Many Tender Ties* is well-known, frequently-used, and transnational. As a result, the overall contours of the scholarship have created nation-specific Wests, in opposition to nation-specific Easts.

6. Gloria Anzaldúa, *Borderlands/La Frontera: The New Mestiza*, 2nd ed. (1987; repr., San Francisco: Aunt Lute Books, 1999), 19. Citation is from the preface to the first edition.

7. On the latter point see such recent examples as Findlay and Coates, eds., *Parallel Destinies*, and Beth LaDow, *The Medicine Line: Life and Death on a North American Borderland* (New York and London: Routledge, 2001), which pay little or no attention to women or gender. The 2004 collection *One West Two Myths* contains only one article dealing with borderlands and gender: Sheila McManus, "Making the Forty-Ninth Parallel: How Canada and the United States Used Space, Race and Gender to Turn Blackfoot Country into the Alberta-Montana Borderlands."

8. See, for example, the work of scholars like Nora Faires, McManus, and the articles in this volume that highlight the analytical advantages of paying attention to gender and borders: Faires, "Poor Women, Proximate Border: Migrants from Ontario to Detroit in the Late Nineteenth Century," *Journal of American Ethnic History* 20, no. 3 (Spring 2001): 88–109; McManus, *The Line Which Separates: Race, Gender and the Making of the Alberta-Montana Borderlands in the Late Nineteenth Century* (Lincoln: University of Nebraska Press, 2005).

9. Anzaldúa, *Borderlands/La Frontera*, 25.

10. Michel Foucault, *The History of Sexuality, Volume I: An Introduction*, trans. Robert Hurley (New York: Vintage Books, 1990), 25; Benedict Anderson, *Imagined Communities: Reflections on the Origin and Spread of Nationalism*, rev. ed. (London and New York: Verso, 1991), 11.

11. Anzaldúa, *Borderlands/La Frontera*, 24.

12. The most thorough critique of this aspect of Canada's Indian Act can be found in Kathleen Jamieson, *Indian Women and the Law In Canada: Citizens Minus* (Ottawa: Advisory Council on the Status of Women, 1978). The most thorough discussion of American Indian policy remains Francis Prucha's *The Great Father: The United States Government and the American Indians*, 2 vols. (Lincoln: University of Nebraska Press, 1984).

13. See, for example, "Report of Commissioner of Indian Affairs E.A. Hayt," November 15, 1879, in U.S. Congress, Department of the Interior, *Annual Report of the Secretary of the Interior,* 46th Cong., 2nd sess., House Executive Documents 1, Part 5, 77; and U.S. Congress, Department of the Interior, *Annual Report of the Secretary of the Interior,* 48th Cong., 1st sess., 1883, House Executive Document 1, Part 5, xi.

14. See, for example, "Report of John A. Macdonald, Minister and Superintendent-General of Indian Affairs," in Canada, Department of the Interior, "Annual Report of the Department of Indian Affairs For Year Ended 31 December 1883," *Sessional Papers* 1884, vol. 3, no. 4, lii–liii, and the Report of W. Pocklington, Sub-Agent for Treaty 7 in the same report, 86.

15. Julia Short Asher, diary excerpts and reminiscence, Short-Knupp Family Fonds, M1137, Glenbow Archives, Calgary, AB (hereafter cited as GA).

16. For three examples of Canadian and American officials complaining about the ongoing cross-border raids of Blackfoot men, see Cecil E. Denny, Report of Agent for Treaty 7, July 10, 1883, in Canada, Department of the Interior, "Annual Report of the Department of Indian Affairs for year ended 31st December 1883," *Sessional Papers* 1884, vol. 3, no. 4, 78–79; R.A. Allen, Report of Blackfeet Agent, 15 August 1885, in U. S. Congress, Department of the Interior, "Annual Report of the Secretary of the Interior," 49th Cong., 1st sess., House Executive Documents 1, Part 5, 344; and Edgar Dewdney, Report of Commissioner of Indian Affairs for North-West Territories, 17 December 1885, in Canada, Department of the Interior, "Annual Report of the Department of Indian Affairs for year ended 31st December 1885," *Sessional Papers* 1886, vol. 4, no. 4, 144.

17. "Report of Father A. Lacombe," 13 July 1885, in Canada, Department of the Interior, *Sessional Papers* 1886, vol. 4, no. 4, 77.

18. U.S. Bureau of the Census, 1880; Canada, 1885 Census of North-West Territories, vol. 1, 10–11.

19. May G. Flanagan, memoirs, SC1236, Montana Historical Society Archives, Helena, MT (hereafter cited as MHS).

20. Mary Ella Lees Inderwick, letter to sister-in-law Alice, ca. Fall 1884, M559, GA.

21. Canada, Department of the Interior, "Annual Report For Year Ending 30 June 1875," *Sessional Papers* 1876, vol. 7, no. 9, p. 6.

22. See Sherry L. Smith, "Single Women Homesteaders: The Perplexing Case of Elinore Pruitt Stewart," *Western Historical Quarterly* 22 (May 1991): 163–84; and Susanne George, *Adventures of the Woman Homesteader* (Lincoln: University of Nebraska Press, 1992).

23. Two of the few specific references to women in the American reports can be found in "Report of Joseph Wilson, Commissioner of General Land Office," 27 October 1870, in U.S. Congress, Department of the Interior, *Annual Report of the Secretary of the Interior*, 41st Cong., 3rd sess., House Executive Document 1, Part 4, 9; and J. Fred Myers, Treasury Department, "Report on Immigration, and the Proper Transportation of Immigrants to and within the United States," in U. S. Congress, "Message from the President recommending Legislation in relation to the transportation of immigrants to and within the United States," 14 May 1872, 42nd Cong., 2nd sess., Senate Executive Document 73, 5. This relative silence, and the focus on women as administrative problems, is a sharp contrast to the Canadian government's reports, which mention women frequently.

24. William Grahame, Report of Duluth Agent, in Canada, Department of Agriculture, "Annual Report of the Department of Agriculture for 1878," *Sessional Papers* 1879, vol. 7, no. 9, 34–35. The scholarship around this growing cultural imperative for white women to marry white men in the Canadian west includes Van Kirk, *Many Tender Ties*; Sarah Carter, *Capturing Women*; and Adele Perry, *On the Edge of Empire: Gender, Race, and the Making of British Columbia, 1849–1871* (Toronto: University of Toronto Press, 2001).

25. Carolyn Abbott Tyler, diary entry September 10, 1862, SC1430, MHS.

26. Mary Douglas Gibson, reminiscence, SC1476, MHS.

27. The numbered treaties were a series of treaties Canada made with First Nations communities across the West and North. The first seven treaties were signed between 1871 and 1877 and covered the whole of the southern prairies. This "peaceful" land grab is

one of the key components of the Canadian myth that their West was kinder and gentler than the American West.

28.   Inderwick, diary entry 29 October 1883, M559, GA.

29.   Short diary, Short Asher reminiscence, M1137, GA.

30.   Alma Coffin Kirkpatrick, reminiscence ca. 1910, includes diary excerpts from 1878, SC940, MHS.

31.   Julia Short Asher reminiscence, Short-Knupp Family Fonds, M1137, GA.

32.   Stocking, diary 29 June 1871, SC142, MHS.

33.   Kirkpatrick, reminiscence, SC940, MHS.

34.   Inderwick, diary 24 January to February 8, 1884, M559, GA.

35.   Sadye Wolfe Drew, reminiscence, SC1532, MHS.

36.   See, for example, Ruth Roach Pierson and Nupur Chaudhuri, eds., *Nation, Empire, Colony: Historicizing Race and Gender* (Bloomington and Indianapolis: Indiana University Press, 1998); Caren Kaplan, Norma Alarcon, and Minoo Moallem, eds., *Between Woman and Nation: Nationalisms, Transnational Feminisms, and the State* (Durham, NC: Duke University Press, 1999); Ida Blom, Karen Hagemann, and Catherine Hall, eds., *Gendered Nations: Nationalisms and Gender Order in the Long Nineteenth Century* (Oxford and New York: Berg Books, 2000); and Himani Bannerji, *The Dark Side of the Nation: Essays on Multiculturalism, Nationalism and Gender* (Toronto: Canadian Scholars Press, 2000).

RE-IMAGINING REGION

SYLVIA VAN KIRK and Susan Armitage, whose essays appear in this section, are senior scholars recognized for unsettling two nations' pasts by casting women as central actors. Armitage, an American historian, and Van Kirk, a Canadian historian, broke historical ground in the 1970s and 1980s by showing how the stories of an androcentric and eurocentric West changed when women joined the cast. U.S. frontiers and the Canadian fur trade had explained how each nation had developed; adding women disrupted those accepted national histories.[1]

Until recently, however, women's historians have accepted as given the western stage on which women acted. We have not really addressed what regions themselves—the West, or the Prairies, or British Columbia, or the Pacific Northwest—might mean, from women's perspectives, or how gender might map regional boundaries. In these articles, Armitage and Van Kirk again take the lead to examine the intersections of region, gender, race, and history.

Gender aside, regions have figured differently in the histories of Canada and the United States. American historians have assumed that the West was a distinct section of the nation, yet they have debated its boundaries and what defined them. Canadian historians have been less concerned with where the West is and have simply divided the Canadian West into the Prairie provinces and British Columbia while they focus on the 49th parallel as the line that divided the Canadian West from the wild region to the South.[2] The important exception for many years was Walter Sage, who argued that ongoing migrations back and forth across the Canada-U.S. border connected the frontiers of North America and that each Canadian region—the Maritimes, central Canada, the Prairies, and British Columbia—had more in common with the adjacent American region than it did with the rest of Canada.[3] After World War II, some U.S. scholars, like Herbert Heaton and Paul Sharp, also began to map a continuous North American West, and to follow the people, economies, and social movements that crossed the 49th parallel.[4] In the late twentieth century, awareness of globalization led many historians to consider transnational histories, emphasizing migrations and ecological and economic interdependence.[5] Yet until quite recently, historians have not addressed how gender and place are connected, nor have they considered how gender might change the ways we define regions or write regional and national histories.[6]

Armitage and Van Kirk turn to that little-explored terrain of gender and transnational regionalism. Each considers how gender functioned in the region once known as Oregon Country, a territory that stretched from what is now the southern border of Oregon to the current northern border of British Columbia. Oregon Country demonstrates the difference a national border could make, because in 1846 the 49th parallel divided the territory that native inhabitants had never divided and that Britain and the United States had claimed and occupied jointly.

The two articles in this section complement each other. Susan Armitage considers how gender and race operated as two nation states claimed and divided the land; Sylvia Van Kirk provides a micro-historical illustration of Armitage's regional perspective.

Armitage ambitiously asks how a gendered perspective would change the history of nineteenth-century Oregon Country if that region were viewed as a meeting ground of native peoples, British fur traders, and

British and American colonists. She asks how each people acquired the place, perceived it, and used it, emphasizing that people did not act alone but as members of social networks. Kinship was a crucial social network that had everything to do with gender. Social networks and assumptions, too, could extend far beyond the boundaries of Oregon Country, as assumptions formed in other places affected how the British and Americans saw the land itself, how they allocated it, used it, and bequeathed it. Armitage shows how assumptions about marriage, land ownership, and inheritance all became central concerns as two nations claimed their parts of what had been a common territory. She demonstrates how focusing on gender, marriage, kinship, and other social relationships could change regional histories on both sides of the border.

Sylvia Van Kirk narrows the focus of Armitage's Oregon Country to one family and examines how the shifting meanings of race and gender during the processes of state formation affected the family of one fur-trade couple, Charles and Isabella Ross. The early nineteenth-century fur-trade society had depended on couples like the Rosses, Scottish and French-Ojibwa, respectively, who, far from their birthplaces and families of origin, forged relationships that depended on the skills and interdependence of both partners. Van Kirk's pathbreaking *Many Tender Ties* first focused attention on these intimate relationships between European men and native women that were so central to the fur trade.[7] In her article, which originated as a featured luncheon address at the "Unsettled Pasts" conference, Van Kirk extends her analysis and time frame beyond the fur trade to the era of colonial settlement, after the new international border separated two Hudson's Bay Company forts, placing Fort Nisqually in Washington State and Fort Victoria in British Columbia.

In a region marked by considerable social and political flux, the Rosses' ten Métis children faced very different options than their parents had. In colonial settler societies, race became increasingly important in defining who could possess land and inherit it. Van Kirk deftly illuminates those complex changes through the shifting marital and economic fortunes of the widowed Isabella Ross and her children, some of whom settled in British Columbia, some south of the 49th parallel. The children's class status, marital choices, and the racial ethnic identities that they could claim on either side of the border depended partly on where they settled, and partly on gender. Especially with the surplus of male immigrants to the colony, it seems that sons had great difficulty securing an economic niche for themselves and maintaining their families' status. The daughters fared better, because their ability to operate across cultures made them, for a time, highly regarded marriage partners, at least until the arrival of European women erected new racial hierarchies.

The fortunes of the Ross children, north and south of the 49th parallel, illuminate the concrete experiences of individual human beings who lived the regional history that Armitage outlined. Their options were embedded in how settler societies in the United States and Canada defined race and their differing policies regarding native and Métis peoples. The Ross family's cross-border migrations reinforce Armitage's point that social networks and kinship complicate the boundaries and meanings of regions.

Both articles suggest how colonial and national power affect what stories are preserved as history. Each group with historical claims to Oregon Country passed stories down from generation to generation to explain how they came into the country and claimed it. For each group— native peoples, Métis, the British, and the Americans—gender affected who told these stories and in what contexts. Later, colonial relationships determined whose stories were regarded as folklore, or as family stories, and whose would become histories of European and American settlement. Focusing on gender, then, illuminates not only the history of a transnational region, but also how that history became truncated to stories of white settlers in two separate nation states.

NOTES

1.   See Susan Armitage, "Through Women's Eyes: A New View of the West," in *The Women's West*, ed. Susan Armitage and Elizabeth Jameson (Norman: University of Oklahoma Press, 1987), 9–18; Sylvia Van Kirk, *Many Tender Ties: Women in Fur-Trade Society in Western Canada, 1670–1870* (Winnipeg: Watson & Dwyer; Norman: University of Oklahoma Press, 1980).

2. For debates about mapping the U.S. West, see Donald Worster, "New West, True West: Interpreting the Region's History," *Western Historical Quarterly* 18 (1987): 141–56; David M. Emmons, "Constructed Province: History and the Making of the Last American West," *Western Historical Quarterly* 25, no. 4 (Winter 1994): 437–59; "A Roundtable: Six Responses to 'Constructed Province,'" *Western Historical Quarterly* 25, no. 4 (Winter 1994): 461–86; Walter Nugent, "Where is the American West?" *Montana: The Magazine of Western History* 42 (Summer 1992): 2–23.

3. Walter Sage, "Some Aspects of the Frontier in Canadian History," Canadian Historical Association, *Annual Report*, 1928; "Geographical and Cultural Aspects of the Five Canadas," Canadian Historical Association, *Annual Report*, 1937.

4. Herbert Heaton, "Other Wests Than Ours," *Journal of Economic History* 6, Issue Supplement: The Tasks of Economic History (1946): 50–62; Paul F. Sharp, "When Our West Moved North," *American Historical Review* 55 (1950): 286–300; Paul F. Sharp, "Three Frontiers: Some Comparative Studies of Canadian, American, and Australian Settlements," *Pacific Historical Review* 24 (1955): 369–77; Paul F. Sharp, *The Agrarian Revolt in Western Canada: A Survey Showing American Parallels* (Minneapolis: University of Minnesota Press, 1948); Paul F. Sharp, *Whoop-Up Country: The Canadian-American West, 1865–1885* (Minneapolis: University of Minnesota Press, 1955).

5. See the December 1999 special issue of the *Journal of American History*; Bruno Ramirez with Yves Otis, *Crossing the 49th Parallel: Migration from Canada to the United States, 1900–1930* (Ithaca, NY: Cornell University Press, 2001); Randy W. Widdis, *With Scarcely a Ripple: Anglo-Canadian Migration into the United States and Western Canada, 1880–1920* (Montreal: McGill-Queen's University Press, 1998); Paul W. Hirt, ed., *Terra Pacifica: People and Place in the Northwest States and Western Canada* (Pullman: Washington State University Press, 1998); Gunther Peck, *Inventing Free Labor: Padrones and Immigrant Workers in the North American West, 1880–1930* (Cambridge and New York: Cambridge University Press, 2000); Beth LaDow, *The Medicine Line: Life and Death on a North American Borderland* (New York: Routledge, 2001); Theodore Binnema, *Common and Contested Ground: A Human and Environmental History of the Northwestern Plains* (Norman: University of Oklahoma Press, 2001); John M. Findlay and Ken S. Coates, eds., *Parallel Destinies: Canadian-American Relations West of the Rockies* (Seattle: University of Washington Press, 2002); Sterling Evans, ed., *The Borderlands of the American and Canadian Wests: Essays on Regional History of the Forty-ninth Parallel* (Lincoln: University of Nebraska Press, 2006).

6. Two notable exceptions are Sheila McManus and Nora Faires, both of whom have placed gender as a category of analysis at the center of their scholarship on the Canada-U.S. borderlands. See Sheila McManus, "Mapping the Alberta-Montana Borderlands: Race, Ethnicity, and Gender in the Late Nineteenth Century," *Journal of American Ethnic History* 20 (2001): 71–87; McManus, "'Their Own Country': Race, Gender, Landscape, and Colonization Around the 49th Parallel, 1862–1900," *Agricultural History* 73 (1999): 168–82; McManus, *The Line Which Separates: Race, Gender, and the Making of the Alberta-Montana Borderlands* (Lincoln: University of Nebraska Press, 2005); Nora Faires, "Poor Women, Proximate Border: Migrants from Ontario to Detroit in the Late Nineteenth Century," *Journal of American Ethnic History* 20 (Spring 2001): 88–109; and John J. Bukowczyk, Nora Faires, David R. Smith, and Randy Widdis, eds., *Permeable Border: The Great Lakes Basin as*

Transnational Region, 1650–1990 (Pittsburgh: University of Pittsburgh Press; Calgary: University of Calgary Press, 2005).

7.   Van Kirk, *Many Tender Ties*.

3

MAKING CONNECTIONS

Gender, Race, and Place in Oregon Country

SUSAN ARMITAGE

IN AN ARRESTING IMAGE in *Legacy of Conquest*, Patricia Limerick suggests that the West has always been a "meeting ground of peoples."[1] The early nineteenth-century Pacific Northwest was such a meeting ground. Home to three distinct native cultures that anthropologists today call the Northwest Coast, Plateau, and Great Basin peoples, by the 1820s the region was also the westernmost outpost of the British Hudson's Bay Company (HBC) fur-trade empire. Two decades later, it was the edenic agricultural destination of the American pioneers who made their way west on the Oregon Trail in the 1840s.

Oregon Country, as it was known, stretched from the Pacific Coast to the continental divide in what is now western Montana, and from the northern border of Mexican California to the southern boundary of Russian Alaska at 54°40′. With the exception of this northern boundary, which is simply a line on a map, the other boundaries of Oregon Country roughly conformed to natural geographical contours. Oregon Country was jointly occupied by the United States and Britain from 1818 to 1846, a situation unique in North American history. At first, joint occupancy worked because the region seemed remote and useless, but as the fur trade moved west across Canada and as the United States expanded its continental ambitions, Oregon Country became increasingly interesting to both nations. In the 1840s, uncertainty about the future status of the region created a situation in which all three resident groups—native peoples, European fur traders, and American farmers—vied for ascendancy. The political story of the struggle between the American settlers and Dr John McLoughlin, HBC chief factor at Fort Vancouver, has been told and retold,[2] but the social and cultural story of the encounters among the three groups has not. I want to look at the Oregon Country at this moment when the "meeting ground of peoples" was most obvious and to suggest new ways to look at region and regional identity that bring women and gender to the centers of these "meeting grounds."

Environmental historian Donald Worster offers a deceptively simple description of how to think about the notion of region: "What the regional historian should first want to know is how a people or peoples acquired a place and, then, how they perceived and tried to make use of it."[3] We know that perceptions and usages are gendered; we also need to understand that they are not solely individual. Worster speaks of "a people or peoples" who were implicitly connected to each other by kinship or by a common outlook. The significance of these networks has been clearly articulated by Montana writer Deirdre McNamer: "I never set out to deliberately de-mythologize the West but...when you try to make your characters real and layered and tied to other lives in other places—your work has the inevitable effect of dismantling the myth of the West as the home of heroic, loner white guys moving through an unpeopled and uncomplicated place."[4] McNamer's comment adds to Worster's definition the recognition that people do not exist alone but in social networks, and that we must take the various forms of these networks into account as we consider their experience on a particular "meeting ground,"[5] just as we consider the factors of race, gender, and nationality. Armed with these insights, we can ask, "How did people live in this place—Oregon Country—and how did they perceive it?"

Beginning, as we always should, with indigenous peoples, one is immediately struck by their variety and the perils of generalization. Nevertheless, whether speaking of the indigenous peoples of the Northwest Coast, the Columbia Plateau, or the Great Basin, we can recognize everywhere the importance of deep collective ties to their particular homelands. There were good reasons for this. Because each people derived all their food and shelter from it, where they lived was the most important fact of their lives, equaled only by the importance of their kin group, for no single person could survive long alone. How the group as a whole made use of its environment determined the survival of everyone. Thus the coastal Indians like the Tillamook in the south and the Tlingit in the north lived off the richness of the sea, supplemented by greens and berries gathered in the summers. Many coastal peoples were impressive seafarers, who often traveled long distances in huge ocean-going canoes. In the vast inland drainage area of the Columbia River, Plateau tribes like the Chinook and the Yakama who lived along the river depended on salmon, augmented by roots, berries, and hunting; groups situated in the interior of the territory, like the Okanagan, gathered and hunted more intensively. To the south and east, aboriginal peoples in the Great Basin, like the Shoshone, hunted and gathered, surviving in apparently inhospitable arid terrain.

The environment affected social structure directly. Some coastal groups, like the Tsimshian and Haida, were famously rich, trading with and raiding other groups for slaves who remained a permanent, hereditary subgroup of the capturing tribe. Because the environment was so rich in food, slavery allowed coastal peoples to devote their energies to creating an elaborate and stratified social structure, a rich ceremonial life, and elaborate arts. Other native peoples on less hospitable terrain were more egalitarian foragers who devoted almost all of their efforts to food gathering; one such tribe, the North Paiutes of the Great Basin, appeared to be so incessant in their gathering of roots and berries that Americans derisively called them "Diggers."[6]

Familiarity with the land was gendered in obvious ways. Male hunters knew certain territories and the behavior of the animals that populated them, and male fishermen knew the ways of the salmon that made their way up the rivers. Women knew how to fillet and dry the salmon and other fish, and they knew where to dig and gather the roots and berries that could provide 60 per cent of the group's diet. Each sex respected the expertise of the other; their knowledges were complementary, they would have said, and both essential to the whole. Or at least this was the ideal. Of course, real life was much more complicated, and every indigenous group made its own adjustments based upon the environment, circumstances, and individual personalities. But the gendered division of labor, and the gendered expertise that sustained it, remained a basic aspect of indigenous life.[7]

The relationship that each group had with the land went beyond detailed geographic familiarity. Their tie to place was spiritual and collective. Each particular North American Indian group identified itself and its place by telling stories about physical landmarks, animals, and other local phenomena. The Nez Perce of present-day northern Idaho still point to the rock they call "the heart of the monster" and tell the story of how Coyote bested him. The Clallum people, on the other hand, tell a tale that describes Mount St Helens as Loo-wit, a beautiful woman who turned herself into a mountain to escape the courtship of two jealous chiefs, Wyeast, now Mount Hood, and Klickitat, who became Mount Adams. Even after they became mountains, the chiefs continued to quarrel: "They caused sheets of flame to burst forth, and they hurled hot rocks at each other." (It seems that Loo-wit got the last word when she "blew her top" in 1980![8]) These stories about specific places—these ties—were constantly being remade as the stories were passed from one generation to the next or when told to the group on special occasions. Storytelling, too, was gendered: male leaders told or performed stories at ceremonial gatherings, while grandmothers told stories to their grandchildren informally. Everyone knew these stories, and they also knew the appropriate circumstances in which to tell them and, in the telling, to call up the group history of the place. Thus these places, and these stories, were alive with both collective and personal meanings. As Native American poet and writer Leslie Marmon Silko explains, "This perspective on narrative—of story within story, the idea that one story is only the beginning of many stories and the sense that stories never truly end—represents an important contribution of Native American cultures to the English language."[9] By entering the story, one simultaneously entered into a collective and ongoing connection with place. This was the powerful connection between oral tradition and the aboriginal link to the homeland. These ties—living, renewable expressions of group and individual consciousness—were at the heart of indigenous life.

Most native peoples spent their lives within their known tribal areas, simply because that was where their livelihood and kin were. Trading and raiding were the major exceptions. Coastal peoples traveled far to trade with others and to raid for captives to augment their supply of slaves. Women were prominent in both activities: they were sharp and shrewd traders, and they were also the most likely captives of male raiding parties. Plateau and Great Basin peoples had customary seasonal rounds of gathering and hunting. Once horses became available in the 1720s, Plateau groups like the Nez Perce made yearly trips over the Rocky Mountains to hunt buffalo and fight, when necessary, with more eastern tribes, such as the Blackfoot, who objected to incursions into their territory. Some Great Basin groups, such as the Shoshone, became full-time buffalo hunters themselves. In addition, there were recognized trade rendezvous points, the greatest of which was at Ceililo Falls on the Columbia River, which drew peoples and goods from far along the Pacific Coast and from as far as 1,000 miles [1,609 km] inland.[10]

As far as we know, until European contact, indigenous peoples did not have a concept of race: that is, of another, essentially different kind of human. They certainly recognized, however, different cultures, and they had to decide whether or not to treat other groups as potential kin or as foes. Communication among groups led to some blurring of tribal lines, for there was considerable intermarriage, especially among Plateau peoples—so much so that one anthropologist described the region as a "vast kinship web."[11] Perhaps we can postulate that the people within this kinship web had a shared sense of regional identity, but this may be an inappropriately modern concept. We do know that widespread kinship ties facilitated the spread of European diseases. The first smallpox epidemic reached the region in the 1770s, carried by trade networks long before any physical European presence; the second outbreak occurred in 1802. Combined, these two epidemics are estimated to have killed at least half of the indigenous population.[12] Thus kinship, a fundamental pillar of native life, was weakened. With vastly reduced numbers, their use of the land must have changed as well.

Nevertheless, ties to place survived the first period of white-indigenous contact during the fur trade that dominated western North America until the 1840s. In the vast sweep of territory called Rupert's Land, in what is now western Canada, indigenous ways of life and connections to the land survived because the European fur trade depended on native people; traders did not deliberately or directly challenge aboriginal peoples, nor did they force them to leave their traditional homelands. This does not mean that Europeans did not racialize native peoples. As Alexandra Harmon points out in her insightful study of cultural contacts in the Puget Sound area, *Indians in the Making*, Europeans used the generic term *Indian* to refer to all the groups they encountered and relied on the general strategies for dealing with them that had developed over the two-century span of the fur trade. Although not unaware of cultural differences among aboriginal groups, fur traders rarely paid much attention to the details unless they affected trade itself.[13]

The fur trappers and traders associated with the British and Canadian fur trade were the second distinct group to enter Oregon Country in the first decade of the nineteenth century. The most striking fact about these fur traders was the arrangement they made with native peoples, which rested on sexual and familial relationships between European traders and native women. European men deliberately used marriage with native women as a means to gain entry into the indigenous group with whom they traded. By entering into marriage alliances on native terms, the traders accommodated themselves to indigenous cultures and customs, not the other way around. Sylvia Van Kirk insists that these marriages, "after the fashion of the country," were "*the fundamental social relationship* through which a fur trade society developed."[14] Here is a striking example of a gendered cross-racial social network—a connection—that persisted over time because it served the needs of both parties. Practiced over several generations, these marriages created not only cross-racial kinship links, but a distinctive, mixed-race people, the Métis, who formed their own communities in the Red River settlement in present-day Manitoba and elsewhere.[15]

The Hudson's Bay Company became a major force in Oregon Country in 1824, when Dr John McLoughlin was put in charge of what the HBC called the Columbia District. Establishing Fort Vancouver on the Columbia River (near present-day Portland) as his base in 1825, McLoughlin remained in charge of the district until 1845. From Fort Vancouver he directed fur brigades that operated from San Francisco Bay north to the border of Russian Alaska, for the district the HBC called New Caledonia (present-day British Columbia) was soon added to McLoughlin's command. In other words, all of Oregon Country was in his purview. McLoughlin was not a settler. He was a trader and exploiter. He viewed the land primarily in terms of its fur-bearing capacity. This required, McLoughlin asserted, being on good terms with the indigenous groups of the region. He explained, "We trade furs, [and] none can hunt fur bearing animals[,] or afford to sell them cheaper, than Indians. It is therefore clearly our interest, as it is unquestionably our duty, to be on good terms with them… particularly when the disparity of numbers is so great as to show but one white man to 200 Indians."[16]

In addition to the fur trade, McLoughlin was deeply involved in agriculture, an occupation usually associated with permanent settlement. However, McLoughlin's initial aim was simple survival: Fort Vancouver could not survive on the uncertain food supply that was supposed to come on the once-yearly ship from England. McLoughlin established at Fort Vancouver, and later at Cowlitz and other fur posts, extensive farming and dairying operations that provisioned all the HBC employees and, after 1839, the Russian America Company in Sitka, Alaska, as well. He also created a brisk trade in lumber and foodstuffs with Hawai'i. McLoughlin, a trader to his core, moved rapidly from subsistence to commercial agriculture, and he achieved this on a scale not to be matched in the region until the twentieth century. In 1839, there were 1,200 acres under cultivation, producing wheat, oats, barley, peas, potatoes, other vegetables, and fruits; additional acreage provided pasture for cattle, pigs, and sheep. Historian James Gibson says that the agricultural work-force was composed of natives, Hawaiʻians, and French Canadians, but he does not specify their gender. Because the fort produced large quantities of butter and cheese, we can speculate that some employees were women. The British regarded dairying as women's work, even though the effort to import a British woman as dairy manager failed. She disapproved of mixed-race marriages and insisted on returning to England.[17]

Indeed, except for the brief sojourns of the dairy manager and of the equally disapproving wife of a British clergyman, all the women at Fort Vancouver were native or Métis. In 1845, most of the approximately 200 male HBC "servants," themselves a mixture of Indian, French-Canadian, Métis, and Hawaiʻians, were married "after the fashion of the country" to native women. The majority of the women were coastal Chinook (a number of whom brought their slaves with them), while the rest were from other coastal or plateau tribes. We can assume that these women (and, or, their slaves) worked alongside their husbands in the fur trade, and perhaps in agriculture, although HBC officials regarded natives as "lazy" workers.[18]

Marguerite McLoughlin and Amelia Douglas, wives, respectively, of the Chief Factor and his assistant, James Douglas, were Métis. Their lives, although luxurious by local standards, were much more restricted than those of the native women who clustered around Fort Vancouver. The male-dominated fur trade was organized in military fashion, with strict discipline and rigid adherence to rank and status, complemented by homosocial male rituals, a prime example of which was the all-male officers mess. An 1839 visitor, Thomas Farnham, left us a vivid word portrait of McLoughlin standing at the twenty-foot [six meter] table in the Big House, "directing the gentlemen and guests to their places according to rank," while his wife and children, who also lived in the house, remained secluded. Indeed, Marguerite McLoughlin, Amelia Douglas, and their female children seem to have spent most of their time in seclusion, except when horseback riding, at which both women excelled.[19]

Aside from this limitation, the most serious concern of these elite Métis women must have been the future of their children. Although fathers in these elite fur-trade marriages often arranged extensive and expensive schooling for their sons, Sylvia Van Kirk argues elsewhere in this volume that Métis daughters, not sons, had a greater likelihood of operating effectively in white society. Perhaps this was true because racial categories tightened with the advent of white settlers, who were excluded from Rupert's Land until the 1830s. But it seems equally plausible that marriage, "after the fashion of the country," which had begun in mutuality, was reshaped over time at the elite level to serve the needs of the British officer ranks. Métis daughters of HBC officials were obvious partners for the young European men who made up the officer class, and they were trained by their native or Métis mothers for this position.[20] But British officers moving into the territory did not bring daughters with them, nor would they have happily married them to Métis men. Race and gender operated within a class system that privileged the social, sexual, and material desires of white men.

The Hudson's Bay Company was a far-flung but closely-knit social network. It appears that the identification of officers and "servants" was not grounded in a particular place but in the trade itself, which functioned by ignoring racial distinctions that prevailed elsewhere. But while these distinctions were ignored within the trade, the racial assumptions of the Imperial homelands were not transformed. Nothing showed the distinctiveness of the HBC more than the dilemma officers faced when they retired: they could choose to retire to Montreal or to England, but because of European racial prejudice, they could not comfortably bring their Métis wives and children with them. Some men abandoned their "country" families, but a surprising number, John McLoughlin among them, retired where they were. McLoughlin, who retired in 1845, was following the example of a number of former HBC employees who, with their Indian wives, were the first settlers in the agriculturally rich Willamette Valley of Oregon in the 1820s. Here, then, was a multiracial social network of men, linked by kinship and common work histories, who chose in retirement to become settlers—subsistence farmers—in a favorable location. McLoughlin himself, true to his trader background, opened a store.

The third players in the Northwest "meeting ground of peoples" were Americans. Methodist missionary Jason Lee arrived in the Willamette Valley in 1834, and although he did little farming and even less missionary work, he did play a major role in publicizing the agricultural potential of the valley to Americans. In the 1830s other missionaries arrived, the most famous of whom were Marcus and Narcissa Whitman, who settled near present-day Walla Walla. They, too, struggled as missionaries, and gradually diverted most of their attention into recruiting American settlers to the region.[21]

American settlers began to arrive in numbers via the Oregon Trail in the early 1840s—100 in 1842, over 900 in 1843, and even more in the years to follow. These people differed markedly from the HBC officers and servants: they were family groups, they were farmers, and they intended to stay. Many were instantly suspicious of McLoughlin, for he represented Britain, against whom many Americans harbored colonial resentments dating back to the Revolutionary War. In reality, many settlers owed their survival to him, for as the exhausted and desperate condition of the pioneers became apparent, McLoughlin began the yearly practice of sending rescue parties back along the trail, providing boats for the trip down the Columbia River from The Dalles to Portland, and providing food, medical treatment, and temporary employment once they arrived at Fort Vancouver.[22]

The epic journey over the 2,000-mile [3,219 km] long Oregon Trail has been described, analyzed, and explained at length by many historians, but in the end a mystery still remains: why did so many ill-prepared people undertake such a dangerous journey?[23] In the early years, the journey west on the Oregon Trail was a much more terrible ordeal than upbeat retrospective accounts have led us to believe. At least in the early years, those who arrived in Oregon were stripped of their material wealth, their physical health, and their emotional reserves.[24] Families were fortunate to survive the journey without the death of at least one relative. Humans are resilient and most people recovered in time, but it may be that the very difficulty of their journey led the American pioneers (as they called themselves) to stake their claim to the land—still jointly occupied by Britain and the United States—with special fierceness.

In his memoir *Traplines,* Idaho writer John Rember describes how his family claimed their land by deliberately obliterating traces of earlier occupation, marking it as their own, as if to insist that they were the first to live there. Much later, Rember tried to reconstruct the lives of the family that had lived there previously, only to be defeated by his own family's successful efforts at obliteration.[25] There is a metaphor here: the Oregon Trail pioneers, the Johnny-come-latelies to the Northwest, asserted their claim with particular vehemence, and they prevailed in part because of sheer numbers and in part because of diplomatic determinations decided far from Oregon. Much to the disappointment of McLoughlin and other HBC officers, who had hoped for a division at the Columbia River, the boundary was set at the 49th parallel, with a dip to allow British occupation of Vancouver Island and to provide access to Puget Sound. The HBC formally transferred the headquarters of its Northwest operations to Fort Victoria on Vancouver Island, and it appointed James Douglas, McLoughlin's long-time assistant, to head it. By 1850, the HBC's control over the lower half of what had been Oregon Country was over.

The group that suffered most as a result of this changeover was not the HBC, but the local indigenous groups with whom the HBC had always cultivated friendly relations. The American settlers had no such sociable inclinations. Most Americans had been taught to be both suspicious and contemptuous of "Indians," although few had ever had much contact with them until their overland journey.[26] At first there were few problems, because the tribes that occupied the Willamette Valley had been so devastated by disease that they could not resist white occupation. But the larger and stronger tribes to the East—the Cayuse, the Yakama, the Nez Perce—were increasingly alarmed at the size of the annual Oregon Trail migrations. These fears, coupled with their anger over the differential effects of disease—whites sickened but survived, while natives died—exploded in the killing of the Whitmans and thirteen others by

Cayuse Indians in 1847. In the American retribution that followed, the Cayuse were the first native group in Oregon Country to be formally deprived of all of their land, which was promptly opened for white settlement.[27] Separation from the land, or confinement to only a small portion of the traditional homeland, was to be the fate of all of Oregon Country's surviving native groups. Throughout the region, sporadic warfare, much of it vicious, occurred from 1847 to 1877 as different tribal groups tried desperately to resist white encroachment.[28] Devastated by disease, often separated from their lands and traditional livelihoods, native peoples were regarded as inferior by whites and were subjected to relentless pressure to conform to European cultural standards rather than their own.[29] North and south of the new border, it was official and deliberate policy, in the name of "civilization," to deprive indigenous peoples of their identities, which had once been so firmly rooted in kinship and place. A racial border between whites and Indians existed that had not been there before.

The Oregon Trail pioneers were primarily farmers: they had a passion—indeed, one might say a greed—for land that made them markedly different from those who had lived in the region before them. Many genuinely believed that the nomadic ways of the "Indians" (as they generically called them) represented an improper use of land that ought properly to be owned and cultivated.[30] Yet historian Peter Boag cautions us not to view these early settlers simply as rapacious conquerors. In his environmental study of pioneers in a part of the Willamette Valley, Boag highlights an enlightening contrast: while nomadic Indians obtained what they needed from many ecosystems, the settled nature of Euro-American agriculture required settlers to search with "painstaking" care for a single piece of land that would supply wood and water, grazing land for stock, and well-drained land for crops. Although settlers were attracted to the broad valley bottoms of the area, they rapidly discovered that this land was too wet to farm without drainage. They therefore chose drier land at the base of the foothills, where their basic needs could be met. As Boag says, "In daily activities...earliest settlers developed an intimate connection with the foothills, though they also looked to the plains as the future."[31]

At the very moment when settlers were adjusting to a new climate and new land conditions, they were already planning ahead to the broad pastoral plains of the future, once they had the time and resources to begin draining the bottomland. Boag tells us that within fifty years the goal was achieved: the foothills were left behind, and large farms, communities, industries, infrastructure, and connections with the wider world were established on the plains. With this shift, he says, came a change of attitude: "The settlers had once considered the landscape to be in some ways separate from humans, and in many ways something on which humans depended; over time, though, the landscape increasingly became just the object of utilitarian desires and economic demand."[32] American settlers began, then, in a state of dependence on nature not so different from that of the natives they displaced, although in the settlers' case much more shallowly rooted because so recent. But because they brought with them a pastoral vision of the land, the settlers worked hard to create that vision, and in so doing they came to believe they had control over the land.

If there were ever a group of people whose "lives were tied to other lives in other places," to use McNamer's phrase, it was these migrants. Tied by kinship and custom to the places they left behind, migrants brought their old ways to their new homes, where they faced the challenge of adapting old practices to new circumstances. As much as possible, they tried to replicate old ways rather than invent new ones. The Oregon pioneers followed this rule in agriculture and elsewhere. It is no surprise to learn, then, that the first provisional government set up by settlers in 1843 was modeled on laws found in *Organic Laws of the State of Iowa*, the one law book the settlers had brought with them.[33]

It may be more surprising to learn that Oregon pioneers followed the most common pattern of migration, known as chain migration, in which people move to join kin or members of their original communities. Most people assume that the celebrated Oregon Trail migrants of the 1840s were individuals or nuclear families. They are mistaken. Lillian Schlissel, in *Women's Diaries of the Westward Journey*,[34] points to evidence of many multigenerational families in the Oregon migration. William Bowen's demographic study of early settlement, *The Willamette*

Valley, confirms Schlissel's observation. Bowen's careful study of the 1850 census shows a clear pattern of "clustering" in rural neighborhoods based on kinship or place of origin. Even with the sketchy sources available, Bowen found that at least 45 per cent of Willamette Valley households had blood ties in 1850. Bowen claimed that other social ties—religious, fraternal, business, neighborhood ties—all of which he terms "clan" relationships, were also present and significant. Bowen's estimate is almost certainly low, because there is no means, based on the census alone, to identify kinship ties between sisters who took different last names when they married. Nevertheless, from the census data Bowen was able to clearly distinguish two kinds of settlement: "one, a rural frontier characterized by clans of westerners; the other, an urban frontier drawing its members disproportionately from the ranks of unmarried men from the Northeast or abroad."[35]

Just as had been true on earlier frontiers and in the fur trade, this demographic pattern meant that the quickest way for an unmarried man to get ahead was to marry the daughter of an established family, thereby gaining access to the family network.[36] Fundamentally, then, just as marriage "according to the custom of the country" was the basic institution of the fur trade, so too did marriage knit the pioneers into community in the Oregon of the 1840s. The vital connection of marriage was epitomized by a novel land policy: the 1850 Donation Land Claim Act, which confirmed the land use policies informally in use since the early 1840s. Preceding the Homestead Act by twelve years, the Donation Land Law was the first U.S. law to offer settlers free land—and lots of it. Every white male citizen over the age of 18 who had arrived in Oregon before December 1, 1851 (later extended to 1855) could claim 320 acres for himself; remarkably, his wife could claim another 320 acres in her own name. By the time the law expired in 1855 nearly 7,500 successful claims to 2.5 million acres of land (which required residence on the land and cultivation for four years) had been filed.[37]

There were several novel aspects of the Donation Land Claim Act. First, contrary to official policy, it confirmed the homestead claims of the pioneers before the U.S. government signed any Indian treaties. Second, the law established whiteness as the norm: only white male citizens and their wives could claim land, thereby excluding native, black, and Hawai'ian men from doing so; in a shrewd political concession, however, the law allowed retired HBC employees, including Métis men, to claim land if they renounced their British citizenship. Third, the law made a direct link between legally-recognized marriage and land ownership. It excluded all marriages that existed "according to the custom of the country" and other, looser forms of sexual relationships that were still common between European men and native women throughout Oregon Country. By demanding a marriage certificate, the law made European-style marriage, almost always between two white people, the norm. Thus it was a crucial tool in replicating American norms on what was now American soil.

Finally, the period of the Donation Land Law's enactment was the only period in the history of U.S. land law when married women were able to claim land in their own name. The later, more famous, Homestead Act allowed single women and widows to file, but not married women. Historians have tended to favor the sentimental explanation that lawmakers wished to acknowledge the role women had played in the Oregon migration, but the truth is surely more prosaic. By restricting the claim to married women, the Donation Land Law had the effect of increasing the "family" (read male) claim to land without increasing female autonomy. In fact, anecdotal evidence indicates the law caused a spate of marriages between adult males and girls as young as twelve or thirteen. The unbalanced sex ratio would have put pressure on young women in any case; whether or not this pressure was exacerbated by the Donation Land Law has not been studied by demographers.[38]

How did the pioneers come to think of Oregon as home? While it is certainly true that the Oregon Trail settlers regarded their very presence as proof that Oregon should belong to the United States, it took longer—perhaps several generations—for a sense of personal connection to establish itself and to create a genuine sense of regional identity. That personal connection was based, more than anything else, on familiarity with the geographic and natural characteristics of the particular place. But regional identification goes beyond this to include a sense of congruity with the ways of similar people with whom one shares a place.

The Oregon Trail pioneers achieved that sense of congruity rapidly, by sheer force of numbers and by establishing familiar institutions and legal forms, all aided by vociferous American nationalism. In the process they displaced and racialized the indigenous people, and they allowed themselves to imagine a "white" community that ignored the continuing reality of cross-race sexual relationships throughout the rest of the nineteenth century.[39]

In the northern part of Oregon Country, regional identity was harder to achieve, and a very different history followed. The region that we now know as British Columbia began as a fur-trade society, which was destabilized by the Fraser River gold rush of 1858. Throughout the rest of the nineteenth century, it remained an uneasy hybrid of miners and traders, with a racially mixed population on whom British authorities sought to impose the patterns and behaviors of a white settler society.[40]

Under the direction of Chief Factor James Douglas, after 1848 the HBC reconstituted its headquarters at Fort Victoria on Vancouver Island, re-established its agricultural enterprises, and provided a locus around which retired company "servants" could settle—while all the while continuing to direct the fur brigades that pursued their trade throughout the New Caledonia region. The census of 1855 showed the success of these efforts, recording 200 non-native inhabitants of the fort and village, 350 on nearby farms, and another 150 in the settlement of Nanaimo. With the exception of a few occupants of HBC fur forts, there were no Europeans on the mainland; there were, however, between 300,000 to 400,000 native inhabitants.[41]

This was the customary fur-trade situation: vastly outnumbered by the native population, HBC officials limited their contact with them to trade and did not interfere in tribal affairs. Personal behavior common to the fur trade continued: European men continued the practice of making marriages with native women "according to the custom of the country." The "society" that grew up around Fort Victoria was led by a fur-trade elite made up of European men and their Métis wives and children. But in the 1850s, the vocal presence of British missionaries and other "civilizers" injected a new note of race consciousness, and elite Métis children became subject to special scrutiny. As Sylvia Van Kirk's article in this volume shows, all Métis daughters survived this scrutiny and married European men. But Métis sons, whom their fathers had sought to educate to become professional men, failed to join the white elite. In subsequent generations, the color bar was raised further, and the elite of the territory became all white (or claimed they were). This result conforms to a worldwide colonial pattern recently discerned by feminist scholars. As Ann Stoler explains, "it was not the progeny of [mixed race] unions who were problematic, but the possibility that they might be recognized as legitimate heirs to a European inheritance."[42] Because under British law women could neither inherit nor own property, female Métis progeny were acceptable in ways that their brothers were not. At the same time, another double standard continued to flourish: native women were objects of sexual desire for European men, while the reverse, the potential for native men to be sexual partners for European women, was impermissible.

In 1858 the fur-trade society was overwhelmed when gold was discovered along the Fraser River. Within a year, the mainland population had swelled to 30,000, composed largely of American men. The Fraser River gold rush reverberated throughout the region that had made up the undivided Oregon Country. Large armed parties of men traveled overland through parts of what is now eastern Washington and British Columbia on their way to the Fraser River mining camps. These would-be miners were imbued with what Daniel Marshall calls the "California mining culture," comprising equally the desire for gold and hostility toward native peoples. As these overland parties moved north, they often shot natives on sight and raided native villages for food, thereby provoking the Indian wars of 1858 in Washington Territory and the miner-native skirmishes known as the Fraser River War of the same year.[43] In the Fraser River, Marshall claims the ultimate result was "a typical California landscape segregated by race and ethnicity, an extension of the American West, and one in which native peoples were quickly compartmentalized and reduced to a matrix of Indian reserves."[44]

We must question whether the violence unleashed by the miners during the California gold rush can be attributed solely to their nationality or to the California location. It is more plausible to look to their actions rather than their national origin as a cause. After all, gold mining was the ultimate extractive industry: miners did not care about the land, only about the gold it might contain, and everywhere in the world that gold miners gathered, they left damaged landscapes and tailings behind. Although individual miners might live in tidy houses and plant gardens, the sheer numbers involved in gold rushes damaged the land and overwhelmed native populations, usually violently. This gold rush result was a worldwide phenomenon and cannot be blamed solely on the California gold rush and, or, American propensities toward violence.[45]

The miners' nationality notwithstanding, missionaries and other British spokesmen regarded the homosocial culture of the large groups of male miners clustered along the lower Fraser River and further north, at Cariboo, with deep suspicion. It was not natural, they argued, for so many men to live without the influence of good women—for indeed, almost all the women in the mining camps were prostitutes. Territorial authorities were doubtless greatly relieved when the mines played out in the 1860s and most of the miners returned to the United States or moved on to gold strikes elsewhere.[46]

What worried British officials in 1858 was the ease with which American miners crossed the border. In reality, many of the miners were recent Cornish, Scottish, or Irish immigrants to the United States, and they scarcely regarded themselves as "American." They were just following the gold. Nevertheless, fearing the possibility of American annexation, the British government moved quickly to create the British colony of British Columbia, uniting Vancouver Island and the mainland under the governorship of James Douglas, who retired from the HBC to take the position.[47] Thus in a political sense, the European inhabitants of the new British Columbia found their initial regional identity in a determination not to be American. In a social sense, the gold rush upset the equilibrium of fur-trade society and forced the authorities to consider other ways to make British Columbia viable. Their answers were deeply gendered.

One solution was to find ways to control the native population, which, although decimated by disease, was much larger than the number of

Europeans or Americans. British authorities granted missionaries and Indian agents authority to reshape native life. Marriage was an institution of great interest to them. Not only did missionaries regard customary HBC marriages "according to the custom of the country" as illicit, they insisted that all unions, native as well as mixed-race, conform to European standards of monogamy and longevity.[48] The missionaries correctly believed that the terms of marriage represented particular kinds of gender relations, and they were determined that those terms would be European rather than native. We might call it marriage "*not according to the custom of the country.*" This attack on native gender relations may be taken to symbolize the end of the fur-trade era and the beginnings of full-blown colonialism. The effects of this policy were to discourage interracial marriage and to segregate the native population. As Adele Perry explains, as long as European and native populations were joined in marriage or in short-term sexual liaisons, "imperial visions of orderly, white communities buttressed by distant and quiescent First Nations populations" remained out of reach.[49]

What missionary efforts did *not* do, at least initially, was to curb the migrations of native peoples across the international border. John Lutz tells us that beginning in the 1850s, coastal peoples from as far north as the Tlingit, in the Alaskan panhandle, to those in the south on Vancouver Island and the adjacent mainland began the practice of annual migrations to Victoria, the lower Fraser Valley, and to Puget Sound. They went for a reason new to them: wage work—the men worked in the mills, the women as domestic servants or as sex trade workers, often cohabiting with white men for the summer, and then returning to their homelands in the fall. But they also migrated for traditional reasons, namely to gather wealth and slaves to continue their customary potlatches. Lutz estimates that in 1885, as many as six thousand native people made the annual migration to Puget Sound.[50]

Here, then, is a significant rationale for the massive missionary interference in native cultures: the prohibition of the potlatch and other native customs was regarded as the only way to force "Canadian Indians" to stay at home. Missionaries and Indian agents imposed European cultural standards in an effort to shape the regional identity of British Columbia, but other steps seemed to be necessary.

The continuing dilemma of British Columbia was plain: there simply were not enough permanent European settlers to control the native people or to discourage American annexation schemes. First the HBC, and later the British Government, attempted to attract settlers, but other places (including the U.S. Pacific Northwest, with more generous land policies) were more attractive. Finally, it was decided to import white women from England to remedy both the gender imbalance in England, where women were a majority, and that of British Columbia, where white men vastly outnumbered white women. Four times between 1859 and 1870, "assisted immigration" of white British women occurred; in all, about one hundred women arrived in British Columbia via "brideships," as they are known in British Columbian lore. As was true of a similar female immigration scheme in Washington Territory— the "Mercer's Belles"—the motives and character of these immigrating women were the subject of much media attention and titillation, and in the larger scheme of things their scant numbers made little difference.[51] But symbolically their presence made a huge difference in British Columbia, for, as Anne McClintock puts it, these women became the "boundary markers of empire" between the minority white and majority native populations.[52]

The importation of white women signified the determination of British authorities to segregate the white and native populations and especially to discourage the growth of the mixed-race population that had resulted from earlier relationships between white men and native women. In the heyday of the fur trade at Fort Vancouver in the 1830s, the aversion of the British dairy manager and the minister's wife, mentioned earlier, to mixed-race marriages had been unwelcome, and they left in a huff; thirty years later the importation of white women symbolized the determination of British authorities to create a white settler society in spite of the numerical predominance of Native peoples. Finally, in the 1890s, successful efforts to encourage migration from England tipped the cultural balance of the province and established the dominance of

British customs and institutions that remain to this day. At the time, proponents of immigration saw it as a means to prevent an American effort to annex the province. Today, exercising those same British customs (paying for an elaborate high tea at the Empress Hotel in Victoria, for example) is touted as a means to attract American tourist dollars north of the border.[53]

How did these British immigrants come to feel at home in British Columbia? With difficulty. British Columbia author Ethel Wilson, well known for her insights, spelled out the emotional aspects that historians sometimes overlook. Wilson regarded developing an attachment to a known landscape as a vital way for lonely newcomers to begin to feel at home. In her novel *Swamp Angel*, published in 1954, Wilson deeply embedded her human story within the patterns of the natural world—the migration of birds, the swimming of fishes—to make her point about cosmic connections.[54] As her heroine builds a "fictive" family to replace the one she has lost, she comes to realize that life—human and animal—is a "web" of relationships, of which she is part. That Wilson means the web to be inclusive is shown by the presence of a young Chinese boy in the fictive family, but there are no native people in the story. And even the heroine's heartfelt connection to the natural world does not make her relationships with other humans less difficult. Wilson's emphasis on the natural world helps us to see that all migrations begin in strangeness and loneliness and move toward a search for connection with the new place. Personal connection with a place—to its geography, its flora and fauna, its remembered associations with human events—can run very deep and may not vary much from individual to individual. But the social connections, their breadth or narrowness, their traditionality or innovation, can very enormously.

In the preceding pages I have focused on a particular time period, the early nineteenth century, and on a moment of dramatic transition. Following Worster's lead ("what the regional historian should first want to know"), I have shown how fur-trade culture at first accommodated native cultures, only to be swamped by American settlers in the lands south of the 49th parallel. North of the new border, the slower transition of British Columbia's fur-trade society into a properly British settler society clearly shows the steps by which a native population was segregated from white culture and dispossessed of their lands, although not fully controlled. I have also shown, following Adele Perry, the ways in which "gender is key in charting the particular trajectories of local colonial projects."[55] The resulting story is very different from that customarily offered in regional textbooks, and to my mind a much richer one, for it tells us how ordinary people, not their governments, made a new place their home. Coming to Oregon Country as members of pre-existing social networks, different groups frequently—and deliberately—destroyed older networks and peoples to forge new regional identities, that is, connections to each other and to the land.

NOTES

1. Patricia Nelson Limerick, *Legacy of Conquest: The Unbroken Past of the American West* (New York: W.W. Norton, 1987).

2. For the historiography, see Chad Reimer, "Borders of the Past: The Oregon Boundary Dispute and the Beginnings of Northwest Historiography," in *Parallel Destinies: Canadian-American Relations West of the Rockies,* ed. John M. Findlay and Ken S. Coates (Seattle: Center for the Study of the Pacific Northwest in association with University of Washington Press; Montreal: McGill-Queen's University Press, 2002), 221–45.

3. Donald Worster, "New West, True West: Interpreting the Region's History," *Western Historical Quarterly* 18, no. 2 (1987): 149.

4. Deirdre McNamer, "Comment," *Aunties Newsletter* (Spokane, WA: Aunties Bookstore, 1996).

5. For an example of the many ways social networks interact with race and gender, see Elizabeth Jameson and Susan Armitage, eds., *Writing the Range: Race, Class, and Culture in the Women's West* (Norman: University of Oklahoma Press, 1997).

6. For much fuller information about specific indigenous groups, see William C. Studevant, ed., *Handbook of North American Indians* (Washington, D.C.: Smithsonian Institution, 1990), especially vols. 7, 11, and 12.

7. See, for example, the gendered limits described in Margaret B. Blackman, *During My Time: Florence Edenshaw Davidson, a Haida Woman* (Seattle: University of Washington Press, 1982; Vancouver: Douglas & McIntyre, 1982).

8. *Guide to the Nez Perce National Park* (Washington: National Park Service, 1983); Ella Clark, *Indian Legends of the Pacific Northwest* (Berkeley: University of California Press, 1953), 20–23.

9. Leslie Marmon Silko, *Yellow Woman and a Beauty of Spirit* (New York: Touchstone, 1996), 50.

10.   Elizabeth Vibert, *Traders' Tales: Narratives of Cultural Encounters in the Columbia Plateau, 1807–1846* (Norman: University of Oklahoma Press, 1997), 124.

11.   Vibert, *Traders' Tales*, 132.

12.   Vibert, *Traders' Tales*, 50–58.

13.   Sylvia Van Kirk, *Many Tender Ties: Women in Fur-Trade Society in Western Canada, 1670–1870* (Winnipeg, MB: Watson & Dwyer Publishing; Norman: University of Oklahoma Press, 1980); Alexandra Harmon, *Indians in the Making: Ethnic Identities and Indian Identities Around Puget Sound* (Berkeley: University of California Press, 1998), 16–17.

14.   Sylvia Van Kirk, "From 'Marrying-In' to 'Marrying-Out': Changing Patterns of Aboriginal/Non-Aboriginal Marriage in Colonial Canada," *Frontiers: A Journal of Women Studies* 23, no. 3 (2002): 1–11.

15.   Jacqueline Peterson and Jennifer S. H. Brown, *The New Peoples: Being and Becoming Métis in North America* (Winnipeg: University of Manitoba Press, 1985).

16.   McLoughlin to the HBC Governor and Committee, November 15, 1843, quoted in Dorothy Nafus Morrison, *Outpost: John McLoughlin and the Far Northwest* (Portland: Oregon Historical Society Press, 1999), 174.

17.   James R. Gibson, *Farming the Frontier: The Agricultural Opening of the Oregon Country, 1786–1846* (Seattle: University of Washington Press, 1985), 31–43; John A. Hussey, "The Women of Fort Vancouver," *Oregon Historical Quarterly* 92, no. 3 (Fall 1991): 292–93.

18.   Vibert says that in 1835 "there were 218 Canadians, 138 Scots and other Europeans, 55 Hawai'iians, and 47 Métis and eastern Native men on servant contracts in the Columbia and New Caledonia districts," Vibert, *Trader's Tales*, 41.

19.   Hussey, "The Women of Fort Vancouver"; Vibert, quoting American visitor Thomas Farnham in 1839, Vibert, *Trader's Tales*, 112; Morrison, *Outpost*, 148.

20.   Sylvia Van Kirk, "A Transborder Family in the Pacific North West: Reflecting on Race and Gender in Women's History," this volume.

21.   Carlos Schwantes, *The Pacific Northwest* (Lincoln: University of Nebraska Press, 1987), 80–84; Julie Roy Jeffrey, *Converting the West: A Biography of Narcissa Whitman* (Norman: University of Oklahoma Press, 1991).

22.   Morrison, *Outpost*, 380–82.

23.   Of the hundreds of volumes devoted to the Overland Trails, the most comprehensive and balanced is generally agreed to be John Unruh, *The Plains Across: The Overland Emigrants and the Trans-Mississippi West, 1840–1860* (Urbana: University of Illinois Press, 1979); the pathbreaking study of gender roles on the trail is that of John Mack Faragher, *Women and Men on the Overland Trail* (New Haven, CT: Yale University Press, 1979). The fullest exploration of the meaning of women's diaries is Lillian Schlissel, *Women's Diaries of the Westward Journey* (New York: Schocken Books, 1982).

24.   Contemporary accounts and letters were often candid about these conditions, but by the time histories of Oregon were written, the hardships had apparently receded from memory and a much more upbeat tone prevailed in works like H. H. Bancroft, *History of Oregon* (San Francisco: History Company, 1886), which was written by Frances Fuller Victor.

25.   John Rember, *Traplines* (New York: Pantheon, 2003).

26.   See Unruh and Faragher on the unfamiliarity with Indians.

27. Malcolm Clark Jr., *Eden Seekers: The Settlement of Oregon, 1818–1862* (Boston: Houghton Mifflin, 1981), 214.

28. Jean Barman, *The West Beyond the West: A History of British Columbia* (Toronto: University of Toronto Press, 1991), 58; Schwantes, *The Pacific Northwest*, 116–20.

29. Barman, *The West Beyond the West*, 154–57.

30. Barman, *The West Beyond the West*, 154.

31. Peter Boag, *Environment and Experience: Settlement Culture in Nineteenth-Century Oregon* (Berkeley: University of California Press, 1992), 73.

32. Boag, *Environment and Experience*, 139.

33. Schwantes, *The Pacific Northwest*, 97.

34. See Schlissel, *Women's Diaries*.

35. William A. Bowen, *The Willamette Valley: Migration and Settlement on the Oregon Frontier* (Seattle: University of Washington Press, 1978), 51–53.

36. This was standard practice, learned on earlier frontiers. See, for example, John Mack Faragher, *Sugar Creek: Life on the Illinois Prairie* (New Haven, CT: Yale University Press, 1986), 144–45.

37. Schwantes, *The Pacific Northwest*, 103. However, Dorothy O. Johansen and Charles M. Gates point out that the 7,500 is a surprisingly small proportion of the nearly 30,000 people who came to Oregon before 1855. *Empire of the Columbia: A History of the Pacific Northwest* (New York: Harper and Row, 1957), 231–34.

38. Bowen says that, overall, there were 154.2 males per 100 females; but that the gender balance was closer—58 per cent male to 42 per cent female—in rural areas. Bowen, *The Willamette Valley*, 53–55.

39. Alexandra Harmon demonstrates this reality for Puget Sound.

40. Adele Perry, *On the Edge of Empire: Gender, Race, and the Making of British Columbia, 1849–1871* (Toronto: University of Toronto Press, 2001).

41. See Barman, *The West Beyond the West*.

42. Ann Laura Stoler, "Rethinking Colonial Categories: European Communities and the Boundaries of Rule," *Society for Comparative Study of Society and History* 31, no. 1 (1989): 148.

43. Daniel P. Marshall, "American Miner-Soldiers at War with the Nlaka'pamux of the Canadian West," in *Parallel Destinies*, ed. Findlay and Coates, 31–79.

44. Marshall, "American Miner-Soldiers," 65.

45. Recently, the complexity of the California Gold Rush has been explored by Susan Johnson, *Roaring Camp: The Social World of the California Gold Rush* (New York: W.W. Norton, 2000); and the authors in Kenneth Owens, ed., *Riches for All: The California Gold Rush and the World* (Lincoln: University of Nebraska Press, 2002). The staid aftermath has been described by Ralph Mann, *After the Gold Rush: Society in Grass Valley and Nevada City, California, 1849–1870* (Stanford: Stanford University Press, 1982).

46. Perry, *On the Edge of Empire*, 20–47.

47. Barman, *The West Beyond the West*, 52–71; Perry, *On the Edge of Empire*, 10.

48. Perry, *On the Edge of Empire*, 97–123.

49. Perry, *On the Edge of Empire*, 111.

50. John Lutz, "Work, Sex and Death on the Great Thoroughfare: Annual Migrations of Canadian Indians to the American Pacific Northwest," in *Parallel Destinies,* ed. Findlay and Coates, 80–103.

51. Perry, *On the Edge of Empire,* 138–66; Lenna Deutsch, *The Mercer's Belles* (Pullman: Washington State University Press, 1992).

52. Anne McClintock, *Imperial Leather: Race, Gender and Sexuality in the Colonial Conquest* (London: Routledge, 1996), 24–25, quoted in Perry, *On the Edge of Empire,* 175.

53. Barman, *The West Beyond the West,* 129–50.

54. Ethel Wilson, *Swamp Angel* (New York: Harper & Brothers, 1954); Desmond Pacey, *Ethel Wilson* (New York: Twayne Publishers, Inc., 1967).

55. Perry, *On the Edge of Empire,* 7.

4

A TRANSBORDER FAMILY IN THE
PACIFIC NORTH WEST

Reflecting on Race and Gender in Women's History

SYLVIA VAN KIRK

IT HAS BEEN OVER TWENTY YEARS since the publication of *Many Tender Ties,* my study on the role of women in the western Canadian fur trade. At that time, the field of women's history was still in its infancy, so one of the book's major goals was to put women into the history—to demonstrate the error and inadequacy of envisioning the fur trade as an archetypal male frontier. Since that time, my own research has been extended in both its time frame and analysis. Recent articles have been concerned with what happened to elite HBC–native families as they moved from fur-trade post to colonial settlement. Further consideration of what happened to the children of these families illuminates the importance of a gendered analysis because significant differences emerge in the experiences of sons and daughters in the second generation.[1] I remain fascinated by the complexities of individual lives. This case study of the Charles Ross family provides an opportunity not only to examine the usual dynamics of gender, race, and class, but to consider the "transborder experience" as another variable. Charles and Isabella Ross raised their family in the Pacific North West in the mid-nineteenth century: the life of this family is intertwined with the histories of Fort Nisqually at the bottom of Puget Sound and Fort Victoria at the southern tip of Vancouver Island. Both forts were established by the Hudson's Bay Company, but the division of the Columbia District between Britain and the United States in 1846 resulted in the former ending up in Washington State and the latter in British Columbia. The differing regional cultures created by the border, as discussed in Sue Armitage's essay in this volume,[2] certainly contributed to the varying experiences of the Ross family.

Charles Ross was a Highland Scot, born in Kingcraig, Invernessshire, who entered the service of the Hudson's Bay Company in 1818. Early in his career, Ross was stationed at Rainy Lake (in southwestern Ontario) where he met Isabella, the daughter of a French-Canadian trader named Joseph Mainville and his Ojibway wife, Josette. Like many Métis girls, Isabella became a wife and mother at a young age: she was about sixteen when she and Ross were wed *à la façon du pays* (according to fur-trade marriage rites) in 1822. Marriage soon took this French-Ojibwa woman far away from her own kin, for most of Ross's career was spent west of the Rockies, including long stints in New Caledonia and the Columbia Department. Over the next twenty years, Isabella bore a family of ten children: six boys and four girls who all survived to adulthood. We catch glimpses of the Rosses' married life through her husband's correspondence. It is apparent that there was a strong attachment and that Isabella was a valued partner. As Ross wrote to his own sister who had settled in Ontario: "I have as yet said nothing about my wife, when you would probably infer that I am rather ashamed of her—in this, however, you would be wrong. She is not, indeed, exactly fitted to shine at the head of a nobleman's table, but she suits the sphere she has to move in better than any such toy—in short, she is a native of the country, and as to beauty quite as comely as her husband."[3] Furthermore, Isabella's courage at

Fort McLoughlin (up the West Coast) even attracted Governor Simpson's notice. In 1841, when her husband was absent, some Indians who were trading with her son drew their knives on the young man. His mother rushed to his aid, according to the account, and "pike in hand, chased the cowardly rascals from post to pillar, till she drove them out of the fort."[4]

But like other country wives, Mrs Ross had had to bear the brunt of racist slanders from the first British missionary at Fort Vancouver in the mid-1830s. As a result, her husband, like several other officers, agreed to a formal Anglican marriage at the fort in 1838. Isabella and her five youngest children were baptized at the same time. Isabella signed her marriage certificate with an X at this point, although she became literate later, after settling in Victoria.

The fortunes of the Ross family seemed to be looking up when the father was promoted to Chief Trader in 1843 and sent to build Fort Victoria on Vancouver Island. That same year Ross, who showed great concern for his children's education, made arrangements for two sons and a daughter to be sent to England for schooling. Colleagues were aghast at the expense, but Ross had hopes that they would do well with his nephew in London. A touching letter written to his "honoured Father" by eighteen-year-old Walter indicates that he had found a good placement as a wool merchant's clerk and that his brother and sister were "much improved in their learning." Their progress was cut short, however—Ross never received the letter, having died the previous year, and relatives were soon expressing their dissatisfaction with the children, whom they found "extremely indocile and addicted to habits incompatible with a residence in this country."[5]

Ross's premature death in June of 1844 left Isabella a widow in her mid-thirties with a large family; in fact, her youngest son William was born after the death of his father. She then had to cope with her three teenage children being sent back from England, as well as with the little ones, though by this time her eldest son, John, had been taken into the service of the company. In the late 1840s, family fortunes focused on Fort Nisqually and the prospects offered by the Puget Sound Agricultural Company. John Ross, accompanied by his mother and younger siblings, took up land offered by the Company, which was trying to forestall the impact of American immigration by settling its employees north of the Columbia. Several other sons were also employed around Fort Nisqually: Walter was employed as a clerk, and Charles Jr appears numerous times in the fort journal doing routine servant tasks.[6]

The marriages of the older Ross children reveal what a truly multi-cultural community was growing up around the fort.[7] In 1848, the eldest daughter, Elizabeth, married the Métis settler Charles Wren, who had come out to Oregon from Red River with his family in 1841. In 1851, eldest son John Ross married Genevieve, a Métis daughter of Simon Plamondon, who had become a major settler on the Cowlitz Plain after leaving the service of the HBC. While intermarriage among fur-trade families was common, a new trend among acculturated families was for daughters to marry incoming white settlers; thus did a younger daughter, Catherine, marry Englishman Henry Murray in 1851. The rapid Americanization of the Oregon Country brought increasingly hostile attitudes toward miscegenation, and by the mid-1850s Indian/settler relations had badly deteriorated. This must have created a particularly difficult situation for Charles Ross Jr, who had married into the local Nisqually tribe around 1850. His wife was Catherine Toma (Tumalt), whose mother was a Nisqually named Quatan and whose father was French-Iroquois, having come west as a company engagé.[8]

Although initially the Ross family appeared to be prospering in the Nisqually region, and a small community called Rossville had sprung up around John Ross's property, the deteriorating racial climate, which resulted in actual warfare with the Indians in 1855, made the family consider the new colony across the border a more inviting location. On Vancouver Island, which had been designated a British colony in 1849, Hudson's Bay Company ties still counted for a great deal. Significantly, three of the younger Rosses (Alexander, Francis, and Flora) were among the first pupils at the school opened for officers' children by Anglican missionaries at Fort Victoria in 1850.[9] HBC officers appear to have looked out for the welfare of the Ross family, and Isabella Ross, who returned to Victoria in 1852, already had a network of female friends among the Métis wives. Such women as Josette Work and Amelia Douglas were known to her from her days at Fort Vancouver. In 1852, when the HBC opened up its lands for sale, its retired officers moved quickly to become the landed gentry of the colony by buying themselves substantial estates. Notably, the Widow Ross was able to participate in this venture, purchasing several hundred acres along the Strait of Juan de Fuca, which made her the first independent female landowner in the colony. Documents from the 1850s show her actively involved in commercial transactions, selling farm produce and livestock.[10] She also became a stalwart member of the Anglican Church. Indeed Victoria seemed a haven from the troubles south of the border. Elder sons John and then Charles Jr, and a Métis son-in-law (Charles Wren), all sold up and brought their families north to British territory. In 1858 John Ross expanded the family holdings in Victoria by purchasing a 200-acre farm known as Oaklands.

With their HBC and Scottish background (in which the Ross family took considerable pride), colonial Victoria may have provided a more amenable community for the family, but even here they would have to deal with the racist currents that were beginning to percolate through this society. In the 1850s, the younger Ross daughters, Mary Amelia and Flora, were featured at the balls given by the officers of the British Navy, but they did not have a father to match-make for them as their Métis contemporaries did. According to one observer, the Rosses were very fine looking girls, but "they had a great deal of Indian blood in them and were supposed to be only on the edge of society."[11] It could not have helped matters much that their two youngest brothers were also getting a reputation for being wild and spendthrift young men about town.[12] It is perhaps indicative of the unsettled prospects of the family at the time that in 1859 the youngest daughter, Flora, who was then only eighteen, made an ill-judged match with a man much older than herself. He was a brash American frontiersman named Paul K. Hubbs, who was for a time collector of customs on San Juan Island and had such extensive trade ties with native people that he was dubbed "a white Indian."[13]

However, Flora's choice paled in comparison to that of her widowed mother, who in her mid-50s succumbed to the attentions of a young suitor from Eastern Canada—one Lucius Simon O'Brien, whom she married in 1863.[14] The new stepfather was soon at odds with the family, especially

Alexander, the eldest son at home, as it became apparent that O'Brien was intent on defrauding them. The conflict resulted in much unfavourable publicity. Isabella's distress resulted in her temporarily running away, whereupon O'Brien stooped to vicious racial slurs as he sought to tarnish her character. He publicly denounced her as "a drunken squaw" in the Victoria *Daily Chronicle* in April 1864, declaring that he would not pay any debts she might incur. A few days later, the youngest son, William, denounced O'Brien, charging "His every act since his marriage has been to try to get everything from my mother, and turn us (the children) out of the house;...Will you do me and my mother the simple justice to publish this, as such a statement as O'Brien has made is calculated to injure both her and myself."[15] When the family then began proceedings against O'Brien to prove that he was actually a bigamist, he apparently deserted up island, where he came to an untimely end a few years later. Isabella, quite thankfully widowed again, reassumed her status as the widow of Charles Ross.[16] The only portrait of Isabella Ross was likely taken in Victoria at this time. It shows her in her widow's weeds: her dignity, but also the sadness resulting from so many difficulties, can be read in this picture. (See Figure 4.1)

Certainly, family tragedy continued. Eldest son John, who had assumed leadership of the family, was only forty when he died in 1863. A few years later, after numerous brushes with the law, the two youngest sons, Francis and William, were convicted of robbing a Chinese man and sentenced for five years at hard labour. This harsh fate aroused public sympathy, and a widely-supported petition to the governor asked for their release, claiming that their health was suffering. Sir James Douglas testified that he had known their "most respectable parents" and that these young men were not the blackguards they were made out to be.[17] After serving about two years, the Ross boys were released on condition of their banishment from the colony and may have gone back across the border to the Puget Sound area.

>FIGURE 4.1: *Isabella Ross.*

[*Permission from British Columbia Records and Archives Service, 7049N: F-01280*]

Isabella Ross must have suffered considerable anguish over these events, but she does appear to have found some solace in religion. The Anglican clergyman Edward Cridge used to make regular visits to Mrs Ross to read and pray with her, and when Cridge broke with the Anglican Church to form the Church of Our Lord in 1874, Isabella Ross was among the initial pew holders.[18] By the early 1870s, the Victoria Rosses had had to sell off a good deal of their property. The remaining son, Alexander, apparently settled down and married in 1868, but he was not well off, being employed as a labourer on the neighbouring Pemberton estate when he died suddenly of a heart attack in 1876.[19] Now only the youngest daughter, Flora, and the widowed daughters-in-law remained in Victoria. The Ross family lost the rest of its property, and Isabella Ross ended her days in a little cottage on the grounds of the convent of the Sisters of Saint Ann, where she died in 1885 at the age of seventy-eight.[20]

Flora was the only child able to provide financial assistance to her mother in her last years, as she had gone on to make an unusual career for herself. Although she had had a son in 1862, Flora had been so badly treated by her husband that by 1868 they had been divorced, and Flora, like her mother, reassumed the family name of Ross. Interestingly enough, she also changed her son's name, giving him the name of her father instead of her husband's. In 1870, Flora Ross was appointed matron of the Victoria jail, primarily to look after several female mental patients who were then housed there. She then became the matron of the Provincial Asylum, which opened first in Victoria and was then moved to New Westminster in 1878. Living quarters for herself and her son were provided at the institution, and although she lacked professional training, she ultimately won considerable respect for her humane and efficient management of the women's ward. Nonetheless, as a native woman with a son to raise on her own, she had to fight to maintain her reputation and her position. While still in Victoria, a newly-arrived superintendent had suggested that she was ill-suited to the job because she was an "immoral Indian," insubordinate, and too fond of fraternizing

>FIGURE 4.2: *Flora Ross.*

[Permission from British Columbia Records and Archives Service, 7052N: A-02445]

with half-breeds. The superintendent, however, little understood the make-up of Victoria's society at the time; Flora Ross had influential friends and retorted that the "half-breeds of whom he spoke were in fact ladies...of the highest respectability, most of them moving in the best society of Victoria."[21] She won the battle with the superintendent and remained in her position well into the 1890s. A stylish portrait of Flora Ross taken in the 1890s captures her own strength of character and Victorian respectability. (See Figure 4.2) She died in 1897 at the age of fifty-five.

Family correspondence in the next generation reveals that there was considerable travelling between branches of the family, back and forth across the border in the ensuing decades. Little is known of the other two Ross daughters, except whom they married. Catherine had never come to Victoria, having married a white settler, Henry Murray, and settling in Pierce Country in Washington State. The remaining daughter, Mary Amelia, had actually married her brother-in-law, Charles Wren, after her sister died in Victoria in 1859, and she thus became stepmother to her four nieces. This branch of the family returned to Washington State, as did Charles Ross Jr and his family. Neither of these branches of the family had prospered in Victoria. In studying the sons of elite fur-trade families in colonial society, it appears that racism could have a differential impact on gender roles. Especially with the surplus of male immigrants to the colony, it seems that sons had great difficulty securing an economic niche for themselves and maintaining the family's status. A clue to the family's aspirations and their emphasis on Scottish ethnicity is evident in this remarkable family portrait of Charles Jr and his family, which was taken during their time in Victoria. (See Figure 4.3) It is certainly ironic, then, that upon returning to Washington State it was to be the wife's Indian heritage that provided a land base. Through Catherine Toma, the family was settled on a homestead on the Nisqually Indian Reservation in 1884. There, Charles Jr and Catherine, who ultimately

<FIGURE 4.3: *Charles Ross, Jr. with his family.*
[*Permission from British Columbia Records and Archives Service, 97185 N: H-04646*]

had eleven children, lived (unlike many of his siblings) to a venerable old age. Charles died in 1904 and his wife in 1914. This land, too, was lost, but descendants of this family today are proud of their membership in the Nisqually Indian band. It is significant to observe, here, that had Charles Ross Jr married a Canadian aboriginal woman, she would have lost her Indian status, as would her children. Under the Canadian Indian Act, any Indian woman who married a white man or non-status Indian was no longer legally considered an Indian and thus lost the right to live on reserve lands.

This brief overview of the Charles Ross family highlights the fascinating dynamics of a mid-nineteenth-century family in the emerging Pacific Northwest. These lives were not only complicated by their mixed ancestry, but by their transborder experience.

NOTES

1. See Sylvia Van Kirk, "Tracing the Fortunes of Five Founding Families of Victoria," *B.C. Studies: The British Columbian Quarterly* 115/116 (Autumn/Winter 1997/98): 149–79; and "'What if Mama is an Indian?': The Cultural Ambivalence of the Alexander Ross Family," in *The New Peoples: Being and Becoming Métis in North America*, ed. Jacqueline Peterson and Jennifer S. H. Brown (Winnipeg: University of Manitoba Press, 1985), 207–17.

2. See Susan Armitage, "Making Connections: Gender, Race, and Place in Oregon Country," this volume.

3. "Five Letters of Charles Ross, 1842–1844," *British Columbia Historical Quarterly (BCHQ)* 7, no. 2 (April 1943): 109.

4. George Simpson, *Narrative of a Journey Round the World, During the Years 1841 and 1842* (London: H. Colburn, 1847), 204.

5. Walter P. Ross to Father, 1 March 1845, Charles Ross Clipping File, British Columbia Records and Archives Service, Victoria, BC (hereafter cited as BCARS); Walter P. Ross and Mary Tait to HBC Secretary, 13 June and 7 August 1845, A.10/19 & 20, Hudson's Bay Company Archives.

6. Cecelia Svinth Carpenter, *Fort Nisqually: A Documentary History of Indian and British Interaction* (Tacoma, WA: Tahoma Research Service, 1986), 132–33.

7. For further discussion of the communities growing out of the fur trade in this region, see John C. Jackson, *Children of the Fur Trade: Forgotten Métis of the Pacific Northwest* (Missoula, MT: Mountain Press Publishing Co., 1996).

8. Carpenter, *Fort Nisqually*, 133–34.

9. School Register, Ft Victoria, 1850–1852, M-2774, BCARS.

10. Augustus Pemberton Diary, 1856–1858, Augustus Frederick Pemberton Papers, E/B/ P37A, BCARS.

11. Philip Hankin Reminiscences, 166, BCARS.

12. *The British Colonist*, 30 April 1859, 2 and 20–21 May 1862, 3. See also several entries in the Charge Books of the Victoria Police Department from 1858 to 1860, BCARS.

13. Marriage Register, Christ Church Cathedral papers, M-0520, BCARS; Gordon Keith, ed., *The James Francis Tullock Diary, 1875–1910* (Portland, OR: Binford & Mort, 1978), 16.

14. Marriage Register, 29 June 1863, Christ Church Cathedral Records, BCARS. O'Brien is identified as the eldest son of Dr Lucius O'Brien of Quebec, QE.

15. *Victoria Daily Chronicle*, 4 May 1864. See also *Daily Chronicle*, 30 April 1864; *The British Colonist*, 26 August 1863, 3; 1 September 1863, 3; 27 September 1864, 3.

16. Vancouver Island, Supreme Court, Cause Books, 616–7, BCARS; Colonial Correspondence, John Morley, File 1170, Inquest into the death of Lucius O'Brien, 1866, BCARS.

17. Colonial Correspondence, File 1352, Petitions (1866), BCARS.

18. Bishop Edward Cridge Papers, Vol. 7 (1868): 68, 89, M-0320, BCARS.

19. *The British Colonist*, 23 September 1876, 3.

20. *Victoria Daily Chronicle*, 24 April 1885; Carrie to Isabella Ross, 17 August 1880, Wren Family Papers, Q/F/L12, A/E/R731, BCARS.

21. Mary-Ellen Kelm, "Flora Ross," *Dictionary of Canadian Biography,* vol. XII (Toronto: University of Toronto Press, 1991), 929–30.

PEOPLE, PLACE, AND STORIES

THE "GREAT MAN" APPROACH to history has largely fallen out of favour among historians. The assumption that one powerful man's life could, by itself, explain key eras and events was recognized as too limited, and the assumption that lone, powerful individuals made history by themselves has been criticized for ignoring the ways that history is made in local and daily contexts. The articles in this section, collective biographies of women in three different times and places, are a refreshing reminder of the powerful insights that can be gained by bringing individual lives into focus.

The power of these essays lies partly in the fact that they do not attempt a "great woman" approach. Rather, they examine stories and lives that reveal something more general about women's experiences in their particular Wests, and about histories that comprise thousands of interesting and illuminating individual stories. These individual stories, so easy to lose in the sweeping narratives the West invites, can also re-shape those narratives in small but critical ways and re-tell them to reflect their different realities.

The title of Jean Barman's article, "Writing Women into the History of the North American Wests, One Woman at a Time," is particularly apt for this trio that illustrates the process through which focussing on individual women's lives had led historians to questions older interpretations of women's lives and their larger historical contexts. They also illuminate the process through which individual women's lives and the perspectives of individual historians interact to produce new histories and new questions.

Jean Barman focuses serially on five women who lived in British Columbia from 1849 to 1941: Emma Douse Crosby, Maria Mahoi Douglas Fisher, Annie McQueen, Jessie McQueen, and Constance Lindsey Skinner. With birth dates ranging from 1849 to 1877 and an equally diverse range of personal backgrounds, these women participated in the major decades of British Columbia's colonization. The last decades of the nineteenth century were critical years for the province, and that history looks different when seen through the life of a teacher born in Nova Scotia, a missionary's wife born in Ontario, a bi-racial Aboriginal and Hawai'ian woman, or a New York writer born in the Cariboo. Each life opens a new window on the roles of individual women within particular historical contexts, on the limiting effects of social structures, and on the power of individual choices to make a difference. The fact that all five lived lives far removed, literally or figuratively, from their birthplaces speaks to the choices they made given the constraints into which they were born. Each woman, at some point, took charge of her own life, making at least one choice that was contrary to the expectations of the day.

Barman shows how paying careful attention to the "traces" that women left behind, whether in the form of voluminous personal correspondence or the oral testimony of their descendants, can shine a light on the ways in which they did and did not conform to the expectations placed on them. When seen through the lenses of these women's stories, the history of British Columbia looks quite different. Barman's narrative shifts from woman to woman, to recreate a stage in women's historical writing sometimes referred to as "add a woman and stir."[1] As each life was added, the story might appear unconnected. It was only after adding a number of women to inherited histories that the larger picture might be imagined in new ways.

The power of an individual narrative is even more evident in Molly Rozum's "'That Understanding with Nature': Region, Race, and Nation in Women's Stories from the Modern Canadian and American Grasslands West." Whereas Barman's five biographies had to be teased from the "traces" they left behind, the three women Rozum chronicles consciously wrote their individual experiences into bigger narratives. North Dakotan Era Bell Thompson's *American Daughter* was published in 1946, Manitoba–North Dakota resident Thorstina Jackson Walters' *Modern Sagas* appeared in 1953, and Alberta's Annora Brown published *Sketches from Life* in 1981. Thompson, Walters, and Brown shared a time (the mid-twentieth century) and a place (the northern edge of the continent's grasslands), but each wrote what might have been a shared history from her own unique perspective.

To one degree or another, all three texts engage the themes of race, women's relationships to western land, and the standard narratives of the Canadian and American Wests, probing their connections to place, the power of western masculinity to constrict the wide open spaces for women, and the meanings of borders—rural and urban, national and social—in their lives. Rozum's close analysis of these three narratives suggests that women in the twentieth-century North American West paid more attention to gender and race than nationalism, and that they forged their own intense connections to the West in defiance of Western narratives that said that women and minorities did not belong. Their combined stories offer a strong corrective to the dominance of male-centred, white-centred, and nation-centred Western narratives.

Joan Jensen's article narrows the focus even further by tracing Jensen's own distinguished career writing the history of rural women. This article makes explicit the connections between the historian's own intellectual and personal history and the process of historical inquiry. Jensen links the journey of her German grandmother, who immigrated to northern Wisconsin in the 1890s, and her own family's history across the Canada-U.S. border with the development of the broader field of rural women's history. By tracing her own intellectual autobiography, she reminds us that the questions historians ask and the stories we tell are connected in some ways to our own lives and to the search for new connections between women's memories and the histories of the places we have called home.

As historians begin to pay more attention to the scholarly output on both sides of the border, Jensen cautions us to beware of the risk of fantasizing or romanticizing women's lives by idealizing a richer, simpler, irretrievable past. The power of truthful storytelling is to reveal the complicated, difficult, and often mundane choices that made up western women's individual lives and our collective past. The power of Jensen's advice lies in how clearly she grounds it in her own history and her own choices as a historian.

These articles remind us, too, that individuals do matter. If history is the sum of each individual's story, then each story can re-shape what "history" looks like. An individual doesn't have to be a "great man" or a man at all, or even "great," to say something significant about history or to help make it.

NOTES

1.   See Gerda Lerner, *Teaching Women's History* (Washington, D.C.: American Historical Association, 1981). For a discussion of this process, see for instance Gerda Lerner, "Placing Women in History: Definitions and Challenges," in Lerner, *The Majority Finds Its Past*, 145–59, esp. 145–48. An earlier version of this article was presented as a paper at the Second Berkshire Conference on the History of Women, 1974; it was originally published in *Feminist Studies III*: 1&2 (Fall 1975): 5–14.

5

WRITING WOMEN INTO THE HISTORY OF THE NORTH AMERICAN WESTS, ONE WOMAN AT A TIME

JEAN BARMAN

IT IS A TRUISM that women were long absent from the ways in which we wrote the history of the North American Wests. The reason lies in how we conceived the past. We considered politics and economics to be the most important subjects to write about. Gender assumptions determined that women would play no, or little, role in the public domain. Even where they did so, as with many indigenous women, their lives have been understood as if their activity was largely confined to the home. Because women were viewed as having only a domestic role, their lives were not considered much worth remembering. When archives were formed, it was the records of male accomplishments that were collected. For the most part, women accepted men's version of what was important and so were less likely to keep traces of their lives with the intention of passing them on to some public location.

So what do we do? How do we write women into the past? Two approaches are possible. The first is to look for women within existing records. We can tease out what they say about women as well as about men. The second is to search out traces that speak to individual women's lives. We write women into the past one woman at a time, as I have been doing recently for five women living in British Columbia between 1849 and 1941.[1]

Both approaches are valuable. Looking for women in existing records, we gain an appreciation of the larger structures that have constrained or liberated women through time. Attention to individual women turns our attention to human agency. We come to understand how women, regardless of their location in historical time, have acted in their own and others' interests. Structure and agency jostle up against each other in every life. The ways in which they do so reveals much about the times and also about the person.

The interplay between larger structures and personal agency is in no way foretold. The process is dynamic and unfolding. If we each think about our own lives, be we women or men, we all come to some point in time when we did the unexpected. We took charge, we exercised agency, we surprised ourselves. It is these moments of change as well as the continuities that characterize the history of women in the North American Wests.

To write about individual lives, we need a trace.[2] If most women die without one, others do not. Traces survive in two principal forms. The first are as written accounts. Particularly for the nineteenth and early twentieth centuries, we are primarily restricted to women sufficiently literate to write as a matter of course and placed well enough that their writing survives. All the same, we should not diminish such accounts.[3]

The second kind of trace comes through oral accounts intended to get at women's experience from their own perspectives. Oral data has the great advantage of extending the range of persons about whom we can write. There are also downsides. Most conversations are perforce retrospective, and we know that human memory is fickle. We want to be seen as rational, sensible beings and tend to construct our pasts in ways that are comprehensible in the present. In general women have seen their everyday lives as possessing less worth than those of their men folk, which puts a great onus on the interviewer. There are, nonetheless, impressive examples of what can be accomplished.[4]

It is with such written and oral traces that I have been engaged, off and on, over the past several years. I did not set out to look at individual lives, but came upon traces in the course of other research that were so engaging, so revealing, I could not resist the opportunity. Five women dogged me. They were so persistent, even waking me up in the middle of the night, I was almost literally forced to make meaning of their lives.

My principal interest as a historian was, up to the time I encountered the five women, less with agency than with structure. In writing about the history of the North American Wests, mostly British Columbia, I was primarily concerned with these places' overall nature through time.[5] I only slowly realized that writing about women, or for that matter about men, was indeed writing about the larger structures as well.[6] The key lies in looking at individual lives, both as ends in themselves and as parts of larger wholes.

We each exist within social contexts. The agency we possess by virtue of our humanity is exercised within settings over which we often have no or very little control. Sometimes we are even unaware of the whole range of larger factors affecting our lives. The two that most often came to the fore for the five women had to do with gender and race, each of which was tempered by place and time. Women's obligation was to uphold the structures put in place by their men folk and to create a home for their families in whatever place they might find themselves. Race was equally fundamental in structuring individual lives. The concept of colonialism was premised on the right of persons perceiving themselves as being of the palest tones, or "white," to dominate their darker, indigenous counterparts around the world to their own political and economic advantage. Just as women were expected as a matter of course to defer to men's presumed superior capacity, persons having a darker skin colour were meant to be subservient to those of lighter pigment.

At the time the five women came of age, the subordination of indigenous peoples was not yet complete in the North American Wests. Location gave the key. The Wests hovered on the edge of a continent. British

Columbia, in particular, was bounded on the east by high mountains, on the west by water and then Asia, and on the north and south by the United States. It took a special effort, and a good reason, such as the fur trade and the gold rush, to head to British Columbia, particularly given its tiny arable land base. Persons came with a purpose, and often that purpose was fairly transient in its appeal. Fur traders mostly moved on at the end of their contracts, gold miners upon becoming disillusioned.

British Columbia was an extreme case of what occurred more generally across the North American Wests. To the south, greater opportunity for agriculture attracted newcomers from the 1840s onward, exemplified by epic treks over the Oregon Trail. Although men outnumbered women there as well, more men came with families in tow. It was not until the completion of the Canadian transcontinental railroad in the mid-1880s that intact families began to arrive in British Columbia in considerable numbers. Up to the First World War, until the five women were between their late thirties and mid-sixties, British Columbia still contained two or more men for every woman. The proportions only evened out in the mid-twentieth century.[7]

The relationship between structure and agency is never static. The nature of the place that was British Columbia encouraged some newcomers to conceive of it as a frontier, a place in space and time where traditional expectations for right gender behaviour were not quite as circumscribed as in areas longer settled by newcomers. Women as well as men considered themselves to possess more personal agency than would otherwise have been the case.

Change over time meant that the force of race and gender affected the five women differently. For that reason they are best considered in birth order to examine how each mediated the structures impinging on her life. Their persons survive through time in their first names, which they did not have to abandon upon marriage as with their birth surnames, and for that reason I prefer to use them here and in my other writing about them. Overall, all five conformed, but also at some point likely surprised even themselves, in effecting change.

Approximate Number and Proportion of Women in the Non-Aboriginal Adult
Population of British Columbia, Washington, and Oregon, 1870–1950/1951
(to the nearest thousand)[8]

	British Columbia	Washington	Oregon
1870	2 (27%)	4 (27%)	19 (36%)
1880–1881	5 (26%)	14 (31%)	38 (35%)
1890–1891	14 (25%)	79 (32%)	81 (38%)
1900–1901	34 (29%)	130 (37%)	116 (41%)
1910–1911	90 (30%)	328 (39%)	201 (41%)
1920–1921	150 (42%)	431 (44%)	259 (46%)
1930–1931	217 (43%)	537 (47%)	336 (47%)
1940–1941	288 (46%)	641 (47%)	410 (48%)
1950–1951	410 (49%)	835 (48%)	544 (49%)

EMMA DOUSE CROSBY (1849–1926)

THE EARLIEST of the five women who have intrigued me and my
co-author, Jan Hare, was born in today's Ontario in 1849. When we look
at the lives of women like Emma Douse Crosby in retrospect, they seem
pretty inevitable in the way they unfolded. Emma was the daughter of a
leading Methodist minister who got his start as a missionary, making it
unsurprising she would marry someone with a similar orientation. She
did so, but all the same, at least from her perspective, it was a conscious
decision. She considered she exercised agency and, I suspect, surprised
herself by her willingness to act.

Emma Douse was in her mid-twenties, a very appropriate age for marriage for women in Ontario, when she took the initiative. In late January
1874, a dynamic missionary, with eyes that seemed to see right through
one, came to speak at the women's college in Hamilton, where Emma
taught. For a decade Thomas Crosby had been converting Aboriginal

people in British Columbia to Christianity and arrived at the college with a powerful message about the perils of savagery, as he saw them. It was just three years since the British colonial possession of British Columbia had joined the Canadian Confederation, and the new province was virtually impossible to reach from the rest of the country. No one in "civilized" Ontario knew much about this faraway place, except that it was a frontier, populated by a handful of former fur traders and gold miners and lots and lots of Indians. Emma was entranced.

Very importantly, the missionary who gave the talk, Thomas Crosby, needed a wife. From a much more modest Ontario family than was Emma, he was converted in his mid-teens and headed west in the hope of saving gold rush souls. Gradually he got the attention of the few Methodist ministers who had made their way there and managed to get himself ordained. The next step was to find a wife. The missionary enterprise gave priority to right behaviour, which, combined with fear of unconstrained sexuality, put the onus on missionaries to be wed. Not only did being married prevent temptation on their part, it served as a model for the Aboriginal people they sought to convert. The skewed sex ratio among newcomer adults in British Columbia put white women at a premium. The difficulty of finding a suitably Christian wife there was in good part responsible for Crosby's trip back home to Ontario. He lit on Emma, with impeccable Methodist credentials, including a father able to further a son-in-law's career, and did his best to convince her that her future lay at his side.

Short weeks after Crosby spoke at Emma's college about supporting the missionary effort, she wrote home to her mother: "Would it grieve you very much—would you be willing to let me go to British Columbia, not exactly as a missionary on my own responsibility, but to be a help and a comfort, if possible, to a noble man who has been there working for years by himself?"[9] Emma dared to exchange one place for another about which she knew virtually nothing.

<FIGURE 5.1: *Emma Douse Crosby.*
[Permission from Helen and Louise Hager and UBC Library, Special Collections]

To make a long story short, Emma married her missionary and spent the next quarter century at Fort Simpson, just outside of the future Prince Rupert on the British Columbian north coast. Her life there, as well as her courtship, we can follow through the letters she regularly wrote home to her mother, which her granddaughter and great-granddaughter considered important enough to keep, and then to grant permission for their publication.[10] They have been co-edited from a dual perspective, my own as a British Columbian historian and that of my colleague Jan Hare, from an Aboriginal point of view. The letters emphasize the great extent to which women bore the everyday burden of changes in place.

And what about Emma? Not surprisingly, given that women were meant to live in the shadow of their men folk—at least in public—Emma, in the main, did so. She let the glory go to her husband, so much so that it is his name that survives as one of the principal missionaries among Aboriginal people in British Columbia and not hers as it also should do.

Emma Crosby's letters to her mother make clear her contribution to the missionary enterprise. The adventure many men found in challenging the unknown was far more trying, and sometimes heartbreaking, from the perspective of women expected to make homes for their husbands, whatever the circumstances. It was Emma who managed everyday life while Thomas went on grandiose conversion expeditions along the coast. It was Emma who originated a girls' home and then a residential school named in honour of her husband. Emma may have written, she certainly edited, the reports in which her less-well-educated husband celebrated his supposed achievements in converting the Tsimshian people of the British Columbian north coast. In line with the gender expectations of the day, Emma took care to buttress her husband's authority rather than give any indication she might be challenging or competing with it.

Emma Douse Crosby's life matters both in and of itself—she gave birth to eight children, of whom she saw four buried while at Fort Simpson—and for the larger understandings it gives about British Columbia history. Emma's life testifies to the importance of structural factors in explaining why women, and men, acted as they did in past time. Having come west due to the province's gender imbalance, she remained for a very good reason, from her perspective. All her life, until her death in 1926, she sustained the gender and racial attitudes of the day. Emma made a difference by virtue of doing so.

MARIA MAHOI DOUGLAS FISHER (c.1855–1936)

MARIA MAHOI DOUGLAS FISHER is Emma Douse Crosby's mirror image. Her inheritance puts her among the objects of conversion of women like Emma, who thought they had a mandate to change other people's outlook according to their own likes and beliefs. What we see when we turn to Maria (pronounced Ma-RYE-ah by those who knew her) is that she very much had a will of her own and was not about to be hassled by anyone else unless she wanted to be. She had agency in spades. Maria acted despite being illiterate. All her life, she signed with her mark, an X.

An X is a pretty slim trace from which to infer a life. Maria survives, to the extent she does, through the voices of others. For a good decade I have had the privilege of listening to stories about Maria told by her many descendants and by descendants of her friends. The stories' survival among so many different persons, in much the same form, is the best possible testament to Maria's having been a tough, resourceful, and thereby memorable woman.

Much of Maria's life remains in the shadows. She was born in the mid-1850s to a Hudson's Bay Company labourer from the Hawai'ian Islands, likely working in the fur trade at Fort Victoria. The company signed on numerous indigenous men in Honolulu, and one of them, named Mahoi, had a child, Maria, by an unknown Aboriginal woman living nearby. The Hawai'ian presence across the North American Wests speaks to the area's distinctive location on the edge of a continent.

How Maria was brought up we have no idea because she never dwelt on the past. Rather, as a grandson who spent much of his childhood in her presence explained to me, she "was always thinking ahead of time,

preparing for the next day, the next time." Maria enters newcomers' record keeping at about age sixteen when she gave birth to the first of seven children by a sea captain from Maine. Abel Douglas had been enticed to Victoria by the possibility of starting a whaling business. The industry fizzled after a few years, but he stayed on—likely because of Maria. The paucity of newcomer women was once again a fundamental influence on the course of a woman's life. Maria, Abel, and their growing family set up house on southern Salt Spring Island. All apparently went well until the mid-1880s when Douglas walked. He abandoned Maria and their seven children, or perhaps she turfed him out.

It is at this point that Maria made clear she was her own person. First, and very importantly, she did not crumple, but very quickly found herself another man—ten years younger than herself and very well educated—by whom she proceeded to have six more children. George Fisher was, like Maria, a child of the colonial encounter. His father was a wealthy young Englishman, his mother an Aboriginal woman. Racial prejudice was endemic against persons of mixed race, such as George and Maria were. Their maternal Aboriginal heritage was scorned, as were their fathers for having deigned to consort with such persons as their mothers. Given these attitudes and the gender imbalance, George Fisher had virtually no possibility of finding a partner from among the relatively small number of newcomer women. He spent much of his youth caught between the two components of his heritage, and Maria may have promised him a solidity that he could not otherwise acquire. She was, once again, the beneficiary of structural factors.

Second, Maria managed, despite her illiteracy, to get herself an island of her own. An elderly Hawaiʻian named William Haumea lived on Russell Island just off south Salt Spring. He left the island in his will to his daughter by an Aboriginal woman. It is almost certain historically that Maria was not his biological daughter, yet she convinced the British Columbia court and her newcomer neighbours on Salt Spring, who

<FIGURE 5.2: *Maria Mahoi Douglas Fisher.*
[*Permission from Violet and Larry Bell*]

testified on her behalf, that she was, and that it was her island.[11] Her well-educated husband may have played a role in the proceedings, but it was principally her own grit and determination that caused her to win out.

Maria, her husband, and younger children moved to Russell Island just after the turn of the century. There they created a little world of their own, secure from the racism against Aboriginal and mixed-descent people that gripped British Columbia during these years. Newcomer families had no sense of, or interest in, the province's past. They did not care to understand the structural reasons numerous newcomer men had opted for Aboriginal women or why there existed a whole generation of mixed-race offspring entering adulthood. Such persons were almost wholly thrust aside by the dominant society and it was only in the small spaces persons like Maria created that they had any possibility of finding their own middle way.

Maria gave her children such strong senses of self that they went on to participate in all aspects of British Columbian society. And here I come full circle, for the way in which I initially encountered Maria was through her great grandson, a prominent British Columbian politician wondering about a possible Aboriginal heritage deliberately kept from him. Many years earlier, a visiting uncle had taken him aside and confided there might be "Indian blood" in the family. His uncle thought he should know, "just in case." All he had to share with me was a faded death notice of his grandmother Ruby's brother. From this small beginning I stumbled on Maria, whose daughter Ruby had, like her mother, protected her children as best she could—in her case, by shedding her Aboriginal heritage. In the anonymity Vancouver offered, Ruby refashioned herself as white and thereby made it possible for her descendants to take advantage of opportunities rather than be tainted by the accident of birth. Maria was waiting to be found, and I became the agent for doing so.[12]

JESSIE McQUEEN (1860–1933) AND ANNIE McQUEEN GORDON (1865–1941)

THE THIRD AND FOURTH women who have engaged me are the McQueen sisters. Jessie and Annie are emblematic of the migration west from within Canada that followed the completion of the trans-continental railroad in 1885–1886. Between 1881 and 1891 the number of persons in British Columbia born elsewhere in Canada skyrocketed from just 3,500 to over 20,000. Each of them has a story to tell about how they came to change their place of living.

To understand the McQueen sisters' reasons for leaving Nova Scotia for British Columbia, we need to go back a generation to their parents. Jessie and Annie grew up in a place and time where God was not to be thwarted. The same virtuous Christianity grounded in racial superiority that propelled Emma to British Columbia also sent the McQueen sisters west.

Born in 1860 and 1865, respectively, Jessie and Annie were raised in Pictou County, which was almost wholly Scots Presbyterian in its outlook. Their parents, and especially their mother Catherine, ensured they considered their lives to be guided by providence, by God's will acting through them, so that they would always behave in accord with God's wishes for them. As part of that obligation, the children kept in close touch with their parents, by letter when not at home. Well over a thousand letters survive between members of the family. It is this remarkable trace, now available on the web through the University of New Brunswick, which grounds my understanding.[13]

From an early age the McQueen children learned the value of hard work on their modest family farm, and on reaching their mid-teens they were expected to go out to teach to bring in a few extra dollars. Jessie and Annie were the two youngest of five daughters, each of whom was released to marry as the next younger entered the classroom. It was within this context that they became sojourners to British Columbia. In Nova Scotia during the 1880s a teacher got $60 for a term of half a year; in British Columbia, even in small rural schools, wages were $60 a month.[14] The money was not for the sisters to spend on themselves but to send home, where they themselves were expected to return. The sisters were permitted to leave by virtue of Presbyterian ministers from Pictou County having gone west before them, men who sought to staff the province's public schools with virtuous young women. Jessie and Annie's mother could not resist the ministerial entreaties any more than she could afford to turn down the money.

The McQueen sisters were part of a larger demographic shift. Following the railroad's completion, British Columbia's newcomer population exploded. At the time Emma Crosby arrived in the early 1870s, there were only about 10,000 non-Aboriginal people in the entire province. By 1891 the number had risen to 70,000 before doubling to 150,000 by 1901. Even as numbers grew, the proportion born elsewhere in Canada doubled from 15 to almost 30 per cent.[15] The shifts were not sufficient to even out the gender imbalance, but they did moderate somewhat its skewed character.

Emma Crosby had had to go by train through the United States and then by boat, north, from San Francisco. It was now possible for the McQueen sisters to catch a train from just outside of the family farm and end up at Kamloops in the British Columbian interior, near where the sisters' one-room schools were located. Jessie's postcards home in March 1888 attest to how the sisters became caught up in a westward movement much larger than themselves. They shared their trip with thousands of others during the rail line's teething years, yet it was also a highly individual experience. Each aspect opened up possibilities less circumscribed than those available back home in Nova Scotia, from "cutting delicate slices of tongue (an inch thick)" to a fellow passenger "eating 'jam' with his scissors!"[16] Whipping off a note from Swift Current, Saskatchewan, Jessie was already reflective: "I believe I will be sorry when the trip is done."[17] Despite arriving at what was still a frontier with all of the freedom for action that the term implied, the sisters soon became embedded, and constrained, within a larger movement intended to transfer west Nova Scotia ways of being, including racial and gender expectations. One place was layered on the other.

The McQueen sisters' story makes an important point about human agency. Even where biology and upbringing is similar, we take different paths that reflect our willingness, or lack of it, to act for ourselves. Jessie and Annie both began as teachers in the Nicola Valley near Kamloops,

>FIGURE 5.3: *Jessie McQueen.*
[*Permission from Bridget Gordon Mackenzie*]

but their paths soon diverged. The presence of far fewer newcomer women than men gave both of them more opportunities for marriage than they would have had at home where the gender ratio was roughly equal. By the Nova Scotian order of things, the older Jessie should have been the first freed from teaching, but Annie, the youngest, jumped the queue. Within a year of arriving in British Columbia, at the age of twenty-three, instead of the Nova Scotia standard age for marriage of twenty-six, she found herself a "dude," as she put it in her newly coined frontier talk.

Annie's marriage made Jessie her parents' last employable daughter. Three times she edged toward the married state, but was beset by misfortune when the man of her desires died on her, or perhaps he only became such a figure by virtue of being unattainable. Ever the dutiful daughter, Jessie spent her life shuffling between teaching jobs in British Columbia and looking after her parents, and then her widowed mother, in Nova Scotia. She never moved beyond the values of her fairly restrictive upbringing, remaining deferent to her parents' wishes and thereby to the life she considered God had intended for her. She found comfort in adhering to larger structures rather than rebelling against them.

Nevertheless, it was Jessie rather than Annie who took a stand when it came to race. They both assumed their own inherent superiority. All the same, Jessie treated the children of mixed Aboriginal descent in her classrooms with basic human decency. She did so well aware of the assumptions of the day, musing how some of her pupils "have attended school for years but in spite of that they still have the squaw looks & manners."[18]

Annie was, for her part, absolutely determined to keep her own children uncontaminated. She held firmly to this priority despite being repeatedly uprooted, as her Ontario-born husband tried a bit of everything to make a living. At the time of their marriage, James Gordon had a furniture store in Kamloops, enticed there by its location along the newly built rail line. After a short, unsuccessful stint in small-town Ontario, the Gordons returned west, but could not make a go of the Salmon Arm,

<FIGURE 5.4: *Annie McQueen Gordon.*
[*Permission from Bridge Gordon Mackenzie*]

British Columbia, farm they took up so optimistically. Jim then wrangled a job with Canadian Customs that carried the family throughout the Kootenays area of southeastern British Columbia.

Like many Canadians of her day, Annie was suspect of the other side of the border her husband managed. Most lives were in practice virtually identical, but that did not prevent women like Annie from searching out differences as a means to legitimate the way of life that they found themselves living. Even though "the American town" was a mile south of the Gordons' home, she fretted over "all the houses of prostitution and saloons and dance-halls in Gateway, Montana," over which she had twice as little control by virtue of being a woman and being Canadian. Annie could only express indignant relief: "the construction boom is over, and the dance hall girls have gone, the prostitutes have nearly all gone, and there are *only* four saloons there now."[19]

Wherever Annie found herself, she ensured her three children would not mix with anyone she considered their inferiors. The local school was in her assessment inadequate, in good part because "the Montana teachers are fairly tumbling over themselves" to teach in it.[20] Annie was most suspicious of her children's counterparts with Aboriginal mothers. Her daughter Jessie was nine at the time Annie justified her outlook to her sister, Jane: "I do wish there were some little white girls here for her to play with. I daren't let her go to play with the half breeds for they are liable to pull her hair out by the root, and beat the life nearly out of her, as they did once shortly after we came down here."[21] Annie improvised. She began to teach the children herself at home and continued to do so for the most part until she managed to cajole westward a Maritimes niece as a tutor. Annie's relief was palpable when in 1907 Jim Gordon inveigled a transfer to the provincial capital of Victoria. A quarter of a century later, Annie still took pride in how "she kept her family from 'going Indian,' as so many of the pioneer settlers did."[22]

Annie's life in Victoria gives us a taste of how changing times affected women. By the early twentieth century, many were becoming active in social reform intended to buttress established ways, and so it was with Annie on being widowed in her mid-forties. Named provincial director of the Homes Branch of the Soldiers Settlement Board, founded to encourage veterans to take up farming, she had charge of accustoming war brides of the First World War to Canadian ways. Then, for a decade, from 1927 to 1936, Annie presided over the British Columbia Women's Institute, a very important volunteer organization whose aim it was to sustain farm wives, and women more generally, much as she had done with veterans' wives.

In their very different ways, each of the McQueen sisters made a difference to the lives of others. Jessie, for the most part, buttressed existing structures, whereas Annie repeatedly took the initiative. Many more women in the past were Jessies than Annies, and it is through their everyday acts of courage, as with Jessie in the classroom, that change also occurs.

CONSTANCE LINDSAY SKINNER (1877–1939)

CHANGE OVER TIME becomes particularly important with the fifth woman, Constance Lindsay Skinner. She is, along with Maria Mahoi, the most consummate British Columbian in her origins. Maria came from a humble background, Constance a genteel one. Her paternal grandfather was one of three English gentlemen farmers brought out from England with their families by the Hudson's Bay Company in the early 1850s to encourage class-based newcomer settlement in the fur-trade colony of Vancouver Island. Her maternal grandfather was enticed by the gold rush, but as a merchant with a family.

Constance was born in 1877 in the Cariboo, where her father ran the Hudson's Bay trading post. She had a stronger sense of self than any of the other four women, both because she was just that much younger and also because she was a pampered only child. From a young age she was determined to have her way. Her parents moved to Vancouver when Constance was twelve, and she was soon writing for the *World* newspaper. Women were still expected to be modest in their behaviour, so she used various pen names in doing so.

Constance told a story later in life that is indicative of her character. It was in the mid-1890s, when she was in her teens, that her self-described "first work of fiction" was printed in a Vancouver Sunday newspaper under a pseudonym. "Considered risqué in those days," the article, to quote Constance, was about "the 'worser' whites mingling with the natives along the coast." In other words, she was writing about the kind of life that Emma Crosby was experiencing first hand at Fort Simpson at precisely the same point in time. She later recalled what happened the day her article appeared: "With heart athrill [I] listened to a guarded discussion of it by [my] parents" and asked to see the paper. "'No,' said mother kindly,...'It is not the sort of thing I want you to read. You are far too young.'"[23]

Generational change was in the air. Increasingly dissatisfied with the narrowness she saw in Vancouver, Constance moved in her early twenties to California. Unlike Annie McQueen a few years earlier, she had no hesitation about experiencing the other side of the border. Within the year she was the drama and music critic for a Los Angeles newspaper owned by up-and-coming publisher William Randolph Hearst, and soon thereafter a Hearst "sob sister" putting out human interest stories about celebrities and part of writer Jack London's coterie. Still dissatisfied, in 1912 she moved to New York City, where she made her living as a writer for the rest of her life.

Constance Lindsay Skinner became sufficiently important for her papers to survive in the New York Public Library, which is where I encountered her. They, together with the three million words of hers that made it into print, make it possible to retrieve her story. What is important in terms of the serendipity that permits us to write about some women's lives and not others is that she did not choose that her papers should be there. It was her male publisher who salvaged everything in her Manhattan apartment when she died suddenly, long since estranged from her birth family.

Constance both sustained and challenged the gender and race assumptions of the day. As to gender, she lived a contradiction. Her years as a

> FIGURE 5.5: *Constance Lindsay Skinner.*
[*Permission from New York Public Library, Special Collections*]

Hearst journalist combined with her singleness to make her, outwardly, "a new woman" daring to be her own person. At the same time, her writing celebrated the married state, due in part to publishers' expectations. Constance always had to scramble to survive financially and, like many others, responded to the expansion of mass-market magazines in the early twentieth century. One of their staples was short stories designed to entertain. As Constance once explained, "A good story serves a useful purpose, if it makes one forget the cares of his daily life."[24] Her prototype couple was affected by modern times, perhaps even got divorced, but in the end reconciled, for the married state was the natural order of things.

The tug of war between structure and agency that existed for Constance with respect to gender is exemplified in "The Torch in the Mist," published in 1915 in the popular women's monthly *Smith Magazine*. The listless wife of a lumber baron learns to appreciate her husband's physicality even as her younger sister discovers the downside of being a suffragette, what their mother terms "the last hope of the ugly woman." The younger sister sees the wrongness of her ways and declares by story's end, "I only *pretended*—that I was really free. I wasn't... Not being married didn't make me free. What is the use of all that talk, when it is *in* a woman, in her nature and a part of her, to *belong* to the man she loves?"[25]

Constance was braver in respect to race. She repeatedly drew from her British Columbian childhood to depict Aboriginal persons not as victims, as was the practice of the day, but as protagonists. Constance got her first international triumph as a writer when in 1913 her submission won the "twenty-one guineas prize poem competition" of *Bookman*, a London review of new literature. The contest attracted two thousand entries from around the world, among them Constance's "Song of Cradle-Making," which divided the first prize. The poem included a note explaining that "the language is that of a British Columbian coast tribe (Kwa'kiutl)." It was written from the perspective of a pregnant Aboriginal woman hoping, in line with the gender expectations of the day, to bear her husband a son:

When I lifted the little cradle,
The little cradle I am making for thee,
I felt thee!....
Oh, I know not if thou be son—
Strong Chief, Great Fisher, Law of Woman,
As thy father is;
Or only Sorrow Woman, Patient Serving Hands,
Like thy mother.[26]

A year later Constance had a cycle of her Aboriginal poems, entitled "Songs of the Coast-Dwellers," accepted for publication in the leading American magazine *Poetry*. Among the fifty-some poets appearing in the same volume featuring Constance were Rupert Brooke, D. H. Lawrence, Vachel Lindsay, Amy Lowell, Ezra Pound, and Carl Sandburg. In the cycle of nine poems, Constance again wrote in the first person, adopting, among other identities, that of a Kwakiutl chief at prayer after the salmon catch, and a tall, proud Haida describing himself as a "conqueror of women."[27] Later that year she beat out, among others, T. S. Eliot's "The Love Song of J. Alfred Prufrock" for second prize for best poem published that year in *Poetry*. Constance's much praised poems, written from an Aboriginal perspective, continue to be reprinted.[28] By present-day standards, Constance's Aboriginal poems can be dismissed as appropriation, but in the time she wrote they were daring for their respect of Aboriginal people.

REFLECTIONS

THESE THEN ARE THE FIVE WOMEN I have sought to write into British Columbian history. In each case I started with a trace. In reading through it, or in uncovering it in the form of recollections, I became aware that each of the women did far more than decorate the edges of the past, so to speak. They were as integral as were men, with their more public contributions, to the history of British Columbia and of the North American Wests more generally.

Each of the five women made a difference to those around her and, in some cases more than others, to the larger society. All five were agents of colonialism. Emma's missionizing helped to reform the Tsimshian people, just as Jessie and Annie did the children in their classrooms. In their very separate ways, Emma, Jessie, and Annie contributed mightily to the making of newcomer society at the expense of Aboriginal peoples, whose continuing presence, all the same, is exemplified by Maria and put into print by Constance. As did Jessie, Maria moderated the worst consequences of racism for those around her.

Emma, Jessie, and Annie each took west established ways of life, much as their American counterparts did travelling the Oregon Trail. Despite British Columbian upbringings that could not have been more different from each other, Maria and Constance both largely took for granted the assumptions that the others brought from elsewhere. Emma and the McQueens helped to transfer assumptions across generations through schooling. Maria acted through her family, Constance through her pen.

Each of the five women's lives was circumscribed by race and gender, as well as by other factors, all intersected by time and place. The British Columbia into which Maria was born in the mid-1850s and where Emma arrived a decade and a half later was very different by the time Constance came of age at the end of the century. Whatever the time period, none of the five spent their adulthood in a single place. As women they each bore the brunt of the moves that marked their lives. Even Constance, who made her own decisions, had to regroup each time she hopped from one opportunity to the next.

All five women lived in a terrain constructed by men. The skewed gender differential in the North American Wests, which was accentuated in British Columbia, gave a particular complexion to relationships between the sexes. It was precisely for that reason Thomas Crosby lured Emma west. Maria and Annie both discovered that the options for finding a man were greater than they would have been in longer settled areas. It is probable that Maria was much more acceptable to the two men in her life than she would have been had there been other, more racially desirable women to choose from.

Whatever the time and place, women were expected to defer to male wishes, and Emma certainly did so wholeheartedly; the other women did so a little less, in part because they were born in a later era. The gender expectations applied to married women put on them the burden of making a home wherever they found themselves. Jessie, in contrast, was repeatedly made aware that she was homeless. Constance, too, suffered from the consequences of singleness, and wrestled in her writing with its implications, just as she did in her private life. All five were much more constrained than comparable women living later in time.

Two of the five remained single, but the reasons Jessie and Constance did so were quite different. Jessie's familial status required her to provide support, which impeded her marriage. The three times she came close, she was beset by misfortune. It is very possible that only in retrospect, after the death of the man of her desires, did she actually consider him marriageable, precisely because a wedding was no longer possible. Jessie remained all her life her parents' daughter. So did Constance, but in a quite different way. Her familial status as a cosseted only child encouraged her to feel special—so special that no man entirely met her expectations. She measured them by her much loved father: "Physically, mentally, morally, he remains my standard of a man."[29] Anyone who did manage the feat of living up to him may well have been scared off by Constance's very strong sense of self.

Race also links the five women. Their lives all passed during a time period when visible distinctions based in skin colour were almost wholly accepted as the principle measure of human beings' worth. Each of the women was captured by racial assumptions. The worldwide colonial advance in which Emma engaged had as its justification the superiority of the newcomer's way of life, particularly their religious predilections, to those of indigenous peoples. Emma did not question committing her life to converting the Tsimshian to Christianity because she genuinely believed that her race had a divine mission to do so.

The activity Emma facilitated in the religious realm, women like the McQueen sisters furthered in the educational dimension, and writers like Constance in the literary domain. Jessie and Annie assumed, as did

Emma, the rightness of their way of life, grounded in their Scots Presbyterian upbringing, and they transported this to the classrooms of British Columbia as a matter of course. Annie followed up in later life by isolating her children and then moving into social reform, by which means she sought to form a generation of women in her own image, which was very much that of the dominant society. While Constance was attentive to the role of Aboriginal people, her preference was for white heroes and heroines.

The activities of these women assumed the colonizers' racial superiority. They should therefore have won out, but did they? We need to return to Maria, who made it clear, time and again, that the people we usually think of as being acted upon were very much actors themselves. Her life should give us pause, for even while identified by those around her as inferior, she repeatedly manoeuvred to make a satisfactory life for her family and community of friends, as did her daughter, Ruby, by throwing off her Aboriginal inheritance.

For all of the constraints exercised by race and gender, each of the women, at some point in her life, took charge. She exercised agency in surprising fashion. Emma decided to become a missionary wife. Maria found two respectable husbands and then an island of her own. In the marriage stakes Annie outmaneuvered her sister Jessie, who quietly continued to exercise what little agency she took to herself. Constance overthrew expectations for marriage to claim a writing life.

The more we write women into the history of the North American Wests, the more we realize that all women, and men, matter. We each, at some point in time, do the unexpected. We should see elements of ourselves in at least one of these five women. Some of us act quietly, mostly behind the scenes, as did Emma, Maria, and Jessie. Others of us like to make a noise, as did Annie and Constance. Whatever our disposition, we are part of larger wholes, and by virtue of our lives we, too, are part of the history of the North American Wests. We each make a difference.

NOTES

1. Jean Barman, *Constance Lindsay Skinner: Writing on the Frontier* (Toronto: University of Toronto Press, 2002); Jean Barman, *Sojourning Sisters: The Lives and Letters of Jessie and Annie McQueen* (Toronto: University of Toronto Press, 2003); Jean Barman, *Maria Mahoi of the Islands* (Vancouver: New Star, 2004); Jan Hare and Jean Barman, *Good Intentions Gone Awry: Emma Crosby and the Methodist Mission on the Northwest Coast* (Vancouver: UBC Press, 2006).

2. For diverse examples of what can result from even very small traces, see Katie Pickles and Myra Rutherdale, eds., *Contact Zones: Aboriginal and Settler Women in Canada's Colonial Past* (Vancouver: UBC Press, 2005); Sarah Carter, Lesley Erickson, Patricia Roome, and Char Smith, eds., *Unsettled Pasts: Reconceiving the West through Women's History* (Calgary: University of Calgary Press, 2005); Elizabeth Jameson and Susan Armitage, eds., *Writing the Range: Race, Class, and Culture in the Women's West* (Norman: University of Oklahoma Press, 1997); Glenda Riley, *A Place to Grow: Women in the American West* (Arlington Heights, IL: Harlan Davidson, 1992); Susan Armitage and Elizabeth Jameson, eds., *The Women's West* (Norman: University of Oklahoma Press, 1987); Sylvia Van Kirk, *Many Tender Ties: Women in Fur-Trade Society in Western Canada, 1670–1870* (Winnipeg: Watson & Dwyer Publishing; Norman: University of Oklahoma Press, 1980). Also impressive, among other sources, are Kathryn Bridge, *By Snowshoe, Buckboard and Steamer: Women of the Frontier* (Victoria: Sono Nis, 1998); Sandra L. Myres, *Westering Women and the Frontier Experience, 1800–1915* (Albuquerque: University of New Mexico Press, 1982); Lillian Schlissel, Vicki L. Ruiz, and Janice Monk, eds., *Western Women: Their Land, Their Lives* (Albuquerque: University of New Mexico Press, 1988); and Kenneth L. Holmes, ed., *Covered Wagon Women: Diaries and Letters from the Western Trails, 1840–1890*, 10 vols. (Glendale, WA: A. H. Clark Co., 1983; Lincoln: University of Nebraska Press, 2003).

3. As examples, Phoebe Goodell Judgson, *A Pioneer's Search for an Ideal Home* (1925; repr., Lincoln: University of Nebraska Press, 1984); Margaret Ormsby, ed., *A Pioneer Gentlewoman in British Columbia: The Recollections of Susan Allison* (Vancouver: UBC Press, 1976); Caroline C. Leighton, *West Coast Journeys, 1865–1879: The Travelogue of a Remarkable Woman* (1883; repr., Seattle: Sasquatch Books, 1995); Dorothy Blakey Smith, ed., *Lady Franklin Visits the Pacific Northwest* (Victoria: Provincial Archives of British Columbia, 1974); R. N. DeArmond, ed., *Lady Franklin Visits Sitka, Alaska 1870: The Journal of Sophia Cracroft, Sir John Franklin's Niece* (Anchorage: Alaska Historical Society, 1981); Martha Summerhayes, *Vanished Arizona: Recollections of the Army Life of a New England Woman* (1908; repr., Lincoln: University of Nebraska Press, 1979); Betty John, *Libby: The Alaskan Diaries and Letters of Libby Beaman, 1879–1880* (Boston: Houghton Mifflin, 1987).

4. Margaret B. Blackman, *During My Time: Florence Edenshaw Davidson, a Haida Woman* (Seattle: University of Washington Press, 1982; Vancouver: Douglas & McIntyre, 1982); Bridget Moran, ed., *Stoney Creek Woman: The Story of Mary John* (Vancouver: Arsenal Pulp Press, 1988); Julie Cruikshank, *Life Lived Like a Story: Life Stories of Three Yukon Native Elders* (Vancouver: UBC Press, 1990); Margaret Horsfield, *Cougar Annie's Garden* (Nanaimo: Salal Books, 1999).

5. Especially Jean Barman, *The West beyond the West: A History of British Columbia* (Toronto: University of Toronto Press, 1991; 3rd ed., 2007); also, as examples, "Aboriginal Women

on the Streets of Victoria: Engendering Transgressive Sexuality during the Gold Rush," in *Contact Zones,* ed. Pickles and Rutherdale; "Encounters with Sexuality: The Management of Inappropriate Body Behaviour in Late-Nineteenth Century British Schools," *Historical Studies in Education* 16, no. 1 (Spring 2004): 191–214; "Seeing British Columbia," *BC Studies: The British Columbian Quarterly* 131 (Fall 2001): 9–14; Jean Barman with Bruce Watson, "Fort Colville's Fur Trade Families and the Dynamics of Aboriginal Racial Intermixture in the Pacific Northwest," *Pacific Northwest Quarterly* 90, no. 3 (Summer 1999): 140–53; "What a Difference a Border Makes: Aboriginal Racial Intermixture in the Pacific Northwest," *Journal of the West* 38, no. 3 (July 1999): 14–20; "Invisible Women: Aboriginal Mothers and Mixed-Race Daughters in Rural British Columbia," in *Beyond the City Limits: Rural History in British Columbia,* ed. R.W. Sandwell (Vancouver: UBC Press, 1999), 159–79; "Taming Aboriginal Sexuality: Gender, Power, and Race in British Columbia, 1850–1900," *BC Studies: The British Columbian Quarterly* 115–116 (Fall-Winter 1997–1998): 237–66.

6. On men, see Jean Barman and Bruce Watson, *Leaving Paradise: Indigenous Hawaiians in the Pacific Northwest, 1787–1898* (Honolulu: University of Hawai'i Press, 2006); and Jean Barman, *Stanley Park's Secret: The Forgotten Families of Whoi Whoi, Kanaka Ranch and Brockton Point* (Madeira Park, BC: Harbour, 2005); *The Remarkable Adventures of Portuguese Joe Silvey* (Madeira Park, BC: Harbour, 2004); "Unpacking English Gentlemen Emigrants' Cultural Baggage: Apple Orchards and Private Schools in British Columbia's Okanagan Valley," *British Journal of Canadian Studies* 16, no. 2 (Autumn 2003): 137–49; *Growing Up British: Boys in Private School* (Vancouver: UBC Press, 1984).

7. Barman, *The West beyond the West,* 3rd ed., 435, table 11.

8. Information comes from the federal census, taken in Canada in years ending in 1, and from the United States in years ending in 0. Canadian data is taken from Barman, *The West beyond the West,* 3rd ed., 429, table 5, and 435, table 11; U.S. data from *Historical Statistics of the United States, Colonial Times to 1970* (Washington, D.C.: Bureau of the Census, 1975), series A 195–209, and Campbell Gibson and Kay Jung, *Historical Census Statistics on Population Totals by Race, 1790 to 1990, and by Hispanic Origin, 1970 to 1990* (Washington, D.C.: U.S. Census Bureau, 2002), tables 52 and 62. Persons given as Native or Indian are excluded. Adults are considered to be aged 15 or over.

9. Emma Douse to her mother, Hamilton, 18 February 1874, Thomas and Emma Crosby Fonds, Special Collections, University of British Columbia Library, Vancouver, BC, reproduced in Jan Hare and Jean Barman, *Good Intentions Gone Awry: Emma Crosby and the Methodist Mission on the Northwest Coast* (Vancouver: UBC Press, 2006), 13.

10. Emma Crosby's letters are now available online through University of British Columbia Library, Special Collections.

11. Russell Island, which still contains the house Maria and her second partner built there, is publicly accessible as part of the recently created Gulf Islands National Park Reserve.

12. See Jean Barman, "Encounter," *Beaver* 84, no. 1 (February/March 2004): 51–52.

13. Atlantic Canada Virtual Archives, http//:atlanticportal.hil.unb.ca/acva/.

14. For the McQueen sisters' salaries while teaching in Nova Scotia, see *Journal of Education, Nova Scotia,* 2nd ser.: October 1878–October 1888; for British Columbia salaries, see

British Columbia, Department of Education, *Annual Report*, which lists individual teacher salaries.

15. Barman, *The West beyond the West*, 3rd ed., 429, table 5, and 430, table 7.

16. Jessie McQueen to her sister Mary Belle, LN, 29 March 1888, McQueen correspondence, Nova Scotia Archives and Records Management, Halifax, NS. The entire McQueen correspondence is available online at http://Atlanticportal.hil.unb.ca.

17. Jessie McQueen to her mother Catherine, Swift Current, SK, 20 March 1888, McQueen, Lowden Family Fonds, Nova Scotia Archives and Records Management, Halifax, NS.

18. Jessie McQueen to her mother Catherine, Lowe Nicola, 28 May 1888, McQueen family correspondence, MS-0839, British Columbia Archives, Victoria, BC (hereafter cited as BCA).

19. Annie Gordon to her mother Catherine, Gateway, MT, May 1902, 11 January 1903, McQueen family correspondence, MS-0839, BCA.

20. Annie Gordon to Jessie Gordon, Gateway, MT, 21 August 1905, McQueen family correspondence, MS-0839, BCA.

21. Annie Gordon to Jane McQueen, Port Phillipps, British Columbia, 20 February 1899, McQueen family correspondence, MS-0839, BCA.

22. Annie Gordon, quoted in Cecil Scott, "No Royal Road to Learning for This B.C. Lad," *Province*, 20 April 1930.

23. Jean Maury, "From a Fur-Trading Post"; "Woman Debunks the Northwest." *Brooklyn Eagle*, n.d. [March 1929], Skinner Papers, Special Collections, New York Public Library, New York, NY (hereafter cited as NYPL).

24. "Woman Debunks the Northwest," *Brooklyn Eagle*, n.d. [March 1929], Skinner Papers, NYPL.

25. Constance Lindsay Skinner, "The Torch in the Mist," *Smith Magazine* 20, no. 5 (February 1915): 719; 20, no. 6 (March 1915): 1910.

26. "'The Bookman' Prize Competitions, May 1913," *Bookman* (London) 44 (May 1913): 72; "Song of Cradle-Making," 44, Supplement (August 1913): 1, also 4.

27. Constance Lindsay Skinner, "Songs of the Coast-Dwellers," *Poetry: A Magazine of Verse* 5, no. 1 (October 1914): 1–19.

28. George W. Cronyn, *The Path on the Rainbow: An Anthology of Songs and Chants from the Indians of North America* (New York: Boni and Liveright, 1918). Among the reprinted editions are George W. Cronyn, ed., *The Path on the Rainbow: An Anthology of Songs and Chants from the Indians of North America* (New York: Boni and Liveright, 1918; 1934; Van Nuys, CA: Newcastle Publishing Co., 1997); *American Indian Poetry: The Standard Anthology of Songs and Chants* (New York: Liveright, 1934); *American Indian Poetry: An Anthology of Songs and Chants* (New York: Ballantine, 1962, 1970, 1972; New York: Fawcett Columbine, 1991).

29. Robert J. Skinner to Constance Lindsay Skinner, Vancouver, 23 April, 7 August 1902, 26 July 1903; Constance Lindsay Skinner, typescript written for Annie Laurie Williams, n.d. [1937] (emphasis in original), both in NYPL.

6

"THAT UNDERSTANDING WITH NATURE"

Region, Race, and Nation in Women's Stories from the

Modern Canadian and American Grasslands West

MOLLY P. ROZUM

"MY FIRST MEMORY of this quiet home in the Wild West is one of terror," wrote Annora Brown remembering life in southern Alberta, Canada. She and her two sisters had been "turned out for an airing" on their family's homestead circa 1900. All three girls ambled along until, suddenly, one of the sisters "became firmly embedded in mud." Annora recalled the panic in her two-year-old body: "There stood Helen, scream-ing with helplessness, rooted in gumbo. There I stood, rooted to the path, in terror of I knew not what."[1] Sticky gumbo terrified Brown. The pairing of "quiet" and "Wild West" in this memory is clearly meant to be ironic. Readers might have expected marauding cowboys or an encoun-ter with Native Americans to follow her invocation of "terror" in the "Wild West," not gumbo mud. Readers who were familiar with prairie landscapes, however, would have recognized a sticky old foe. Throughout her autobiography, based on a lifetime of firsthand experience and study, Annora Brown asserted her place in the grasslands West by claiming expert knowledge about the region's natural environments.

Women who came of age in the Canadian and U.S. northern grasslands in the first half of the twentieth century left numerous writings that begin to suggest the contours of a post-conquest, modern western regionalism and the significant roles women played in the region's creation.[2] To better understand how women placed themselves in the modern West in relation to the settlement generation, masculine narrative traditions, and American and Canadian national western myths, this essay explores the autobiographical writings of three women, Annora Brown from Alberta (1899–1987), Era Bell Thompson of North Dakota (1905–1986), and Thorstina Jackson Walters, who grew up in a transnational, Manitoba–North Dakota community (1887–1956).[3] These three women are relative contemporaries, each a representative of second-generation grasslands residents (they considered their parents "the pioneers"), but located in diverse communities running from east to west across the prairies and plains, and from north to south over the 49th parallel. Though they published their books at different life cycle moments, the three women shared the same general historic times (the late 1800s to the mid-1940s), their self-identification as westerners, and an attachment to the ecology and history of the continental northern grasslands. Historian Hal Barron has described this period as the "second great transformation in the northern countryside." Regional landscapes were being transformed from wild grasslands to commercial crop acreages, but development had not yet reached the "Great Disjuncture" of the post–World War II years when agriculture consolidated intensely and became fully mechanized.[4]

Annora Brown, who is discussed first, became a regionally known painter of prairie subjects, primarily grasslands flora and Blackfoot Native American scenes. She wrote as she entered her senior years, when memory often becomes both hazy and acute. Working with her memory was "like living with a poltergeist," she said, with "fragmentary memories buzz[ing] about angrily."[5] This essay draws on her ideas about the grass-lands West as she set them out in *Sketches from Life* (1981), her well-documented autobiography, and *Old Man's Garden* (1954), a prairie plant lore collection based on historic observations of the grasslands and legends she collected from the Blackfoot Nation.[6] Brown is discussed first because her narratives provide the clearest evidence of a distinct modern women's way of laying claim to western land. Her writings also best suggest themes important to comparative study of Canadian and American mythic Wests. Era Bell Thompson's autobiography moves the analysis from Canada to the U.S. side of the 49th parallel. She moved from an Iowa city to rural North Dakota when she was a child and published *American Daughter* (1946) in midlife after winning a fellowship for regional writers. Living in Chicago, she wrote explicitly to explain the presence of a Dakota-identified African-American to a nation not too familiar with either a realistic North Dakota or its multicultural population. Thompson wrote the autobiography just before she started a long career as editor for *Ebony* magazine.[7] The final case study focuses on Thorstina Jackson Walters, who lived in Icelandic communities on both sides of the 49th parallel in Manitoba and North Dakota. As a borderland resident she was uniquely exposed to the culture and history of both the Canadian and American Wests. Walters also received a regional fellowship in the 1940s to write *Modern Sagas* (1953), a unique combination of autobiography and Icelandic community history. She collected material for her study for most of her life, first finishing her father's long-time project of recording pioneer family histories of Icelandic immigration to Canada and the United States, then moving beyond him to complete a sociological interpretation of the same community with added analysis of her generation. Until multiple sclerosis began degrading her nervous system, Walters promoted Icelandic-North American history and foreign relations on a lecture circuit that saw her travel among Canada, the U.S., and Iceland.[8]

This sample of three women's autobiographies begins to answer several important questions. Classic Canadian narratives center on a peaceful, orderly West, while the more popularly well-known American West holds violence and risk at its core. Did such national mythologies make a difference in the self-presentation of these three women, though they lived in an ecologically unified region? Canada and the United States share mythic attachments to the West as a "manly" space, even though the conceptions of manhood are not the same. The representative Canadian western man is identified with duty, courtesy, and calm, and can seem almost feminine when compared to the wild, aggressive, ruggedly independent, and too-frequently brutal American western man.[9] Given the persistence of male-inspired icons (and the values, norms, and ideals they stand for), such as the farmer, rancher, cowboy, and Mounted Policeman, how did modern women writers locate themselves in the West? Finally, what, if anything, competes with region, nation, and gender in the ways each woman represented her western life and times?

Examined individually in the sections that follow, the writings of Brown, Thompson, and Walters suggest that their generation claimed the West as a birthright and possessed its land by developing physical and emotional affinities with prairies and plains landscapes. They relied more on regional and racial identities than on national affiliations to represent the lives they lived in their unique corners of the grasslands. If men laid claim to the land with legal titles to farms and ranches, women claimed land by acquiring regional environmental knowledge. Brown referred to this process as becoming "one with Nature."[10] Environmental historian Richard White has called it "knowing place."[11] Many women gained legal title to homesteads, and women may have sometimes thought about land in the same ways men did, hoping, for example, that commercial agriculture would be profitable.[12] Men, too, surely acquired a sense of place. What is distinctive about these women's narratives is the *emphasis* placed on appreciation of a general grasslands aesthetic sense rather than on a profound manly effort to tame the grasslands with commercial agriculture. If Brown, Thompson, and Walters were typical regional representatives, then their narratives show how central an ecological consciousness was to twentieth-century western women's identities. Only racial status concerned them as much.

* * *

AS THE DAUGHTER of a Canadian Mountie, Annora Brown could have employed stock characters and emphasized familiar mythic themes in her autobiography. But she did so only selectively. Instead, sticky gumbo symbolized her place in the West more than her father's service with the North West Mounted Police, the group credited in Canadian history for establishing law and order in the West. She found the iconic Mountie appealing when she was a child. Brown recalled how she used to study old photographs of her father in "scarlet tunics and yellow leg-stripes." Even then, however, it was "in my imagination" only, she wrote, that she could see her father "still in uniform." He had not worn a Mountie uniform since before she was born. She remembered, also, how during childhood she felt that the Mounted Police barracks "belonged to me." Brown, however, never knew her father as a Mountie. In her lifetime her father found duty only in the mundane actions of a town bureaucrat. As an adult, she chose to provide readers with a realistic portrait of him. Brown stressed her father's economic insecurity. An economic depression drove her father out of England to the Canadian West. Then, although he wished to farm in the West, he joined the Mounted Police because he lacked the money to develop a government homestead. He could not even ride a horse before he joined the Mounted Police.[13] Her father's lack of skill and desperate motives for joining the police force do not come across as heroic. Brown could have presented a myth-sustaining story of her father's involvement in establishing law and order in the Canadian West. By locating her awe of the Mountie in her own childhood, however, and then juxtaposing that admiration with a more realistic history of her father, Brown suggested the oversimplification at the core of mythic icons. Her father's story undercuts the standard attributes of the beloved Canadian Mountie. Similarly, when she claimed to be related on her mother's side to the "Colonel William Frederick (Buffalo Bill) Cody of Wild West Fame," Brown invoked a quintessential, popular U.S. western man.[14] Again, however, Brown chose not to engage in mythmaking. The brave, forceful

Buffalo Bill signaled her West no more than a methodical, manly Mountie.

Just as she refrained from turning her bureaucrat father into a mythical Mountie, Brown refrained from telling a traditional western narrative of rural life. Indeed, she depicted her family *leaving* the land for the nearby town of Fort Macleod in her very first chapter. Her clearest memory of leaving centered on patting goodbye the "soft nose of the gentle farm horse" named Queenie.[15] Brown covered in very few lines the rural conquest that typically consumes entire memoirs.[16] She continued to demote the traditional rural homesteading story when she used municipal growth to symbolize conquest. She recalled gazing at streets and avenues laid out but torn apart for the installation of water and sewer pipes:

> Gangs of men laid out straight lines of sticks and cords along the streets and then began to dig deep trenches so the pipes would be safe from winter frosts. With what interest I watched these men disappear! First the feet, then knees and hips, then shoulders, and finally heads; all the while a spray of gravel and earth flew from their shovels to the side of the pit [until,] finally, it seemed to come magically from the earth itself. The head of a shovel, a spray of gravel, emptiness; the head of a shovel, a spray of gravel, emptiness.
>
> ...The prairie sun beat down on a level plain sprinkled with houses. All down the street was a row of trenches ten or twelve feet long, separated by two-foot-long bridges of earth, each trench accompanied by a pile of gravel.[17]

>FIGURE 6.1: *Annora Brown (center) at play on the prairie, Fort Macleod, Alberta. The photograph is taken from one of her scrapbooks, under which is penned, "Rubble from ditch in background."* [Courtesy of the University of Alberta Archives, (83–116–16–2)]

>FIGURE 6.2: *Annora Brown and her father, Edmund Forster Brown, outside their Fort Macleod home in the middle of well-developed gardens and mature trees, "about 1950." In one of her scrapbooks, Brown compares this photograph with another taken at the same location "about 1911," when the only landscape feature was worn-to-the-dirt prairie.* [Courtesy of the University of Alberta Archives, (83–116–17–2)]

Amy   Annora   Kathleen

Rubble from ditch in
background

By connecting the prairie sun with pipes and a level plain with houses, Brown is deliberately pairing nature and development. The beauty she saw was a manmade counterpoint to the "great prairie distances, high skies, foothills, [and] blue mountains" she also admired. Along with water and sewer pipes, Brown noted the introductions of telephones, electricity, plumbing, gas heat, and automobiles. Her West included modern amenities that ran counter to the stereotypical image of the West as an isolated wilderness.[18] The vignette also related the development of Brown's identity as an artist. The memory celebrates her early artistic sight. Indeed, one of the main themes of Brown's autobiography is the process by which she established herself as a professional artist in a male-dominated art world, at a time and in a place where the regional population seemed to her little interested in art generally, prairie landscapes even less.

The stereotypical "wild" and "orderly" opposition between American and Canadian Wests does make one appearance in Brown's autobiography. Brown remembered how she "avidly" listened to stories from her father's "colourful past" and treasured his memories as "the very stuff from which the country had been built." Once she overheard a conversation between her father and another old-timer about when the latter was a young man. The old-timer explained that he left Indiana for the West after his fiancé "was killed." "I was pretty wild," he said. "I come west and I was a pretty wild one.... I was all strung up and nervous and lost my temper easy. 'Dynamite' they called me and I was pretty handy with my gun—too handy with it—but that wasn't me, you know." Later, the man headed north to Canada, where he bought land, married, and helped raise two children. The shift in the man's location from the American West to the Canadian West corresponded to a change, in Brown's words, from "wild one" to "good citizen," the stereotypical opposition between men in the American and Canadian Wests.[19] The anecdote also reinforced belief in a special male healing power intrinsic to North America's

<FIGURE 6.3: *In addition to her prairie flora watercolors, Annora Brown became well known regionally for paintings of Native Americans in the Blackfoot Confederacy, such as this camp scene. She lived near the Piegan Reserve, and her scrapbooks include many photographs of local First Nations peoples and photos of her paintings depicting them.*
[*Courtesy of the University of Alberta Archives, (83–116–17–12)*]

western spaces. A "virgin" territory allowed a broken man to conquer his feelings for a woman as he rebuilt his masculinity. A West where a damaged man might renew himself by acting wild in the wilderness (in the United States) or one where he could start over and settle comfortably as a responsible family man despite injury (in Canada) are two variations of one escapist theme.[20] With this story Brown seems to be supporting national western stereotypes, but it is unclear whether Brown in her recalling or the old-timer in the telling invoked the national difference.

Brown used a specific environmental definition of *wild* that did not mean lawless or uncivilized (in accordance with U.S. tradition). Nor did it mean an uncharted or isolated wilderness (in accordance with Canadian tradition). For Brown *wild* meant the natural prairie, plains, and riverbank environments—the gumbo—of her youth. Most of the autobiography explains how Brown became "one" with the prairie as a girl; how she explored that prairie intellectually and physically as a young adult; and how she retreated to these grasslands with paint and memory for most of her adult life. After witnessing the distress of the 1930s, she described how the "white man hoed out" native grasslands plants "with merciless determination" and provincial agricultural departments classified wild roses as weeds. The familiarity with Blackfoot traditional culture that she gained from her Blackfoot friends helped her to see the conflict in the reclassification of sweet grass from "sacred" plant to "noxious weed."[21] As Brown wrote her autobiography in the 1970s, when many people were awakening to a new environmental awareness, she explained how "much of the public was not yet ready for it" in the 1950s, when she first published her plant lore book.[22]

What Brown termed the "Wild East" tamed her Wild West.[23] To her the "Wild East" consisted of uncontrollable agricultural industrialization represented by increasing crop acreages, unsustainable grazing, and the bulldozers, tractors, and automobiles that rolled over native plant life. Brown wanted to freeze the environmental configuration of the prairie of her youth and halt development *after* conquest admitted her family to the region. She critiqued the industrial culture that destroyed grasslands, but she did not see herself as part of these forces. Brown saw herself as organically prairie, in the same tradition by which Native peoples claimed the place as homeland. She and her Blackfoot friends aligned in attitude against the powers of commercialization that threatened the prairie they all loved. This alliance meant that Brown could deny the differences in status and power that accrued to her from past territorial conquest, which had been rationalized in large part by ideas of racial superiority.[24] Individual claims to the land made by generations of people such as Brown, who were of imperial national heritage but born and raised on the grasslands, served to entrench national claims of ownership by conquest and/or treaty. Even if she considered herself a friend of the Blackfoot, Brown appropriated Native peoples' lands and furthered the conquest of her parents' generation by intellectual and artistic, not treaty and territorial, methods.

When Brown mentioned Old West or mythic themes, she often did so when referring to her parents' generation. Sporadically, Brown noted how her mother and father often shared "recollections" of what Brown called "the old, old West," such as "long lines of oxen-drawn Red River carts" and "precarious crossing of the Lethbridge coulees" in the early years.[25] Accepting her pioneering parents' role in the conquest of the West allowed her to identify with classic western themes *through* them (and the pioneer generation generally), which freed her to write about different themes in her own life. Brown also indirectly challenged the crucial connection between classic western men and their West, agricultural mastery of the land, when she made intimate knowledge of prairie ecology key to a distinctive women's way of claiming regional land.

* * *

"TO MANY, I was the First Black Child in a land that is still burying it's [sic] First White Children," explained Era Bell Thompson of her experiences growing up on the prairies and plains of North Dakota.[26] She titled the first chapter of her autobiography "Go West, Black Man"[27] and placed the decision of her family's move to the West squarely with her father. In this and many ways, Thompson's is a typical prairie story.

American
Daughter
THOMPSON
THE UNIVERSITY
OF CHICAGO
PRESS
American
Daughte
ERA BELL THOMPSO

The family followed her father's brother, who had migrated before and steadily praised Dakota land and life. In anticipation of the move, her mother had "tears in her eyes" and worried about howling coyotes and social isolation. However, Thompson's autobiography also continues the post-Civil War journey of African-Americans to find a secure place in America. Her grandparents left Virginia to find opportunity in the "great Northwest," and Thompson's father wandered all over the country working as a cook, restaurant owner, and janitor before settling in Iowa, where Era Bell was born. Expecting the U.S. West to be marked male more than white, Thompson's father embraced the profession of farming as one of the few respectable occupations open to black men. Thompson recalled her father trying to convince her mother that they should, as he said, "take the boys to Dakota." Thompson explained that the move was the last hope of her father "to find a new home in the wide open spaces, where there was freedom and equal opportunity for a man with three sons. Three sons and a daughter," she added, including herself, though her father seemed little concerned about her when he made the decision to "go west."[28]

Thompson carried with her to North Dakota many romantic and racist images of the U.S. West. One theme of her autobiography is the gradual throwing-off of western stereotypes. To begin with, the move evoked fantasies of "going to fight the Indians, and ride the range in search of buffalo." But snow was not an appropriate setting for "dreams of Indians." An ill-fated search for Indians continually interrupts her story. Once she thought she saw a settlement of Indians, but the mass of tents turned out to be pitched for a religious revival. She dreamed frequently of escaping to "live with the Indians." Instead she found Indians confined to reservations and day schools. The "little girls in pale blue dresses" at the Indian school did not measure up to her preconceptions. Horse rides

<FIGURE 6.4: *A mock-up of the dust jacket for the 1946 University of Chicago Press publication of Era Bell Thompson's autobiography,* American Daughter. *Thompson received a fellowship from the Newberry Library's "Midwestern Studies" initiative, funded in turn by a grant-in-aid from The Rockefeller Foundation in New York City.*

[*Courtesy of the Newberry Library Archives, Office of the President, Stanley Pargellis Papers (03/05/03, Box 3, Folder 94), and also courtesy of the University of Chicago Press, Illinois*]

caused her to imagine herself amidst "cowboys in a Western thriller." Since no Indians ever chased her, she also remembered the difficulty she had sustaining this western fantasy. When she attended the Mandan rodeo, she "loved" the "Indian war dances" most. It was a "picturesque thing, weird and exotic," with "bloodcurdling yells" and "chiefs and warriors wearing long headdresses and carrying hatchets in their fringed buffalo pants." All of her childhood searching, however, led to no buffaloes, "no wigwams, no squaws, no warriors," and no "red" faces.[29] Even a college-aged Thompson imagined "Indian ceremonial fires" in the burning surface-coal mines of the prairie night and "could almost see the red men dancing about the blaze, copper bodies bending, hatchets shining in the eerie light." Though she showed empathy in wanting to "live with the Indians," Thompson also resisted a direct association. She recalled one celebration when she joined a circle dance with "the squaws," but noted also how she quit when "some brash individual asked what tribe I belonged to."[30]

As her sensitivity to racial classification indicates, skin color distinguished her family in the Dakota West. U.S. law did not bar the Thompson family from owning western land, but Era Bell and her brothers suffered many incidents of racial prejudice and much *de facto* segregation. Children stared and voiced racial slurs. One even screamed at the sight of a young Era Bell. A theater manager refused her a main floor seat. Her school textbooks argued blacks were innately inferior.[31] But Thompson also took some comfort in the "the world," as she phrased it, that truly lived in North Dakota. She lived with only handfuls of African-American and Jewish people, but found diversity in the state's large European immigrant and Native American populations. Thompson was not the only girl who *looked* different. Indians "wore native clothes" and Icelandic, German-Russian, and Norwegian immigrants donned Old World costumes. Many people sounded different as they "spoke the mother tongue," and families celebrated a host of different traditions according to various "ways of the fatherland." She recalled how she felt she could "share" their "foreign peasantry." Thompson identified with what she called the "second generation," a cohort of young people making their way in

America between two worlds, the Old and New, only her two worlds were white and black.[32]

Although Thompson appreciated the diversity she found in North Dakota, she still felt compelled to try living in a predominately African-American community. One by one she saw her brothers leave the farm to join black communities in St Paul, Minnesota, and elsewhere. She soon followed them to St Paul, but where her brothers found fellowship, she felt "hemmed in, apart from the rest of the world." She found herself surrounded by Minnesota's verdant growth, but longing to see "one ragged tumbleweed" and "one alkaline slough."[33] She viewed a life in North Dakota with more ambivalence than did her brothers. Thompson explained, "Three times I came down from the prairies to live with 'my people' and twice I returned to my plains."[34]

Thompson's attachment to what she called "my plains" competed with a desire to live in an African-American community. Looking back from the middle of the twentieth century, Thompson realized that the sensory complexity of what she called "prairie silence" became a force pulling her home to the grasslands. She described "still days, silent, hot, motionless days when not a blade of grass stirred, not a stalk of grain moved. You didn't talk much then, you hated to break the prairie silence, the magic of its stillness, for you had that understanding with Nature, that treaty with God." Silence magnified the details of the land: "tumbling tumbleweeds," wild roses, purple crocuses, and even snow appeared quietly striking. But silence also had qualities one could feel and see—the "warm silence of twilight," for example. And silence could be seen and heard in the hills of grain fields "whispering gold, undulating ever so softly in the bated breeze." She explained to readers that although "the silence wore hard on those who did not belong," it was essential for those suited to the place. When she visited two friends, single sisters, on their homestead, she recalled that the three of them automatically "lapsed into prairie silence."[35]

Thompson laid claim to land in the West as she explained the growth of an affinity with "prairie silence" that no other member of the family *but* her father, ironically, seemed to share. "Something in the vast stillness," she understood, "spoke to Pop's soul."[36] He had believed he and his sons would share the West, but in the end it was he and his daughter who developed the same attachment. After his sons left, her father moved into town. His vision did not include a land-inheriting daughter. Thompson enjoyed the countryside and felt at home in it, but there is no evidence she pursued or even desired a homestead of her own. Her sense of the land signaled a feeling of place in a way that legally owned land sometimes did not. She developed a visceral attachment to the natural environment, including the "nature"[37] of commercial grain fields. Her West privileged the senses, not gender or race.

Thompson's environmental West also included a popular West. Even as she began to substitute real Native Americans for those of myth and to comprehend the complexity of the grasslands' natural habitat, Thompson began to embrace popular western imagery anew. Only now she did so from an insider's perspective, one that let her use such imagery to entertain her readers. This "popular" West was already thriving on the grasslands when Thompson and her family arrived. She recalled how on winter evenings her uncle told "hard-to-believe" pioneer tales, and her cousin played on the harmonica sad, slow "cowboy laments" about the "lone prairies." Stories and lyrics about stock western characters—the pioneer and the cowboy—kept mythic imagery alive and appreciated on a tale-telling level. As tourism began to develop in the early twentieth-century West, western peoples used mythic Wests to their advantage.[38] Thompson recalled how American Indians near Mandan left their reservations "to greet the tourist trains." In her late teenage years, Thompson, already a budding writer, began to fictionalize the "commonplace events" of her extended family in the West for the prominent African-American *Chicago Defender* newspaper. The popularity of her father's manly West lived on in the "colored pen pals beyond the hills" who wrote to her literary persona "Dakota Dick," a man she identified as "a bad, bad cowboy from the wild and wooly West." Looking back on this creative endeavor, she observed "The Mandan Chamber of Commerce could not have done better," presumably to distinguish and sell the small western city.[39] The "commonplace" situations she fictionalized in a mythic West style as a teenager involved some of the same people and places she wrote about at midlife in her autobiography. In this way, both myth ("Dakota Dick") and anti-myth (her autobiography) were real in the twentieth century, because Thompson had embraced both the popular West she hawked to eager readers *and* the realistic day-to-day West in which she once lived. She hoped mid-twentieth-century readers would find the latter an appealing story too. By the early twentieth century, western residents like Thompson could embrace popular western elements without feeling that such imagery defined genuine life in the West.

As much as Thompson embraced the stock characters of the U.S. mythic West, she did not seem aware of any myths associated with Canada's West. Other than a train trip through Canada, her only mention of the Canadian West involved an incident she had with 1920s U.S. Prohibition-era, law-breaking Canadian "rum runners." The episode occurred at a time when she had returned to her father's home to be with him when he died (of natural causes) and while she was living in his used furniture store. The "booze truck began making regular runs from Canada," she explained, and continued on to describe a special clientele that loitered around her father's store, waiting for deliveries. She slept with a "revolver under my pillow." Expecting a drunken attack one night, she stood at the screen door with the gun in hand. When her cat scared her, she pulled the trigger, fainted, dropped the gun, and woke up later wondering what had happened. Although the incident provides comic relief in the middle of one of her most serious chapters, the humor emerged as she thought back on that girl with a gun, not from what she actually experienced at that time in her life.

Thompson could have engaged in mythmaking or debunking, but she chose not to take or did not recognize the opportunity. Certainly, Thompson's boundary "runners" do not conform to the law-abiding men of Canadian myth (though their clients seem to fit stereotypical "wild" American men).[40] Nevertheless, the realistic rendition of this illegal exchange has the effect of undermining classic icons key to a popular U.S. West. A cat, a truck, and an armed girl injected a subtle realism that ran counter to popular expectations for mythic cowboys with guns and horses. Similarly, inebriated men and illegal transactions might be set in an Old West saloon, but not outside a furniture store. Thompson's insistence that the West provide the frame for her life story, together with her realistic style, however, worked against widespread mythic preconceptions that she argued were *part* of the reason she desired to publish her autobiography.

Thompson explained to the regional fellowship committee that she wanted to write about both the "remote and isolated" North Dakota (a "little known state...God Forgot") and the "humorous incidents" of her "Negro family" in the West.[41] Many people she encountered, black *and* white, felt that *anyone* who came from Dakota, regardless of race, must have lived in the "strange white world." It was odd to meet a black self-identified Dakotan, but the state's reputation as a "frozen wilds" of ice and snow made all of its residents exotic.[42] Thompson wanted these people still caught up by a mythic West to know a realistic Dakota environment and to know also that a black woman claimed this western region as her own.

As she told her life story, Thompson critiqued American race relations as well as the U.S. West. Indeed, publishers seemed more interested in what her life revealed about race relations than they were in what she said about the West. (Never mind that regional life ostensibly was the primary focus of the fellowship program that supported her writing.) One publisher remarked that "between the lines of her narrative, one can see her solution [to America's race problem], although she never presses it or uses sociological language."[43] But Thompson gave race and region nearly equal importance. She described the grasslands as a "country that is new and free and strangely beautiful."[44] These words flow out of classic manly western themes of starting over, taming wilderness, and finding freedom. When it was Thompson, and not her brothers, however, who laid claim to the land by embracing its environmental aesthetic, she indirectly challenged the manly West that originally pulled her father and his family to Dakota. Even the simple inclusion of a moderately successful "middle class" black family in the West countered dominant perceptions of the West's whiteness. The uncle and other black families who made appearances in her western story and the persistent attention she paid to the multicultural population of Dakota argued that diversity was central to the *real* West and, by extension, to America. Her mother and father both died and were buried on the prairie, providing her a lasting tie to a grasslands West. Nevertheless, the lack of opportunity her brothers found in the West and the racism Thompson experienced in "free" Dakota showed that troubled race relations had a history in all of America's regions, not only the South. Racist people and ideas lived even in the West, the archetypal place of American opportunity. Thompson herself struggled with the country's deeply condoned racism against Native peoples as they appeared in the mythic U.S. West she once embraced (until she became an insider and had real relationships with Natives). Thompson eventually left the prairie and settled in Chicago, the city she described as "the crossroads of America," where she found black communities as well as a multicultural diversity similar to that of North Dakota.[45] Although she left the place physically, the important roles the West and its environment played in her narrative suggest that Thompson's departure from the grasslands West was never complete.

* * *

THORSTINA JACKSON WALTERS situated her narrative of Icelandic immigration in a western frame but, like Thompson, her story of Icelanders in North America focused as much on racial identity as it did on laying claim to western land. Walters made clear her western roots in the title of her introductory chapter, "I Grew Up with the Pioneers." Similarly, using classic manly West phrasing, she cited an 1860s Icelandic proponent of immigration who, she said, urged, "Go to America, young men."[46] For Walters, the Wests of Canada and the United States became one denationalized *Ameríku,* a word used to denote all of the North American West. When Icelanders "felt the urge to take up the trail to the West," they started by crossing an ocean. Once in *Ameríku,* Icelanders lived an international cultural life, crossing and re-crossing the 49th parallel. In the 1880s a religious dispute, for example, sent Icelanders from Winnipeg, Manitoba, to North Dakota, while during the early twentieth century Icelanders from North Dakota moved back to Canada to claim newly opened prairie. Walters' father immigrated to Winnipeg, then to North Dakota (where Thorstina was born), and retired in Winnipeg. Walters grew up in North Dakota but attended college in Winnipeg. Well into the twentieth century, she claimed, this North American immigrant population operated as "loosely federated Icelandic colonies in the U.S. and Canada."[47]

Walters argued that Icelanders shared with their regional neighbors a common "desire to conquer a wilderness," but when she explained what motivated Icelanders in the North American West, she turned to what she held to be the core Icelandic ideals of "liberty, culture, advancement."[48] She claimed agriculture as "the staff of life" and asserted that Icelandic "heritage" was one of a "rural civilization," using language that suggests a strong connection to the theme of manly land transformation. But she mentioned her father's work as farmer in North Dakota only once. Instead, she praised her father's library and language skills, and her mother's milkhouse and midwifery expertise. Walters' father found his most important place in the family living room, reading aloud from traditional Icelandic sagas, while her mother prepared traditional foods and sang ballads. The Icelanders of her generation had a western "Adventure in Education," which frequently took them, the sons *and* daughters of the pioneers, off the land into the professions as scholars, doctors, writers, musicians, and lawyers. Even the farmers of her generation had the "desire for education in agriculture" and became "Master Farmers" who contributed to the "scientific development of American agriculture."[49] Walters created a uniquely Icelandic western persona based on cultivation of the intellect first, and the land second. Both women and men could become her typical, idealized westerner: educated, good-natured, and poetic.[50]

Walters passed over opportunities to distinguish between American and Canadian Wests, which suggested that she and the community she

> FIGURE 6.5: *A young Thorstina Jackson Walters with her father, Thorleifur Jóakimsson.*
[*Courtesy of the Institute for Regional Studies, North Dakota State University, Fargo (2010.2.1)*]

presented did not absorb nation-specific western imagery and ideas (at least on a level that was important enough for her to include). She noted, for example, that "disregard for the law of the land was all too prevalent" in the United States, as represented by the "berserk shooting and robbing" as committed by iconic western outlaws Frank and Jessie James. She showed no awareness, however, that regard for the law was any different in the Canadian West (though this may have been implied in her exclusion of Canada in this observation). "Custer's last stand against their [Indians'] fury was still on everybody's lips," and the "warlike mood" of the "Indians" in Canada that led to the 1885 Riel Rebellion, according to Walters, seemed to cause equal anxiety in early Icelandic settlers. Walters recalled visiting Métis communities in her North Dakota neighborhood and referred to them as "French-Canadian half breeds." That there were Canadian-identified Natives on the U.S. side of the international boundary did not seem unusual to her. In this Manitoba–North Dakota borderlands area, both Métis and *Ameríku*-Icelanders had "people...scattered on both sides of the boundary line."[51] Walters did write of the historic competition by Canada and the United States for Icelanders who would "populate and build up the vast areas of the central part of the American continent." She related one occurrence when an immigrant agent "in the service of the Dominion Government" and a representative from the U.S. Icelandic community both met a group of "165 Icelanders who had just landed on the Canadian shores at Quebec." The group split, with the majority staying on in Canada, and 50 crossing the boundary to the United States.[52] Here Walters emphasized the positive qualities of Icelandic immigrants, not those ideals voiced by the agents of the two nations vying for settlers.

Loving reminiscences of their family home, made from "hand-hewn oak logs," and a chapter titled "The Winding Road from the Log Cabin," about the rise to prominence of Icelandic youth, however, suggest that Walters knew classic U.S. symbolism well.[53] The log cabin had been linked to U.S. westward expansion as far back as the eighteenth century, when immigrant settlers flowing through the Delaware valley (originally New Sweden) picked up the Finnish design and building method as they made their way to the backcountry West.[54] Walters talked about "us who lived on the fringe of the frontier" and viewed Theodore Roosevelt's well-known cowboy tradition in North Dakota's western badlands as a version of her own heritage. She "never tired of hearing my mother tell about her journey from Iceland to the Dakota plains," a story reinforced by her father's collection of "pioneering" tales.[55] With these reference points, Walters attached the Icelandic immigrant experience in the West to the traditional American ideal of opportunity for all.

Unlike the serious tone of her discussion of pioneer success, which seemed to accept western myth uncritically, Walters told other stories in a way that undermined mythic West meanings. These tales focused on incidents passed down in the Icelandic community and were collected from the experiences of her contemporaries. For example, she turned her good friend's experience herding cattle one summer when he was a boy into what she called a typical "Wild West thriller." Walters emphasized how this young "cowboy" fought "relentless" mosquitoes by wearing a hat of blue netting for protection. This was not a typical mythic story that revolved around a rugged cowboy donning a Stetson hat and fighting "Indians." She did something similar to a story passed on in the Icelandic community about a North Dakota 1880s "Wild-West frontier town." While Walters included all of the classic elements of a mythic western, mentioning a "new saloon," "beer bottles," and people in the streets "shooting revolvers into the air," this "wild" town turns out to be holding only a "noisy" celebration for the grand opening of the new tavern. It was only friendly revelers with no targets who shot their guns. Moreover, the central character of this story, a preacher, sought a "peaceful haven" on the edge of town "near the tent of the Indian," the opposite of what might happen in a cross-cultural encounter in the U.S. mythic West.[56] With this type of vignette Walters had fun with western myth and with her readers, too. By linking classic western language with realistic stories of day-to-day living in the West, Walters indirectly challenged myth.

The majority of Walters' narrative, however, focused on the serious value of Icelandic democratic and racial cultures to North American communities. She argued that both the United States and Canada came to value Icelandic settlers because they already "had a democratic appreciation of other people's achievements." Walters asked readers to recall that it was the Norse Vikings in 930 who established in Iceland "the first democratic body of its kind North of the Alps." Icelanders indeed, according to ancient sagas, belonged in both Canada and the United States, because "Leif Ericsson and other Vinland heroes" had originally discovered the New World.[57] Traditional Icelandic democratic experience related to what Walters implied was the very important racial fitness of Icelanders for the continent. She argued that Icelanders aimed only to give "the best in the Icelandic racial inheritance to the adopted country," and as late as the 1950s she wrote that "individualism is still their most pronounced racial trait." Walters never thought of Icelanders as ethnic, she always identified them as a race. It is probable that part of Walters' emphasis on racial characteristics came from living the prime of her life during a time when scientific racism rose in acceptance.[58] A heritage of "Viking blood and its pristine purity," she implied, meant Icelandic stock could replenish blood clouded by the supposedly less-advanced races.

The promotion of the purity of the Icelandic race also may have grown out of fears that came with original Icelandic North American settlers. Walters repeated stories passed down from the 1870s that suggested how Icelanders might be targeted for violence, "eaten alive by red-skinned savages" in the "far West," or "worse yet, be driven to the deep South of the United States and thrown into slavery like Negroes." The first Icelanders feared they could become a race classed forever apart from

>FIGURE 6.6: *Thorstina Jackson Walters delivered lectures to promote better relations among the people of Iceland, Canada and the United States. The back side of this pamphlet includes endorsements for Walters' talks from, among others, Arctic explorer Vilhjalmur Stefansson, Isaiah Bowman, director of the American Geographical Society, Louis C. Tiffany of New York City, and a representative of Duluth State Teachers College. Listeners described her lectures as "interesting," "instructive," and "entertaining." One audience member thought her presentation "unite[d] the best tradition of the Icelandic family sagas with the finest spirit of American democracy." Stefansson, a personal friend, grew up in the same Icelandic Manitoba–North Dakota community as did Walters (he is the young "cowboy" who fought "relentless" mosquitoes in what Walters dubbed a typical "Wild West thriller").*
[*Courtesy of the Institute for Regional Studies, North Dakota State University, Fargo (Mss 630, Box 3, Folder 3)*]

THORSTINA JACKSON WALTERS

Author and Translator

Lecturer and Traveller

TWICE DECORATED BY THE
KING OF DENMARK AND ICELAND
FOR HER WRITINGS AND LECTURES ON

ICELAND

THE "HERMIT OF THE NORTH ATLANTIC"

Will the mellow culture of the past blend with the practical spirit of the modern age, proving there is poetry and idealism in action, and thus guard the charm of "Sagaland" and prevent it from being lost in materialism, now that "Young Iceland" has embraced the era of "modernism" with all the enthusiasm of youth.

the mainstream, rather than how Walters wanted to present Icelanders, that is, as a race simultaneously capable of assimilation and of making cultural contributions that would strengthen the continent's peoples. This older fear echoed during World War I, and Walters recalled how her generation "proceeded very cautiously" in the promotion of heritage organizations, such as the Icelandic National League. For her own part, Walters thanked her mother for early instruction on "racial equality" (she had been "frightened" by Métis children she encountered when her mother was delivering a baby, and questioned whether God had made "those black children").[59] The perceived potential for established North American societies to exclude Icelanders based on race shaped Walters' writing, rather than a desire to prohibit other races from taking their equal place.

Even though Walters' main agenda was to praise Icelanders as desirable settlers, she too, like Brown and Thompson, used the idea of becoming "one" with land to define a western identity. Her grasslands identity existed alongside pride in her Icelandic heritage. She viewed the "bright summer nights and the flaming Northern Lights of the winter season" in Iceland as parallel to "the opalescent colors of daybreak" and "the fiery brilliance of the sunset" in North Dakota. Similarly, she explained how her husband, the painter Émile Walters, observed that North Dakota's badlands and Iceland's sub-artic terrain created similar artistic "problems"; the two areas attracted him because of their similar "stark," lonely qualities. But Thorstina was also quick to highlight the willingness of her people to exchange Icelandic poppies for prairie roses and thrush for robins. She recalled fondly local rivers, "mighty oaks," serviceberry bushes, "banks upon banks of clouds," "the level plain," rolling hills, and the colors, deep blue and purple, of distance. Her personal claim to the land rested in these environmental elements. The initial "confusion" by the first Icelandic settlers over an environment that seemed "prodigal," she explained, gave way as they gradually "learned to recognize" the "possibilities and limitations" of the grasslands. Walters' definition of the region's "natural" environment included the "first nature" of grasslands habitat and the "second nature" of commercial crops. Understanding the grasslands allowed Icelanders to better subdue the countryside with "larger fields, more equipment…and greatly increased livestock." Over time and generations, Icelanders succeeded in building the same "communion of nature" with the prairie environment as earlier generations had done long ago back in Iceland.[60]

Thorstina Jackson Walters claimed a prominent place for Icelanders in *Ameríku* by weaving their history into a generic western "pioneering" experience. Walters used classic western content to link Icelanders to major founding events in the history of both Canada and the United States. Her trade in imagery and mythic West themes seem more pronounced than either Thompson or Brown's narrative use of mythic Wests. Moreover, she reinforced the mythic West's whiteness when she suggested that the biology of Icelanders made a renewing contribution to North American peoples. Nevertheless, on occasion, Walters challenged stock western language when she tied mythic West imagery to realistic day-to-day western living. Also, her emphasis on education and intellect created space for women in Icelandic definitions of western success, which in turn indirectly challenged dominant male assumptions tied to popular Wests. Finally, when she attached herself to the grasslands environment, she participated in what seems to be a common female narrative strategy for claiming land and a place in the West.

* * *

WHILE ANNORA BROWN, Era Bell Thompson, and Thorstina Jackson Walters each referred to both Canadian and American western content in their autobiographical writings, these women did not construct their narratives with *steady* awareness of competing national western mythologies. Brown suggested some knowledge of stereotypical Canadian and American Wests when she linked divergent manliness ideals with opposite sides of the 49th parallel. Only Brown, however, wrote specifically against a Canadian mythic West. Thompson included Canada only when Canadians happened to cross her path and as one place she visited among many (including New York, the South, and California). Walters' unique experience as a member of the transnational northern borderlands Icelandic community caused her to recognize historic events and persons in western Canadian and American history, but her "saga" overall exhibited little awareness of any significant differences between the two nations. Her combination autobiography–community history suggests that some immigrants may have identified with variations on western myth, as in Walters' case with an Icelandic version.

When they thought in regional labels, they identified with the geographic label *West*. The generally cursory references to the details that would distinguish American and Canadian mythical West traditions suggest these women may have condensed many mythic elements into a simple, sometimes inconsistent, generic North American West.[61] But they redefined older meanings of the "West" as they delivered New West messages about environmental activism, racism, and the value of immigrant populations. They contextualized Old West imagery with the details (the gumbo mud, a cat and a truck, and mosquitoes) of everyday life. They used humor and irony to expose the fictional components of such imagery. However, in the end these women critiqued more by implication than by directly challenging either the Canadian or American mythic Wests.

While these narratives suggest that Brown, Thompson, and Walters developed a distinctive way to lay claim to western land by growing close attachments to its environment, their narratives also reveal an important subordinate point about western myth's racial assumptions. Whiteness marked grasslands space for these women. Race for this generation of women proved to be a powerful category. By right of common birthplace, Brown minimized racial conflict by aligning herself *with* Native peoples of the region, all of them *against* the commercial destruction of grasslands habitat. Her lack of attention to race generally suggests how well her own English racial heritage matched the whiteness of the myth. Thompson's characterization of Dakota as a "country that is new and free and strangely beautiful" suggests that she shared Brown's feeling of regional ownership, one that denied the long history of Native peoples to which the same places would have seemed *old* and *occupied*. Thompson, too, aligned herself with Natives (and also Old World immigrants) on the basis of their shared generational status. As an African-American, however, Thompson also shared with Natives and immigrants an uncertain racial status. The potential for exclusion based on national origin drove Walters to draw constant positive parallels between Icelanders and their Old World heritage and the dominant white "Americans," so as to be admitted *because of* race. The whiteness of Icelanders, according to Walters, made them perfect for either American or Canadian citizenship.

The development of a personal attachment to the grasslands environment explored and asserted to differing degrees by Brown, Thompson, and Walters, if they are representative, suggest that modern western women developed a distinct way of laying claim to western land. Brown called this environmental attachment "oneness." She became environmentally aware by studying and painting the details of flora and wild grasses as they changed over the seasons. Thompson referred to "that understanding with Nature." She appreciated a "strangely beautiful" place rather than land acquisition. Walters wrote about a "communion with nature." For her, successful immigrant integration into North American society included the essential step of comprehending the "limitations and possibilities" of the environment. They all claimed to know a regional aesthetic. Their emphasis on environmental consciousness shaped a modern regionalism that included women in the role of typical westerner. These case studies of women's voices suggest complexities worth considering in the search for the roles western women played in the construction of a modern sense of North American Wests.

AUTHOR'S NOTE

Thanks to Laura J. Moore for helping me impose order on the larger free-ranging exploration from which this essay is drawn, to Jennifer Ritterhouse and Regina Sullivan for helpful suggestions, and to Betsy Jameson and Sheila McManus for careful readings of earlier drafts. Thanks a second time to Sheila McManus for comments and questions that improved the clarity of this essay considerably.

This article began as a very different exploratory paper delivered at the "Unsettled Pasts" conference held in Calgary, Alberta, in June 2002. In the conference paper I compared Lillian Smith of the United States' Deep South to Canadian Annora Brown's Grasslands West. (See

Lillian Smith, *Killers of the Dream* (1949; 1961; repr., New York: W.W. Norton & Co., 1994). The larger project and this essay are designed to move beyond what Robin W. Winks long ago identified as the tradition of "insularity" endemic to regionalism studies. See his "Regionalism in Comparative Perspective," in *Regionalism and the Pacific Northwest,* ed. William G. Robbins, Robert J. Frank, and Richard E. Ross (Corvallis: Oregon State University Press, 1983), 13–36.

NOTES

1. Annora Brown, *Sketches from Life* (Edmonton, AB: Hurtig Publishers, 1981), 11–12.

2. For an introduction to Canadian-American comparative work, see Sterling Evans, ed., *The Borderlands of the American and Canadian Wests* (Lincoln: University of Nebraska Press, 2006); C. L. Higham and Robert Thacker, eds., *One West, Two Myths: II* (Calgary: University of Calgary Press, 2007); Higham and Thacker, eds., *One West, Two Myths* (Calgary: University of Calgary Press, 2004); Higham and Thacker, eds., "One Myth, Two Wests: Special Issue on the West(s)," *American Review of Canadian Studies* 4 (Winter 2003); and William G. Robbins, "The American and Canadian Wests: Two Nations, Two Cultures," in *Colony and Empire,* ed. Robbins (Lawrence: University Press of Kansas, 1994).

    Both nations have a long tradition of thinking in regional terms. For a quick history of regionalism in the United states, old and new, see Brown's "The New Regionalism in America, 1970–1981," in *Regionalism and the Pacific Northwest,* ed. Robbins, Frank, and Ross, 37–96; Peter S. Onuf, ed., *All Over the Map* (Baltimore, MD: Johns Hopkins University Press, 1996); Robert L. Dorman, *Revolt of the Provinces* (Chapel Hill: University of North Carolina Press, 1993); and for a discussion of the way humans "think" regions into existence using the U.S. central grasslands, see Elliott West, *The Contested Plains* (Lawrence: University of Kansas Press, 1998). An important caution to the recent growth in the study of regions is Robert Maria Dainotto, "'All the Regions Do Smilingly Revolt': The Literature of Place and Region," *Critical Inquiry* 22 (Spring 1996): 486–505.

    For Canada, see Winks "Regionalism in Comparative Perspective," Gerald Friesen, "Defining the Prairies: Or, Why the Prairies Don't Exist," in *Toward Defining the Prairies,* ed. Robert Wardhaugh (Winnipeg: University of Manitoba Press, 2001), 13–28; Peter McCormick, "Regionalism in Canada: Disentangling the Threads," *Journal of Canadian Studies* 24 (Summer 1989): 5–21; Richard Allen, ed., *A Region of the Mind* (Regina, SK: Canadian Plains Studies Centre, 1973).

3. On autobiographical writing see Jill Ker Conway, *When Memory Speaks* (New York: Alfred A. Knopf, 1998); Helen M. Buss, *Mapping Our Selves* (Montreal: McGill-Queen's University Press, 1993); Ruth E. Ray, *Beyond Nostalgia* (Charlottesville: University Press of Virginia, 2000); Patrick B. Mullen, *Listening to Old Voices* (Urbana: University of Illinois Press, 1992); and Jacquelyn Dowd Hall, "'You Must Remember This': Autobiography as Social Critique," *Journal of American History* 85 (September 1998): 439–65.

4. Hal S. Barron, *Mixed Harvest* (Chapel Hill: University of North Carolina Press, 1997), 10; Mary Neth, *Preserving the Family Farm* (Baltimore, MD: Johns Hopkins University Press,

1995), 4; and John L. Shover, *First Majority—Last Minority* (De Kalb: Northern Illinois University Press, 1976), xiv.

5. Brown, *Sketches from Life*, 10.

6. Brown, *Sketches from Life* and *Old Man's Garden* (Toronto: J. M. Dent & Sons, 1954). Brown's personal scrapbooks and period correspondence complement both of her books. See Annora Brown Manuscript Collection (AB 83–116), The University of Alberta Archives (BARD), Edmonton, Alberta; and Canadian Artist Gallery, Annora Brown (File 31, M8403) and Annora Brown Photograph Collection (NC–10), Glenbow Archives, Calgary, Alberta.

7. Era Bell Thompson, *American Daughter* (1946; repr., St Paul: Minnesota Historical Society, 1986). Period correspondence supports her stated autobiographical intentions. Stanley Pargellis Papers, RG 03, SG 05, Series 3, Box 4, Folder 136 "Erabell [sic] Thompson," Newberry Library Archives, Chicago, Illinois (hereafter cited as Pargellis Papers). Subsequent publications help to sketch an outline of her career. By 1947, Thompson was associate editor for *Ebony* magazine, which began circulation in 1945; her articles appear occasionally up to the mid-1970s. She also edited with Herbert Nipson, *White on Black: The Views of Twenty-Two White Americans on the Negro* (Chicago: Johnson Publishing Company, 1963) and authored *Africa: Land of my Fathers* (New York: Doubleday, 1954).

8. Thorstina [Jackson] Walters, *Modern Sagas: The Story of Icelanders in North America* (Fargo: North Dakota Institute for Regional Studies, 1953). The book is supported by the Thorstina Jackson [and Émile] Walters Papers (Mss 630), North Dakota Institute for Regional Studies, North Dakota State University Libraries, Fargo, ND. Debilitating illness also seems to heighten memory; Walters' chapter, "I Grew Up with the Pioneers," bears a reflective distance to past events similar to parts of Brown's autobiography.

9. Sarah Carter has summarized the different qualities of the Canadian and American western men outlined by John Herd Thompson at the conference "One West, Two Myths: Comparing Canadian and American Perspectives," The Buffalo Bill Historical Center, Cody, Wyoming, May 2002, in "Transnational Perspectives on the History of Great Plains Women: Gender, Race, Nations, and the Forty-ninth Parallel," *American Review of Canadian Studies* 4 (Winter 2003): 565–96.

    On masculine-centered landscape discourse see Krista Comer, *Landscapes of the New West* (Chapel Hill: University of North Carolina Press, 1999), 11, 13–14, and 27. Both Canada and the United States drew on language inherited from European imperial "landscape discourse" to define the links between men, women, and nature. See also Catherine Cavanaugh, "'No Place For A Woman': Engendering Western Canadian Settlement," *Western Historical Quarterly* 28 (Winter 1997): 493–518; Joan M. Jenson, *One Foot on the Rockies* (Albuquerque: University of New Mexico Press, 1995); Carolyn Merchant, *Earthcare* (New York: Routledge, 1995); Vera Norwood, *Made From This Earth* (Chapel Hill: University of North Carolina Press, 1993); and Virginia J. Scharff, ed., *Seeing Nature Through Gender* (Lawrence: University Press of Kansas, 2003).

    Glenda Riley argues that women naturalists "feminized public images of western environments" and "envisioned a feral yet accessible west that neither deterred nor intimidated women…" (5) and further, women's attitudes toward nature changed between 1870 and 1940. Women's writings "generally lacked the twin themes of conquest and domination of land that marked so many men's works of the same era" and "stressed [instead] the beauty and spirituality of nature women emphasized the necessity of living with the demands of the physical world rather than subduing them, which allowed women to perceive the violent side of nature without feeling overwhelmed or threatened by the environment" (13). See her "'Wimmin is Everywhere': Conserving and Feminizing Western Landscapes, 1870 to 1940," *Western Historical Quarterly* 29 (Spring 1998): 4–23.

10. Brown, *Sketches from Life*, 42.

11. Richard White, "'Are You an Environmentalist or Do You Work for a Living?': Work and Nature," in *Uncommon Ground*, ed. William Cronon, (1995; repr., New York: W.W. Norton, 1996), 171–85.

12. For a good summary of the U.S. Homestead Act (1862) and Canadian Dominion Lands Act (1872), including their different provisions for women, see Sheila McManus, *The Line Which Separates* (Lincoln: University of Nebraska Press, 2005), 37–41. Basically, single women in the United States could file on government land, while, with a couple of exceptions, in Canada they could not.

13. Brown, *Sketches from Life*, 14–18.

14. Brown, *Sketches from Life*, 71. Although Buffalo Bill Cody is a classic U.S. mythic West reference point, he was well known throughout the continent. Buffalo Bill toured Alberta. Jim and Stasia Carry, Brown's contemporaries, were famous Wild West performers in Canada and both had links to the U.S. Wild West tradition. See Lorain Lounsberry, "The Real Wild West of Jim and Stastia Carry," *Glenbow* 17 (Summer 1997): 23–25.

15. Brown, *Sketches from Life*, 12.

16. Many contemporary autobiographies either focus on a family's move and eventual departure from a homestead, in Canada or the United States, or cover only the years up to the author's departure from the family homestead, even if others remained. For a sampling see Hal Borland, *High, Wide and Lonesome* (Philadelphia: J.B. Lippincott, 1956); Nell Wilson Parsons, *Upon a Sagebrush Harp* (Saskatoon, SK: Western Producer, 1969); Sarah Ellen Roberts, *Alberta Homestead* (Austin: University of Texas Press, 1971); Faye Cashatt Lewis, *Nothing to Make a Shadow* (Ames: Iowa State University Press, 1971).

17. Brown, *Sketches from Life*, 47–48.

18. Brown, *Sketches from Life*, 6, 54, and 67–68.

19. Brown, *Sketches from Life*, 210–12.

20. See Carter, "Transnational Perspectives" and Henry Nash Smith's classic study, *Virgin Land* (1950; repr., Cambridge, MA: Harvard University Press, 1978). The archetypal story fits a pattern popularized by Theodore Roosevelt's 1880s tenure in (North) Dakota Territory. It is well known that Roosevelt built his body and proved his manliness (at least to himself) in the U.S. West, but it is less often observed that he headed West after the near simultaneous deaths of his first wife and mother. See David H. Murdock, *The American West* (1988; repr., Reno: University of Nevada Press, 2001).

21. Brown, *Old Man's Garden*, 59, 196, and 151.

22. Brown, *Sketches from Life*, 217. *Old Man's Garden* was reissued in the 1970s.

23. Brown, *Sketches from Life*, 37.

24. For a discussion of the links between territorial conquest and ideas of racial superiority in Canada see Doug Owram, *Promise of Eden* (1980; repr., Toronto: University of Toronto Press, 1992), especially 70–100. For a similar brief discussion of U.S. racial attitudes see Richard White, *"It's Your Misfortune and None of My Own"* (Norman: University of Oklahoma Press, 1991). See also C. L. Higham, *Noble, Wretched, and Redeemable: Protestant Missionaries to the Indians in Canada and the United States, 1820–1900* (Albuquerque: University of New Mexico Press, 2000).

25. Brown, *Sketches from Life*, 7, 37, 66, 69, and 73.

26. Thompson to Pargellis, May 24, 1944; "Report on Era Bell Thompson, American Daughter," n.d. [1945?], Pargellis Papers.

27. The classic U.S. West phrase "go west, young man" has been attributed since the 1850s to Horace Greeley, editor of the nationally influential newspaper the New York *Weekly Tribune* and strong supporter the Homestead Act. He took the phrase from an Indiana newspaper. See Robert V. Hine and John Mack Faragher, *The American West* (New Haven, CT: Yale University Press, 2000), 331–33.

28. Thompson, *American Daughter*, 13, 27, 30, 93–94, 14, and 21–22.

29. Thompson, *American Daughter*, 128.

30. Thompson, *American Daughter*, 26, 86, 47, 63, 42, 190, 149, 128, 149, 27, and 190. Thompson revealed, however, that her family ancestry included Native Americans (13).

31. She cites many incidents of racism. See Thompson, *American Daughter*, 83, 86, 117, 126, 128, 139, 151, 141, and 143.

32. Thompson, *American Daughter*, 147–48, 164, and 214.

33. Thompson, *American Daughter*, 164.

34. Thompson to Pargellis, May 24, 1944, Pargellis Papers.

35. Thompson, *American Daughter*, 50, 46, 42, 52, 100, 58, 66, 47, 50, and 190–91.

36. Thompson, *American Daughter*, 23–24.

37. William Cronon, *Nature's Metropolis* (New York: W.W. Norton, 1991), 56–57. Cronon discusses the difference between "first" and "second" natures, arguing that locals "often forgot the distinction between them. Both seemed quite 'natural.'" Commercial grain fields, "designed by people and 'improved' toward human ends," constitute a "second nature" laid overtop a "first nature," the "original landscape."

38. For the rise of tourism in the United States in the post–Civil War years and the way it challenged already established senses of place in the West, see Hal K. Rothman, *Devil's Bargains: Tourism in the Twentieth-Century American West* (Lawrence: University Press of Kansas, 1998). When Thompson (and others) began to promote a popular West by catering to tourists and outsiders, they engaged, I believe, in what Hal K. Rothman described as the "innocuous" "initial development of tourism." "The embrace of tourism," Rothman argued, "triggers a contest for the soul of a place" (11). Rothman continued, "The railroad made tourists out of travelers, especially in the western United States. To be a tourist meant to be divorced from the realities of any visited place, to re-create its essence in the context of the cultural baggage brought along in a manner previously impossible." In this way, residents of any place with tourist activity live with both the image created and a reality grounded in a non-tourist "social shape" embedded in a specific "economy, environment, and culture" distinct from the image (39).

39. Thompson, *American Daughter*, 33, 145, and 152. Thompson turned to the stock cowboy character when her opinions on Marcus Garvey's "Back to Africa" movement received criticism. Her account of this newspaper column is brief.

40. Thompson, *American Daughter*, 204–05. Some fifty years earlier the Canadian government organized the North West Mounted Police force in part to control illegal U.S. liquor distribution to Native Peoples in Canada. Now in the 1920s, it was Canadians who supplied the liquor, albeit to still law-breaking Americans south of the border. See Stephen T. Moore, "Refugees from Volstead: Cross-Boundary Tourism in the Northwest during Prohibition," in *The Borderlands of the American and Canadian Wests*, ed. Evans, 247–61; Paul F. Sharp, *Whoop-Up Country* (1955; repr., Helena: Historical Society of Montana, 1960) and Walter Hildebrandt and Brian Hubner, *The Cypress Hills* (Saskatoon, SK: Purich Publishing, 1994). Thompson seems unaware of these parallels.

41. Thompson to Pargellis, May 24, 1944; Joseph A. Brandt to Thompson, August 4, 1945; [Rosemary B. York] to Thompson, March 5, 1945, all in Pargellis Papers. Brandt changed the name from "I Found It Fun" to "American Daughter."

42. Thompson, *American Daughter*, 7, 26–27, and 194–95.

43. The "tone" of her work, she wrote to a potential publisher who praised her for her "lack of a 'chip on the shoulder attitude,'" "is the thing I most wanted to stress." The style "make[s] the reader like you," one editor told Thompson. It seemed an "unusual" tale with "no bitterness as in Richard Wright," observed another. Thompson to Pargellis, May 24, 1944; [Rosemary B. York] to Thompson, March 5, 1945; Thompson to York, March 10, 1945; [Pargellis to Guggenheim Foundation?, Recommendation Letter?, n.d., October 1945?]; Pargellis to Thompson, June 11, 1945; Doris Flowers to Stanley Pargellis, February 15, 1946, all in Pargellis Papers.

44. Thompson to Pargellis, May 24, 1944, Pargellis Papers.

45. Thompson, *American Daughter*, 294.

46. See footnote 28 above.

47. Walters, *Modern Sagas*, 33, 14–15, 31, 84, 178, and 150. The family histories collected by Walters' father, Thorleifur Jóakimsson (Jackson), reveal that the destination *Ameríku* stood in for most places in Canada and the United States.

48. Walters, *Modern Sagas*, 46 and 136. The quote is the motto of an early short-lived immigrant self-help society; Walters felt the edict "lived on" in the Iceland community at large. These Icelandic principles might be compared to those of "peace, order, and good government" for Canada and "life, liberty, and pursuit of happiness" for the United States. For standard characterizations of Canadian and U.S. political values, see William H. Katerberg, "A Northern Vision: Frontiers and the West in the Canadian and American Imagination," *American Review of Canadian Studies* 4 (Winter 2003): 543–63.

49. Walters, *Modern Sagas*, 116, 177, 12–13, 2–3, 102, 141–76, and 179–80.

50. Her gender-neutral westerner was unlike the "wild" and "orderly" model males of the U.S. and Canada's Wests, respectively. The Icelandic ideal westerner might be comparable to the law-abiding Mounted Policeman and the rugged, aggressive U.S. cowboy.

51. Walters, *Modern Sagas*, 116, 117, 4, and 32. Walters made reference to the possibility that Canada was a safer place than the United States only once. She mentioned 1870s

immigrants thought their money might be safer in "British banks in Canada, asserting that in their opinion they were on a firmer foundation than the American banks" (42).

Custer and Riel received Walters' equally perfunctory treatment. Her understanding of the Riel Rebellion may have been quite rudimentary, because she thanks a few Canadian informants for their assistance in explaining this history. She does not elaborate on Custer either. Her slight mentions may show how little an educated Icelandic person who considered herself "western" may have understood the history of even the most prominent actors in U.S. and Canadian narrative traditions.

Métis peoples had traveled through the land that became North Dakota between Selkirk, Manitoba, and what became St Paul, Minnesota, since the early nineteenth century. There were Métis settlements at Pembina, south of the 49th parallel and south of Devils Lake, in the future North Dakota. See Robinson, *History of North Dakota*, 65–67, 105, 110–11, and 118–20.

Despite efforts by Mounties to educate new immigrants "about what set Canadians apart from other men," that is, an "orderly and law-abiding" nature, Walters did not seem to have absorbed the Canadian nationalist lesson. R.C. Macleod discusses the influence of nationalism among immigrant populations in "Canadianizing the West: The North-West Mounted Police as Agents of National Policy, 1873–1905," in *The Prairie West: Historical Readings,* ed. R. Douglas Francis and Howard Palmer (Edmonton: University of Alberta Press, 1992), 229. Walters' North Dakota publisher no doubt also influenced the construction of her West.

52. Walters, *Modern Saga,* 41.

53. Walters, *Modern Saga,* 11, 14, and 1.

54. William Henry Harrison also used the log cabin symbolically in his successful 1840 presidential campaign. The log cabin's association with the West became complete when Congress passed the 1841 preemption land law, known widely as the "Log Cabin Bill." See Robert V. Hine and John Mack Faragher, *The American West* (New Haven, CT: Yale University Press, 2000), 72–73 and 331.

55. Walters, *Modern Saga,* 11, 14, and 1.

56. Walters, *Modern Sagas,* 1, 141, 189, 77, and 117.

57. Walters, *Modern Sagas,* 13, 15, and 18–19. She noted there had been no "scientific retracing" of Ericsson's journeys (29).

58. Nordic peoples, according to one popular theory of the 1920s, for example, existed at the top of a white racial hierarchy (over Alpine and Mediterranean peoples), while all of the white races ranked above African-Americans, Africans, Asians, and Native Peoples. See Mathew Frye Jacobson, *Whiteness of a Different Color* (Cambridge, MA: Harvard University Press, 1998); John Higham, *Strangers in the Land* (1955; repr., New Brunswick, NJ: Rutgers University Press, 1998); April R. Schultz, *Ethnicity on Parade* (Amherst: University of Massachusetts Press, 1994); and Howard Palmer, "Strangers and Stereotypes: The Rise of Nativism, 1880–1920," in *Prairie West,* ed. Francis and Palmer, 308–34. Walters did not wholly embrace the idea that Icelanders contained "pure" Nordic blood; she argued that Icelandic blood could not have remained pure over some nine centuries. She also referenced debates in the Icelandic community over whether Viking blood was pure or

had grown "mixed" and "thin" over time (191). She does not argue against concepts of race tied to blood, and she clearly considered Icelanders to be good stock.

59. Walters, *Modern Sagas,* 79, 16, 33, 192, and 3–4.

60. Walters, *Modern Sagas,* 167, 1, 17, and 75–76.

61. The mythic symbols of the U.S. West may have been more pronounced in this generic version than their Canadian counterparts because it is likely that the former were more visible in popular North American media and entertainment, but the sample of women studied here is not large enough to reach any conclusion. As early as 1927 American companies controlled Canadian movie theaters and their screenings. When A.D. Kean, whose "goal as a filmmaker was to make films about Canada, shot in Canada, and presented on Canadian screens," tried showing a Canadian "epic feature film that chronicled the formation of law and order in the Canadian West," he found only one movie theater in Canada, in Toronto, willing to show it (6). See Melanie Kjorlien, "Cowboy Kean," *Glenbow* 17 (Summer 1997): 6–7. For the influence of U.S. popular culture in Canada see Lee Clark Mitchell, *Westerns* (Chicago: University of Chicago Press, 1996); and Pierre Berton, *Hollywood's Canada* (Toronto: McClelland and Stewart, 1975).

7

THE PERILS OF
RURAL WOMEN'S HISTORY

(A Note to Storytellers Who Study the West's Unsettled Past)

JOAN M. JENSEN

I HAVE ALWAYS CONSIDERED the writing of history to be a process of crossing borders and comparing cultures. The boundaries in my work have usually been within the United States: the social borders of race, class, region, and ethnicity. Over the years I have consciously narrowed my field of interest, starting out to study European history, then refocusing on the United States to ask a question that social historians had been asking for years about Europe. How had social institutions taken form? Looking at the United States and adding questions raised by historians of gender, I found a world wonderfully complex, one that faced inward and outward. This focus began in graduate school and intensified in subsequent years as I adjusted, unlearned, and expanded my formal education. In 1963, when I received my PhD in history, there were almost no studies of social or women's history, little rural history (as distinct from agricultural history, which then considered farming solely a male occupation), and relatively little immigration history. I was trained to write white male political history. Nevertheless, I began a history of Asian Indian immigrants which took me, eventually, across the Canadian border as I researched these men who sought work in the United States and Canada and faced similar discrimination in each. But when women's history expanded as a field, I gladly turned to the task of writing about rural women in the United States, indigenous and settler, immigrant and native-born. Rural women, the majority of women for most of U.S. history, seemed to be entirely neglected.[1]

I specifically chose rural women as my focus, but I chose the time and region almost by chance. The Regional Economic History Research Center at the Eleutherian Mills-Hagley Library was offering grants on the industrializing of the mid-Atlantic region. I suggested they support my research into the question of what happened to rural women during this process. By chance, then, I used this region to explore my own questions about rural women. The result of my research was *Loosening the Bonds*, a study of rural women in southeastern Pennsylvania, an area in which a Quaker culture had been well established by 1750.[2]

That book completed, I focused westward, looking for a new group of rural women to continue my story. I chose north-central Wisconsin, an area in which German immigrants replaced the predominantly native-born Yankee settler culture after the 1850s. I began my study there, thinking I could combine this second volume of rural women's history with my own family history. My grandmother, a German Bohemian farm woman, had crossed the Atlantic to settle in this midwestern region in the 1890s. There she raised her eight children, among them my mother who, at sixteen, left for St Paul, Minnesota, where she married an urban Italian-born immigrant in 1925. My mother was one of the thousands of rural women who sought jobs in urban areas, married, and chose city life over farming.[3]

I never expected this project to stretch over a decade, or to bring me to new indigenous/settler borders, or to consider again the Canadian/ United States border, over which I found that my mother's and other families frequently crossed in the early twentieth century seeking economic opportunity. My European-born German relatives did not find the same discrimination as those born in Asia. In fact, authorities in Western Canada welcomed these European immigrants as a buffer against the need for Asian immigrant labor.

Between 1900 and 1910 there was a "Canada craze" in northern Wisconsin. German immigrants who were still arriving and the children of earlier immigrants found U.S. land prices rising and market prices depressed. Families sought less costly land in Canada. A friend of my aunt moved to Canada with his family in 1910 because he was one of five sons in the family, all of whom wanted their own land to farm. He returned to marry her and she farmed there with him for forty years. Other neighbors followed them. I myself might have been born in Canada, had my grandfather been able to convince my grandmother to move north when he caught the "Canadian craze" in 1905, two years after my mother's birth. Grandma refused to budge. Instead Grandpa traveled north to the wheat harvest in Canada each year. He liked the excitement of the harvest and perhaps played his accordion in the granary that my aunt and her husband opened each harvest for dances. Grandpa Schopp did not like the everyday life of a farmer, and Grandma eventually kicked him off the land that she had inherited from her first husband and passed it on to her first-born son. Thus my own rural family history remains rooted in northern Wisconsin instead of across the border in southern Canada.

Still, I have photographs to prove that my parents took me across the border to visit my aunt in that small town of Browning, Saskatchewan, in the summer of 1937. I was two and one half years old when my Canadian uncle perched me atop a huge work horse and steadied me while my father took the photograph. We crossed the border easily if not often. My aunt visited us in St Paul at Christmas time the next year. We thought nothing of borders except the space that would separate my mother from her sister once we moved west to southern California. The ties then seemed broken, but I still remember writing to my aunt in the 1940s, worrying that the letter with the simple address "Mary Sacher, Browning, Saskatchewan," with no street or house number, would arrive safely. I know she got the letters, though I have none of hers to prove that she wrote back.

We forget about borders until reminded by some special event. Recently, when I crossed the northern border to find my aunt's Canadian history for my Wisconsin book, I began to think about how to share part of the thirty years of writing rural women's history in a way that might be helpful to historians on both sides of this particular border. I am not sure how our comparative Canadian–United States rural women's history will develop. I know I have gained insight from reading Canadian First Nations history and theory, from studies of rural Canadian sexuality, and from articles on Canadian settlement in the west. Yet in a recent bibliography that I helped create, we only referenced four items on Canadian rural women, two of them presented at Rural Women Studies Association conferences and published by *Agricultural History*. Only one of the articles was on Western Canada. While a number of scholars contributed to that bibliography, none challenged our oversight. United States historians are still not as aware of Canadian scholarship as they should be. Conversations about comparisons have hardly begun.[4]

My reading list on Canadian rural women has lengthened considerably in the past few years. I read Joy Kogawa's moving story *Obasan*, about the lives of rural Japanese Canadians forcibly removed from urban life to rural towns and farms in the 1940s. In it Kogawa asks, "If I could follow the stream down and down to the hidden voice, would I come at last to the Freeing word?" Kogawa writes of silence and silencing, and like her we must follow the stream to recover the voices of rural women on both sides of the border.[5]

As we go about this task, I would like historians on both sides of these national borders to be aware of what I call the six "perils" of writing rural women's history. Analyzing these perils can serve as a starting point for a dialogue on writing across the border as we search for and tell the stories of rural women. I have categorized these perils as fantasizing, romanticizing, victimizing, rationalizing, personalizing, and politicizing. I do not know if these categories apply equally in every place. I write from my own self-analysis, the urges I have had to resist as I study rural

women's history. Fantasizing is the urge to blur the rough edges, to simplify to achieve a story that pleases me, one that neatly divides rural and
urban, and accepts this division as a constant in the lives of rural women.
Romanticizing is often a fatal attraction for me, seeing the loss of rural
life as the story of one group losing out, the world we have lost. Victimizing
emphasizes that these people were defeated and did not survive culturally. Rationalizing means I impose a view that events are natural, inevitable,
and universal rather than specific, nuanced, and varied, that we object-
ify as we recover stories. Then we risk personalizing: in our efforts to
find the individual words and voices, we make public what once was private. How do we use that information in a responsible way? Many writers
use novels to combine and rearrange family history into fiction. But as
historians we want to leave specific information distinct and separate.
Finally, in politicizing, we may impose politics, wishing that rural women
had shared certain views, or chastise them for not having these views.
Let me elaborate a bit on why each of these approaches presents perils.

FANTASIZING

I WRITE ABOUT THE PAST of small rural communities, mostly
now obliterated by the urban technological society. In doing so, I try to
resist the temptation to fantasize, while at the same time preserving
what I can of their past. To me it seems that most of the cultures I study
wanted technology, but wanted to use it at their own pace for their own
needs and somehow lost control of it. And in the losing they also lost
much of their own culture and their control over their land. But history
is never as clear and cleanly cut as fantasy. I try to remember that.

Recently, I have been reading a book titled *The Telling* by Ursula Le
Guin, the well-known writer of science fiction and fantasy. *The Telling*
centers on Sutty, an Anglo-Indian from Vancouver, who has left Terra
(earth) for the planet of Aka where she is an official Observer for Ekumen,
an intergalactic federation. The Corporation State has controlled Aka
for seventy years, during which time it has imposed an industrial technological mode and remade culture. Sutty, who has studied ancient scripts
of Aka, is sent by Ekumen historians to find out more about Aka culture,

for they believe "a useful knowledge of the present is rooted in the past." When Sutty arrives, she can find almost no trace of the old culture in the capital city, Dovea. The Corporation has destroyed the old language and pulped the old books to use as insulation in buildings. All the people who told the stories of the past are gone. Sutty's job is to look for these stories and any people who tell them. To do so, she travels up the river by boat for ten days to a provincial town called Okzat-Ozkat. There she finds "the tellers," known as the maz. The maz continue to tell the old stories and the people maintain a secret life in which they listen to the stories and practice the old culture. In this old culture, people seek a spiritual and physical satisfaction that does not serve the growth of society's material wealth and complexity as the Corporation demands. The old stories often denounce excess profit making. The people have taken what they can preserve of the old books of Aka culture up to a cave in the mountains where the people go to study and read the books. Sutty goes there and learns about the history of the Aka culture, then attempts to negotiate its preservation.[6]

I loved this book. How could I not? It portrays a rural culture where mind is memory, honor comes from truth, and storytellers are respected for sharing the past and holding no secrets about it. And that is the peril. Reading fantasy is not enough. I may use Le Guin's Asian-Canadian scholar who explores other worlds as a model, but I must find this world's details of history and not create a fantasy. As a historian, I cannot set out to find Le Guin's fantasy community. It simply does not exist. Her model of a scholar/explorer can, however, help me to see different aspects of cultures more clearly and give me the courage to continue listening for the stories.

In the area of Wisconsin that I research, many family and community stories simply are not shared. Or they are contradictory. Or incomplete. Or untrue. I wish it were not this way, but it is. And I have to find ways to ground my stories in these realities. Minnesota writer Carol Bly talks about the problem of describing a midwestern culture that has developed a way of deflecting realities. They want to talk nice. But many of the things that go on in all cultures are not nice: racism, family violence, community ostracism of those who are different. How do we reveal these without giving the impression that this is the most important part of a culture?[7]

ROMANTICIZING

BELIEVING THAT RURAL PEOPLE lost out, that a rich, simple way of life is gone forever, is another peril. I find it difficult to avoid romanticizing rural women. I do it and I think many historians of rural people do it. We identify with the subjects of our stories in reaction against their being portrayed as unimportant to urban people and their historians. I sometimes catch myself believing that because rural people had to leave their land, they did not carry their cultures into the mainstream. I sometimes think in a sort of dualism, rural vs. urban, or good vs. bad. The trick is to see rural history as multidimensional.

And also multicultural. I also have a tendency to want to write about the majority, or only one group. I think it is important for people to write their own stories, but I also believe that people do not have to write only their own stories. To write only about one group seems to me to deny the reality of a huge and very diverse group of people interacting in complex ways. If I write only about settlers and not Indigenous people, native born and not immigrant, white and not people of color, I miss the vital edges where people come together, mix, and clash or cooperate. And if I write about the United States and not Mexico, the United States and not Canada, I miss the vital edges where national borders meet and people cross them.

One of the reasons my Wisconsin book has taken so many years to complete is that I have moved away from the center to the margins. When large numbers of German families arrived in the 1890s, earlier Yankee settlers did not welcome this new minority. Land agents and lumber companies wanted to sell their land to these new immigrants. One contemporary wrote that the purchase of land and settlement of communities by these new immigrants lowered land values of the already settled farmers. The saga of struggling European-based frontier immigrant folk seems an easy story to tell. Yet if we ignore conflict among

European immigrants, we miss an important part of their story. Polish immigrants resisted attempts by German immigrants to dominate. Polish immigrants arrived later than the Germans, most from areas of German-occupied Poland. Conflicts ran deep, even separating Polish nuns from German nuns and causing schism in northern Wisconsin: Polish nuns wanted to learn to teach, while the German nuns relegated them to tasks in the kitchen.[8]

So now I had early French and Irish Canadians, Yankees, Germans, and Poles on this bit of Wisconsin land. I kept reading about the "disappearance" of Native people in this region. Yet Native American writers testify to the survival of their ancestors in these regions. The story of Native removal, if romanticized, can also mask or remove conflict from the settler story and eliminate the story of how indigenous people responded to settlers.

When settlers intruded into Native lands in the woodlands area, one response was the creation of the Dream Dance, which spread throughout Wisconsin, other north-central states, and into the Canadian province of Manitoba in the 1880s. The Dream Dance paralleled the pan-Indian movement of the Ghost Dance of the Plains. Yet it is seldom discussed in historical accounts. This religious revival was started by the Sioux woman Red Feather Woman, who preached cooperation among Native tribes. Red Cloud Woman, the Menominee who recounted Red Feather Woman's story to anthropologist Leonard Bloomfield in 1920, said the Spirit was quite explicit in giving instructions: "You will tell your men-folk to go slay the creature [a deer] that you are to use on this drum, so that you may make a drum. Let them hurry about it. Then when they have completed the drum, they will dance together." The purpose of the Dream Dance ceremony, Red Cloud Woman went on, was to encourage Indians to "deal kindly with each other, that they may never fight each other, exchanging things by way of reciprocal gifts." Native people were also to share the Dream Dance by making a second drum to pass on to a new group along with instructions for the dance. In 1910 anthropologist Frances Densmore had witnessed such a passing on of a Dream Dance drum from the Lac du Flambeau Ojibwa to the Menominee. Other drums passed north among the Plains Ojibwa in Manitoba.[9]

Native peoples belong to Nations that still oppose the arbitrary Canadian-U.S. boundaries that cut through their homelands. The Tuscarora, for example, celebrate Border Crossing Day every July to honor their right to trade and cross the United States border unhindered by government officials. Settlers, too, once ignored abstract national boundaries and crossed freely from one nation to the other. Their loyalties to one or another were not firmly established. They had left their native lands and were raising Canadians and Americans, often of mixed ethnic and racial heritage—their languages, customs, and loyalties still in a wonderfully complex flux. Native-born children, of all ethnic and racial groups, were a new generation with experiences different from those of their parents and grandparents.[10]

It is true that I risk distortion and omission with inclusion. Yet if I identify only the majority, it is easier to ignore the parts of the community that might be the most critical of it and from whom I can learn much. Studying different parts of a community helps keep me from romanticizing one part of it. Including cross-border conversations can lead to important insights. A case in point is the cross-border historical discussion that has developed around the history of mixed-heritage women in Canada and the United States. These discussions began in earnest with the 1980 publication of Sylvia Van Kirk's *Many Tender Ties* and Jennifer Brown's *Strangers in the Blood*. Since these early attempts to describe women's roles in an economy and culture that crossed borders, more recent accounts have broadened, deepened, and become more complex as the descendants of these women have joined the discussion about how best to write about how their ancestors developed trade and founded bicultural communities. The Métisse, as scholars sometimes refer to these earlier mixed-heritage women, continued to influence women's history through their female descendants long after Canada and the United States divided up the fur-trade territory. My analysis of mixed-heritage twentieth-century women has been clarified by listening to these dialogues and by entering into discussion and debate.[11]

One of the hardest things for me is to accept criticism and to risk criticism from one group or another, and to learn how to use that criticism. Almost always, I instinctively want to avoid drawing connections between categories and populations because these invite controversy, not only between cross-border elements, but between rural–urban, good–bad, white and non-white. I find it difficult to pursue questions of how choices are made and who passes into one culture or the other, how people maintain bicultural or multicultural heritages. Yet these are the very questions that keep us honest, keep us from suppressing the parts we do not want to deal with—the prejudice, the mistreatment, the scorn, the indifference that exists in small rural communities just as it does in cities.

VICTIMIZING

WHY IS IT that I always believe losing control of land is bad and that people who lose it are victims? I often write with the assumption that leaving the land is a sort of defeat. I hate policies of the United States government that have assumed some people should be moved off the land, either to have others take their place, such as replacing Indigenous peoples with settlers, or replacing settlers with agribusiness or suburbs. And yet I know that many of the people who left, especially women, including my mother, have felt they prospered by leaving rural areas.

And perceptions change. I have been going back through a number of books written about Native Americans, and the feeling of victimization is present in almost all of them. Recent Native American writers, while careful to tell the story of occupation and conquest, frequently choose not to dwell on their losses but to emphasize survival. I am trying to learn from them to counter-balance the loss of land and the sense of victimization by looking at how people survived and what they wanted.

People can be both victims and victimizers. I learned from my study of Native history that settlers were not innocent, but they also became victims of government policies that controlled and neglected their health and welfare. In northern Wisconsin, lumber companies sought German immigrants to sell them cutover land. They sold the land cheaply, with easy credit, but the settlers received a piece of stumpy land. These early settlers worked incredibly hard for very little. Most had escaped countries where they had no access to the land at all. They often had to accept difficult and dangerous factory or mine work in America. Property values did increase in parts of northern Wisconsin, but in much of the cutover the settlers simply lost their land in the economic depression of the 1930s and had to abandon all the money and effort they had invested.[12]

I began my current research into family history because my mother had seemingly passed on so little to me. She said little about growing up poor in a log house in Wisconsin. Other family members seemed equally reluctant to share memories. Two of my aunts, including the one who migrated to Canada, had no children who might have helped me recreate the family's past. Only my uncle Frank, who had lived on in that log house on the family farm, had a fund of stories to tell me about my grandmother and mother. His daughter Mary Ann had listened to these stories and others as she cared for him in old age. Much of my family had abandoned stories of place and ethnicity when they left for the city. Two wars with Germany undoubtedly made these descendants of late nineteenth-century German immigrants reluctant to discuss their heritage with their second-generation children. I have found convincing evidence that the German oral culture that survived into the twentieth century was already deeply embedded in and adapted to a larger midwestern culture before these wars, and I believe it survives there yet. But it did not survive as a distinct culture transmitted among descendants who scattered off the land. Probably more is being done to recover this culture by the third and fourth generations than by those who left the land.

Other cultures have survived within families even when they have left their homelands. The Diné photographer Hulleah Tsinhnahjinne once told me about a visit to New Zealand and the contact she made there with a Maori woman from Tasmania. They were looking over photographs in the archives and the woman showed Hulleah one identified as "The Last of the Tasmanians." Hulleah said she was ready to get sad after looking at the photograph. But her friend laughed and said, "We're not gone." And that mental image has stayed with me, as it did with Hulleah. My job is to trace the movement and transformation of rural people, not to proclaim them victims and announce that they are "gone" when they leave the land. Colonialist attitudes not only erased the continuing presence of Indigenous women, but they erased the white settler women who also had to leave the land. The people have survived and changed, but their cultures have lived on in their descendants.[13]

RATIONALIZING

IF I RATIONALIZE rather than sympathize, I also run the risk of distortion and oversimplification. I can explain away all policies and all treatment by providing a universal context, by making the decisions of government and dominant settler communities seem rational. There may be alternative histories that avoid both victimization and rationalization of events, a way to show both the effects of colonization on rural communities and how some survived. A recent PBS program, *Ancestors in the Americas*, contained one part titled "Chinese in the Frontier West: An American Story." This part traced Asian immigrants in the Americas and dealt with the treatment of Chinese in the American West. It discussed the optimistic men leaving for the Gold Fields and the discrimination and violence faced once they arrived. Then it asked what might have been if Chinese men had been joined by their wives and families and led more normal lives. Scholars had discovered a community of Chinese families living at Point Alones, near Monterey in California, and the descendants of some of its members. One was a physicist. Her grandparents had settled in this small fishing community and prospered until 1906. Then a fire had wiped out the community. The railroad, which controlled the land, kept the community from rebuilding its town and remaining on the land. But for the many years before the fire they had settled there; these Chinese families lived as an intact community, maintained many of their cultural traits, and adopted whatever they wished from the host culture. Dispersed families had then continued the process of maintenance and adoption after leaving the land. By emphasizing this type of survival, the documentary avoided both victimizing and rationalizing. It took the viewer into a community constructed in one physical space that had escaped much violence and persecution directed at Asians by the dominant culture and had survived intact longer than other Asian communities of the time. Then it showed the lives of individuals who had formed the culture of the next generations.[14]

When I applied that technique to my own work, I began to look more carefully for ways in which communities and families survived and to find their descendants. The Lac du Flambeau Band of Lake Superior Chippewa Indians found ways to preserve old and new. I interviewed Dorothy Thoms, who traced her lineage back to her grandmother Isabella Wolfe St Germain. Isabella arrived in Lac du Flambeau in the 1890s to work as the nurse at the government boarding school during a brief period when the Indian Agent there was hiring educated Native women for jobs as nurses, teachers, and matrons. Isabella had grown up in North Carolina, her father a proud Cherokee, her mother a white woman who joined his community and saw that Isabella learned traditional Cherokee culture. Isabella received a good education at the local Cherokee school and worked there for several years before going on to receive formal training as a nurse.

Isabella worked at the Lac du Flambeau boarding school for almost two years before resigning to marry into the St Germain family. Evidence in government records revealed her excellent performance as a nurse and awards she received later at annual fairs for canning, sewing, creating basketry and beadwork. In addition to maintaining Cherokee traditions (her baskets were probably Cherokee), Isabella learned beading and other traditions from her Chippewa mother-in-law. Isabella continued to practice nursing and traveled on snow shoes all over the community to deliver babies using both traditional Native and settler healing techniques. Known simply as "Grandma St Germain," Isabella was a woman renowned in the community for her healing skills. Her granddaughter showed me a photograph of Isabella standing proudly in front of her huge lilac bush. Then she took me to Isabella's land where the lilac bush still stood. Isabella's family, which had moved from North Carolina to Tennessee, had sent the lilac cuttings. In turn, Isabella gave cuttings of her lilacs to the many neighbors who admired them. Every May, her lilacs still bloom all over the community.[15]

I realize now that this is the type of story that I should be looking for. It gave me a context for what was a short-lived but potentially positive government policy that was not pursued because the government decided Native women should not be employed in most positions of responsibility. It also showed me that the community provided for most of its own health needs. The government had contracts with physicians to attend seriously ill people in the community. A number of them were well regarded by the people at Lac du Flambeau. But for most of their health care needs they turned to Grandma St Germain—to birth their children, to diagnose their illnesses, to advise them on how to restore good health. A rational view might have told only the story left by the government documents. An oral history might have floated alone as only a family story. Together they led me to the rich texture created by the concrete and specific details of a woman's life that Isabella's family offered me. I am continuing to share my research with her family, which hopes there will be a place for Isabella's story in both her community and in my history.

PERSONALIZING

I HAVE A RESPONSIBILITY to the families who share their private histories with me. I have to present that material as accurately as I can, allow family informants to remain anonymous if they would like, and to accept their role as keepers of family history who share only the information they wish me to have. Historians of women are still working out ways to tell more about women's personal lives so we can better understand how these lives affect women's public lives. Often this effort takes us into sensitive areas, into personal lives that families wished to keep private because of the ways in which family and community enforced, or tried to enforce, limits on the activities of women. Courts and administrative agencies impose privacy restrictions. Beyond these legal restrictions, we face ethnical questions regarding what we have access to and how we use this material in our work. How far does the right of privacy extend into personal lives for which we have no legal guidelines or restrictions? Many of us wish to open these areas of women's lives, whether historical or contemporary, to the light of analysis and possibly change. We try to develop new language with which to describe women's lives that is more neutral than popular language. We try to avoid the pejorative terms that have been used to control women's lives in the past. We try to expand the limits of what may be safely discussed publicly because many of us feel that secrets and silences are often the result of socially sanctioned constraints that make it more difficult for women to live full, creative, and satisfying lives, lives that are not crippled because of events both within and outside their control.

When I wrote my book on mid-Atlantic women, I had only a few documents that discussed women's sexual activities. I chose to discuss the activities, without pseudonyms or entire names, either surnames or family names. I used the initial of their first name, and a full citation to the document, assuming any historian trying to locate the information for further research could easily find it and that using an initial was enough for my readers to know. In my current work, I have in many instances tried to use the full name of the woman, and the first name and last initials in others, even though these events are closer in time. Most events took place over one hundred years ago, and I have set my own ethical limits tighter than most legal limits of privacy. I have documented considerable violence toward women in the rural areas I have been studying: incest, sexual abuse of young women by neighbors and kin, improper abortions. I have tried to discuss these "personal" issues with a combination of objectivity and concern for the women who went through these experiences.[16]

Lately, I have been looking more closely at my own family's history. Like most rural families, mine has become urban. Using family history as I am in my current work makes it difficult in new ways. How much family history belongs to me? Just because I experience it, do I have a right to these family stories? Of course. But where do I end the stories? An aunt talked to me one afternoon about her experiences in the city of Milwaukee in the 1910s and 1920s. There was nothing I felt uncomfortable writing about. Yet she worried that I might write about her life and was reluctant to discuss it at all. She was a very private person. She died a few years ago and I want to use parts of that conversation in my work, in this case to discuss violence toward women in the city.

The issue is how much violence did rural women encounter in cities? It is not the kind of material that is easy to come by means other than legal documents. One historian uncovered a memoir in which a Swedish immigrant woman discussed her concern about walking alone on city streets. How much danger did city streets present to young rural women who went there to work? My aunt seemed to think there was relatively little in Milwaukee in the 1920s. She went everywhere, on foot and by streetcars, by day and by evening, seemingly without concern about possible violence to herself. My aunt did usually go out with a female friend, but they thought nothing of going to dances, meeting young male strangers, and accepting rides home from them. Several of my aunts met their future husbands at dances, one at a roller rink. This contrasts with the concern of middle-class reformers about the welfare of young rural women coming to the city, particularly from 1900 and through the 1920s, during the height of progressive reform. How much concern was about real violence, and how much about the freedom that these young women assumed for their own activities? Progressive reformers sometimes called them "women adrift" because they had no families. Some did seek help from city agencies. Violence toward women existed to some extent in all places. The young, the poor, the racially or culturally different, those without adult protectors, have always been especially at risk for this violence. But the women I have talked to, who came from poor rural families, seemed perfectly comfortable in the city and able to care for themselves without help from reformers. They seemed more interested in getting help to obtain better working conditions and wages than help with their private lives.[17]

Because I felt that the issue of violence toward women and how they felt about it was important, I decided to use my aunt's comments about safety in the city. I still hear her voice asking for privacy even though she is no longer living. I choose to compromise with her. I did include her experiences in my analysis because I think it will contribute to a historical discussion of violence toward women in the cities. I did not, however, use her name.

What rights do kin have to privacy about other events in their family history? I have an uncle who was Native American. I have found in public records that he was probably married and had a child before marrying another of my aunts. They were married by a Lutheran minister rather than Catholic clergy, who performed the ceremony for my mother and her other sisters. This aunt had died long before I began this study and we never discussed it. I discovered this information through public documents. Do I use that information as part of my family's story when I have not been close enough to that family to know how they would feel? In this case, I also used the information, but without identifying her explicitly.

A few years ago I shocked some of my aunts (now all dead) by showing how my grandmother, their mother, practiced bridal pregnancy. Grandma Tillie was a German immigrant and I explained that bridal pregnancy was a German cultural custom at that time, marrying only after a woman *knew* she was pregnant. I saw nothing wrong with the practice. My nieces and nephews thought the custom similar to today's practice. My aunts thought it contradicted their conception of their mother as very religious and therefore at odds with the conventions that they had learned as second-generation immigrants of German heritage. No sex before marriage. No premarital pregnancy without shame.

My mother's family was very poor. It was incredibly difficult for my grandmother to care for eight children when her husband, a bad second choice after her first husband died, refused to farm or to bring home money from any other work. Neither the state nor the church provided assistance for such poor families in the early twentieth century. Families have been taught to conceal such poverty in their past. Yet as a historian I think it important to reveal the lack of support that women had in caring for their children, whether married or unmarried. I have used my own family history, in part, because so much of rural women's history is invisible, because there are fewer documents than for urban women, and because family history can uncover issues that do not appear in the documents that do exist. Family history took me beyond the women who did not enter the public record, but it did not make my life as a historian easier. It forced me to come to terms with family history that some members wanted to keep private.

Where do my needs and interests end and those of others in the family begin? This is, perhaps, yet another borderland to be negotiated.

My family story crosses national and state borders, rural and urban cultural borders, and the borders between public and private. Each border shifts in importance with time and circumstance. Consciousness of these shifts for me and my readers, be they kin or colleague, helps me to make decisions about what I include and how I present it in my narrative.

POLITICIZING

I WAS TRAINED to write white male political history. I was also trained to be critical of government policies and to analyze them. I knew when I decided to write about rural women that I was abandoning most of the women's political history as I had known it. By this I mean the type of political history that I had written emphasized women's activities in demanding the right to campaign for peace, expanded rights for women workers, and for access to full citizenship rights. When researching my book *Loosening the Bonds*, I was fortunate to find Quaker women in the region who participated in the women's rights movement of the early nineteenth century. These women formed organizations to obtain those rights and described in writing their thoughts and actions.

I suppose I thought I would somehow discover similar political women in Wisconsin, despite the fact that my mother never showed much interest in formal politics beyond voting. In her personal life, she resisted a very authoritarian husband and negotiated a lifestyle that met her needs and wants perhaps as much as his. Still my mother never talked politics the way my father did when he was with his brothers. I opened a file called "politics" for my Wisconsin book and waited for it to fill. It did, eventually. But it had very little of the ordinary type of women's political history—labor activism, middle-class reform, suffrage.

I did, however, find some very important political activities by women. School superintendent Mary Bradford developed tactics to achieve reform in the schools. Nellie Kedzie Jones wrote about strategies for women to join together in clubs and to assume a greater role in family farm business decisions. Ho-Chunk administrator Mary Ann Paquette, employed by the United States Bureau of Indian Affairs, worked to achieve the best possible environment for Native children to learn, despite an authoritarian government boarding school that forced their attendance.

Among settler women in Wisconsin, I found the formal suffrage movement did very little to promote their participation in public affairs. The Royal Neighbors of America (RNA) encouraged them to organize as women and to engage in public displays of their unity. The RNA began as an auxiliary to the Modern Workmen of America (MWA) in the 1890s. It soon took on a life of its own with the goal of providing life insurance for rural women who were prohibited by insurance companies from insuring their own lives. Its social component brought women out into the streets in drill teams and on floats for community picnics and Fourth of July celebrations. Such street performance had been reserved for men previously. Benefits included those long available to men through fraternal lodges—not only payments on death, but financial support and sisterly aid in times of illness and injury, and a lively social agenda that included frequent suppers for members and their families. RNA was still selling insurance as of 2002 and some women still met, although membership was aging in most rural areas as the population aged. It would be good to know if similar groups were formed across the border in Canada.[18]

The American Society of Equity (ASE) offered even more opportunities for rural women to organize. The ASE was the largest farmers' movement in Wisconsin, Minnesota, Iowa, and other midwestern states between 1900 and 1920. It was dedicated to developing a cooperative union for producing and consuming. Like the RNA, women formed as an auxiliary, but the ASE women continued to function only as an auxiliary. While it lasted, the Women's Auxiliary of the ASE (often called simply the WA) offered a public venue to work on public political and economic issues with male family members. Women had to be related to male members to form their own auxiliaries, which meant both wives and husbands and fathers and daughters might belong.

The women of the ASE also had their own convention where they raised issues of equity within the ASE. Because the texts of these women's addresses were preserved, both in the columns of the *Equity News* and in typescript records, we can get some sense of their political interests.

Wisconsin farmer Caroline Emmerton, who worked on the family farm and with her father in the ASE, wrote to *Equity News* in 1913: "Women who share the burdens of producing wealth upon the farms, should be admitted to full fellowship in the co-operative movement." ASE women never achieved that full fellowship, but they passed resolutions opposing discrimination against women in banking and in citizenship (the Cable Act of 1922, for example, reversed earlier laws that had stripped citizenship from United States women who married aliens ineligible for citizenship). Women members claimed the right to leave their never-ending work routines to meet and discuss the "welfare of the home and the Nation." Leaders urged women to speak up in the ASE and elsewhere. Adelaine Junger, the state president of the Minnesota WA, whose husband headed their local ASE, told delegates in 1917, "You are always telling us that the hand that rocks the cradle rules the world. Now, how do you account for the fact that if we are rocking the cradle and ruling the world, women have nothing to say."[19]

Canadian historians were among the first to point out this type of grass-roots organizing among rural women. In 1976 the Toronto Women's Press published *A Harvest Yet to Reap*, in which the authors pointed out that Women's Institutes had organized in all three prairie provinces by 1910. Formed first in 1897 by the Canadian government, it expected this women's auxiliary to be passive and concern itself with educating women as homemakers. Women refused to be controlled by officials at the top and moved toward what historians have called "social feminism." They assumed the right to speak out on national issues because these issues affected conditions in their homes. Canadian women also joined the United Farm Women of Alberta and the Women Grain Growers' Association of Saskatchewan, which were women's sections of the farm protest movement there. These women did not think of themselves as a women's auxiliary but as partners in protest who preferred to work together in reforming the economic and legal conditions affecting them as rural women. The United Farm Women of Alberta also took an active part in debates on women's legal status.[20]

Rural women along with urban women organized during World War I to support reforms and tried to obtain changes in health and welfare policies at the local level. These women claimed the right to meet to exchange information on the farm economy, to discuss the politics of farm life, to organize public activities, as well as to support each other when in need. In Wisconsin, the government sponsored no rural women's groups until agricultural extension began to organize rural women into clubs in 1918. The American government expected Home Demonstration Agents to keep women focused on homemaking skills, but at least some early agents assumed these rural women's clubs would operate much as urban clubs had done, taking an interest in a wide range of social and legal reforms. When the United States extension service organized animal breeders' clubs in the 1920s, women also insisted on joining. They claimed the right to share responsibility with men for the good health of their farm animals and the economic welfare of their farms. These women saw to it that their daughters were admitted to mixed youth groups, not just to those that encouraged them to improve domestic skills. Their daughters raised and exhibited calves with the young boys, won prizes for their skill in breeding animals, and shared public recognition.[21]

I admit that I am still struggling to understand the roles of Native women in matters of political activity. Like settler communities, Native communities had a division between formal power and personal or familial power. Many Native women worked within their families and communities to see that young people would be prepared to go off reservation to obtain education if they wished. They cultivated a sense of mutuality that allowed them to influence tribal policy even if the U.S. government would not acknowledge Native women publicly as leaders and reinforced the idea that only men should participate in public debate over policy. In the end I found a kind of political bedrock provided by women despite attempts by the government and many of their kin to weaken their influence on public policies. They could not be ignored in the making of public policy even if they were, in theory, to have no influence.

CONCLUSION

WHERE IS THE PERIL? Trying to force issues upon past rural women and expecting them to respond as I would wish is futile. I have to accept the possibility that I may be wrong, that these women may, in fact, have had less influence than I think or wish they had. I tell myself that what I am doing must not be only wishful thinking, but true understanding of how women within rural communities worked for change and for continuity of cultural values and practices they considered important. Sometimes these women had little influence over activities they felt were truly important in their cultures. In this they must have felt as I often still do.

Wish me luck. The movie heroine whose perils kept me enthralled as a child seemed to end each episode strapped to the rails facing an oncoming train. Unfortunately, she had to wait for some male hero to rescue her from these perils. I've been more fortunate. As a teenager I had Nancy Drew who always solved her mysteries. And now I also have Sutty, Ursula Le Guin's intrepid Anglo-Indian observer who has reminded me of the importance of research into a culture's past. Learning the stories of western women and being an audience that asks the storytellers to retell those stories is surely worth the risks.

AUTHOR'S NOTE

This paper was first delivered at the Unsettled Past conference in Calgary, Alberta, Canada in June of 2002; in September 2003 and July 2004 it was revised, expanded, and submitted for publication in the book *One Step Over the Line: Toward a History of Women in the North American Wests.*

NOTES

1.   Joan M. Jensen, *Passage from India: Asian Indian Immigrants in North America* (New Haven, CT: Yale University Press, 1988).

2.   Joan M. Jensen, *Loosening the Bonds: Mid-Atlantic Farm Women, 1750–1850* (New Haven, CT: Yale University Press, 1986).

3.   I have used family and archival history to recreate this rural-urban migration in Joan M. Jensen, "Out of Wisconsin: Country Daughters in the City, 1910–1925," *Minnesota History* 59, no. 2 (Summer 2004): 48–61.

4.   Joan M. Jensen and Anne B.W. Effland, "Introduction," in "Rural Women," special issue, *Frontiers: A Journal of Women Studies* 22, no. 1 (2001): 1–20; Karen Dubinsky, *Improper Advances: Rape and Heterosexual Conflict in Ontario, 1880–1929* (Chicago: University of Chicago Press, 1993); Terry Crowley, "Experience and Representation: Southern Ontario Farm Women and Agricultural Change, 1870–1914," *Agricultural History* 73, no. 2 (Spring 1999): 238–51; Linda M. Ambrose and Margaret Kechnie, "Social Control or Social Feminism: Two Views of the Ontario Women's Institutes," *Agricultural History* 73, no. 2 (Spring 1999): 222–37; and Catherine A. Cavanaugh, "No Place for a Woman: Engendering Western Canadian Settlement," *Western Historical Quarterly* 28 (1997): 493–518.

5.   Joy Kogawa, *Obasan* (New York: Godine, 1982; New York: Anchor Books, 1994).

6.   Ursula Le Guin, *The Telling* (New York: Harcourt, 2000).

7.   Carol Bly, *Letters from the Country* (New York: Harper & Row, 1991).

8.   The conflict between Polish and German nuns is recounted in Michael J. Goc, *Native Realm: The Polish American Community in Portage County, 1857–1992* (Stevens Point, WI: Worzalla Publishing; Friendship, WI: New Past Press, 1992), 83–88.

9.   Red Cloud's story is in Leonard Bloomfield, *Menominee Texts*, vol. 12, *Publications of the American Ethnological Society*, ed. Franz Boas (New York: Stechert, 1928), 107. Densmore's observations are in her Diary of 1910, Densmore Papers, American Ethnological Society Records, National Anthropological Archives, National Museum of Natural History, Washington, D.C.. The reference to Manitoba is in Thomas Vennum, *The Ojibwa Dance Drum: Its History and Construction* (Washington, D.C.: Smithsonian Institution Press, 1982), 70.

10.   Lindi Schrecengost, "Tuscarora," in *The Gale Encyclopedia of Native American Tribes*, 4 vols., ed. Sharon Malinowski and Ann Sheets (Detroit, MI: Gale, 1998), 1:308.

11.   Among the early published sources of this debate are Sylvia Van Kirk, *Many Tender Ties: Women in Fur-Trade Society in Western Canada, 1670–1870* (Winnipeg, MB: Watson & Dwyer Publishing; Norman: University of Oklahoma Press, 1980); Jennifer S.H. Brown, *Strangers In Blood: Fur Trade Company Families in Indian Country* (Vancouver: University of British Columbia Press, 1980); Jacqueline Peterson and Jennifer S.H. Brown, *New Peoples: Being and Becoming Métis in North America* (Lincoln: University of Nebraska Press, 1985); Sarah Carter, "Categories and Terrains of Exclusion: Constructing the 'Indian Woman' in the Early Settlement Era in Western Canada," *Great Plains Quarterly* 13 (Summer 1993): 147–61; Jennifer S.H. Brown and Elizabeth Vibert, *Reading Beyond Words: Contexts for Native History* (Peterborough, ON: Broadview Press, 1996); and Lucy Eldersveld Murphy, "Public Mothers: Native American and Métis Women as Creole Mediators in the Nineteenth-Century Midwest," *Journal of Women's History* 14, no. 4 (Winter 2003): 141–66, continued the discussions. Heather Devine and I joined Murphy to review some of this cross-border research at the "Women's and Gender Historians of the Midwest Conference" in Chicago, Illinois, during the summer of 2004 in a session titled "Re-thinking Métis Women's Experiences."

12.   Robert Gough, *Farming the Cutover: A Social History of Northern Wisconsin, 1900–1940* (Lawrence: University of Kansas Press, 1997).

13.   Hulleah Tsinhnahjinnie, interview by author, 29 May 1999, Rough Rock, Diné Nation.

14. "Chinese in the Frontier West: An American Story," *Ancestors in the Americas*. Dir. Loni Ding. 3 Programs. PBS. KRWG-TV, Las Cruces, NM, 28 May 2002.

15. Dorothy Thoms, interview by author, 10 July 2003, Lac du Flambeau, WI.

16. Joan M. Jensen, "The Death of Rosa: Sexuality in Rural America," *Agricultural History* 67, no. 4 (Fall 1993): 1–12; "'I'd Rather be Dancing': Wisconsin Women Moving On," *Frontiers: A Journal of Women Studies* 22, no. 1 (2001): 1–20; and "Sexuality on a Northern Frontier: The Gendering and Disciplining of Rural Wisconsin Women, 1850–1920," *Agricultural History* 73, no. 2 (Spring 1999): 136–67.

17. See Jensen, "Out of Wisconsin," for a more detailed discussion of urban reformers.

18. The Royal Neighbors are still going strong. See their webpage. They have an extensive archive at their headquarters in Rock Island, Illinois.

19. *Equity News* 6, no. 5 (10 July 1913): 85. American Society of Equity, Wisconsin State Union Records, 1916–1934, Wisconsin Historical Society Archives Division, Madison, WI.

20. Linda Rasmussen, et al., *A Harvest Yet to Reap: A History of Prairie Women* (Toronto: Women's Press, 1976), 88, 122; Ambrose and Kechnie, "Social Control or Social Feminism: Two Views of the Ontario Women's Institutes," 222–37; and Cavanaugh, "No Place for a Woman," 507–12.

21. Home Demonstration Agent Mary Brady's Annual Reports of 1 December 1918 and 11 December 1919 for Marathon County, Wisconsin, explain these organizing plans. College of Agriculture, Agricultural Extension, County Agricultural Agents, Annual Reports, 1914–1952, Series 9/4/3, Steenbock Memorial Library, University of Wisconsin, Madison, WI. See the same series for the reports about the activities of women and girls in these clubs.

PUSHING THE BOUNDARIES

SOME LINES can never be crossed and can only be pushed, leaned against like a barbed wire fence: flexible to a point, but a nasty bite nonetheless. Race relations in the North American West have generally worked like this, as whites and people of colour bumped up against each other, pushed and resisted, accommodating but only to a point. It is a prickly and painful story, with more than enough villains and unhappy endings to go around.

The U.S. West in the late nineteenth century and the west coast of British Columbia in the mid-twentieth century had few things in common, but among those few things were contentious race relations and the unexpected centrality of education to political debates about race. Educators and the education system worked to build fences as often as they worked to bend them or tear them down. The articles in this section offer two new ways of seeing how educators reinforced or resisted the boundaries of race. Margaret Jacobs and Helen Raptis take us to the heart of these tensions as they discuss two different kinds of educational reformers in two very different Wests.

Shifting U.S. policies toward Native Americans gave education a new prominence after 1880, and Jacobs shows how central white women reformers were to this process. By portraying native mothers as dirty or heathens or immoral, and therefore unfit to raise their own children, white women invented and justified their "duty" to re-educate Indian children. However noble their intentions, Jacobs shows how "great white mothers," no less than the "great white father," acted as agents of white colonialism.

Edith Lucas, the subject of Helen Raptis's article, was a rather different sort of educator who spent her career challenging racist inequalities. British Columbia's physical and social geography worked against the aims of a public education system, yet Lucas devoted her career to finding ways to challenge those obstacles. Her successes might have been unexpected, given that she was only one of three women to head a branch of the province's education department when she was appointed in 1941. Raptis probes the particular bureaucratic circumstances that enabled Lucas's efforts. The challenges of serving Japanese Canadians in World War II relocation camps and, later, new immigrants who arrived after the war, illuminates racial divides in British Columbia. It also invites comparisons with the policies of the United States toward Japanese Americans during the war and would-be immigrants after 1945.

These two very different chapters in the history of western women educators are vivid reminders of the power of education to reinforce or to bridge the boundaries of race. Both articles highlight the centrality of children to the state's plans. In both cases the state was trying to punish the parents—for being Japanese and therefore a supposedly unassimilable threat to the nation, or for being native and therefore an obstacle to the nation's development. And in both instances, the profession that empowered some women could not eradicate the racism that constricted other women and their children. In neither instance could the racial boundaries be entirely overcome. Reformers could only choose to push the boundaries, push the people they sought to serve, or be pushed.

8

THE GREAT WHITE MOTHER

Maternalism and American Indian Child Removal

in the American West, 1880–1940

MARGARET D. JACOBS

IN 1892 members of the Women's National Indian Association (WNIA), a white women's reform organization, discussed the need for temperance work among the Indians. One reformer, Miss Frances Sparhawk, "suggested...finding homes in good families for Indian children exposed to the vices seen in homes of intemperance." Mrs William Green asked, "Is it necessary that Indian children should be returned to savage homes?" Mrs Plummer replied, "It is difficult and perhaps wrong to evade the parental authority brought to bear to enforce their return." Finally, Mrs Frye "spoke of the great fondness for their children which she had observed in her visits among Western tribes."[1] Neither at this meeting nor at subsequent conventions did the WNIA ever come to a consensus about whether it was proper to remove American Indian children from their homes. Their polite exchange in 1892, however, reveals a little-known aspect of white women reformers' work in the American West—their role in promoting, implementing, and sometimes challenging the policy of removing American Indian children to boarding schools. A rich historiography has accumulated regarding American Indian boarding schools and the experience of Indian children within them. Western women's historians have also studied many white women who were involved in efforts to advocate for American Indians. Yet, in general, these two historiographical tracks have developed along parallel lines without intersecting. This essay argues, however, that white women were integrally involved in the removal of American Indian children to boarding schools and that their involvement implicated them in one of the most cruel, yet largely unexamined, policies of colonialism within the American West.

Through a politics of maternalism, many white women reformers claimed for themselves the role of a "Great White Mother" who would save her benighted Indian "daughters."[2] Ironically, however, while these reformers venerated motherhood in their political discourse, they often failed to respect the actual mothering done by many native women. Instead, many reformers portrayed American Indian women as unfit mothers whose children had to be removed from their homes and communities to be raised properly by white women within institutions. And as white women articulated a sense of difference between themselves and native women as mothers, they helped to construct racial ideologies that deemed Indian peoples to be in need of "civilization" by their white benefactors. Thus, much of white women's advocacy for Indians in the West ultimately reinforced the very racial notions that contributed to the ongoing colonization of native peoples in the region.

In the late nineteenth century, after decades of Indian wars, government authorities turned to an assimilation policy as the solution to the so-called "Indian problem." Beginning about 1880, the U.S. government began to promote boarding schools for American Indian children, modeled on Captain Richard Henry Pratt's Carlisle Institute in Pennsylvania, as a primary means to assimilate Indian children.[3] By 1900 the government had established about 150 boarding schools (including twenty-five off-reservation schools) as well as another 150 day schools for about 21,500

Native American children. Officials sought to remove every Indian child to a boarding school for a period of at least three years.[4]

The subject of Indian boarding schools has generated many scholarly and autobiographical works. Some scholars have focused on the origins of assimilation policy, the founding of boarding schools, and the often oppressive nature of the schools.[5] Though critical of the overall assimilation policy, other writers have focused on the unintended and seemingly positive consequences of the boarding schools—the fostering of a strong peer culture and the accompanying emergence of a pan-Indian identity. Several scholars have demonstrated the ways in which Indian communities began to embrace and use some of the boarding schools for their own benefit and purposes.[6] This literature has had a significant impact in moving the field away from seeing Indian peoples as simply passive and reactive victims of government policy. Yet, curiously, scholars have focused only briefly on how Indian children were taken to boarding schools.[7] This essay and the larger project from which it derives—comparing the role of white women in the removal of indigenous children from their families and homes in the United States and Australia—is an attempt to examine Indian child removal not just as a by-product of the federal Indian policy of assimilation, but as a key practice of colonialism.[8]

Countless Indian autobiographies and archival records include accounts of the forced removal of children to boarding schools. For example, when she was growing up on the Navajo Reservation in the early twentieth century, Navajo (Diné) Rose Mitchell recalls: "the agents were sending out police on horseback to locate children to enroll [in school]. The stories we heard frightened us; I guess some children were snatched up and hauled over there because the policemen came across them while they were out herding, hauling water, or doing other things for the family. So we started to hide ourselves in different places whenever we saw strangers coming toward where we were living."[9] As a Hopi child growing up at the Oraibi village, Helen Sekaquaptewa remembers how, "Very early one morning toward the end of October, 1906, we awoke to find our camp surrounded by troops who had come during the night from Keams Canyon. Superintendent Lemmon...told the men...that the government had reached the limit of its patience; that the children would have to go to school....All children of school age were lined up to be registered and taken away to school....We were taken to the schoolhouse in New Oraibi, with military escort." The next day government authorities, along with a military escort, loaded Helen and 81 other Hopi children onto wagons and took them to Keams Canyon Boarding School.[10]

Yet not all Indian children's journeys to the boarding schools were forced. Rose Mitchell relates in her autobiography, in fact, that she begged her parents to let her attend school, and she describes in later chapters her willingness to allow some of her own children to attend boarding schools.[11] Many Indian authors also recount their Indian school days with a degree of nostalgia and fondness for certain aspects of their experience.[12] Over time, as many scholars have shown, some Indian communities began to send their children to the schools willingly, even to claim the schools as their own.[13]

Although some Indian peoples grew to accept the schools, we should not lose sight of the initial motivation for establishing the schools and the ways in which the government forced many Indian children to attend them. The case of the Mescalero Apaches in the late nineteenth century illustrates the coercive nature of the assimilation policy in practice. When the acting Indian Agent at the reservation in New Mexico encountered resistance from "the men to having their hair cut, and from...the women to having their children compelled to attend school....The deprivation of supplies and the arrest of the old women soon worked a change. Willing or unwilling[,] every child five years of age was forced into school."[14] To compel Indian parents to send their children to school, government agents commonly withheld annuity goods, including food, that had been guaranteed by treaties.[15]

As evident in the methods government authorities employed, the policy of Indian child removal possessed a harshly punitive quality. In fact, government efforts to punish Indians for their past resistance and to prevent their future opposition appear to have strongly motivated officials to adopt Indian child removal as policy. Government officials and reformers believed that, as the WNIA put it, "The Indians at Carlisle and Hampton [Institutes] are rising; and the more they rise there, the less uprising there will be on the Plains."[16] The government, in fact, targeted particularly recalcitrant Indian nations for child removal. The Commissioner of Indian Affairs expressly ordered Pratt to obtain children from two Great Plains reservations with hostile Indians, the Spotted Tail agency among the Lakotas and the Red Cloud agency of Lakota, Cheyenne, and Arapaho people, "saying that the children, if brought east, would become hostages for tribal good behavior."[17]

As American Indian child removal became systematized as federal policy, many white middle-class women became intent on addressing what they saw as the plight of Indian women. Several seasoned women reformers formed the WNIA in 1879, and it would play an influential role in moving the government to adopt an assimilation policy. Some of the historiography on the WNIA and other white women involved in Indian reform has characterized the women reformers in much the same terms as they represented themselves—as admirable champions for an oppressed race.[18] Yet other women's historians have critiqued the ways in which white women sought to impose a notion of nineteenth-century white middle-class ideals on Indian women.[19] Many scholars have examined how native women understood and negotiated white women's reform efforts, finding that native women strategically selected what they found useful in the white women's reform agenda.[20] In general, most women's historians have agreed that white women's reform for Indian women was well-meaning but ultimately ethnocentric and limiting. An analysis of white women's role in American Indian child removal, however, reveals a more sinister side to white women's reform efforts.

In the face of ideologies that deemed women's role to be in the home, white women often justified their political reform activity by asserting the need for their traditional feminine values and skills as mothers to be extended beyond the home into society to uplift women and children of other races and classes whom they characterized as oppressed. For example, the WNIA's president, Amelia S. Quinton, in 1899 proclaimed the WNIA to be the "nation's...motherhood for helping, saving the native race."[21] In recent decades, many women's historians have dubbed

Quinton's perspective "maternalism" and gone on to examine maternalist discourse and politics. Except for the work of Benson Tong, Karen Anderson, and Peggy Pascoe, however, most American scholarship on maternalism has focused on middle-class white women reformers in the eastern United States and their activism on behalf of poor single mothers.[22] As defined by Sonya Michel, *maternalism* is a "politics that claims a position of authority for women in their 'natural' roles as wives and mothers and seeks to protect the health and welfare of women and children."[23] Women's historians who have studied maternalism argue, as does Michel, that the "politics of maternalism...accepted the notion that mothers properly belonged at home with their children."[24] Indeed, much of the work carried out by eastern white women maternalists revolved around a campaign for mother's pensions, which enshrined in legislation the notion that poor single mothers belonged in the home with their children, not in the paid workforce.[25] As this essay makes evident, however, maternalism by white women on behalf of American Indian women in the American West manifested itself quite differently.

Instead of promoting the notion that "mothers properly belonged at home with their children," most reformers who advocated for Indian women supported the removal of the latters' children. Because motherhood and maternalism was such a crucial construct to white women's identities and reform efforts, one might expect to find such women in opposition to removing indigenous children to institutions. Instead, many reformers supported the position of reformer and government administrator Estelle Reel, who affirmed that "the Indian child must be placed in school before the habits of barbarous life have become fixed, and there he must be kept until contact with our life has taught him to abandon his savage ways and walk in the path of Christian civilization."[26]

Many white women reformers who worked as teachers or matrons within the boarding schools envisioned themselves as the children's surrogate mothers, who would properly train indigenous children for their new roles in society. Eleanor E. Bryan, a matron at the boarding school in Grand Junction, Colorado, asserted,

I would raise the dignity of matronhood and compare it favorably with that of motherhood....

[The matron] of our Indian Government schools...must try to accomplish the same for her Indian girls and boys as the sweet and noble mothers of our land achieve for their children. When a little child at the tender age of 3 or 4 years is taken from its Indian mother, placed within a boarding school, and kept there until he has attained the age of 21, if, during that period, he has been deprived of a good school mother's refining influence and love, he has necessarily missed from his character an additional force he should have known.[27]

In fact, the government's need for personnel to carry out assimilation policy dovetailed with white women's own ambitions. White women comprised the majority of boarding school employees and acted as the primary day-to-day contacts with indigenous children who had been removed and institutionalized.[28] The government seemed to agree with most reformers that middle-class white women were particularly suited to act as "the great white mother" to the Indian "race."

Some white women played an active role in Indian child removal—not just as caregivers of removed Indian children but as their actual *recruiters*, the euphemistic term reformers used. Alice Fletcher, a reformer and early ethnologist, hired on with Captain Pratt in 1882 to remove Plains Indian children to attend both Carlisle and Hampton Institutes.[29] It is hard to know exactly how many children Fletcher "recruited" over the course of several years. In 1882 alone, she removed at least thirty-six Omaha children. Amelia Stone Quinton lauded Fletcher for bringing these Omaha children to Carlisle and Hampton, "herself raising $1800 with which to meet the expenses of other Indians who begged to join the party and seek an education. She persuaded General Armstrong to undertake at the Hampton school, the training of young Indian married couples, in cottages built by funds she raised for their training, and by the success of this experiment introduced the department of Indian Home Building into the Women's National Indian Association."[30]

In her first decades of work with American Indians, Fletcher sub-scribed to a maternalist ideology, casting herself as mother to her Indian children. She repeatedly told audiences that she had first found the Omahas in 1881, "waiting for her to act 'with all the confidence of chil-dren for their mother.'"[31] Fletcher remarked in 1891, "The Indians cling to me like children, and I must and will protect them."[32] Joan Mark asserts that given Fletcher's traumatic childhood, which showed signs of abuse by a stern stepfather, she had difficulty relating to other people in any way except as "a dependent child or as a mother." Fletcher, according to Mark, felt "comfortable" in the role of mother, "bringing aid and giving instructions, firmly directing other people's lives."[33] Given the widespread practice of maternalism in the late nineteenth century among white women, Fletcher's maternalist impulses should be examined as part of a broad social current rather than simply the result of individual psycho-logical development.

Estelle Reel also played an active role in Indian child removal. Emerging from the women's reform movements of the late nineteenth century, Reel was superintendent of Indian education from 1898 to 1910. One of her major efforts in her early years in office was the promotion of a com-pulsory schooling law for Indian children. "If the Indian will not accept the opportunities for elevation and civilization so generously offered him," Reel asserted, "the strong hand of the law should be evoked and the pupil forced to receive an education whether his parents will it or not."[34]

Reel's personal papers reveal her to be a consummate politician; she carefully crafted her public image by penning articles about herself in the third person, then having journalists print them under their own by-lines. In fact the paper that printed her obituary prefaced it by say-ing, "This article was written several years ago by [Estelle Reel], with the apparent intention that it be used as her obituary. It was completed except for a blank space where the date of her death was to be inserted."[35]

In her articles, Reel frequently referred to her role in taking Indian children to boarding schools. She often portrayed herself as a motherly figure who could easily convince the Indians to relinquish their children to her care. In "Woman's Great Work for the Government," she claimed, "Miss Reel is popular with the Indians. She is known as the 'Big White Squaw from Washington.' So fond of her are some of the Indians that they are willing she should take their children away, and one Indian woman insisted that she should carry a pair of fat papooses to President Roosevelt. She doesn't have to bribe the Indians with promises and presents to send their children to school now."[36]

Many other white women also actively promoted the removal of Indian children. Cora Folsom, for example, who worked in the Indian education division of Hampton Institute in Virginia for over forty years, made over a dozen "recruiting" trips to the west.[37] Thus white women played an integral role in the practice of Indian child removal, both as active "recruiters" and as the caretakers of the children removed to the schools.

Both reformers and officials employed a rhetoric of humanitarianism in justifying their policies of Indian child removal. They routinely characterized the removal of American Indian children as an act of benevolence aimed at "rescuing the children and youth from barbarism or savagery."[38] This rhetoric rested on a racialized discourse that deemed indigenous peoples to be lower on the scale of humanity than white Anglo-Saxon, middle-class Protestants. As both reformer and anthropologist, Alice Fletcher played a key role in constructing this racial hierarchy. For example, in her lecture "Our Duty Toward Dependent Races," Fletcher asserted,

In this march of progress thru the centuries the victory has been with the race that was able to develop those mental forces by which man is lifted above his natural life, which enabled him to discern the value of work....

Looking back over the ages, there is little doubt that to the white race belong the great achievements of human progress. The religions of the world have sprung from this branch of the human family, the higher arts and sciences are its children, and it is also true that this race has held possession of the best portions of the Earth's surface.[39]

While Fletcher and other reformers associated the "white race" with "the great achievements of human progress," they often equated indigeneity with backwardness, poverty, immorality, and parental neglect. For example, the missionary John Lowrie argued that civilization "can only be effectually accomplished by taking [Indian children] away from the demoralizing & enervating atmosphere of camp life & Res[ervation] surroundings."[40]

Agreeing with Lowrie, many white women maternalists supported indigenous child removal based on several powerful and interrelated tropes. First, they portrayed indigenous women as the powerless drudges of their men. Mary Dissette, who worked for many years at Zuni Pueblo in New Mexico, pronounced that in Indian tribes "the male is supreme and all that contributes to his comfort or pleasure is his by right of his male supremacy. The female is taught this from early childhood."[41] Helen Gibson Stockdell, a missionary for the Trinity Mission at Lemhi Indian Agency, in Idaho, believed that Indian women "make slaves of themselves for the men."[42]

This trope rested on another related one: the belief that sexual and marriage practices among indigenous groups particularly degraded indigenous women. In Alaska, the WNIA alleged, "girls from a few months old and upward are sold as wives," and "girls from 10 to 15 years of age are rented by their parents to white men." WNIA reformers took over the custody of some of these Native Alaskan girls whom they considered "deserted child-wives" because, they argued, such girls were "without kindred who care for [their] welfare."[43] Helen Tyler Griswold claimed with alarm that among the Utes "Polygamy is common....The men marry at 18 and the women at from 13 to 16. A Ute squaw who remains unmarried at 20 is a pariah in the tribe, and is well on the way toward being condemned to death as a witch ere she is 40 years old."[44]

In other contexts, white women reformers represented indigenous women not as the passive victims of indigenous male sexual privilege but as sexually immoral actors. In a typical comment, Amelia Quinton, the WNIA's president, claimed that Navajo women were promiscuous and therefore "good morals are next to impossible. For children from such homes, the day school can do far less than the boarding school."⁴⁵ Many reformers believed it was essential to remove Indian children, particularly girls, from their families to protect them from what white women perceived to be oppression, abuse, and immorality.

Some white women regularly employed another common trope, alleging that indigenous women did not know how to properly care for their children. Catherine Haun, for example, as she traveled across the continent to settle in the West in the nineteenth century, described a scene of an American Indian mother and her child: "The squaws carried their pappooses [sic] in queer little canopied baskets suspended upon their backs by a band around their heads and across their foreheads. The infant was snugly bound, mummy-fashion with only its head free. It was here that I first saw a bit of remarkable maternal discipline, peculiar to most of the Indian tribes. The child cried whereupon the mother... stood it up against a tree and dashed water in the poor little creature's face."⁴⁶ White female reformers and missionaries expressly condemned the use of cradle boards, these "queer little canopied baskets." One missionary, Miss Howard, wrote, "I found a woman with a sick baby not yet three weeks old; of course it was strapped upon a board; and it was moaning with fever."⁴⁷

Reformers also implied that indigenous women did not provide a proper home for the upbringing of their children. Loulie Taylor, describing her experiences at Fort Hall Reservation in Idaho, wrote,

we had...the advantage of seeing just how the Indian lives in his tepee, and what had been the life of these children before coming to the mission.

What a contrast! The smoking fire in the centre of the tepee, and on it the pot of soup stirred by the not over-clean squaw, whose black hair fell in as she stirred; men, women, and children lolling on the ground, a few blankets the only furnishing of the tepee; and then to think of the neat, comfortable home at the mission, with the uplifting of its daily prayer offered to their Great Spirit, our Heavenly Father. We realized what a blessed work these faithful missionaries...were doing in giving to these poor, neglected children...some of the light and blessing that had been given to them.[48]

Thus, at the same time as they sacralized and politicized white motherhood, many white women activists pathologized indigenous motherhood, constructing indigenous mothers as degraded and sexually immoral, misguided and negligent, and even cruel and unloving. Such representations contributed to justifying state policies of indigenous child removal. "If we do not educate Indian children to our civilized life," argued the WNIA, "their parents will continue to educate them to their savagery."[49]

To many in the WNIA, and other reformers, Native American mothers had failed to fulfill their motherly role. It was thus necessary for white women to step in as surrogate mothers. As one WNIA article put it, the Indian "girl has never had a bath in her life; she has never slept in a bed or eaten from a table; was never in childhood taught to say a prayer or tenderly kissed and snugly tucked into bed....She does not know a single letter of the alphabet, or a hymn. She has never been to a birthday party, nor a Thanksgiving dinner, nor a Fourth of July celebration; she has never heard the sweet story of Christmas....Who will carry the light to these dark sisters?"[50] Many WNIA members and other reformers believed that white women, in either institutions or homes, would make better mothers for Indian children, at least until Indian women could be properly trained. Mary Watkins, a teacher at Mesa Grande School in California, fantasized, "Think of sending *true* women to teach the poor, ignorant, mothers whose babies are born but to *die* or grow up to disgrace their Ind. homes after $2000.00 of Govt money has been spent on them."[51] As this comment suggests, many reformers seemed to evince little sympathy for the Indian women who were asked to relinquish their children. Indeed, many white women activists deemed Indian children to be free for the taking. In an article she titled "My Indian Children," Alice Larery, a missionary at the Fort Hall Reservation in Idaho, asserted, "No longer are [the Indian children at the mission school] merely the children of a few isolated Indian tribes but...[they] have become members of the world's great family of children."[52]

Maternalist discourse also rested on the notion that proper motherhood formed the basis for a sound, efficient, and orderly nation. Thus many reformers believed that if they could remove young indigenous girls and train the future mothers of an indigenous nation, they could radically transform the Indian "race." Estelle Reel argued, "industrial training will make...the Indian girl more motherly. This is the kind of girl we want—the one who will exercise the greatest influence in moulding [sic] the character of the nation....Thus will they become useful members of this great Republic, and if compulsory education is extended to all the tribes, there is little reason to doubt that the ultimate civilization of the race will result."[53]

Reel's comment reveals another underlying motivation for promoting indigenous child removal: to make indigenous children "useful." Through the "outing" program at most boarding schools, instructors trained the children in various menial labor, then placed them as servants and laborers in white homes.[54] One white woman corresponded with Alice Fletcher and Carlisle founder Richard Henry Pratt about obtaining an Indian girl as a domestic:

> I was seriously thinking it was my duty to take one of the Indian girls—to train for usefulness....Miss Fletcher wants Mary to have a friend that will be a mother to her perhaps you had as well send her to me....
>
> There is only one thing that I do require, that is, an honest girl....She is but a child and needs play as well as work. And several years more experience before I would expect her to bear any responsibility.
>
> I do not keep servants, my family is small....I can teach the Indian girl all the lessons she will want. And I will teach her all kinds of house work by having her assist me, also dress-making.[55]

Although this woman cloaked her request in the rhetoric of maternalism, her remarks that she would "train [the girl] for usefulness" and would eventually expect the girl to bear some responsibility in the household, as well as her admission that she does not keep servants, all point to this woman's intention to employ the girl as a servant, for little or no pay. Hence, alongside a desire to punish Indians for their recalcitrance and to prevent their future resistance, a belief that it was necessary to bring Indian people into the modern American economy as cheap laborers also motivated the enactment of child removal policy.

Although white women reformers emphasized the differences between native and white women as mothers, they also routinely evoked motherhood as the universal experience of women that bonded them together. Thus reformers proceeded as if they knew what Indian women wanted and that they could speak for them. Yet, as Patricia Hill Collins points out, "racial domination and economic exploitation profoundly shape the mothering context, not only for racial ethnic women in the United States, but for all women." Collins identifies three main issues that challenged the maternal empowerment of women of color: the struggle to control their own bodies, namely whether to become a mother; "the process of keeping the children that are wanted"; and "pervasive efforts by the dominant group to control children's minds." Collins astutely acknowledges that "physical and/or psychological separation of mothers and children, designed to disempower individuals, forms the basis of a systematic effort to disempower racial ethnic communities."[56] As Collins's analysis makes clear, motherhood, far from uniting women across lines of color and race as a universalizing experience of women, became a primary force for dividing white from indigenous women.

Many indigenous women fiercely resisted the removal of their children. Among the Mescalero Apaches, "Every possible expedient was resorted to by [the women] to keep their children from school." Agent V. E. Stottler claimed that Mescalero women "would brazenly deny having children despite the evidence of the accurate census rolls and the ticket on which they had for years drawn rations. Children were hidden out in the bushes; drugs were given them to unfit them for school; bodily infirmities were simulated, and some parents absolutely refused to bring their children in."[57]

Many Indian women also bitterly contested the maternalism of white women. Her public persona as the "Big White Squaw" aside, Estelle Reel admitted in her reports the great difficulty she had working with Indian women. The Indian mother, she wrote, is "much more opposed, as a rule, to allowing her children to accept the white man's civilization, than is her spouse."[58]

One Omaha woman, Lena Springer, wrote in great anger to Captain Pratt at Carlisle regarding what she considered to be Alice Fletcher's role in the death of her daughter, Alice, at Carlisle: "I had [no] idea of sending my children there, but Miss Fletcher got round Elsie and persuaded her to go and then Alice wanted to go with her. It was Miss Fletcher's doings that they went, and now my husband is grieving all the time. I do not see why the government put so much power and confidence in Miss Fletcher, as we think she does no good to the Omahas but much harm. She cannot be trusted. Please do not deny our request, if you have any regard to a Father's and Mother's feelings."[59]

Other Native American women tried to appeal to white women using the very maternalist rhetoric favored by them. The Indian secretary of a local branch of the Woman's Christian Temperance Union in Warm Springs, Arizona, for example, emphasized that "the mother, be she white or red, has the same heart-aches over her boys."[60] Clearly motherhood became a primary battleground upon which native women fought to secure their rights to raise their own children. In doing so, they articulated a new type of maternalism. As Lisa Udel reveals in her article "The Politics of Native Women's Motherwork," motherhood and maternal politics have thus been integral to Native American women's activism.[61]

As can be seen in the debate among white women of the WNIA that opened this article, some white women themselves contested the removal of indigenous children. White women care-givers and the indigenous children in their care often developed complicated relationships that sometimes undermined colonial aims. Miss Worden, who worked at the Santee School in Nebraska, believed that her "highest aim is to fit these boys and girls for work among their own people. We do not believe in having them absorbed in Eastern civilization. We propose to teach the fifth commandment at Santee. And how can boys and girls honor their fathers and mothers if they are not where their parents are?"[62] Within these "intimacies of empire," as Ann Laura Stoler refers to them, colonial strategies of rule were enacted and reinforced, but they were also constantly negotiated and contested. Indeed, through their interactions with indigenous children and women, many white women developed their own critique of indigenous child removal policy, and by the mid-twentieth century they had taken steps to oppose it formally.[63]

A few critics also came from the ranks of women reformers who had no association with the boarding schools. Constance Goddard DuBois became involved in the Connecticut Indian Association, a branch of the WNIA. In 1897 she ventured to southern California for a summer, where she worked to help the Luiseño and Diegueño peoples of the area. Thereafter she spent almost every summer with them and almost every winter advocating their cause. In the early 1900s, she conducted fieldwork on the Diegueños and other Mission Indians off and on under the direction of Alfred Kroeber, head of the University of California's Anthropology Department in Berkeley and also recorded songs and myths and collected "specimens" for Clark Wissler of the American Museum of Natural History.[64] Through her close association with a group of indigenous people, and no doubt through her exposure to the new anthropological theories of her day that promoted cultural relativism over a belief in cultural evolution, DuBois became vehemently opposed to child removal. She particularly targeted Reel's proposed compulsory schooling law for Indian children.

Instead of relying on maternalist rhetoric, DuBois used what we might call a materialist and an equal rights discourse to counter Reel's proposed law. First she argued that the law would "turn the Indians into a scattered remnant of homeless vagrants, cheap laborers, or paupers, without land." Then, she challenged the notion that extending a compulsory school law to Indians was no different than similar laws for white children. "No white child can be forcibly carried from his home without the consent of his parents," wrote DuBois, "taken to a school inaccessible and remote, and kept a prisoner under close restraint during the term of his education." She concluded, "let no law be placed upon our statute books that shall mete out to the Indian treatment which would outrage every sentiment of humanity if applied to ourselves." DuBois agreed that Indians should be provided with education, but she insisted that "the school should be brought to the Indian, not the Indian to the school."[65] DuBois' opposition to Indian child removal did not stem from maternalist sentiment, which emphasized differences between native and white women; instead, it was grounded on the principle that Indian children and their parents deserved equal treatment under the law.

As we scrutinize the work of white women who advocated the removal of American Indian children to institutions, we can see the inadequacy of maternalism as it is currently defined. For all their maternal rhetoric, the maternalism practiced by many reformers in the West looked quite different from that practiced by white middle-class women in the East. Rather than promoting a motherly and domestic role for American Indian women, reformers participated in dispossessing Indian women of their children. White women maternalists in the West did not "accept the notion that mothers properly belonged at home with their children." This does not mean, however, that the concept of maternalism is useless in studying western women's history; rather, it reveals the limited nature of many current studies of maternalism and the need to redefine and transform the concept. Further work on maternalism in the West will challenge dominant narratives about maternalism that have derived primarily from studies in the East and have largely focused on class rather than race. The distinctive racial dynamics of the American West—that complicate and transcend the black-white dichotomy of the East—shifted maternalist efforts in a different direction than similar campaigns in the East that targeted working-class women.

At the same time, attention to maternalism may enrich the field of western women's history. The politics of maternalism enabled many white women in the West to gain positions of power and influence, but often this was achieved by denying the actual practice of mothering to the Indian women for whom they supposedly spoke. Through their work on behalf of Indian women in the West, reformers often couched their work in benevolent and charitable terms. As historians we would be shirking our scholarly responsibilities if we simply accepted these women's pronouncements as proof of their concern for Indian women. A steadfast belief in the superiority of white womanhood and a desire to reform and control Indian women permeated white women's pronouncements about rescue work.

For some historians it is easy to dismiss these charges by asserting the "woman of her times" argument. As this argument goes, these women were simply unable to escape the racial ideologies of their era, and it is therefore wrong to judge them by contemporary racial ideologies. Yet the active participation of white women in shaping these ideologies, as well as the presence of other white women activists who challenged maternalist practices, shows that the "woman of her times" argument holds up little better than the man of his times thesis. As Louise Newman puts it, "racism was not just an unfortunate sideshow in the performances of feminist theory. Rather it was center stage: an integral constitutive element."[66] Notions of racial difference and hierarchy were fundamental to white women's maternalism in the American West and, in turn, maternalism was a key element in shaping racial ideologies in the late nineteenth and early twentieth centuries.

NOTES

1. *Annual Meeting and Report of the Women's National Indian Association*, hereafter cited as *WNIA Report* (Philadelphia: December 1892).

2. This phrase derives from an article in the WNIA's publication, *The Indian's Friend* 16, no. 5 (January 1904): 5. The WNIA must have been playing on the common phrase the "Great White Father," a term the government often asserted that Indians used to refer to the federal government.

3. Richard Henry Pratt, *Battlefield and Classroom: Four Decades with the American Indian, 1867–1904*, ed. Robert Utley (New Haven, CT: Yale University Press, 1964).

4. David Wallace Adams, *Education for Extinction: American Indians and the Boarding School Experience, 1875–1928* (Lawrence: University Press of Kansas, 1995), 57–58.

5. See, for example, Robert Utley's introduction to Pratt, *Battlefield and Classroom*; Frederick E. Hoxie, *A Final Promise: The Campaign to Assimilate the Indians* (Lincoln: University of Nebraska Press, 1984); Francis Paul Prucha, *The Great Father: The United States Government and the American Indians*, 2 vols. (Lincoln: University of Nebraska Press, 1984); Adams, *Education for Extinction*; Robert A. Trennert Jr, *The Phoenix Indian School: Forced Assimilation in Arizona, 1891–1935* (Norman: University of Oklahoma Press, 1988); Clyde Ellis, *To Change Them Forever: Indian Education at the Rainy Mountain Boarding School, 1893–1920* (Norman:

University of Oklahoma Press, 1996); Scott Riney, *The Rapid City Indian School, 1898–1933* (Norman: University of Oklahoma Press, 1999). More general histories of Indian education that include material on the boarding schools include Margaret Connell Szasz, *Education and the American Indian: The Road to Self-Determination, 1928–1973* (Albuquerque: University of New Mexico Press, 1974); David H. DeJong, *Promises of the Past: A History of Indian Education in the United States* (Golden, CO: Fulcrum Publishing, 1993).

6. See, for example, Brenda Child, *Boarding School Seasons* (Lincoln: University of Nebraska Press, 1998); Tsianina Lomawaima, *They Called it Prairie Light: The Story of the Chilocco Indian School* (Lincoln: University of Nebraska Press, 1994); Michael Coleman, *American Indian Children at School, 1850–1930* (Jackson: University Press of Mississippi, 1993); Hazel Hertzberg, *The Search for an American Indian Identity: Modern Pan-Indian Movements* (Syracuse, NY: Syracuse University Press, 1971). For a beautifully produced and moving book that represents all these approaches, see Margaret Archuleta, Brenda Child, and Tsianina Lomawaima, eds., *Away from Home: American Indian Boarding School Experiences, 1879–2000* (Phoenix, AZ: Heard Museum, 2000).

7. I became interested in this issue when I began to do comparative work on indigenous and women's history in the United States and Australia. On my first research trip to Australia in 1998, I became immediately aware of the "Stolen Generations" as a contemporary and a historical issue in Australia. Aboriginal historians' focus on the actual removal of children helped shift my attention away from looking at assimilation policy or boarding schools, per se, to the actual motivation, justification, and practice of white officials taking Indian children to boarding schools. Moreover, my research into indigenous child removal in Australia encouraged me to look at the Indian boarding school system as a practice of colonialism, not just as American federal Indian policy.

8. See Margaret Jacobs, "Indian Boarding Schools in Comparative Perspective: The Removal of Indigenous Children in the U.S. and Australia, 1880–1940," in *Boarding School Blues: Revisiting American Indian Educational Experiences*, ed. Clifford E. Trafzer, Jean A. Keller, and Lorene Sisquoc (Lincoln: University of Nebraska Press, 2006); Margaret Jacobs and Victoria Haskins, "Stolen Generations and Vanishing Indians: The Removal of Indigenous Children as a Weapon of War in the United States and Australia, 1870–1940," in *Children and War*, ed. James Marten (New York: New York University Press, 2002), 227–41.

9. Rose Mitchell, *Tall Woman: The Life Story of Rose Mitchell, a Navajo Woman, c. 1874–1977*, ed. Charlotte J. Frisbie (Albuquerque: University of New Mexico Press, 2001), 61–62.

10. Helen Sekaquaptewa, *Me and Mine: The Life Story of Helen Sekaquaptewa*, as told to Louise Udall (Tucson: University of Arizona Press, 1969), 91–92.

11. Mitchell, *Tall Woman*.

12. See, for example, Francis La Flesche, *The Middle Five: Indian Schoolboys of the Omaha Tribe*, foreword by David Baerreis (1900; repr., Lincoln: University of Nebraska Press, 1978); Sekaquaptewa, *Me and Mine*; Polingaysi Qoyawayma (Elizabeth Q. White), *No Turning Back: A Hopi Indian Woman's Struggle to Live in Two Worlds*, as told to Vada Carlson (Albuquerque: University of New Mexico Press, 1964).

13. See, for example, Child, *Boarding School Seasons*; Lomawaima, *They Called it Prairie Light*; Ellis, *To Change Them Forever*; Riney, *Rapid City Indian School*.

14. *The Indian's Friend* 10, no. 1 (September 1897): 10. See also Eve Ball, with Nora Henn and Lynda A. Sánchez, *Indeh: An Apache Odyssey* (Norman: University of Oklahoma Press, 1988), 219. Ball notes that at Mescalero, after building a boarding school on the reservation in 1884, agents took children forcibly to school and "incarcerated" them there; "To prevent their escape the windows were nailed shut" (219).

15. See, for example, Leo Crane, *Indians of the Enchanted Desert* (Boston: Little, Brown, and Company, 1925); Henrietta Mann, *Cheyenne-Arapaho Education, 1871–1982* (Niwot: University Press of Colorado, 1997).

16. *The Indian's Friend* 3, no. 4 (December 1890): 4.

17. Pratt, *Battlefield and Classroom*, 202; also see 220 and 227.

18. See particularly Valerie Mathes, "Nineteenth-Century Women and Reform: The Women's National Indian Association," *American Indian Quarterly* 14 (1990): 1–18; Helen Wanken, "'Woman's Sphere' and Indian Reform: The Women's National Indian Association, 1879–1901" (PhD diss., Marquette University, 1981); Valerie Mathes, *Helen Hunt Jackson and Her Indian Reform Legacy* (Austin: University of Texas Press, 1990).

19. See Helen M. Bannan, *'True Womanhood' on the Reservation: Field Matrons in the U.S. Indian Service*, Southwest Institute for Research on Women, working paper no. 18 (Tucson, AZ: Women's Studies, 1984); Lisa Emmerich, "'To respect and love and seek the ways of white women': Field Matrons, the Office of Indian Affairs, and Civilization Policy, 1890–1938" (PhD diss., University of Maryland, 1987); Theda Perdue, "Southern Indians and the Cult of True Womanhood," in *The Web of Southern Social Relations*, ed. Walter J. Fraser et al. (Athens: University of Georgia Press, 1985), 35–51.

20. Lisa Emmerich, "'Right in the Midst of My Own People': Native American Women and the Field Matron Program," *American Indian Quarterly* 15 (Spring 1991): 201–16; Carol Devens, "'If We Get the Girls, We Get the Race': Missionary Education of Native American Girls," *Journal of World History* 3, no. 2 (1992): 219–37; Peggy Pascoe, *Relations of Rescue: The Search for Female Moral Authority in the American West, 1874–1939* (New York: Oxford University Press, 1990); Lomawaima, *They Called It Prairie Light*; Devon Mihesuah, *Cultivating the Rosebuds: The Education of Women at the Cherokee Female Seminary, 1851–1909* (Urbana: University of Illinois Press, 1993); Margaret Jacobs, "Resistance to Rescue: The Indians of Bahapki and Mrs. Annie E. K. Bidwell," in *Writing the Range: Race, Class, and Culture in the Women's West*, ed. Elizabeth Jameson and Susan Armitage (Norman: University of Oklahoma Press, 1997), 230–51; Margaret Jacobs, *Engendered Encounters: Feminism and Pueblo Cultures, 1879–1934* (Lincoln: University of Nebraska Press, 1999); Amanda J. Cobb, *Listening to Our Grandmothers' Stories: The Bloomfield Academy for Chickasaw Girls, 1852–1949* (Lincoln: University of Nebraska Press, 2000).

21. *The Indian's Friend* 1, no. 5 (January 1889).

22. Benson Tong, *Susan La Flesche Picotte, M.D.: Omaha Indian Leader and Reformer* (Norman: University of Oklahoma Press, 1999), 61; Karen Anderson, "Changing Woman: Maternalist Politics and 'Racial Rehabilitation' in the U.S. West," in *Over the Edge: Remapping the American West*, ed. Valerie J. Matsumoto and Blake Allmendinger (Berkeley: University of California Press, 1999), 148–59; Pascoe, *Relations of Rescue*. For literature on maternalism in the East, see Sonya Michel, *Children's Interests/Mothers' Rights: The Shaping of America's Child Care Policy* (New Haven, CT: Yale University Press, 1999); Gwendolyn

Mink, *The Wages of Motherhood: Inequality in the Welfare State, 1917–1942* (Ithaca, NY: Cornell University Press, 1995), especially 5–6; Linda Gordon, *Pitied But Not Entitled: Single Mothers and the History of Welfare* (Cambridge, MA: Harvard University Press, 1994); Molly Ladd-Taylor, *Mother-Work: Women, Child Welfare, and the State, 1890–1930* (Urbana: University of Illinois Press, 1994); Alexis Jetter, Annelise Orleck, and Diane Taylor, eds., *The Politics of Motherhood: Activist Voices from Left to Right* (Hanover, NH: University Press of New England, 1997); Theda Skocpol, *Protecting Soldiers and Mothers: The Political Origins of Social Policy in the United States* (Cambridge, MA: Belknap Press of Harvard University Press, 1992).

23.   Michel, *Children's Interests/Mothers' Rights*, footnote 16, 311.

24.   Michel, *Children's Interests/Mothers' Rights*, 3. See also 18–20, 73–87, 89.

25.   See particularly Gordon, *Pitied But Not Entitled*.

26.   "Her Work for the Indians: Miss Estelle Reel, Genl Supt of Indian Schools, talks interestingly regarding Indian matters, Favors compulsory education and industrial training," n.d., Estelle Reel papers, H6–110, Box 1, "Articles" folder, Wyoming State Archives, Cheyenne, WY (hereafter cited as WSA).

27.   Report of the Supt of Indian Schools for 1898 (Washington: Government Printing Office, 1899), 33, Papers of Estelle Reel, MS 120, Box 2, Folder 70, Eastern Washington State Historical Society, Northwest Museum of Arts and Culture (formerly Cheney-Cowles Museum), Spokane, WA (hereafter cited as EWSHS).

28.   Adams, *Education for Extinction*, 82–94.

29.   "Draft of publication, 'Going Home with the Indians,'" 1882, Alice Fletcher Papers, Box 6, National Anthropological Archives, Smithsonian Institution, Washington, D.C. (hereafter cited as Fletcher Papers).

30.   Amelia Stone Quinton, "Care of the Indian," in *Woman's Work in America*, ed. Annie Nathan Meyer (New York: Henry Holt and Company, 1891), 376.

31.   Quoted in Joan Mark, *A Stranger in Her Native Land: Alice Fletcher and the American Indians* (Lincoln: University of Nebraska Press, 1988), 107–08.

32.   Quoted in Mark, *A Stranger in Her Native Land*, 197.

33.   Mark, *A Stranger in Her Native Land*, 3–16, quote 14.

34.   Report of the Supt of Indian Schools (Washington: Government Printing Office, 1900), 15, Papers of Estelle Reed, MS 120, Box 2, Folder 72, EWSHS. For more on Reel, see K. Tsianina Lomawaima, "Estelle Reel, Superintendent of Indian Schools, 1898–1910: Politics, Curriculum, and Land," *Journal of American Indian Education* 35 (Spring 1996): 5–31.

35.   "Mrs. Cort Meyer Prepared Own Obituary," *Toppenish (WA) Review*, 6 August 1959, Papers of Estelle Reed, MS 120, Box 1, Folder 6, EWSHS.

36.   "Woman's Great Work for the Government," draft of article, n.d., Estelle Reel Papers, Box 1, "Articles" folder, WSA.

37.   Donal F. Lindsey, *Indians at Hampton Institute, 1877–1923* (Urbana: University of Illinois Press, 1995), 199, 250–52.

38.   T. J. Morgan, "Indian Contract Schools," *Baptist Home Mission Monthly* 18, no. 2 (December 1896): 392.

39. Alice Fletcher, "Our Duty Toward Dependent Races," draft of lecture, n.d., Fletcher Papers, Box 11.
40. Quoted in Devens, "If We Get the Girls," 158.
41. Dissette to Miss Willard, 3 March 1924, Indian Rights Association papers (Glen Rock, NJ: Microfilming Corporation of America, 1975), reel 40.
42. Helen Gibson Stockdell, "Woman's Work for Women on the Lemhi Reservation," *The Woman's Auxiliary* 67, no. 1 (January 1902): 53–54, MSS 91, Box 64, Archives of the Episcopal Diocese of Idaho, Special Collections, Boise State University, ID.
43. *The Indian's Friend* 1, no. 7 (March 1889).
44. Helen Tyler Griswold, "Utes of Colorado," *Los Angeles Sunday Times*, 26 January 1902, Papers of Estelle Reed, Box 1, Folder 41, Newspaper Clippings, EWSHS.
45. *The Indian's Friend* 3, no. 10 (June 1891): 4.
46. Catherine Haun, "A Woman's Trip Across the Plains in 1849," in *Women's Diaries of the Westward Journey*, ed. Lillian Schlissel (New York: Schocken Books, 1982), 174–75.
47. WNIA *Report* (Philadelphia: November 1884), 33–34.
48. Loulie Taylor, "What a Diocesan Officer Saw on an Indian Reservation," *The Woman's Auxiliary* 67, no. 3 (March 1902): 208–09, MSS 91, Box 64, Archives of the Episcopal Diocese of Idaho.
49. *The Indian's Friend* 2, no. 2 (October 1889): 1.
50. *The Indian's Friend* 12, no. 4 (December 1899): 10.
51. Letter from Mary Watkins, Mesa Grande school, to Charles Lummis, 1 August 1902, Papers of Charles Lummis, 1.1.4543, Braun Library, Southwest Museum, Los Angeles, CA.
52. Alice M. Larery, "My Indian Children," *The Woman's Auxiliary* 87 (October 1922): 653, MSS 91, Box 64, Archives of the Episcopal Diocese of Idaho.
53. "Her Work for the Indians: Miss Estelle Reel, Genl Supt of Indian Schools, talks interestingly regarding Indian matters, Favors compulsory education and industrial training," n.d., Estelle Reed Papers, Box 1, "Articles" folder, WSA.
54. Adams, *Education for Extinction*, 54, 155–63.
55. Mrs Young to Pratt, 12 May 1883, Fletcher Papers, Box 1.
56. Patricia Hill Collins, "Shifting the Center: Race, Class, and Feminist Theorizing about Motherhood," in *Mothering: Ideology, Experience, and Agency*, ed. Evelyn Nakano Glenn, Grace Chang, and Linda Rennie Forcey (New York: Routledge, 1994), 45, 53, 54.
57. *The Indian's Friend* 10, no. 1 (September 1897): 10.
58. Untitled draft of article, beginning with "She believes in giving the Indian child...," n.d., Estelle Reed Papers, Box 1, "Articles" folder, WSA.
59. James Springer and Lena (signed Lenora) Springer to Pratt, 20 November 1883, Fletcher Papers, Box 1.
60. WNIA *Report* (1897), 26.
61. Lisa J. Udel, "Revision and Resistance: The Politics of Native Women's Motherwork," *Frontiers: A Journal of Women Studies* 12, no. 2 (2001): 43–62.
62. *Proceedings of the 11th Annual Meeting of the Lake Mohonk Conference of the Friends of the Indian* (1893), 30.

63. See Ann Laura Stoler, *Carnal Knowledge and Imperial Power: Race and the Intimate in Colonial Rule* (Berkeley: University of California Press, 2002); Ann Laura Stoler, "Tense and Tender Ties: The Politics of Comparison in North American History and (Post) Colonial Studies," *Journal of American History* 88, no. 3 (2001): 829–66.

64. See Kroeber to DuBois, 4 December 1902, 15 December 1902, 22 December 1902, 6 Feb 1903, 19 Feb 1903, 14 March 1903, 19 May 1906, 29 May 1906, 20 and 27 June 1906; and Wissler to DuBois, 23 June 1905; in Constance Goddard DuBois Papers, #9167, Division of Rare Books and Manuscript Collections, Cornell University Library, Ithaca, New York, formerly located at the Huntington Free Library, Bronx, New York.

65. Constance Goddard DuBois, "A New Phase of Indian Education," *City and State* (7 June 1900): 363; Papers of Estelle Reed, Box 1, Folder 30, Newspaper Clippings, EWSHS. As far as I can tell, DuBois was successful in preventing the passage of this law.

66. Louise Michele Newman, *White Women's Rights: The Racial Origins of Feminism in the United States* (New York: Oxford University Press, 1999), 183.

9

PUSHING PHYSICAL, RACIAL, AND ETHNIC BOUNDARIES

Edith Lucas and Public Education in British Columbia, 1903–1989

HELEN RAPTIS

THE HISTORY OF EDUCATION in British Columbia is marked by the boundaries of race, ethnicity, gender, and geography. Although historians have devoted much time to documenting British Columbia's turbulent ethnic, racial, and gendered relations, they have spent comparatively little time examining the impact of the province's forbidding geographic landscape on its education system.[1] Yet since the inception of the first public schools in 1872, government and school officials have wrestled with the challenge of providing educational services to a thinly scattered population across a province that measures almost one million square kilometres [386,000 square miles] in size.[2]

Due to the isolation of British Columbia's scattered communities, government officials have had difficulty attracting and retaining competent teachers, a situation first dubbed "the rural-school problem" in 1920 by

Kelowna school inspector Alexander Lord. Edith Ethel Lucas was one such educator, and her story is one of sustained resistance to the geographic, racial, and ethnic constraints that bounded her students' lives. In 1941 Lucas became one of only three women then directing a branch of government within British Columbia's education department.[3] She presided over the department for twenty-four years and managed some of the province's greatest social challenges. An immigrant to Canada herself, Lucas used her power within the bureaucracy to ameliorate the lives of learners who, without the branch, might have been denied an education due to barriers of race, geography, and ethnicity. During her tenure as director of the high school correspondence branch from 1941 to 1963, she ensured provision of educational opportunities for British Columbians in remote regions of the province, including Japanese-Canadian high-schoolers who were interned during World War II, and to the steady flow of postwar immigrants who fled their war-ravaged homelands to settle in British Columbia. Lucas's desire to assist the province's marginalized populations was surely shaped by her personal experiences of leaving Ireland to settle in a city whose inhabitants, at the time, were considered "more English than the English."[4] This paper will argue that Lucas's ability to exercise so much autonomy in government was facilitated by the era in which she worked—a time described by British Columbia historian Tom Fleming as the "Imperial Age of School Administration." By the time Lucas left government in 1963, this age of autonomy was already beginning to dissolve.

Edith was the fourth of seven children born to John and Mary Ann Lucas in Ireland in 1903 (Figure 9.1). Her father, a gamekeeper on a moderately-sized estate, was left crippled after a serious bout of rheumatic fever in 1910. Realizing that his gamekeeper now presented him with a liability, the earl of the estate provided the Lucas family with passage to Canada. On 18 April 1913, the outcast Lucas family set sail for Canada on the *Empress of Ireland* and arrived in Victoria, British Columbia, on 2 May.[5] Reflecting on the experience later in life, Edith's older sister Evylin described the scene like this: "With 'homesick feet upon a foreign shore' five of us children stood in a row on the sidewalk outside the CPR (Canadian

FIGURE 9.1: *The Lucas Family in County Wicklow, Ireland, 1908. Edith is standing, second from right.* [Courtesy: Barry and Lorna Lucas]

Pacific Railway) station building on Belleville Street in Victoria. Mother, with Rachel and Edwin in tow and Father hobbling along behind on his two walking sticks, had gone to look for a place to spend the night." Curious passers-by questioned the children's unsupervised presence and, upon learning that they had just arrived from Ireland, responded with a "sniff," for, according to Evylin, Victoria at the time "was largely populated by zealots who referred to England as home."[6]

John Lucas was never able to secure work after arriving in Canada, and Mary Ann supported the family by undertaking housecleaning and sewing repairs for the well-to-do families in Victoria. All the while, she encouraged her children to study hard in order to escape the poverty to which the family was now destined. Edith attended North Ward Elementary

School, noted at the time for its diverse immigrant population, and graduated from Victoria High School at age 16. (Figure 9.2) Her teachers immediately recognized her academic capabilities and encouraged her in several academic areas.[7] As testimony to her hard work, Lucas's name still adorns the honour roll in the school's main entrance way. The commentary in her high school yearbook describes Edith as an outstanding scholar, "inclined to studious habits" with a mind "set to learn and know."[8]

After graduating high school, Lucas earned first-class honours degrees in French and Latin from the University of British Columbia and received the Governor General's Gold Medal—the province's highest recognition of academic excellence.[9] From 1925 to 1927, Lucas taught French at Powell River High School. She then applied for and won the Nichol Scholarship for postgraduate studies. In three short years, Lucas completed her doctoral studies in French Literature at the Sorbonne in Paris (Figure 9.3a and 9.3b). With her PhD in hand, Lucas returned to Canada and "stepped right in to the depression of the thirties."[10] Reflecting on her experiences several decades later, Lucas reported that she was "lucky" to have been granted the "only French position in the province at Chilliwack."[11]

In 1931 Lucas accepted a teaching post at Prince Rupert High School and became principal in 1933. During her time in Prince Rupert the provincial Department of Education contracted Lucas to write the first senior French language correspondence courses.[12] The high school correspondence branch had been established in 1929 to reduce the educational inequities that had plagued the geographically remote areas of the province since public education's inception in 1872. Because many settlers would not have ventured into British Columbia's hinterland without assurance of education for their children through correspondence, the branch became instrumental in the government's plan to address the "rural-school problem."[13] Lucas's success in course writing led to an invitation to join the British Columbia education department full time in

>FIGURE 9.2: *Edith Lucas at graduation in 1920.*
[*Courtesy: Barry and Lorna Lucas*]

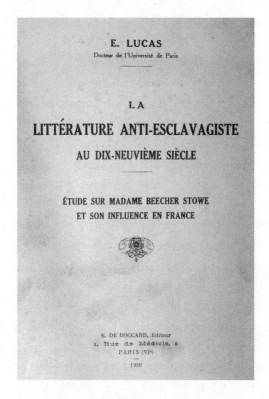

E. LUCAS
Docteur de l'Université de Paris

LA
LITTÉRATURE ANTI-ESCLAVAGISTE
AU DIX-NEUVIÈME SIÈCLE

ÉTUDE SUR MADAME BEECHER STOWE
ET SON INFLUENCE EN FRANCE

E. DE BOCCARD, Éditeur
1, Rue de Médicis, 1
PARIS (VIᵉ)
1930

FIGURE 9.3B:
Copy of the cover of Edith Lucas's doctoral thesis completed in 1930.
[*Courtesy: Barry and Lorna Lucas*]

1937, and in 1941 she replaced John Gibson as director of the high school correspondence branch.[14]

Within a year of assuming the directorship, Lucas found herself at the centre of a political tempest over the internment and education of children of Japanese ancestry. Anti-Japanese sentiment in British Columbia began long before World War II, and it tended to rise during economic downturns, periods of increasing immigration, and contentious provincial elections.[15] By January 1942, after the bombing of Pearl Harbor and Canada's declaration of war against Japan, anti-Japanese hysteria was sweeping the province.[16] In the face of severe public pressure, the Canadian government moved the first 100 men of Japanese ancestry from coastal areas to work camps in the province's interior on 24 February 1942.[17]

<FIGURE 9.3A: *Edith Lucas while studying in Paris, 1929.*
[*Courtesy: Barry and Lorna Lucas*]

At that time, the Dominion government assigned the men "to work on completing the Jasper–Prince George Highway, a road considered vital to British Columbia's defence,"[18] but it did not intend to relocate women or children. However, events unfolded rapidly over the next eleven months and culminated in the evacuation of some 22,000 people of Japanese descent from British Columbia's coast, including women and children. As its first step, the federal government established the British Columbia Security Commission (BCSC) and granted it the power to remove any residents of Japanese origin from their homes. Next, the BCSC transported Japanese evacuees from coastal points outside British Columbia's lower mainland to Hastings Exhibition Park in Vancouver before sending them to abandoned mining towns and other interior areas.[19] The government confiscated their property and belongings and sold them below market value without consent or recompense. Some 6,000 Japanese Canadians were "repatriated" to Japan, and most of the rest were scattered throughout Canada. Few remained in British Columbia.[20]

The internment seriously compromised the education of children of Japanese ancestry. There were just over 5,000 Japanese-Canadian school-children in British Columbia when the government announced the evacuation.[21] They had earned reputations as intelligent, hardworking, and well-behaved, and as having above-average ability.[22] Reports indicated that the Japanese-Canadian students were active in every aspect of school life and that they mixed well with other children.[23] Teachers spoke fondly of them, and as anti-Japanese sentiments increased in 1938, the British Columbia Teachers' Federation defended them, condemning anti-Japanese policies as "dangerous and un-Christian."[24]

Teachers and administrators who worked closely with Japanese pupils also sought to protect their students' academic status. In April 1942, A. R. MacNeill, the popular principal of Richmond High School, informed S. J. Willis, provincial superintendent of education, about his concern over the rumoured removal of the Japanese students. He inquired about the proper procedures regarding students qualifying for university entrance and argued that if the students were evacuated they should be given correspondence courses free-of-charge for the remainder of the term to maintain their academic studies.[25] Unfortunately, the province's elected politicians were not as supportive of the rights of these pupils as their educators. The provincial government maintained that because the Canadian government had orchestrated the relocation, the province was no longer accountable for educating children of Japanese ancestry.[26] This was partly because many schools in British Columbia's interior did not have the physical capacity to accommodate the Japanese children, although small numbers of children were "squeezed in" where possible.[27] One of the provincial government's main concerns, however, appears to have been a lack of human and financial resources. Provincial education minister H.G. Perry estimated that the total cost of educating the roughly 5,000 interned school children would be $343,026—of which approximately $230,000 was needed to construct new buildings in the interior settlements and the rest going to "teachers' salaries, textbooks and incidental expenses." Perry and his government argued that such spending was unwarranted because the evacuees no longer paid property taxes, and revenues could not be generated to cover the costs of their education.[28]

The educational problems generated by the war did not affect the interned students alone. Throughout World War II, education in British Columbia suffered from a lack of human, financial, and material resources. In August 1942, the *Vancouver Sun* newspaper announced that the "harassed Department of Education" was making "desperate attempts to secure instruction" for children whose teachers had left teaching to support the war effort. Approximately fifty provincial schools were closed as the Department of Education "appealed for former teachers in British Columbia and elsewhere to help out."[29] By refusing to permit British Columbia teachers to instruct Japanese children removed to rural areas, the department was following its strategy to "conserve teachers" for geographic areas with higher student populations.[30] In an attempt to ensure equity throughout the province, the government encouraged students in teacher-less schools to enrol in correspondence courses through the education department's high school correspondence branch, which had increased its production capacity significantly to meet increased demand. In light of these widespread hardships, Roman Catholic,

Anglican, and United Church groups offered to provide facilities for educating some of the evacuee children.[31]

The anti-Japanese sentiment characteristic of some politicians and the public has been well documented in British Columbia's historical literature. Less well documented, to this point, is the history of various civil servants who were sympathetic to the Japanese evacuees. According to historian Patricia Roy's account of the internment, it was "the civil servants in the BCSC [who] persuaded their political masters that educating children in the interior housing settlements was 'a matter of fairness to the future of the children' and 'in the national interest.'"[32]

As a result of this persuasion, on 18 September 1942, the BCSC announced that it would cover the cost of elementary correspondence programs for interned pupils up to grade eight. Letters between Anna Miller, director of elementary correspondence, and the BCSC indicate that as early as July 1942 the branch provided marking support for lessons in elementary literature, language, health, social studies, grammar, and general science.[33] Although Miller informed the BCSC education supervisors on several occasions that course materials and supplies could not be sent, this was usually due primarily to shortages brought about by the war.[34] For example, in August 1942, Miller wrote to W.S. McRae, supervisor at Hastings Park, Vancouver, stating that she could not provide a marking key for mathematics because the branch had only one set. Two months later the branch notified the BCSC that compasses had become scarce and it was likely that drawing sets would no longer be supplied.[35]

According to historical accounts of the internment, "high school students—[unlike their primary counterparts] were [officially] left to fend for themselves through correspondence courses—at their own expense."[36] These accounts appear at odds with education department correspondence involving Edith Lucas. In April 1942, provincial School Superintendent S.J. Willis informed Lucas that the BCSC was considering correspondence education for high school students in the internment camps.[37] By 15 June 1942, plans were approved for correspondence courses to "be made available to high school students under supervisors, with regular hours of study."[38] Under this arrangement—referred to as the "group plan"—individual correspondence lessons were purchased and shared by several high school students working under the supervision of Japanese-Canadian adults.[39] This "user pay" system was not unlike the system in which many non-interned, geographically remote students enrolled in and paid for their own high school correspondence courses.[40] At the start of the war in 1939, the branch enrolled 3,101 such pupils. The total jumped to 3,982 in 1941 as branch staff scrambled to accommodate additional pupils whose schools were forced to close due to wartime teacher shortages.

By February 1943, Edith Lucas and Cleo Booth of the BCSC's department of education were corresponding at length regarding arrangements for end-of-year high school examinations.[41] What is significant is that Lucas and her colleagues set and marked the exams, not only for official registrants of the correspondence courses, but also for evacuee students who were not officially registered.[42] Furthermore, in response to a request from internee supervisors, Lucas and her staff postponed end-of-year examinations from June to August to accommodate evacuees whose educational progress had been hampered by administrative "delays and other handicaps" brought about by the evacuation.[43]

Lucas and her colleagues in the high school correspondence branch were not alone in their attempts to help evacuee children. Other educational administrators within and outside of government also assisted in the interned children's education. In a letter to Anna Miller in October 1942, the BCSC indicated that 2,418 elementary school students had benefited from correspondence lessons at a total cost to the commission of $3,344.45.[44] Later that month, J. A. Tyrwhitt of the BCSC wrote to Miller to indicate his need for approximately 1,020 copies of *New Canadian Arithmetic,* books I and II, because the books were no longer prescribed by the provincial education department and were no longer available from the textbook branch.[45] Since correspondence lessons were based on the old texts, Miller appealed to H. N. MacCorkindale, superintendent of the Vancouver schools, to supply the branch with any surplus copies.[46] Nine days later superintendent MacCorkindale had provided Miller with 1,020 texts that she then dispatched to the BCSC.[47] Further assistance was extended to the evacuees by the faculty of the Vancouver Normal School, which held annual summer school courses at New Denver to accommodate BCSC school instructors.[48]

Nevertheless, British Columbia's original government policy was to not educate the evacuees and to not permit them to enrol in correspondence courses.[49] However, the Department of Education was caught in a dilemma, with educators such as Lucas, Miller, and MacCorkindale working to overcome the political circumstances to assist the interned students where they could. Although the full extent of these educators' efforts may never be known, a letter from Harry Shibuya, supervisor at Alpine Lodge, Cascade, British Columbia, suggests that Lucas's assistance was much appreciated. Shibuya stated that Mr J.A. Tyrwhitt of the Securities Commission had "acquainted" him with the effort Lucas had "exerted on behalf of the Canadians of Japanese parentage, in the matter of their education." He closed the letter by extending thanks for her "sense of justice and fair-play," which she showed on "behalf of the unfortunate children of evacuees."[50]

British Columbia's historical literature has failed to record the positive contributions of Lucas and her colleagues to the education of the Japanese Canadians. Instead, accounts have focused more directly on the actions of the individuals who orchestrated the internment for reasons that might include racism, military defence, or political expediency. In contrast, the actions of Lucas and her colleagues seemed motivated by a strong sense of social justice, civic fair-mindedness, and a general sense of fair play. These same qualities served Lucas well after the war, when the deputy minister of education assigned her the daunting task of coordinating the province's English and citizenship program during a high point of immigration. Lucas met the challenge and built the high school correspondence branch into an internationally prominent organization.

As part of the post–World War II resettlement of "displaced persons," an influx of non-English-speaking European women came to British Columbia in 1948 seeking work as domestics. The Young Women's Christian Association (YWCA) in Victoria, where most of these women settled, "undertook, among other things, to give them classes in English." YWCA volunteer teachers were soon overwhelmed by the magnitude of this work and the insufficient resources, prompting the deputy minister of education to request that Edith Lucas "take charge of the program in English and citizenship." Lucas quickly recognized the sheer size of her task, given that there was "no book on the market suitable for teaching English to intelligent adults of a different tongue."[51]

Although Lucas, a seasoned teacher and principal, had never before prepared lessons for adult immigrants, she knew that these learners' needs differed from those of children and adolescents. Finding no suitable resources for adult language instruction, Lucas devised her own strategy. On her own time, Lucas organized a class of newcomers to meet in the evenings in her Victoria office, a stone's throw from the YWCA. Once she had prepared and "field tested" a lesson with her own students, she had it "mimeographed and sent to the YWCA classes for their guidance."[52] Each lesson consisted of formal grammar, a vocabulary drill, and pages of reading material about a fictitious immigrant family experiencing various aspects of Canadian life, such as government, banking, property insurance, taxation, home decoration, and workmen's compensation. Lucas eventually compiled her lessons into three books, titled *English I*, *English II*, and *English III*, each totalling over 300 pages.[53] Upon completing *English II*, students could sit an examination that entitled them to a "certificate in English and citizenship," a document they could present as evidence of readiness when applying for Canadian citizenship. By 1954, more than 115 night schools in British Columbia used Lucas's textbooks, which she described as "instruction in the rights and responsibilities of Canadian citizenship, teaching at the same time practical English and our customs."[54]

As a member of the Canadian Citizenship Council and an immigrant to Canada, Lucas considered the development of English I, II and III to be a "labour of love"—produced mostly during her own unpaid time. Lucas preferred to produce her own materials from scratch, because she disapproved of many of the available language texts whose pages were rife with stilted, formulaic phrases, such as "the pen of my aunt is under the lilac bush." Lucas took pride in her works, which were well illustrated with phrases built around the daily needs of the adult immigrants "in the sort of sequence in which they are naturally spoken."[55]

Although first, and always, an educational civil servant, Lucas proved adept at marketing her books and the other resources produced by the correspondence branch. With information provided to her by the federal citizenship and immigration branch, Lucas would write to Canadians sponsoring or employing recent immigrants offering them her English language materials. By the early 1950s, Lucas was receiving requests for her materials from public school teachers.[56] Requests for advice and materials came from as far away as California.[57] In keeping with official custom of the time, Lucas replied personally to all requests, sending information and materials free of charge.

During her time as a civil servant, Lucas's department handled over 100 different correspondence courses that addressed a range of topics, from "mathematics and French to steam engineering and frame house construction."[58] A 1941 survey of student enrolment revealed a highly varied student population, of which 27 per cent of the 3,900 enrolled were adults. Many of Lucas's enrollees were physically marginalized from mainstream society, including 273 who were confined to hospital beds, 104 British Columbia Penitentiary inmates, and twenty inmates from Oakalla prison. A further eighteen students were enrolled from the Girls' Industrial Home, and twenty were from New Haven, the boys' home. Many enrollees not only passed their senior matriculation, they won scholarships and other honours.[59] One such award went to Horst Kramer, a Rumanian immigrant, who won a major university entrance bursary for academic excellence in 1956. He had taken all of his high school education through correspondence—beginning with Lucas's *English for New Canadians I* and *II*.[60]

Lucas's correspondence branch also helped many new settlers endure the hardships experienced in some of Canada's most geographically remote areas. In 1941 there were but three non-native women in the Fort Selkirk district of the Yukon. They would meet on Thursdays to sew and knit for soldiers abroad. One of the three, Mrs Kathleen Cowaret, took up the study of French through Lucas's correspondence education school. Through Cowaret's "delightful, chatty letters," Edith Lucas learned of the lonely life in the Far North for those women whose husbands were absent on trapping expeditions for lengthy periods of time.[61] Over the years, appreciative parents informed Lucas that "without assurance of education for their children through correspondence, they never would have ventured into remote parts of B.C."[62]

By the time Edith Lucas left the civil service in 1963 (Figure 9.4), she had spent over 25 years building the reputation of British Columbia's high school correspondence branch into "international prominence."[63] The branch grew from serving 2,000 pupils in 1940 to 20,000 in 1963.[64] Through her publications in scholarly journals and talks she provided when invited, on topics such as correspondence schooling and adult education, Lucas extolled the virtues of correspondence education.[65] At the 1959 annual convention of the British Columbia School Trustees Association, Lucas lectured school board members that, in regular schools, "there is a tendency among students to expect the teacher to do all the work."[66] In contrast, Lucas asserted, correspondence students "learn quickly to stand on their own feet," and in so doing develop perseverance and willpower that helps them excel at their studies.[67] Not surprisingly, Lucas sought to foster in her students the discipline and resourcefulness that she had learned as an immigrant child—the qualities that had taken her from a working-class neighbourhood in Victoria to the classrooms of the Sorbonne, and the independent mindedness that she had demonstrated throughout her career in government as she sought to surmount the rural, racial, and ethnic inequalities that divided British Columbia society as surely as its great mountain ranges. In 1960, as testament to her international stature, the Ford Foundation selected her to set up a correspondence program for the West Indies.[68]

In 1963, Lucas decided to retire early for two reasons. Troubled throughout her life with a serious goitre, her physical energies had begun to wane. In addition, the provincial education department was on the verge of reorganization. She felt that after such a reorganization, the branch should be in the hands of younger people. With her usual blend of

humour and humility, she noted that she did not want to "crawl to the goal post."[69]

On 3 February 1989—two months before her eighty-sixth birthday—Edith Ethel Lucas passed away.[70] Newspapers noted her passing with headlines lauding her as a "famous educator" with an "honoured career."[71] These records testify that Lucas was an outstanding scholar and a pioneering educator who made significant contributions to provincial, national, and international communities. No doubt Lucas's first-hand experiences as an Irish immigrant in the very "English" city of Victoria, and later on as a graduate student alone in France, fostered her empathy for "outsiders." And, like other educational and social reformers of her time, Lucas was evidently motivated by a strong desire to serve others.[72]

Edith Lucas's story provides contemporary researchers with a window into a forgotten world of educational government—a world controlled almost entirely by "professionals" inside the system.[73] Lucas's ability to "push" the physical, racial, and ethnic boundaries that would otherwise restrict the lives of her learners was greatly facilitated by the "unbounded" autonomy that government granted civil servants of the time. From her position inside the education department, Lucas could, and did, bypass government's official policy not to educate the Japanese-Canadian internees. As a senior civil servant, she could, and did, make decisions that mattered to youngsters, as she did in postponing the 1943 year-end examinations. Unable to find a suitable textbook with which to teach English to adult immigrants, she simply created her own. In short, Lucas's achievements on behalf of the province's marginalized learners were the consequences of a combination of two factors: a socio-political context that bestowed unbridled latitude on senior civil servants, and Lucas's personal drive to improve the lives of British Columbia's marginalized learners, among whom she had once been counted.

<FIGURE 9.4: *Edith Lucas in 1965, two years after her retirement.*
[*Courtesy: Barry and Lorna Lucas*]

AUTHOR'S NOTE

I would like to express my gratitude to Dr Thomas Fleming, whose support has been invaluable. I would also like to thank Dr Jean Barman for encouraging me to explore Edith Lucas's life further. Thanks are also due to Edith Lucas's nephew, Barry Lucas, and his wife, Lorna. Without their generosity I would not have been able to understand Edith's personal drive to better the lives of immigrants.

Segments of this chapter were originally published in my article "A Tale of Two Women: Edith Lucas, Mary Ashworth, and the Changing Nature of Educational policy in British Columbia, 1937–1977," *Historical Studies in Education* 17, no. 2 (Fall 2005). These segments are reprinted with permission.

NOTES

1.   See, for example, Peter Ward, *White Canada Forever: Popular Attitudes and Public Policy Toward Orientals in British Columbia*, 2nd ed. (Montreal: McGill-Queen's University Press, 1990), and Timothy J. Stanley, "White Supremacy and the Rhetoric of Educational Indoctrination: A Canadian Case Study," in *Children, Teachers and Schools in the History of British Columbia*, ed. Jean Barman, Neil Sutherland, and J. Donald Wilson (Calgary: Detselig Enterprises, Ltd., 1995). For historical perspectives on gender and British Columbia's public schools, see Thomas Fleming and Carolyn Smyly, "The Diary of Mary Williams: A Cameo of Rural Schooling in British Columbia, 1922–1924," in *Children, Teachers and School*, ed. Barman, Sutherland, and Wilson, 259–84; and Thomas Fleming and Madge Craig, "Anatomy of a Resignation: Margaret Strong and the New Westminster School Board, 1911–1915," in *School Leadership: Essays on the British Columbia Experience, 1872–1995*, ed. Thomas Fleming (Mill Bay, BC: Bendall Books, 2001).

2.   Province of British Columbia, *A Legacy for Learners: The Report of the Royal Commission on Education* (Victoria, BC: Queen's Printer, 1988), 26. See also F. Henry Johnson, *A History of Public Education in British Columbia* (Vancouver: UBC Press, 1964), and Thomas Fleming, "The Imperial Age and After: Patterns of British Columbia School Leadership and the Institution of the Superintendency, 1849–1988," *BC Studies: The British Columbian Quarterly* 81 (1989): 50–76. See also Thomas Fleming and Tara Toutant, "A Modern Box of Magic: School Radio in British Columbia, 1927–1984," *Journal of Distance Education* 10, no. 1 (Spring 1995): 53–73.

3.   In 1941, men held seven of the existing directorships. Numbers compiled from tables in British Columbia Department of Education, *Public Schools of the Province of British Columbia, 1970–71* (Victoria, BC: Queen's Printer, 1972).

4.   See Terry Reksten, *More English than the English: A Very Social History of Victoria* (Victoria, BC: Orca Books, 1986).

5.   I am thankful to Barry and Lorna Lucas, Edith's nephew and his wife, for this information provided during an interview on 21 June 2004.

6.   Quoted from Evelyn (Lucas) Fleischmann, *"Leaves from An Old Tree": Memoirs of the Lucas Family*. Memoirs provided to me by Barry and Lorna Lucas. Evelyn's perceptions of the English in Victoria may have been influenced by her feelings for the earl for whom her

father had worked until he was crippled; the earl was originally from England. According to Evelyn's description, "He and his Countess and their family spent part of the year on the Continent and in England, went up to Lond[on] for the 'Season,' spent some time in their mansion in County Wicklow and spent most of the shooting season (August) at a secluded country house not far from where we lived. With their entourage of servants they moved from place to place, depending on the season, or on their fancy." Quoted from Fleischmann, *"Leaves from an Old Tree,"* 16.

7.   Fleischmann, *"Leaves from an Old Tree,"* 16.

8.   *The Camosun, 1919–1920,* 26. Courtesy of the Victoria High School Archives.

9.   "Personality of the Week: Dr. Edith E. Lucas," *Victoria Colonist,* 3 February 1952, 16.

10.   "Personality of the Week: Dr. Edith E. Lucas," *Victoria Colonist,* 3 February 1952, 16. The title of her dissertation was "La Littérature Anti-Esclavagiste au Dix-Neuvième Siècle: Etude sur Madame Beecher Stowe et Son Influence en France, 1930." Dissertation provided to me by Barry and Lorna Lucas.

11.   "Personality of the Week: Dr. Edith E. Lucas," *Victoria Colonist,* 3 February 1952, 16.

12.   "Personality of the Week: Dr. Edith E. Lucas," *Victoria Colonist,* 3 February 1952, 16.

13.   Jean Barman notes that the province's establishment of correspondence education was rooted in a broader post–World War I social reform movement that sought, among other goals, to improve the welfare of children. Jean Barman, *The West Beyond the West: A History of British Columbia,* rev. ed., (Toronto: University of Toronto Press, 1995), 226–29.

14.   "Dr. Edith Lucas Gets School Post," *Vancouver Sun,* 20 August 1941, 9.

15.   Ward, *White Canada Forever,* 128–29.

16.   Peter W. Ward, "British Columbia and the Japanese Evacuation," *Canadian Historical Review* 57, no. 3 (September 1976): 298. See also Patricia Roy, "B.C.'s Fear of Asians," in *A History of British Columbia—Selected Readings,* ed. Patricia Roy (Toronto: Copp Clark Pitman, Ltd., 1989), 291.

17.   "Plan to Move 100 More Japs Every 2 Days," *Vancouver Daily Province,* 24 February 1942, 8.

18.   "Advance Party of Japanese Leaves Vancouver for Jasper," *Vancouver Sun,* 24 February 1942, 17.

19.   Thomas Berger, "The Banished Japanese Canadians," in *Ethnic Canada,* ed. Leo Driedger (Toronto: Copp Clark Pitman Ltd., 1987), 387. See also Ninette Kelly and Michael Trebilcock, *The Making of the Mosaic: A History of Canadian Immigration Policy* (Toronto: University of Toronto Press, 1998), 294; "Entire Japanese Community Will Take Over Ghost Town," *Vancouver Daily Province,* 12 June 1942, 5.

20.   Toyo Takata, *Nikkei Legacy: The Story of Japanese Canadians from Settlement to Today* (Toronto: New Canada Publications, 1983), 141.

21.   H. K. Hutchison, "Dimensions of Ethnic Education: The Japanese in British Columbia, 1880–1940," (master's thesis, University of Victoria, 1972).

22.   See M. Ashworth, *The Forces Which Shaped Them* (Vancouver: New Star Books, 1979); J. Dahlie, "The Japanese in B.C.: Lost Opportunity? Some Aspects of the Education of Minorities," *BC Studies: The British Columbian Quarterly* 8 (Winter 1970–1971): 3–16. Patricia Roy, "'Due to Their Keenness': The Education of Japanese Canadian Children in the British Columbia Interior Housing Settlements During World War Two," in *Children, Teachers and Schools,* ed. Barman, Sutherland, and Wilson, 375–92.

23. In addition, see Peter L. Smith, *Come Give a Cheer! One Hundred Years of Victoria High School, 1876–1976* (Vancouver: Evergreen Press, 1976), 103. See also, "A Lesson in Brotherhood: Children of 31 Nations Mix Happily in Strathcona School," *Vancouver Daily Province*, 22 January 1940, 20.

24. "Isn't It About Time That We Spoke Up?" Editorial, *The B.C. Teacher* 18 (October 1938): 287.

25. MacNeill to Willis, High School Correspondence, 1942–1951, File: Japanese GR1219, British Columbia Archives, Victoria, BC (hereafter cited as BCA).

26. Ken Adachi, *The Enemy That Never Was* (Toronto: McClelland and Stewart Inc., 1991), 263–65; Patricia Roy, et al., *Mutual Hostages: Canadians and Japanese During the Second World War* (Toronto: University of Toronto Press, 1990), 131; Roy, "Due to Their Keenness," 375; "Japanese Education Held Ottawa Charge," *Victoria Colonist*, 20 August 1942, 2; "Japanese Exodus Speeds Up to Meet Sept. 30 Deadline," *Vancouver Sun*, 1 September 1942, 13.

27. Alice Glanville, *Schools of the Boundary: 1891–1991* (Merritt, BC: Sonotek Publishing Ltd., 1991), 87. See also Willis to Tyrwhitt, Correspondence Courses, GR1219, BCA; "Special Grade Schools Planned for Jap Children at B.C. Points," *Vancouver Daily Province*, 15 June 1942, 5. A severe teacher shortage in British Columbia due to the war also prevented the government from hiring extra Caucasian teachers in the interior settlements. See Roy, "Due to Their Keenness," 379.

28. "Japanese Education Held Ottawa Charge," *Victoria Colonist*, 20 August 1942, 2.

29. "Government Widens Plan to Recruit More Teachers: Stopgap Methods May Assist Rural Schools To Combat Shortage," *Vancouver Sun*, 28 August 1942; "Japanese Education Held Ottawa Charge," *Victoria Colonist*, 20 August 1942, 2.

30. "Government Widens Plan to Recruit More Teachers: Stopgap Methods May Assist Rural Schools To Combat Shortage," *Vancouver Sun*, 28 August 1942, 17.

31. Jorgen Dahlie, "The Japanese in BC: Lost Opportunity? Some Aspects of the Education of Minorities," *BC Studies: The British Columbian Quarterly* 8 (Winter, 1970–1971): 13; Glanville, *Schools of the Boundary*, 86–89.

32. Roy, "Due to Their Keenness," 376.

33. Miller to McRae, 29 July 1942; Miller to Tyrwhitt, 6 August 1942; Miller to McRae, 6 August 1942, Correspondence Courses, GR1219, BCA.

34. See Unsigned letter to Tyrwhitt, 9 October 1942, Correspondence Courses, GR1219, BCA.

35. See Unsigned letter to Tyrwhitt, 9 October 1942, Correspondence Courses, GR1219, BCA.

36. Ken Adachi, *The Enemy That Never Was* (Toronto: McClelland and Stewart Inc., 1991), 263–64; "Japs' Chances for Education Better Than B.C. Whites," *Vancouver Daily Province*, 22 May 1943, 8. Adachi is not alone in concluding that high school students were left to "fend for themselves." See J.D. Wilson, "Review of *The Forces Which Shaped Them: A History of Minority Group Children in British Columbia*," *BC Studies: The British Columbian Quarterly* 46 (1980): 91–96.

37. Willis to Lucas, 12 April 1942, Correspondence Courses, GR1219, BCA.

38. "Special Grade Schools Planned for Jap Children at B.C. Points," *Vancouver Daily Province*, 15 June 1942, 5; "Will Educate the Japanese," *Victoria Colonist*, 19 September 1942, 1; "Japs' Chances for Education Better Than B.C. Whites," *Vancouver Daily Province*, 22 May 1943, 8.

39. Lucas to Takimoto, 29 September 1942, Correspondence Courses, GR1219, BCA.

40. "Japs' Chances for Education Better Than B.C. Whites," *Vancouver Daily Province,* 22 May 1943, 8.

41. Booth to Lucas, 1 February 1943, Correspondence Courses, GR1219, BCA. Other letters exist in the file as well.

42. Lucas to Booth, 4 February 1943, GR0128, BCA.

43. Booth to Lucas, 26 April 1943; Lucas to Booth, 11 May 1943, GR1219, BCA.

44. Tyrwhitt to Miller, 22 October 1942, GR1219, BCA. Noted that the BCSC provided lessons to teachers and not directly to individual students, who were not officially permitted to enrol.

45. Tyrwhitt to Miller, 6 October 1942, GR1219, BCA.

46. Miller to MacCorkindale, 6 October 1942, GR1219, BCA.

47. MacCorkindale to Miller, 15 October 1942, GR1219, BCA.

48. Roy, "Due to Their Keenness," 379.

49. Willis to Tyrwhitt, 6 October 1942; Miller to Tyrwhitt, 19 October 1942, and Miller to Ovans, General Secretary of the BCTF, 20 February 1945, GR1219, BCA.

50. Shibuya to Lucas, 10 November 1942. Correspondence Courses. GR1219, BCA.

51. "Book Enables 'New Canucks' To Outshine 'Old Canadians,'" *Vancouver Sun*, 7 January 1956, 11.

52. "Book Enables 'New Canucks' To Outshine 'Old Canadians,'" *Vancouver Sun*, 7 January 1956, 11.

53. Published in Vancouver by Dent and Sons, the three books' dedications read as follows: "To all non-English speaking immigrants, this book is lovingly dedicated. May they find in its pages the help they need in learning our language, and may skill in our language enable them to prosper in this land of freedom and opportunity."

54. "Personality of the Week: Dr. Edith E. Lucas," *Victoria Colonist*, 3 February 1952, 16.

55. "Personality of the Week: Dr. Edith E. Lucas," *Victoria Colonist*, 3 February 1952, 16.

56. Couling to Lucas, 30 October 1959; Anderson to Lucas, 22 March 1950, GR1219, BCA.

57. Lucas to Allyn, 3 April 1950, GR1219, BCA.

58. "Personality of the Week: Dr. Edith E. Lucas," *Victoria Colonist*, 3 February 1952, 16.

59. "Spirit of Yukon Maintains Wide Interest in World Affairs," *Vancouver Daily Province,* 13 September 1941, 14.

60. "Book Enables 'New Canucks' To Outshine 'Old Canadians,'" *Vancouver Sun*, 7 January 1956, 11.

61. "Spirit of Yukon Maintains Wide Interest in World Affairs," *Vancouver Daily Province*, 13 September 1941, 14.

62. "B.C. Correspondence Course Students Soon Learn to Stand on Their Own Feet," *Victoria Colonist*, 22 October 1959, 7.

63. "Lighting a Torch for Learning," *Victoria Times*, 25 October 1963, 4.

64. "Dr. Edith Lucas Resigns From B.C. School by Mail," *Vancouver Province*, 23 October 1963, 3.

65. Lucas to Allyn, 3 April 1950, GR1219, BCA; "Famous B.C. Educator Closing Honored Career," *Victoria Colonist*, 23 October 1963, 8.

66. "B.C. Correspondence Course Students Soon Learn to Stand on Their Own Feet," *Victoria Colonist,* 22 October 1959, 7.

67. "B.C. Correspondence Course Students Soon Learn to Stand on Their Own Feet," *Victoria Colonist,* 22 October 1959, 7.

68. "Woman Educator Gets Assignment in West Indies," *Victoria Times,* 7 December 1960, 21.

69. "Famous B.C. Educator Closing Honored Career," *Victoria Colonist*, 23 October 1963, 8.

70. Lucas-Wells, Edith—Obituary, *Victoria Times-Colonist*, 23 February 1989.

71. See, for example, "Top Educator to Quit B.C.'s Biggest Class," *Victoria Times,* 23 October 1963, 17; "Famous B.C. Educator Closing Honored Career," *Victoria Colonist,* 23 October 1963, 8.

72. American historians David Tyack and Elisabeth Hansot show that women were winning an increasing share of leadership positions during the Progressive Era of the early twentieth century. See David Tyack, *Managers of Virtue: Public School Leadership in America, 1820–1980* (New York: Basic Books, Inc., 1982), 187. For a more recent story of one such reformer in Canada, see Anna Lathrop, "Portrait of 'A Physical': A Case Study of Elizabeth Pitt Barron (1904–98)," *Historical Studies in Education* 11 (1999): 144. In the U.S. see also Kathleen Weiler, "Corinne Seeds and the Avenue 21 School: Toward a Sensuous History of Citizenship Education," *Historical Studies in Education* 12 (2002): 191–218.

73. According to Lucas's nephew, Barry Lucas, the autonomy that Edith exercised within government was "much discussed in the family." Among the family members it was generally felt that Lucas was much more competent than her political superiors and, thus, had to "engage in frequent, tactful circumvention of their authority." Interview with Barry and Lorna Lucas, 21 June 2004.

BORDER CROSSERS

EVERYONE WHO CROSSES a border is a transgressor of one kind or another, either entering or departing a space that is not "theirs." At the same time, borders are never more real than when they are crossed, even if the crossers flout them. The articles in this section consider three different groups of border crossers and border transgressors, three different groups of Americans who entered the Canadian West: prostitutes, club women, and African Americans. Each group made specific and strategic uses of the border to suit its own needs, build particular identities, and resist particular circumstances.

A number of western industries crossed the 49th parallel. The fur trade, logging, ranching, mining, and agriculture all crossed the line, pushing and pulling trappers, loggers, cowboys, miners, and harvest hands to wherever they could sell their skills on either side of the border. Char Smith follows the migrations of the women sex workers whose work was so closely tied to western industries that drew disproportionate numbers of men to the ranges, mining camps, and forests of the North American West. Unlike the male workforce, however, women in the highly stratified sex trade crossed the class lines of their clientele.

No other transborder labourers were as reviled as the American prostitutes who crossed the western Canadian-American border. Their journeys illuminate the intersecting boundaries of sex and class, public morality and private behaviour. They illuminate, too, the various meanings of border crossings, those that the women chose voluntarily, to work, and those they endured involuntarily, as Canadian authorities deported them. National identity and citizenship, too, became more complex: a means to attract customers, or for the state to deport the women back to the United States. So, too, did the treasured concept of western mobility suggest different meanings for women who simply moved to work and for whom the border was just one more line to be crossed.

The genteel club women discussed in Nora Faires' article present a quite different example of experiences had by a group of American women in western Canada, and a very different connection between identity and mobility. Americans were a significant minority in Calgary, making up more than 13 per cent of the city's foreign-born population in 1911, with a political and economic influence far beyond their numbers. The American Women's Club of Calgary, founded in 1912, was dominated by well-to-do married white women for whom the Club erected protective boundaries that reinforced American identities and promised an eventual return to homes south of the border. Unlike the American prostitutes who had to or were forced to stay on the move, the Club women chose to see themselves as being on the move even when they clearly weren't, because only then could they retain their American identities. As women crossed the Club threshold, they found a haven from conflicting national demands for their loyalty and their identity.

Cheryl Foggo's family was not as unwanted as the prostitutes nor as valued as the elite American club women from whose social circles they were excluded. Foggo, a fourth-generation Canadian, tells her own story of growing up Black in the Canadian West, where racist social boundaries "fenced out" African Canadians, both subtly and blatantly. Foggo, an author and filmmaker, screened portions of a film about her family's history in Alberta at the "Unsettled Pasts" conference. For this volume, she graciously allowed us to reprint excerpts from her autobiography, *Pourin'*

Down Rain, and wrote a new introduction for the article. Foggo probes her own identity, her family's historic ties to Canada, and her own, the cross-border migrations and the cross-border movements through which she crafted her own identity as an African Canadian woman in Alberta.

The excerpts from *Pourin' Down Rain* chronicle the complexities of African Canadian history and identity, as Foggo uncovers progressive layers of her own awareness of race, of racism in the United States and Canada, and sources of Black identity and strength that also crossed the 49th parallel. The narrative of her own maturation, and her reflections from a 2006 perspective on the autobiography she began to write in 1985, further emphasize the importance of time and place—of history and context—to how we understand ourselves and our pasts.

These three groups of border-crossers and -transgressors highlight the multiple meanings that can be attached to or derived from that crossing. Each group made different uses of the border and different uses of their American identities once they had crossed the line. The prostitutes were never going to be considered talented or charming, and were never going to be welcome despite their best efforts to stay. They used the line in a manner nation states feared—as something that could enable and only occasionally hinder their work in the sex trade. They also occasionally used it as a source of identity and pride, for marketing purposes, which would have horrified the club women. They crossed the border in addition to transgressing many other boundaries of gendered and racialized propriety. By contrast, the Club women could move in some of the highest social circles in Calgary but saw themselves as sojourners even when they weren't. They used the border the way their class, gender, and race wanted it to be used: as a marker of national and personal identity one could be proud of, as a marker of difference-but-sameness, as a line that could reinforce other hierarchies (like class, race, and gender). They tended to stay put once they had crossed the line, yet they carried the border with them always—to remind themselves that they were not "home," that they were "outsiders" despite racial and class privilege. For Foggo, the borders of race remained even when the national border had been crossed, yet racism was performed differently in Canada than in the United States, a difference that mattered, even if Canada did not fulfill the dreams that drew Black Americans north. Like African Americans, African Canadians always contend with issues of belonging, and of the intersecting histories and identities of being Black while being Canadian, or being American. Nowhere do the histories of border crossings become more complex, or more densely clear, than in the difficult histories of forced migration from Africa to North America, and the efforts to forge Black communities and identities across those difficult social and historical borderlands.

10

"CROSSING THE LINE"

American Prostitutes in Western Canada, 1895–1925

CHAR SMITH

BORDERLANDS STUDIES have traditionally focussed on the movement of ethnic groups over national boundaries. For example, Gloria Anzaldúa's *Borderlands: La Frontera*, a path-breaking study of movement across the U.S.-Mexican border, examined the effects of the border on ethnicity and the construction of identity, shifting cultural practices and language.[1] While ethnicity affected some groups' experiences in the borderlands, as a category of analysis ethnicity is less useful when studying a group of people who arguably had little in common— American prostitutes who crossed the western Canadian-U.S. border. While groups of marginalized people in borderlands studies often have similar backgrounds, the women in this study came from many different class and ethnic groups. They also worked in the sex trade at different levels, from the brothel madams, who were some of the wealthiest residents of the towns, to the women working in the cribs or on the streets.

Prostitutes' position within the community and their financial success, contact with authorities, the formation of relationships and personal safety, and their experience of crossing the border into a new country were all affected to some degree by class, ethnicity, and stratification of the sex trade. By focussing on the role of the border in the lives of American prostitutes who crossed the line into western Canada, this article examines how women negotiated various types of border crossings and how nationality affected women's experiences and their construction of identity in the borderlands.

The transnational movement of women can easily be related to the standard national frameworks of resource and economic development. Just as we can trace the movement of American capital and people into British Columbia and Alberta (from urban development in the lower mainland, to gold and coal mining in the Kootenays and southern Alberta), so too we can follow the immigration of prostitutes into the boomtowns.[2] Yet this framework often leads to the standard narrative of western frontier prostitution in which women of loose morals followed the men into the resource extraction areas to turn a quick buck and leave the area as soon as the "civilizing influence of women of good character" started to filter into the towns.[3] A study of American prostitutes in western Canada suggests that the "standard narrative" based on geographic and economic models needs to be reconsidered when examining prostitutes who crossed national borders to conduct their trade.[4]

So what drove American prostitutes across the border? Following economic models, historians often argue that prostitutes came north to seize the opportunity of engaging in a lucrative, if temporary, business.[5] There are many stories on both sides of the border of the whore with a heart of gold, the Mae Wests who were fixtures in the frontier towns, providing feminine care and companionship in the rough and ready male world of cowboys, miners, and lumberjacks, outlaws, and even Mounties. These women are often depicted as beautiful, well dressed, independent, and even powerful within their communities. As with any stereotype, my research found that there was some truth to these representations, but they did not tell the whole story.[6] Like other immigrant groups,

American prostitutes came North for a number of reasons. Wealthy brothel owners in Rossland clearly saw economic opportunity in the British Columbian mining booms. Some women crossed so often that the border may have been meaningless, while others capitalized on their nationality by catering to the large number of American men in the Canadian West. Personal ties, too, may have drawn prostitutes into British Columbia and Alberta. Border crossings were relatively easy in the early years of fluid migration, and many women had family and friends on both sides of the border.[7] Some prostitutes used the border to escape their pasts, elude the law, or give in to a restless mobility, common for many women who lived life on the margins. Finally, some sex trade workers were subjected to involuntary border crossings as police increasingly exercised deportation as a viable tool for the removal of undesirable women from western Canadian cities and towns.

Popular cultural representations of wealthy and beautiful brothel madams are very similar on both sides of the border. While contemporary stereotypes in Canada are fed in part by the importation of American cultural icons like Mae West, historically, the transnational movement of prostitutes may have contributed to the stereotype. Sid, Dora, and Stella were all wealthy brothel owners in Rossland in the 1890s through the 1910s.[8] All had travelled from the western states during a mining boom in which Rossland was called "the new Eldorado." Along with the American miners, capital, and expertise that crossed the border in the early years of the rush, these prostitutes also crossed the line, bringing their own capital or making enough money to open up brothels in the boomtowns. In an atmosphere of intense competition, the brothels began to develop specific clienteles. Stella's Vancouver House was on the "respectable" edge of a large block of tenements used as cribs.[9] Close by were numerous saloons, hotels, a bowling alley and poolroom, lodging houses, and miners' rooms over offices and stores. Her customers were the men who spent their leisure time in the downtown core, as well as her hotel guests—in many cases the "elites" or the wealthiest in the town.[10]

Dora's and Sid's brothels were located in the southern end of the city, almost beyond the city limits in 1897. Far from the bustling downtown saloons and hotels, their brothels likely catered to workingmen coming from the smelter in Trail and to travellers.[11] They were located half a block away from the passenger platform of the Columbia and Western Railway that traversed the southern edge of the city on its route to Trail, with important connections south to Washington state and north to steamer connections on the Arrow Lakes.[12]

Sid, Dora, and Stella were all white madams from middle-class backgrounds between the ages of thirty and fifty who had sold properties in the United States before relocating to Rossland. Although the records do not provide much detail, they appeared to have followed the mining booms as they moved across the western United States. Certainly by the time they reached Rossland, all were experienced businesswomen. They provided a variety of services, offering their customers lodging, meals and drink, laundry services, companionship, entertainment, and (of course) sexual services. These madams appear to have maintained their American connections, and prostitutes coming from the United States quickly found a warm welcome in Rossland brothels, especially in Stella's hotel, which had a high turnover of American women.[13]

Nationality was important for women who sought to capitalize on it by catering to the migrant men who populated the Canadian boomtowns. In the police records, many of these women chose to identify themselves as Americans, and like the woman who renamed herself "Texas" when she crossed the border proudly proclaimed, it was their place of birth. There may have been significant benefits for American madams. Many boomtowns attracted large numbers of American immigrants, and "Texas's house" reportedly offered the reassuring sounds of a true southern drawl, along with its other services.[14] Nationality thus became significant for women who in many other ways were nameless, existing on the outside margins of society, and identified only by the category of "prostitute." Police recognized that women frequently used aliases, and in the monthly collection of fines, nationality and location were more significant identifiers for police than names. But nationality may have had multiple meanings for the women in the borderlands.

For some women, ethnicity may have been as important as nationality. In all the towns of the Kootenays, and in city police records in Victoria,

Vancouver, and Calgary, police identified brothels as Asian, Black, or ethnically grouped, such as the women described as "Italian" in Greenwood's police records and newspapers or "French Mary's" house in Rossland.[15] Police recognized and used the names of "characters" like Texas and Stella; however, anonymity was often protection for women of ethnic minorities. Police seldom identified individuals in ethnically grouped brothels, more often using locations rather than names. Thus, "Japtown whorehouses" appeared in Calgary records, and "the houses on Dupont [Street]" referred to brothels in Vancouver's Chinatown. Rarely are women in these brothels mentioned by name except in the regular collection of fines, and the frequency of some names in certain brothels suggests the ease with which women changed names and nationalities.[16] Ethnicity was less easy to hide. So when the North West Mounted Police closed down a Japanese brothel just outside of Calgary due to an outbreak of syphilis, the women had fewer options and less mobility than other prostitutes and remained in the house until their symptoms appeared to go away and they had passed a medical inspection, allowing the house to reopen.[17] While increased marginalization in ethnically grouped brothels may have worked to strengthen the bonds of identity, the women in most brothels came from a wide variety of backgrounds, and some of the most successful brothels may have purposely offered a selection of women of different nationalities. For women who were cut off from their past and exiled from their nation of birth, however, personal connections may have become more significant than national or ethnic identity.

If we complicate national models of western expansion and the economic analyses of resource development with an examination of the individual experiences of prostitutes who crossed the line, it becomes clear that personal connections played a role in drawing women into the borderlands. By frequently using aliases and refusing to provide personal information to the police, or by quickly moving on to the next town when they found themselves under surveillance, prostitutes often avoided contact with police by maintaining their anonymity. In contrast to the brothel prostitutes who had proudly proclaimed their nationality, when women chose a transient lifestyle, or when they were driven out of towns as police closed vice districts, their identities became less connected to national or ethnic markers and more closely tied to the personal relationships they developed.

At first glance, public fights, abusive language, and thefts appear to characterize prostitutes' relationships with each other. Rossland police records show twenty-seven instances of fights between prostitutes between 1898 and 1902 and numerous cases of stolen property. One example is the charge brought against Irene by a fellow prostitute for stealing a silver tray valued at $4. Also typical were the results of the case—the plaintiff decided to drop the charge and the case was dismissed the next day.[18] But not all prostitutes' relationships were characterized by violence, jealousy, and competition. Marion Goldman notes that structural aspects of the trade led to the formation of long-lasting friendships between women. Women living and working together in brothels or as independent prostitutes forced into close proximity in restricted districts led to "isolation from the respectable community, [which] created a bond among them."[19] In western Canada, instances of this type of bond became apparent when prostitutes travelled together over long periods of time, protected each other from the hazards of the trade, provided charity to co-workers in times of need, and responded emotionally in times of extremity.

In the records of monthly fines, occasionally it is possible to identify prostitutes who had a family connection through the uniqueness of their surnames. Gay and Marion, for example, crossed the line into Grand Forks and travelled together throughout the Kootenays, changing residence frequently, but always appearing together until they left the area one year later.[20]

Similarly, Blanche and Louise fled Vancouver together and opened up a brothel in Hedley in the aftermath of a very public trial of Louise's alleged husband, Desire Brothier. In 1904, Brothier received seven years for forgery, procuring, and buggery. At the time, Brothier's sister and brother-in-law were also charged in connection with the forgery of a medical certificate that claimed Blanche was free of disease, but the charges were dropped when they fled to Montana. The persistent efforts of Brothier's brother-in-law and new evidence of the sister's involvement in the forgery led to Brothier's release after serving just two years. Blanche and Louise remained together for the duration of his incarceration and disappeared from British Columbia immediately upon Brothier's release, presumably to return with him to the United States.[21]

At times, prostitutes assisted their colleagues, even when it was dangerous for them to do so. Mrs Welsh was fined for running a bawdy house because she opened her doors to a fellow American prostitute who had no other place to go, ensuring "she would no[t] be drove [sic] around like a dog when she had not done anything."[22] In the same spirit of sisterhood, a group of prostitutes in Nelson raised money for a madam "to provide her with the necessities of living, she being sick and destitute with a large family, and no one to assist her but the charitable."[23]

Although prostitutes' isolation may have led to the formation of stronger personal ties, it likely made things like child-bearing and motherhood more difficult. Children appear in the records in connection with prostitutes quite regularly, and there are several stories of neglected children who police believed were endangered by the involvement of their mothers in the sex trade.[24] Yet the sources also indicate that prostitutes may have had a broader range of options for caring for their children than is often suggested. For example, Minnie, a brothel madam in Golden, took care of a young prostitute's child for many years, eventually sending him to live with Minnie's mother in Spokane, Washington. This type of arrangement would usually be hidden from public view, except Minnie became annoyed when the young mother quit paying for the boy's monthly room and board and took her case to the local justice of the peace.[25]

While personal ties may have drawn some prostitutes into western Canada, others used the border to escape their pasts. In the West, the presence of men in the brothels in the roles of lovers and pimps is apparent, though not all that common in the earlier years. Further, charges of "living off the avails of prostitution" may have included many types of relationships other than the obvious one involving economic exploitation and physical abuse. In Desire Brothier's case, procuring appears to have concerned a relationship with Blanche and Louise that transcended even a few years in jail. A letter from one of Brothier's former prostitutes, who fled to France to escape testifying against him, declares her undying love and an offer to send letters or money if doing so would help him gain his freedom.[26]

Many prostitutes who travelled with men may have benefited from their protection. In Rossland there were two husband and wife teams operating brothels, and police remarked on the lack of conflict in those houses compared to others in operation at the time. Jennie, a Japanese prostitute in Revelstoke, who had came to British Columbia from Seattle in 1900 with her husband, appeared to have a stable relationship in which she controlled the couple's finances. Yet her husband's presence did not prevent her murder in 1905.[27] For the occasional woman who might have gained from long-term connections with men, many suffered from abusive, violent relationships—and some paid the price with their lives.

There are many tragic stories of domestic and physical abuse of prostitutes in western Canadian legal records. While some women sought to escape their pasts, not all were successful. Annie was a Black American prostitute who had travelled to Phoenix with an entertainment troupe in 1903. From all accounts she had a beautiful voice. She had sought to escape the memories of an almost fatal stabbing in Spokane, Washington, for which her live-in companion, Joshua Bell, had done time. But she did not run far enough. Just one year later, Bell arrived in Phoenix with an American prize-fighting outfit that had toured the West, presumably on a hunt for Annie. When he found her, he planned a cold-blooded murder, waiting in hiding for her to come out of her brothel and "stabbed her in the breast with a knife, and then kicked in her teeth." Bell tried to flee back across the border but was quickly caught. His hanging made big news in all the British Columbia newspapers, with race and nationality the dominant themes in the narratives. Some editors even indulged in the opportunity to add to the rampant anti-Asian rhetoric by calling for the deportation of all people of colour who had come from the United States. For Annie, the Canadian borderlands were no safe haven from the violence that followed her.[28]

Whether prostitutes crossed the line for economic gain, to capitalize on their nationality, re-establish personal ties, or to run away from the past, mobility was pervasive in the trade. Except for a lucky few who were able to achieve financial success, sex trade workers suffered from a general lack of stability caused in part by the marginalization of women who existed outside the law and outside the bounds of accepted morality. In the late 1800s, as resource booms occurred across western Canada, many American prostitutes voluntarily crossed the line on a regular basis. Structural changes in the trade in the early twentieth century, when brothels were shut down and streetwalking increased, led to greater mobility. But this mobility was increasingly restricted within national boundaries when the police began to deport "undesirable" prostitutes and used the border to limit re-entry. Border crossings were also made more difficult with the implementation of changes to the Immigration Act in 1906, which halted the earlier policy of free entry. By 1914, the prohibited classes increased from those who might become public charges or infirm to include persons convicted of "any crime involving moral turpitude, prostitutes, pimps, professional vagrants or beggars..."[29] Police then had a powerful weapon with which to fight morality crimes, and in a climate of social change they began to use that weapon more frequently.

Their considerable mobility makes it very difficult to trace prostitutes who travelled in the West; most worked alone and may have had very good reasons to maintain their anonymity. Fortunately, prostitution was not just a profitable business for the women. The police and town councils also made a lot of money regulating the sex trade, and they left extensive records. Just like other national myths, western Canada's law-abiding reputation does not hold up well in an examination of the police court dockets, which are full of charges for prostitution, theft, gambling, assaults, and even the occasional murder. And the sex trade was certainly one of the steadiest sources of income for the fledgling western cities.[30] For example, when John S. Ingram took over as chief constable of the Rossland Police, he systematically collected fines from all the brothels and cribs on a monthly basis, filling the city coffers with well over $1,000 per month. To maintain this source of revenue for the city, Ingram and his constables kept extensive records tracking the movements of prostitutes in and out of the city, many of whom were

Americans.[31] To control the influx of transients into their towns, a regular duty of the lowest constable on the roster in Rossland was to watch passengers as they disembarked from trains, looking for single women who were not met by "respectable" residents.[32] In towns like Princeton, in the Similkameen, where trains came from both Vancouver and from the south through the border crossing of Oroville, Washington, "Specials" were hired to help the single policeman keep an eye on the day and night trains. Once marked, police tended to keep a close watch on these women's activities.[33] For itinerant prostitutes, this intense surveillance usually resulted in charges within a few weeks or even a few days of the woman's arrival, and the prostitute frequently left town immediately after appearing in court and paying her fine.[34] If police felt they did not have enough evidence for a charge of prostitution, they often charged the woman with other offences, which suggests that once a woman was suspected, any means that effectively removed "undesirable" women from the community was deemed legitimate.[35]

Women were frequently on the move throughout the early 1900s, yet they were increasingly restricted within national boundaries as borders were closed down. Social reformers frequently called for deportation as one means to close down the red-light districts. The Vancouver Police Commission's recommendations for "handling the social evil" in 1912 are typical for this era: "The Chairman stated the Attorney General had laid down five different ways or means of bringing about a better condition of affairs viz (1) That all undesirable aliens be stopped at the border and refused admittance into Canada. (2) That these women can be brought up in court everyday and fined, and in time got rid of. (3) You can fine the land-ladies each day and if the fine is not paid you can issue distress warrants on their goods. (4) You take proceedings against the males who visit these places and (5) To prosecute the owners of these buildings for living off the proceeds of crime."[36] On the streets of Lethbridge, Calgary, Vancouver, Nelson, and Victoria, reformers toured the red-light districts, making recommendations to police departments that usually demanded complete suppression of the trade. These tours had dire consequences for prostitutes, as they incited public opinion against the women. As early as 1903, growth in Vancouver's downtown area made the brothels on Dupont Street too visible for the comfort of Vancouver City Council and it decided to force the women to leave.[37] However, council could not decide where to move the women, most of whom owned their properties, and therefore it let the matter rest for almost three years, until moral reformers increased their activities in 1906.

The fight between the prostitutes of Dupont Street and city council began in earnest in 1906 with a letter from a resident of the area to the mayor, claiming that the police chief, reportedly for "mercenary" reasons, had ignored his complaints about a brothel on Dupont. He claimed that the brothel was "conducted by two colored girls, whose conduct is in the extreme reprehensible...they harbour white girls who are visited and debauched by colored men and chinamen who induce them to smoke opium and indulge in many un-natural practices."[38] This inflamed public opinion about the brothels because the complainant focussed on their multi-racial nature in an era when racism, and especially anti-Chinese sentiment, was already heightened in the city.[39] The allegation that Chief North was profiting from the presence of the red-light district caused an investigation that resulted in his suspension in June 1906, and he was replaced by Chief Chisholm.[40]

Despite a legal fight, the women were finally given ten days' notice to vacate their premises.[41] Although it appeared to the public that Chisholm's ultimatum was being adhered to, internal police records suggest that this was not the case. After a city police sergeant was forced to resign for allowing the brothels on Dupont to "[run] full blast," the chief recommended "that his resignation be accepted," and he suggested that "the Commissioners have nothing further to enquire into."[42] Possibly, the chief did not want the commissioners to investigate too closely into where the women had gone when they followed his orders to vacate Dupont Street. In an interview in November 1906, Chisholm said he could not respond to the question of the dispersal of the women: his instructions were to clear the street, and he had obeyed those instructions. When questioned if they would "flit again to respectable sections of the city," Chisholm replied, "I make no concealment of my view...that ultimately one place, one district remote from respectable streets and centres, will have to be set aside for these dames."[43] But this sentiment was in direct opposition to the reform agenda of suppressing vice altogether, and Chisholm did not last any longer as chief of police than had his predecessor, North.[44]

Many of the women who left Dupont moved to Shanghai and Canton streets, also in Chinatown, and by the end of 1906 the whole process began again.[45] First, Chinese merchants began a petition requesting that police "prevent an invasion of undesirable women."[46] Then, moral reformers and aldermen toured the district, finding that conditions in the restricted district were the "worst in [the] city's history."[47] The allegations were brought before the police board, extra police were put on duty in the area, and the brothels were raided regularly.[48] In Vancouver, forcing the brothels to close down and move to a new district every few years had the undesirable result of scattering many of the women who could not afford to buy new houses every time they were forced to move.

With each relocation, more women ended up moving into rooming houses throughout the city. Police thus found it increasingly difficult to regulate the women, and police records correspondingly show a decrease in large groups of monthly fines that were collected from the madams and inmates of brothels as police went house to house. Individual charges for streetwalking increased throughout the period, as did charges for "keeping a bawdy house" that were collected from single women in rooming houses.[49] Increased suppression of the trade had long-range effects on the structure of prostitution in western Canada. From finding some protection amongst the female communities of the brothels, prostitutes were increasingly forced to rely on their own resources as they negotiated their increasingly marginalized status.

The reform movement that led to the closing of formal red-light districts in the cities also affected national identity. Whether forcibly scattering women into new areas in the city, deporting them back to the States, or moving them on to another town, nationality may have become less important as women sought to hide their country of birth to avoid deportation or resigned themselves to accepting a new nationality as borders became harder to cross. While women who seized economic opportunity or formed personal connections voluntarily crossed the line, others were not able to exercise the same degree of agency. A wave of deportations of American prostitutes in the early 1900s from western Canadian cities afforded the women little opportunity to choose their nation of residence. While many could claim at least twenty years' residency in Canada, in the new climate of moral regulation they were uprooted from their homes, families, and friends and unceremoniously dumped on the other side of the border as a means of ending the "social evil."

Charges of "white slavery" were frequently heard in this era as a result of the highly publicized anti-prostitution campaigns in the United States, in which "muckraking journalists exposed the web of corruption between police, politicians, and vice magnates. Novelists and filmmakers sensationalized the traffic in women in lurid tales of abduction, rape, and sexual slavery."[50] Much of the American material, estimated to amount to as many as one billion pages over the period, was incorporated into Canadian publications, with the Methodist Church's Department of Temperance and Moral Reform leading the way in generating numerous pamphlets that were presented in speaking tours across the country. One Methodist publication, Canada's War on the White Slave Traffic, used American estimates that "15,000 foreign girls, and 45,000 native born are the victims every year in the United States and Canada."[51]

Police usually recognized that the stereotypical representation of the "black-hearted man" waiting on the train platform to force an innocent young woman into the sex trade occurred very rarely. Nevertheless, they did use the rhetoric of the white slave trade to assist them in their sweeps through the red-light districts. For example, in 1907 police took a "census of...[Vancouver's] restricted district in Chinatown...found 180 sporting women recently settled there."[52] Fortunately for the police, they found that all but five of the women came from the United States, and thus involved immigration inspectors in the deportation of more than 150 women.[53] This led to an odd kind of cross-border trade—a trade in prostitutes. Once the deportees arrived in Seattle and were released by the immigration officials, they quickly re-crossed into Canada. In late 1907 another census set the number of American prostitutes in Vancouver's Chinatown at 210.[54]

All border towns found deportation a handy way to deal with unwanted prostitutes, although everyone knew they simply re-crossed the line. In Lethbridge, Alberta, after five years of deporting prostitutes across the border only to see them re-enter almost immediately, the newspapers began to call for an end to the expense of using police hours to gather and transport the women to the border. After tossing out the idea of simply sending them en masse to Calgary, the town eventually settled for putting the prostitutes on a train, preferably not at town expense, and sending them east or west.

Whether forcibly scattering women into new areas of the city, deporting them back to the States, or moving them on to another town, increased suppression of the trade had long-range effects on the structure of the trade. After finding some protection amongst the female communities of the brothels, prostitutes were forced to rely on their own resources as they negotiated their increasingly marginalized status. One means was to construct an identity linked to national pride. As expatriates, many American women banded together and proudly proclaimed their national identity. Others found anonymity to be safer and formed connections on the personal level as friends, sisters, daughters, wives, and mothers, choosing to reject nationality as an identifying factor. Some had little choice but to withstand the repeated deportations that might arise from being identified as American.

In common with American settlers and immigrants who came North, prostitutes in western Canada shared the hopes, dreams, and aspirations connected with crossing any border into a new land. But there were important differences too. As women living on the margins, prostitutes also crossed lines of respectability and acceptability, which made their journey across the border that much more difficult.

NOTES

1. Gloria Anzaldúa, *Borderlands/La Frontera: The New Mestiza*, 2nd ed. (1987; repr., San Francisco: Aunt Lute Books, 1999). On transnational approaches to the history of migration see Donna R. Gabaccia, "Is Everywhere Nowhere? Nomads, Nations, and the Immigrant Paradigm of United States History," *The Journal of American History* (December

1999): http://80-www.historycooperative.org.ezproxy.lib.ucalgary.ca:2048/journals/
jah/86.3/gabaccia.html (accessed 1 February 2004).

2. For a good overview of the development of resources in southern British Columbia, see
Jean Barman, *The West Beyond the West: A History of British Columbia* (Toronto: University of
Toronto Press, 1991), especially chapter 6, "The Young Province," 99–128, on the eco-
nomic growth of the era; and Allen Seager, "The Resource Economy, 1871–1921," in *The
Pacific Province: A History of British Columbia*, ed. Hugh J.M. Johnston (Vancouver: Douglas
& MacIntyre, 1996), 205–52. For Alberta, see Gerald Friesen, *The Canadian Prairies:
A History* (Toronto: University of Toronto Press, 1984), especially chapter 12, "Capital and
Labour 1900–40: Cities, resource towns, and frontier camps." On the movement of peo-
ple into southern Alberta, see Howard Palmer and Tamara Palmer, *Alberta: A New History*
(Edmonton: Hurtig Publishers, 1990), chapter 6, "The Boom Years (1896–1913): Politics,
Cities, and Resource Development," 128–66.

3. Dee Brown, *The Gentle Tamers: Women of the Old Wild West* (Lincoln: University of Nebraska
Press, 1958), presents the image of (moral) women as civilizing influences, which
Mariana Valverde examines in *The Age of Light, Soap, and Water: Moral Reform in English
Canada, 1885–1925* (Toronto: McClelland and Stewart, 1991). Marion S. Goldman, *Gold
Diggers and Silver Miners: Prostitution and Social Life on the Comstock Lode* (Ann Arbor:
University of Michigan Press, 1981), takes a hard look at the stereotypical representa-
tions of prostitutes, finding few redeeming qualities in a life of prostitution.

4. One of the most colourful examples of the typical portrayal of prostitutes in western
Canada is James H. Grey, *Red Lights on the Prairies* (Saskatoon, SK: Fifth House, 1971).

5. On the creation of western institutions and the role played by prostitutes in their implementation in western American contexts, see Anne M. Butler, *Daughters of Joy, Sisters of
Misery: Prostitutes in the American West, 1865–90* (Urbana: University of Illinois Press, 1985).

6. Marilyn Wood Hill, *Their Sisters' Keepers: Prostitution in New York City, 1830–1870* (Berkeley:
University of California Press, 1993) also found that the correspondence of Helen Jewett,
a beautiful and wealthy New York prostitute, had to be examined carefully to get
beneath the surface account of her movements in high society and thus contextualize
the events that led to her brutal murder.

7. On the easy cross-border movement of migrant labourers in Montana and western
Canada, see Evelyne Stitt Pickett, "Hoboes Across the Border: A Comparison of Itinerant
Cross-Border Labourers between Montana and Western Canada," *Montana: The Magazine
of Western History* 49, no. 1 (Spring 1999): 18–31. For a general look at American immigra-
tion studies, see David D. Harvey, "Garrison Duty: Canada's Retention of the American
Immigrant, 1901–1981," *American Review of Canadian Studies* 15, no. 2 (1985): 169–87. On
Canadian immigration to the States and open borders see Bruno Ramirez, "Canada in
the United States: Perspectives on Migration and Continental History," *Journal of
American Ethnic History* 20, no. 3 (Spring 2001): 50–70. On women's roles and kinship
networks in the decision to migrate North, see Randy Widdis, "American Resident
Migration to Western Canada at the Turn of the Twentieth Century," *Prairie Forum* 22,
no. 2 (Fall 1997): 237–61.

8. One issue that arises out of the types of sources used in this study is the use of names
and the suppression of personal information. Many of the repositories that hold police

and court records have policies regarding access to personal information. In the attempt to preserve anonymity, I have chosen to use only the first names of prostitutes throughout to adhere to the restrictions where necessary, and to ensure continuity in the work when using public records where full names are accessible. Just as I am aware that the naming and categorization of women may have negative effects, I also realize that there is a danger to removing identity or personhood when denying women the right to their full names, and I hope that my choice does not negatively impact the representation of women whose lives and experiences are the central focus of this paper.

9. *Rossland Fire Insurance Plans* (Toronto: Chas E. Goad, Civil Engineer, 1897), unaccessioned records, Rossland Historical Museum and Archives, Rossland, BC (hereafter cited as RHMA).

10. City of Rossland, Tax Roll, 1898–1901, unaccessioned records, RHMA. Stella owned block 42, lots 18 and 19, and the lot on Queen Street, located in the block behind the main street, which were valued at $3,200 in 1898. One lot contained the Vancouver House Hotel, which was assessed at $1,250, while the other remained unimproved. Stella's property holdings were considerably more than that held by the average female property owner held in 1898. Of the forty-four women on the tax rolls, the average value of land and improvements was $1,343.50. Only eight other women held more property than Stella, and of those, four were hotel owners. Clearly, Stella's holdings were very substantial for the period.

11. City of Rossland, Tax Roll, 1898–1901 and City of Rossland, Arrears of Taxes, 1898–1902, RHMA. Sid sold her property by 1914, and a man named Hop Ching owned block 48, lots 11 and 12, between 1914 and 1917, the next date that tax assessments and collectors rolls for Rossland are available. The majority of Chinese who owned properties had relocated to this area by the 1920s, moving from their former location close to the downtown core in the Sourdough Alley. Kutenai West Heritage Consulting, Summary Report Prepared for the City of Rossland and the West Kootenay Chinese Heritage Society, 29 September 1995, 139.

12. *Rossland Fire Insurance Plans*, 1897, RHMA, and Jeremy Mouat, *Roaring Days: Rossland's Mines and the History of British Columbia* (Vancouver: UBC Press, 1995), 31–33.

13. City of Rossland, Daily Police Report, 13 November 1900 to 17 June 1903, unaccessioned records and *Rossland Fire Insurance Plans*, 1897 and 1912, all RHMA.

14. Typical is this entry in the daily reports on 28 June 1901: "On duty 4 to 12 pm. Called at 11:30 to Texas's house. Couple of fellows broke glass in door, but they moved before I arrived. Quite a few drunks around but are orderly." Texas was frequently involved in altercations with her customers and the police considered her a "character." City of Rossland, Daily Police Report, 13 November 1900 to 17 June 1903, unaccessioned records, RHMA.

15. British Columbia Provincial Police (BCPP), "Greenwood Correspondence Jan 1918–Dec 1919." File 40–3050, R. N. Atkinson Museum and Archives, Penticton, BC (hereafter cited as RAMA); and City of Rossland, Daily Police Reports, RHMA.

16. Sid Horrell notes that "prostitutes frequently changed their names and seemed to prefer diminutive first names like Tilley, Trixie, Georgie, Lulu and Allie that had a friendly

ring of familiarity," in "The (Royal) North-West Mounted Police and Prostitution on the Canadian Prairies," *Prairie Forum* 10, no. 1 (Spring 1985): 105.

17. Superintendent Deane to Commissioner Perry, NWMP correspondence 28 February 1907, RG 18 Vol. 1605 File 133, quoted in Horrell, "The (Royal) North-West Mounted Police," 117.

18. City of Rossland, Police Court, 1 October 1902 to 28 June 1907, entries on 3 and 4 June, 1905, unaccessioned records, RHMA.

19. Goldman, *Gold Diggers*, 117.

20. City of Rossland, Police Court, 30 January 1904 to 29 August 1904, unaccessioned records, RHMA.

21. The details of Brothier's trial are found in *The Daily News-Advertiser*, Vancouver, 10, 11, 12, 15 March 1904 and in the *Vancouver Province*, 2, 13 June 1906, 5 October 1906. The women's activities in Hedley are described in a letter to the Chief of the Provincial Police, Victoria, 28 July 1906 and in reports from the Hedley constable to Superintendent Hussey, BCPP Victoria, 5 September 1906 found in GR0429 Box 13, File 3, Provincial Archives of British Columbia, Victoria, BC (hereafter cited as PABC) Blanche may have returned to Vancouver the next year as a prostitute named Blanche, using the same last name as Brothier's brother-in-law, and is found in Vancouver's Prisoner Record Book, 5 March 1907, City of Vancouver Archives, Vancouver, BC (hereafter cited as CVA), although it is difficult to be certain because all the women connected with Brothier, including his sister, used a number of pseudonyms throughout the trial. The constable in Hedley believed that Blanche and Louise, a.k.a. Bernice or "Mrs. Brothier" in the brothel, were the same women who worked for Brothier in Vancouver.

22. Welsh to E.V. Bodwell, Barrister, Victoria, 29 September 1899 in GR0429, Box 5, File 2, PABC.

23. *The Tribune* (Nelson), 26 September 1899.

24. Thomas H. Long, Chief of Police, Rossland to C.J. South, 26 June 1905, in GR0429, Box 13, File 1, PABC.

25. Golden BCPP, Letter Book 1913, 5 September 1913, unaccessioned records, Golden Museum, Golden, BC.

26. Marcella to Desire Brothier, 1 November 1904, in French, translator unknown, GR0429 Box 11, File 3, Document 1132/04, PABC.

27. *Revelstoke Herald and Railway Men's Journal*, Revelstoke, 20 April 1905. This case is discussed in detail in my thesis, "Regulating Prostitution in British Columbia," (master's thesis, University of Calgary, 2001), 46–47.

28. Annie's story is told in the *Boundary Creek Times*, 19 August 1904 (7 days after the murder), 21 October 1904, and 14 January 1905. Quotation is from 19 August 1904. The events of Joshua Bell's trial and hanging are in the Attorney General's files, GR0429 Box 11, File 5, 3142–04 1904 dated 11 October and 17–25 October, 1904, PABC.

29. *The Immigration Act and Regulations* (Ottawa: King's Printer, 1919), Effective July 14, 1914.

30. Greg Marquis, "Vancouver Vice: The Police and the Negotiation of Morality, 1904–1935," in *Essays in the History of Canadian Law, Volume VI: British Columbia and the Yukon*, ed. Hamar Foster and John McLaren (Toronto: The Osgood Society for Canadian Legal History,

1995), 242–73. Marquis in part examines the profitability of policing the vice trade in Vancouver.

31. On 1 July 1897, John S. Ingram replaced Kirkup as chief constable. With the appointment of Ingram, a new era of policing began in Rossland. Order and accountability became paramount in the newly incorporated city. As a result, regular record-keeping procedures were enacted that make it much easier to trace charges for prostitution-related offences from mid-1897 into the first decades of the twentieth century. These records are available at the Rossland Museum and Archives as Daily Police Reports.

32. Many instances of this type of duty are evident in the Rossland Daily Police Reports.

33. BCPP "Princeton Reports / Crime: Sex Offences 1924–26." File 40–3472, RAMA.

34. While these tactics seem to be in a grey area by contemporary practice of the law, in the *Revised Statutes of Canada, 1927,* Section 225 "disorderly houses" included "common bawdy houses," "common betting houses," and "common gaming houses." The British Columbia Provincial Police used the term consistently to refer to "bawdy houses." A *bawdy house* was defined as "a house, room, set of rooms or place of any kind kept for purposes of prostitution or for the practice of acts of indecency, or occupied or resorted to by one or more persons for such purposes." Thus, almost any women who exhibited suspicious behaviour in any location could be charged with prostitution. For example, Phyllis booked into the Davenport Rooming House in Princeton; she was convicted under Section 229 of the Criminal Code of being an "Inmate of a Disorderly House" the very next day, paid her $25 fine, and immediately left for Seattle via Vancouver. BCPP "Princeton Reports / Crime: Sex Offences 1924–26." File 40–3472, 14 May 1924, RAMA.

35. I examine the treatment of transient prostitutes in more detail in "Policing Prostitution in the Similkameen: Informal Systems of Regulation in the 1920s," in "Regulating Prostitution in British Columbia, 1895–1930," (master's thesis, University of Calgary, 2001), 98–113.

36. "Minutes" Vancouver Board of Police Commissioners, 3 December 1912, 75-A-1 File 3—Minutes June 12, 1912 to November 17, 1920, CVA.

37. "Mayor Says They Must Be Moved," *The Daily Province,* 18 August 1903, 1.

38. "A Citizen," to The Mayor, Vancouver, 2 February 1906, in Vancouver Board of Police Commissioners General Files Correspondence 1905–37, 75-A-5, File 13, "Petitions," CVA.

39. John McLaren, "The Early British Columbia Judges, the Rule of Law and the 'Chinese Question': The California and Oregon Connection," in *Law for the Elephant, Law for the Beaver: Essays in the Legal History of the North American West,* ed. John McLaren, Hamar Foster, and Chet Orloff (Regina, SK: Canadian Plains Research Centre, 1992), 237–73.

40. "Alexander Selected for Police Inquiry," *The Daily Province,* 23 June 1906, 1.

41. *The Daily Province,* 13, 15 August; 7, 11 September; 31 October; 3, 5 November; 4 December 1906.

42. Chisholm to The Board of Police Commissioners, Vancouver, 31 October 1906, "Vancouver Board of Police Commissioners General Files, Correspondence 1905–1937" 75-A-5 File 4, CVA.

43. "Lottie Mansfield the Only One Left," *The Daily Province,* 3 November 1906, 3.

44. "Alexander Selected for Police Inquiry," *The Daily Province,* 23 June 1906, 1.

45. "Deporting From Restricted Districts," *The Province,* 23 January 1908, 8.

46. Chisholm to Police Board, 3 September 1906, "Vancouver Board of Police Commissioners General Files, Correspondence 1905–1937" 75-A-4, File 13, "Petitions," CVA.

47. The Daily Province, 19 November 1906.

48. The Daily Province, 20, 21 November 1906; 24, 28 December 1906; 16 March 1907.

49. "Says Women Must Not Scatter, Mayor is Indignant," The Daily Province, 15 June 1906, 1.

50. Barbara Meil Hobson, Uneasy Virtue: The Politics of Prostitution and the American Reform Tradition (New York: Basic Books, Inc., 1987), 140.

51. Rev. J.G. Shearer and Rev. T. Albert Moore, Canada's War on the White Slave Traffic (Toronto: The Department of Temperance and Moral Reform of the Methodist Church, 1912), 2–3; "Rev. Hugh W. Dobson Papers 1912–26, Western Field Secretary for Evangelism and Social Service," Box A3/File G, United Church Archives, University of British Columbia, Vancouver, BC.

52. The Daily Province, 16 March 1907.

53. "Vancouver's Restricted District," Victoria Colonist, 6 December 1907, 14.

54. "Deporting From Restricted Districts," The Province, 23 January 1908, 8.

11

"TALENTED AND CHARMING STRANGERS FROM ACROSS THE LINE"

Gendered Nationalism, Class Privilege, and the American Woman's Club of Calgary

NORA FAIRES

It is safe to say that in Calgary there are one thousand American women.... Outside of the life of the home what has the American woman who first comes in this country to interest her?...[T]he time has arrived for the former women residents of the United States to band together and do something to make it easier and more pleasant for the American sister upon her arrival in a new country.

—"Organization of a Club for American Women," *Calgary News Telegram,* 26 March 1912

Many prominent Americans...had already established lovely homes [in what] was known as "American Hill." These ladies were anxious to extend a friendly greeting to the many talented and charming strangers from across the line, and they were included in our first roster.... [T]he American Woman's Club of Calgary rejoices in the fact that it is, every day of its existence, proving of value in this far west, to those who are but "ships that pass in the night."

—*Glimpses of the Past*, American Woman's Club of Calgary
Golden Anniversary Booklet, 1912–1962

WRITING IN 1922 for the popular Canadian weekly *Saturday Night*, Toronto journalist Anne Anderson Perry took up the subject of "The American Woman in Canada."[1] Focusing on the five "American Women's Clubs" established in leading Dominion cities during the previous decade, Perry began by placing these organizations in the context of parallel institutions flourishing across the border: "Dotted over the United States are many Canadian Clubs [in which] Canadian men or women, living away from the land of their birth, seek to promote sociability among themselves, to do constructive civic or community work in the cities where their lives are cast." Perry lauded the clubs as sites where "thousands of Canadians avail themselves of the opportunity...to preserve their national sympathies, to feel anew their ties of sentiment with Britain, to reaffirm, in a word, their Canadianism, even though many of them are naturalized Americans and lead the lives of American citizens." She assured her readers that "in this there is nothing amiss, nor is there ever any question among our friendly cousins to the south of the right or rightness of these Canadian Clubs to exist and flourish." The same was true of organizations of Americans living in Canada, Perry maintained, which differed from the Canadian societies in a single key respect: the American clubs "have all been formed by women, for women, and are known as American Women's Clubs."[2]

This essay analyzes the first of such organizations, the American Woman's Club of Calgary (AWC), from its founding in 1912 through the

Second World War. Most of the members of this organization were well-to-do white married women who crossed the international border as dependants of their husbands. They had the leisure time to pursue a round of mannered socializing that included card parties, teas, paper flower-making, travelogues, and cooking demonstrations for elegant repasts. With the means to dispense charity to the needy, they also had the resolve to deny their benevolence to those they deemed unworthy. The club members endeavored to use their gender, race, and class privilege to insulate themselves from pressing economic, social, and political questions, often with striking success. In line with Perry's depiction, these women self-consciously constructed themselves not as settlers to Calgary but as U.S. women whose lives temporarily "cast" them in Canada; their organizational outpost reinforced this gendered, classed sojourner identity, even as some became long-term residents of Alberta.

Meanwhile, the act of establishing the club connected them to the city where they resided (but pointedly refused to call home), enmeshing them in the burgeoning realm of local women's associations.[3] The club's charter inscribes this unstable, marginalized position. Mandating that the organization remain aloof from both religious and political issues in case these might provoke controversy within the group, it also encouraged cooperation with other associations in Calgary engaged in civic and philanthropic causes. Local, national, and international events and concerns at times strained this tenuous and artificial distinction, intruding on the club's devotion to its social routine and destabilizing its members' self-imposed position on the periphery of the community.

My research examines how this group of privileged women negotiated their status as civic outsiders in Canada, and how they created, maintained, fortified, and sometimes transgressed the boundaries of a gendered, sojourner American identity and allegiance. The essay focuses on the tumultuous periods of the two world wars, when nationalisms mattered intensely and when twice the border initially divided a combatant from a noncombatant nation and then designated a boundary between allies waging war against a common foe. In these parallel historical moments of crisis, the AWC's patterns became disrupted: the boundary between the United States and Canada became alternately brittle or blurred, the meaning of "American" complicated and contradictory. AWC members variously conflated nationalism and continentalism, subsumed nationalism under Anglocentrism, and elided the distinction between a mobilized Canada and a noncombatant United States. Yet, even in times of extranational emergency, the AWC remained vigilantly within a framework of bourgeois propriety and gendered gentility, translating the concepts of patriotism and citizenship into its own domestic vocabulary. After sketching the foundation of the club and its membership, I explore episodes that offer insight into the identities of these "talented and charming strangers from across the [border]line." Reconsidering Perry's formulation of the AWC, I conclude by viewing this organization and its members through the lens of growing American hegemony during the first half of the twentieth century.

* * *

WHEN THE SEVENTY-FIVE charter members of the American Woman's Club of Calgary met on April 11, 1912, the city was in the midst of an unprecedented economic boom that transformed its economy and caused its population to skyrocket.[4] As an article appearing in a local weekly in 1913 expressed it, during the past decade the "wild and woolly cow town of four thousand" had become "an up-to-date city of sixty thousand."[5] The expansion of the Canadian Pacific Railway (CPR), a world-wide upsurge in wheat prices, the growth of food-processing and allied businesses, and, especially after 1914, the development of natural gas and oil companies, prompted the city's rapid metamorphosis from a small center in a cattle ranching region to an industrial and financial hub, albeit one particularly prone to cycles of boom and bust.[6]

During these years Calgary grew primarily through in-migration. Settlers from the provinces of eastern Canada, immigrants from across Europe, and European step-migrants who first had made homes in eastern Canada all swelled the ranks of Calgarians.[7] So, too, did immigrants from the United States. In the two decades prior to the Great War, as many as 600,000 Americans flooded into Canada's Prairie West, settling the agricultural frontier and adding to the workforce in the region's extractive, manufacturing, and commercial centers.[8] By 1911 immigrants from the United States comprised more than a fifth of Alberta's population, and in some rural areas Americans made up nearly half of all the province's farmers.[9] In that year more than three thousand Americans lived in Calgary, comprising more than 7 percent of the city's population and 13 percent of its foreign-born residents.[10] Ironically, the establishment of the "Calgary Stampede," a rodeo extravaganza, signaled that Americans had begun to put their stamp on the city. This world-famous exhibition of the "cowboy days" of the Canadian West was created by an American entrepreneur, and even its founding was an exercise in racialized nostalgia, for by 1912 the ranching frontier in Alberta (wrested earlier from First Nations peoples) had given way, for the most part, to farming and gas and oil drilling.[11] American men were prominent in all these economic endeavors, from the ranches, farms, and wells in outlying districts to the banks and businesses lining downtown streets.[12]

Established the same year as the Stampede, the AWC more quietly testified to the substantial presence of Americans in the city. Virtually from inception, the club expressed its identity as a society of American women in Canada by joining both the most prominent umbrella organization of U.S. women's organizations, the General Federation of Women's Clubs, and the Calgary branch of Canada's most important coalition of women's societies, the National Council of Women.[13] When the AWC joined the Local Council in 1913, the group encompassed forty-eight societies, ranging from the Young Women's Christian Association (YWCA) and the Women's Christian Temperance Union (WCTU) to the smaller Society for the Prevention of Tuberculosis.[14] As I discuss below, affiliation with the Local Council sometimes proved problematic for the AWC, since the alliance of Calgary women took on lobbying efforts and social causes that stretched the AWC's boundaries of acceptable activity and engaged the aloof Americans more closely with their Canadian environs.

The attention of these—and other—Americans did not always prove welcome, for intermingled currents of Canadian nationalism, British empirism, and anti-Americanism periodically coursed through Calgary as elsewhere in the Dominion. The Local Council, for example, also included the Woman's Canadian Club of Calgary, established in 1911 to foster patriotism and promote Canadianism.[15] This club regarded the schools as a crucial arena for acculturation, for example offering prizes "to those of the English speaking foreign born students...who have shown greatest progress in the study of Canadian history."[16] Aimed primarily at the children of southern and eastern European immigrants to Calgary, this assimilation project may well have extended to the sons and daughters of Americans. In contrast, the Anglophilia underpinning much of the club's nationalist vision probably exempted the offspring of the city's numerous English settlers from this effort. Indeed, some leading women of British origin or descent (including those born in Canada) conducted their own immigrant assimilation campaigns as members of the Calgary branch of the Imperial Order of the Daughters of the Empire. Affiliated with the Local Council but open to membership only through invitation, this exclusive society's motto—"One Flag, One Throne, One Empire"—at least rhetorically distanced it from the AWC, whose patriotism flouted the superiority and supremacy of the Union Jack.[17]

A major economic dispute in the long-troublesome arena of tariffs between Canada and the United States also shaped opinion about American immigrants. The year before the AWC's founding witnessed the Dominion-wide "Reciprocity debate," a bitter controversy over U.S.-Canadian trade relations that resurrected many Canadians' fears of American imperial designs.[18] In this climate, wealthy Calgary lawyer R. B. Bennett came into national political prominence, winning a seat in Parliament largely by running against a special tariff arrangement with the United States. Bennett, a Conservative, appealed to Albertans to reject tariff "reciprocity" and thereby defy what he deemed yet another annexation effort of Canada by the United States, this time an economic rather than military expression of "manifest destiny."[19] Once in Parliament Bennett decried the continued immigration of the U.S.-born, with their "love of republican democracy" and "spirit of unrest," as one of the "two greatest dangers which threaten the [Canadian] west today." Ironically, as his critics pointed out, the other peril Bennett saw looming was "the ease with which people can get rich"—precisely what Bennett had accomplished by speculating in Albertan real estate, much of it sold to settlers from the United States.[20]

This prosperous and influential politician (who served as prime min- ister two decades later) also led a successful anti-American effort in his home district. Many well-to-do U.S. immigrants lived in a subdivision in the southwest section of the city designated as "American Hill." Believing that they, like other immigrants, should forge loyalties to Canada, Bennett spearheaded a campaign to have the CPR, which owned the land, rename the subdivision "Mount Royal" and give its streets patriotic Canadian names.[21] In a stroke, the "Americanness" of this fashionable ethnic enclave thus was erased from public view, if not social memory or lived experi- ence. For despite the official name change, through the 1940s and beyond, many Americans resided in the substantial homes that dotted the hill- side of Mount Royal. Members of the AWC clustered there and in the stately apartment buildings that lined the numbered avenues just to the north, recruiting neighbors to join the club.[22] Suitably, it was in Mount Royal that in 1938 the AWC bought its own clubhouse, purchasing and refurbishing a snug brick building that had housed a telephone exchange.[23]

The great majority of women who met in the clubhouse and in the rented rooms that served the AWC during the first quarter century of the club's existence were married. Although the announcement of the club's formation explicitly welcomed "all American women, young and old, married or single," like other women's organizations of its ilk during this era, the AWC primarily served as a club for wives.[24] Of the nearly 500 women accepted for membership from 1912 to 1942, 95 percent listed themselves by the title "Mrs" followed by their husbands' names (rather than their own first names).[25] The club founders consisted overwhelm- ingly of women who had arrived in Calgary when their husbands took positions in the city's bustling oil, lumber, milling, construction, and farm equipment firms, in banking, insurance, and real estate, or in the professions.[26] The very first name on the club roster, for example, was that of Mrs A.J. Cumming, who was married to an oil executive. Likewise, other charter members included Mrs Walter F. McNeill, wife of an owner and manager of a coal mine in nearby Canmore; Mrs E.T.

Critchley, married to the managing director of a major lumber company; Mrs Charles E. Fenkell and Mrs. Jacob Stoft, whose husbands were sales managers for a leading paint firm and the CPR, respectively; and Mrs A. McKillop, whose husband owned a wholesale shoe business and was regarded as a "prominent sportsman." Mrs J.M. Streib's husband had a distinctively American occupation: he managed the Calgary Baseball Club, furthering a sport whose popularity already had eclipsed that of Canada's lacrosse.[27] Four unmarried charter members form an interesting contrast. One worked as a stenographer and another gave as her occupation "president West End WCTU"; a third, Dr. Helen E. Walker, was an osteopath who had a private practice in partnership with the husbands of two other founding AWC members; and the fourth, Miss Mabel Childs, was a "comptometer" who soon gave up operating her intricate adding machine to become the wife of S.C. Reat, the American consul to Calgary.[28]

The club continued to have this class and marital profile, with members in the main coming from the ranks of the well-to-do professional and, especially, business elite.[29] Like such privileged women in the United States (and Canada) some of the married members carved out prominent places in the community in their own rights, most through their contributions in the realm of women's clubs. Among the charter members, for example, Mrs E.P. Newhall, a Canadian-born legal secretary who had resided in the United States for nearly thirty years, headed the Calgary Consumers' League.[30] After a distinguished nursing career, Mrs W.J. Selby Walker transferred her talents to the leadership in the YWCA and activism on behalf of the city hospital.[31] Similarly, at least three AWC stalwarts served as presidents of the Local Council of Women, the most celebrated of whom was Alice Jamieson, the Council's inaugural and four-time executive.[32] The widow of the general superintendent of the CPR, in 1915 Jamieson became Canada's first woman juvenile court judge and, two years later, the country's second female police court magistrate.[33]

In terms of place of birth, the AWC comprehended a far-flung membership. During its first three decades the club drew members from twenty-eight states (and the then-territory of Alaska), but disproportionately from the West (Colorado, Kansas, Montana, Nebraska, North Dakota, South Dakota) and, even more, from the Midwest (Illinois, Iowa, Michigan, Minnesota, Missouri, Ohio, Wisconsin).[34] Fully half the members were Midwesterners, and one in six came from Minnesota alone, some of whom must have found Calgary's low humidity and looming mountains a substantial change. Looking at these data from a borderlands perspective reveals that nearly three of five were born in states sharing the boundary with Canada.[35] While some who joined the AWC were born in cities larger than Calgary (including Chicago and Minneapolis), most came from smaller places (including two from the evocatively named Americus, Kansas). Not all members were born in the United States, with the club accepting women born in New Zealand, Australia, Germany, Bohemia, and, perhaps most intriguingly, Canada itself (including Ontario and even Alberta). One declared herself a "naturalized American," but the remainder claimed American nationality—and it would seem, identity—derivatively, stating that one or both of their parents or, twice as often, that their husband was American-born.

For AWC members on the whole, the occupational needs and personal inclinations of their husbands prompted their migration to Alberta. The AWC referred to itself as a "home away from home" and its members as "ships that pass in the night," reflecting the expectation that these women would regard prairie Calgary as a landlocked port of call and would leave, as they came, according to their husbands' itineraries.[36] For many members Calgary apparently did prove a short-term location. The minute books record the departure of members matter-of-factly, their resignations accepted with regret but without surprise. In 1930 the club formalized the ritual of leaving: those with three years' membership received a teaspoon decorated with a bluebird, the club's emblem.[37] Nonetheless some members spent many years in Calgary, at least a few remaining in the city most of their lives. Mrs Roy Beavers, for instance, was born in Illinois, arrived in Calgary in 1911, joined the AWC in 1916, and was a partner with her husband in the Club Cafe, a popular downtown bar and restaurant; she was an AWC member until her death in 1973.[38] Others had similar or even greater longevity in Calgary and in the club: Mrs Clarence Cosgrove, for example, belonged for fifty-four years; Mrs William H. Blatchford, sixty years; and Mrs Walter McNeill, sixty-two years.[39] These matriarchs may have been exceptional in their decades of affiliation, but fragmentary evidence indicates that a sizeable segment of the membership stayed in Alberta, some becoming pillars of the AWC. For instance, the club made a practice of visiting local cemeteries each May to place flowers on the graves of "departed members."[40] The roster of the club's sixtieth anniversary celebration, held in 1972, similarly testifies to some members' residential persistence and enduring organizational attachment. Mrs E.T. Critchley was the only charter member attending the festive gathering, but eight others at the luncheon had been affiliated for more than forty years, another nineteen for at least two decades, and eleven more for at least ten years.[41]

Yet this pattern did not alter the organization's conception that it served American women who found only temporary quarters across the border. In 1960, veteran member Mrs McNeill, whose daughter-in-law also was active for years in the club, reasserted this view, declaring that the AWC was "ever striving to give happiness and friendship to the many Americans who come and go from Calgary."[42] Several episodes in the history of the AWC during both world wars and the interwar years illustrate how these self-proclaimed sojourners expressed their liminal status as civic outsiders in Calgary.

* * *

IN SEEKING TO UNDERSTAND the constructions of national identity of these elite migrant women, I relied on the club's scrupulously kept minute books, attending to disruptions in the club members' comfortable, albeit energetic and time-consuming, routine of benevolent visiting, socializing, and attendance at lectures on a parade of places they clearly deemed exotic (from China and the Soviet Union to Iceland and the islands of the South Pacific). The very orderliness of their doings and the bureaucratic assiduousness with which they recorded their leisure-time endeavors make departures from this routine more remarkable.

The devastating global conflict of the Great War provides the first context in which to trace their negotiations of identity and allegiance.

Beginning in 1914, Calgary's Local Council led the mobilization of women's organizations to aid the war effort and meet the needs of those on the home front.[43] In Local Council meetings and throughout the city, AWC members must have witnessed evidence of Canada's involvement in the war, even while their nation remained a noncombatant until April 1917. To Calgary's west, hundreds of immigrants from the Ukraine and other lands constituting the Austro-Hungarian Empire were incarcerated in a mountainous internment camp. In February 1916 anti-German sentiment in the city fueled a riot, with 1,500 soldiers and citizens destroying two restaurants and a hotel in an immigrant neighborhood.[44] Moreover, thousands of soldiers trained at military bases in Calgary, among them more than 150 Americans, sons of American residents in Canada or men who had left the United States to fight in Canadian regiments against the Central Powers.[45] Some trained locally would not survive: by war's end, Alberta had Canada's highest rates both of enlistments and casualties.[46]

Despite the proximity of massed troops and the visibility of a mobilized homefront, AWC support for the Allied effort was meager prior to U.S. entry into the war.[47] In 1915 the club sponsored a speaker who lectured on "Certain Aspects of the Present World War" and the next summer held a concert to benefit a local Serbian Relief Fund.[48] As wounded soldiers began to fill Calgary hospitals and convalescent homes, the club donated money, exercise equipment, clothing, and reading material.[49] In late October 1916, the club turned over proceeds of another benefit to the Local Council "for the purpose of buying dainties for the soldiers at the front," apparently the club's first direct support for Allied forces.[50] Its timing could not have been more opportune for reassuring a skeptical Calgary public of American virtue: two weeks before, several hundred American volunteers in the Canadian Expeditionary Force had stormed the local barracks of the Royal Canadian North West Mounted Police, protesting the conviction of five of their number who had violated Alberta's liquor law.[51] The club marked the next patriotic occasion, Abraham Lincoln's birthday in mid-February 1917, by hosting a card party to raise funds for Belgian children.[52]

Such small-scale activities helped prepare the club for the intensive work it undertook upon America's declaration of war two months later. The AWC immediately organized a group called the "Daughters of the Allies," led by its members but including other women in Calgary. Reflecting the AWC's organizational prowess, the Daughters of the Allies quickly convened a series of knitting and sewing groups, purchasing machines and supplies, installing the machines in rented quarters, issuing a schedule of times for the groups to meet, and suggesting quotas to fill.[53] The results of their labors proved impressive. In eighteen months the Daughters of the Allies produced nearly 38,000 articles of clothing, the monthly totals made by each group duly logged in the club's minute books. They furnished the U.S. Navy League with only 500 of these articles and supplied the rest, via the Local Council, to the Canadian Red Cross.[54] Their contributions to this charity exceeded that of any other women's organization in Alberta, an achievement of particular pride for the club.[55]

Turning its attention to the home front, in June 1918 the AWC issued the *Daughters of the Allies Conservation Cook Book*, which it "offered to the public as an aid in the conservation of Beef, Bacon, Sugar, and animal fats, which are needed by our soldiers." These self-proclaimed "thrifty housewives of Calgary" assured potential buyers that they had tested the recipes themselves, and dedicated their book to "The Soldiers of the Allies," with the "earnest wish that [it] may be of real assistance in winning the world's greatest war."[56] In response to this shared national emergency, the club seems to have earned the name of its relief organization, the American outsiders becoming allies of their Canadian counterparts.

Notwithstanding this collaboration, the AWC remained detached from most civic activism in Calgary throughout the Great War and into the 1930s. At the same meeting in December 1916, for example, that the club's executive board agreed to continue providing magazines to recuperating Canadian veterans, it refused to endorse a series of measures proposed by the Local Council regarding equal property rights for wives, mothers' pensions, and neo-natal care, deeming these issues "not within our province as a body to discuss or consider."[57] Three years later the AWC shelved an initiative by the Calgary Consumers' League to limit business profits to 10 percent, despite charter member Mrs Newhall's leadership in the League; in 1923 the club tabled a Local Council proposal to abolish capital punishment; and the following year it declined to participate in the District Anti-Narcotic League's campaign "to limit the growth of poppy and coca plants" internationally.[58]

While refusing to support these and other activities defined as beyond its scope, the AWC cooperated with the Local Council and other Calgary groups on selected social issues and benevolent efforts. The club promoted community singing; worked with civic agencies to curb the 1918–1919 influenza epidemic; supported the area chapters of the Salvation Army and Humane Society; and sometimes allocated funds to Calgary's Public Welfare Board for dispersal to the local poor, in part to quell criticism of the club's practice of assisting only indigent Americans.[59] Similarly, in 1925 the AWC helped the WCTU decorate a float for the Stampede Parade by lending it an Uncle Sam outfit.[60] With Prohibition the law of their nation, club members seemed either to have construed this gesture as nonpartisan, despite Alberta having rescinded a ban on the sale of alcohol two years before, or believed the temperance battle, wherever joined, fell within its purview.

Throughout the interwar period, only one major public issue seemed to engage club members' sentiments, occasionally puncturing their civic reserve and garnering their discursive support. The horrific spectacle of the Great War, perhaps glimpsed more fully because witnessed from Canadian ground, seems to have convinced the AWC of the merits of international endeavors to foster peace. Hence, although the United States did not join the League of Nations, American women in Alberta did. For all but a few years, the AWC was an organizational member of the League until the Second World War, and then aligned itself with its successor, the United Nations. An example from the post–World War I period illustrates both how sincere and how circumscribed was the club's advocacy of its most outward-looking cause.

In the early 1920s Alberta suffered from a postwar economic slump and a prolonged drought, leading to business closures and unemployment in Calgary; woman's suffrage recently had been enacted in both the homeland of AWC members and their land of settlement; and international tensions ran high.[61] Meanwhile, as usual, the activities of the club revolved around the hospitality and recreation of its members. But in September 1921 world affairs encroached on this citadel of affluent female American sojourners when one of its members, Mrs H.H. McKinney, the wife of a "life assurance" manager, put forward a bold proposal for the club's endorsement.[62] She urged her club sisters to send a resolution "to the representatives of the land of their birth and the land of their adoption," supporting "the disbanding of armies and navies and the disarmament of the world."[63] It seems that this extraordinary request was met with stunned silence: club members at first took no action on it, instead turning to the planning for the annual Thanksgiving dinner dance, held as per the U.S. custom in November (not October, when the holiday is celebrated in Canada) and then listening to a travelogue on India. But before the meeting adjourned, controversy broke out over the proposed resolution, the details of the disagreement characteristically glossed over in the club's minutes. The upshot of the apparently protracted wrangling, however, is clear: a motion to send the resolution to U.S. Senator Henry Cabot Lodge prevailed. On this occasion, concern about world affairs interrupted the socializing, and in the name of international peace the organization crossed the line into a mild form of political action directed at its own, but not Canada's, government.

During the remainder of the decade the club took no similar action, although it hosted speakers who stressed the need for world peace.[64] But in 1934, as fascism triumphed in Europe and beyond and as the goal of international harmony consequently appeared both more elusive and more urgent, the AWC enthusiastically joined Calgary's newly formed Peace Council.[65] The club embraced the group's plan to hold a city-wide rally in November 1935, the seventeenth anniversary of the end of the Great War, becoming a sponsor of the day-long event. Once again the club took a firm rhetorical stand, this time joining with Canadians to urge the leaders of the Dominion, rather than the American government, to take action. The AWC endorsed a Peace Council resolution that

"Canadian foreign policy should be directed toward the eventual establishment of a world body, clothed with the legal authority to regulate
distribution of raw material in accordance with the needs of mankind,
irrespective of political frontiers."[66] The proposed international body
would exercise sovereignty over the United States as well as Canada, of
course, but for a brief moment the members of the AWC seem to have
allowed concern for global peace to supersede their commitment to maintaining national borders, including the 49th parallel. However fleetingly,
they seem also to have set aside (or perhaps failed to consider) the implications of such a resolution on their own circumstances as wives of men
whose wealth rested to a great extent in controlling the distribution of
just such materials—oil, gas, foodstuffs—as the proposed international
body would regulate. In the next five years, as fascist forces overcame
armed resistance in such far-flung places as Ethiopia, China, and Spain,
the AWC remained active in Calgary's Peace Council; sent dues to the
Women's Peace and Disarmament Committee based in Geneva, Switzerland;
heard lectures on developments in the Mediterranean, Asia, South America,
and, especially, Europe; and, in the wake of the Nazi takeover of Austria,
discussed "Great Britain's foreign policy" and again sent members to a
local peace rally.[67]

High-blown rhetoric about distant conflicts and pie-in-the sky international economic tribunals being one thing, action counter to class
position and ideology quite another, throughout the grim years of the
Depression the wealthy women of the AWC declined to cooperate in efforts
to alleviate Calgary's suffering populace. In 1934, the same year that the
club joined the Peace Council, it resigned from the Local Council of
Women, AWC members voting unanimously to sever the decades-long
tie.[68] The immediate impetus for the break was the Local Council's denun-
ciation of a cut in relief payments to the unemployed, but the AWC had
become restive almost as soon as the Depression hit, rejecting the Council's
advocacy for Calgary's poor and working-class residents as too political.
In 1930, for example, the club refused to participate in Local Council
programs to aid unemployed women and improve local recreation facilities; three years later it declined to join the Council's protest of the

closing of dental clinics and its effort to curtail landlords' seizures of household property from women delinquent in rent.[69] Instead, throughout these hard times the club confined its benevolence primarily to providing charity to needy Americans, a long-standing practice taxed by increasing demand; delivering Christmas hampers to Canadian families it deemed especially poverty-stricken and worthy; and sending books, used magazines, and playing cards to men in relief camps.[70]

When war once more engulfed the globe at the end of the decade, AWC members again confronted the problem of how to situate themselves, as foreigners, in the civic landscape of a combatant nation. Unlike World War I, when the AWC had waited for American entry to undertake its marathon sewing sessions, the club began a sewing campaign in September 1939, when Canada entered World War II. No longer affiliated with their Canadian counterparts through the city's coalition of women's groups, club members perhaps felt their organization's as well as their nation's isolation and sought to demonstrate some immediate support for their neighbor's cause. But six months into this effort (and eighteen months before the U.S. joined the war), charter member Mrs McNeill, now fifty-nine years old, expressed her concern that the AWC was flagging in its duty and urged members to increase their output of caps, sweaters, socks, sheets, dressing gowns, hot water bag covers, and "pneumonia jackets." Invoking the club's proud heritage of production during the Great War, she extolled the attainments of the Daughters of the Allies to an audience largely unfamiliar with the group.[71]

The unhurried pace of the members' sewing machines and knitting needles in early 1940 may have reflected the AWC's then muted and partial sympathy with the Allied cause. The club's day-to-day routines continued much as usual, its minutes omitting even an announcement of Canada's taking up of arms. The first inkling that the Dominion would enter the fray occurred in an off-hand comment made regarding a last-minute "change in program" for a regular meeting of the club's Domestic Science branch. On 5 September 1939, four days after German troops invaded Poland, and just five days before Canada formally joined the Allied war effort, club member Mrs Philips announced with regret that "owing to Mr. Lick enlisting for war service he was unable to carry out [the] Standard Brands demonstration and talk [but that a] demonstrator of Magic Baking Powder" would come instead, adding that she "anticipated an interesting program" despite this substitution.[72]

Similarly, the AWC's bulletin of upcoming club events for the year 1940–1941, printed just a few months after Mrs McNeill's admonition, viewed the catastrophic world situation at arm's length; in contradistinction it lauded the close ties between Canada and the United States. Such annual club calendars had a fairly standard format, with the first few pages typically listing the lyrics to one American and one Canadian patriotic song side by side. The 1940–1941 edition, however, featured a fascinating hybrid consisting of four patriotic songs.[73] In addition to the words for the "Star Spangled Banner" and "O, Canada," the bulletin included "God Bless America," with an introduction alluding to the danger, rather than the actuality, of war "across the sea." The calendar also included a song that interwove the two nation's histories, destinies, and identities. The "International Hymn" began with the first stanza of "America the Beautiful"; continued with the first stanza of "God Save the King"; and concluded with a stanza that celebrated what club members evidently regarded as the common British, English-speaking, Christian heritage that bound Americans with Canadians:

Two empires by the sea,
Two nations, great and free,
One anthem raise.
One race of ancient fame,
One tongue, one faith, we claim.
One God, whose glorious name
We love and praise.

Likewise, the unusual inclusion of a poem entitled "Our Borderline" bespoke the club's sentiment that the international divide separating the United States and Canada proved no barrier to this common heritage but rather symbolized the kinship between nations. In the poem's words, the boundary constituted "three thousand miles" that represent "living proof to all the world of faith in brotherhood." This paean to the 49th parallel concludes by invoking a half-century-old trope of American-Canadian relations: "God speed that surely dawning day—that coming hour divine—/ When all the nations of the earth shall boast such border line."[74]

Thus in the spring of 1940, with the army of the Third Reich already occupying Poland to its east and Hitler secretly planning the invasion of France, members of the AWC held the war-torn world at a distance. Identifying as citizens of a noncombatant nation, they located them-selves outside the global conflict. Simultaneously, they recast themselves as members of a civic society that stretched across the U.S.-Canada bor-der, rhetorically relinquishing their position as outsiders to the nation in which they dwelt.[75] Yet their assertion of an imagined joint Anglophile heritage and mythologized history of continuous harmony between the United States and Canada did not alter the fact that the international boundary then divided a neutral nation from an embattled country, nor did their invocation of a "surely dawning day" of international peace square with the reality that throughout much of the world former bor-ders had become soaked with blood.

By November 1940 the presence in Calgary of their own countrymen as volunteer soldiers, echoing the Great War, seems to have rendered the yearbook's discursive transborder allegiance as well the war itself more palpable for club members. While the AWC declined to help raise funds for Allied aircraft, turning down a member's suggestion that they "spon-sor a Spitfire Drive for Americans," the club took up the entertainment of Americans training nearby, inaugurating a program of twice-monthly Sunday dinners.[76] At first the club hosted only U.S. officers and service-men but soon expanded their guest list to include Australians, New Zealanders, and then Canadians.[77] Perhaps to provide the soldiers with suitably manly conversation, club members also invited their husbands to attend, and out-of-town members, often on the margins of club activities, contributed produce and chickens for the hearty suppers.[78] Then in February 1941 the war for which so many Canadians already had sacrificed became more personal and tangible to the AWC when an American volunteer was killed nearby.[79]

Quentin Burl Chace from Wichita, Kansas, held the rank of Leading Air Craftsman in the Royal Canadian Air Force (RCAF). He and RCAF Sergeant Pilot Alfred Reginbal of Lafleche, Saskatchewan, died while on a training mission, their plane crashing twenty miles [32 km] west of Calgary.[80] In August 1941, along a barren roadside near the crash site, AWC members gathered with local leaders to unveil a stone monument to the American and Canadian fliers, erected by the city's League of Nations chapter. At its regular monthly meeting three weeks later, the club voted to accept custody of the Chace-Reginbal memorial, agreeing to maintain the cairn and decorate it with a wreath on patriotic occasions.[81] The month after the crash, the AWC invited an American woman who was not a club member to be their guest at a Sunday dinner: Mrs S. F. Chace, the young Kansan's widow.[82]

Characteristically, after the U.S. joined the Allies in December 1941, the club's wartime activities accelerated. The AWC stepped up its production of knitted and sewn garments, participated in local anti-inflation and rationing efforts (even forswearing coffee and tea at its monthly meetings), heard speeches on wartime conditions in Europe and Asia, entertained servicewomen and Red Cross volunteers, visited the wounded in city hospitals, and donated funds to help furnish a clubhouse for U.S. officers stationed in Calgary.

Yet even with the United States fully engaged in the war, its homeland rapidly and thoroughly mobilized to support the Allies, the AWC's efforts to support the cause remained saturated with gendered gentility. At least in their official records, club members cast, in wartime even more pointedly than in peace, what historian Laura Wexler has in another context termed the "averted gaze," a look of "domestic sentiment [that] normalize[s]" relations of dominance. In this case, the AWC's averted gaze domesticated global state-sponsored violence.[83] During the war years, for example, the club's Travel Department noted a lecture offered to the group on "Head Hunting in the Solomons" in the same tone (and perhaps with similar racist tinges) as it reported on a slide presentation portraying events at Pearl Harbor and U.S. President Franklin Roosevelt's subsequent signing of the declaration of war against Japan.[84] Other AWC departments seemed to adopt a similarly normalizing view about wartime conditions. The Domestic Science department announced to the club's general membership "an interesting program" of study for 1942 and 1943 that "stress[ed] sugarless cakes, inexpensive dishes and suggestions for overseas parcels."[85] In like vein, the Arts and Crafts department, pursuing the theme of "war and crafts," heard at one of its meetings a "splendid" report that ranged from the difficulty of obtaining spinach seed, to the continued export of fine blankets, lace, and tweeds from Britain, to the status of "brave China," which had "hidden in her hills... 30,000 tiny industries, goods carried in every conceivable fashion...[and people living] in caves—moving from one spot to another when necessary but always with the resolve that the work must go on."[86] Club members translated even the equipment of death into an object of refined discussion. As the naval battle raged in the North Atlantic, in the course of a meeting's usual round of reports club members learned, seemingly with equanimity, that their fundraising "had supplied a depth charge for the Calgary Corvette [sic]." Six months later, tucked into the corresponding secretary's report, is notification of the receipt of a "letter from J. Davis, officer of the ship *La Malbin* [sic] thanking us for the depth charge."[87] To what end that depth charge was put remains unremarked in the AWC records; having raised the monies to provide it and received courteous thanks for doing so, these elite women mentioned the topic no more.

* * *

SUPPORTING THE ALLIED CAUSE, hoping for victory, and perhaps imagining the peacetime world that might ensue, in fall 1942 AWC members held a fundraising tea for the "United Nations," a term coined earlier that year by Franklin Roosevelt to denote the twenty-six countries fighting against the Axis Powers.[88] A photograph of the event printed in a local paper captures the AWC's signature combination of efficient but well-bred organizing, cautious internationalism, sororal

FIGURE 11.1: *On 29 September 1942 the American Woman's Club of Calgary hosted a tea for more than 400 guests at their clubhouse. The club raised funds for the United Nations by selling corsages that incorporated war savings stamps. L. to r: Miss Dorothy Benfield, Mrs S. G. Coultis, Mrs F. M. Motter, and Miss Delores Heiters.*

[*J. L. Rosettis, photographer. Permission of* The Calgary Herald]

if not matronizing admiration for Canada, and ebullient American patriotism.[89] The tea's convener, Mrs S.G. Coultis, and the club's president, Mrs F.M. Motter, wear corsages cleverly fashioned from fresh flowers and war savings stamps and lapel pins with war savings certificates attached, both designed by the club. They are clothed soberly but elegantly in dark dresses and veiled hats. Posed like cigarette girls, two young women, Miss Dorothy Benfield and Miss Delores Heiters (daughter of a prominent club member), flank the AWC officers, holding trays from which they sell the corsages and pins. Bedecked with Uncle Sam hats and clad in satiny, "attractive red, white, and blue star spangled costumes," these stylish vendors sport sashes declaring that they are "Calgary U.S.A. Miss Canadas." All four are smiling, seemingly pleased with and proud of themselves, each other, the club, their endeavor, and their homeland.

FIGURE 11.2: *The executive of the American Woman's Club, May 1956. Mrs V. V. Forcade, far left, presents a gavel to Mrs Wilbur McNeill, second from right. She stands between two charter members of the club, her mother-in-law Mrs Walter F. McNeill (far right) and Mrs E. T. Critchley (second from left). Despite the club's identity as a haven for sojourners, many club leaders persisted for decades in Calgary. 3 May 1956.*

[Jack De Lorme, photographer, The Albertan; permission of Glenbow Archives NA-5600–8449a]

Perhaps at the time of this event the AWC, then fully launched in its country's wartime cause, subsumed the identity of Canada beneath the U.S., erasing the border between the countries in support of a postwar world where a "united nations"—under American hegemony—would prevail. Had she lived to see that day, Mrs H.H. McKinney, who two decades before had swayed the AWC to appeal for disarmament, no doubt would have endorsed the club's reconceptualization, however fleeting, of their allegiance as well their implicit confidence in their nation's leadership in a postwar world.

Rather than simply mirroring elite Canadians residing in the United States, as journalist Anne Anderson Perry portrayed them in 1922, AWC members constituted, intentionally or not, representatives of an increasingly dominant nation whose shadow lengthened across its northern neighbor during the first half of the twentieth century.

Exploring the identities of the elite women who comprised the AWC is one means to shed light on the making of a transnational prairie West and the crafting of a gendered Americanism during the first half of the twentieth century. All the women who belonged to the AWC crossed the international borderline and took up residence in Calgary at least long enough to seek out and affiliate with others of their nationality, race, gender, and class; for some this affiliation lasted for decades, the club becoming an absorbing arena beyond their families and the clubhouse a sustaining female domain. Boasting patriotic corsages and dining at banquet tables resplendent with U.S. flags, these well-to-do American women living in Canada reinforced their national pride in ways that both paralleled and departed from women in other ethnic societies. Resistant to assimilation, seemingly secure in their national superiority, and insulated by wealth, they generally set themselves apart from Canadian women, even those of their social rank. In the dusty prairie city they regarded as a temporary dwelling place, these cosseted ladies attended to their own pastimes and to charity work for needy Americans, largely ignoring the problems and concerns of their neighbors. Occasionally, however, these privileged, self-styled sojourners to a physically proximate, vaguely alien land moved beyond the boundaries they imposed upon themselves and others.

In multiple dimensions the members of the AWC occupied a position of hyper-privilege: as they interacted on apparent terms of ease and social equality with elite women of Calgary, they simultaneously embodied American presence and genteelly extended American power. Hosting Fourth of July galas and emblazoning their clubhouse door with an American eagle, these white-gloved expatriates daintily but deftly stuck the Stars and Stripes into the upper crust of Calgary. In small but telling ways, the club's domestic dramas help to elucidate the complicated meanings and expressions of U.S. nationalism and, perhaps, cultural imperialism in the fifty years that came to constitute the "American Century."

AUTHOR'S NOTE

I undertook this project in fall 2000 while I held the Fulbright Chair in North American Studies at the University of Calgary. Support from the Burnham-Macmillan Fund of the Department of History at Western Michigan University supported a subsequent research trip. I extend hearty thanks to Laurel Halladay, a graduate student in the Department of History at the University of Calgary, for her scrupulous notetaking, insightful commentary, terse lessons in Canadian history, and bracing sense of humor. Thanks also to Sarah A. Carter, Elizabeth A. Jameson, and to other organizers of the conference on "Unsettled Pasts: Reconceiving the West through Women's History," held at the University of Calgary in 2002, where I presented a version of this paper. Other scholars in Calgary who graciously have aided my work are Heather J. Coleman, Richard Sicotte, Frank Towers, Catalina Vizcarra, and especially Jewel L. Spangler. Daniel Lenfest-Jameson was a generous and able assistant at the Glenbow Library and Archives. I appreciate the aid of staff members at the Glenbow, especially Jennifer Hamblin, and at the Calgary Public Library, especially Jennifer Bobrovitz. I received thoughtful comments from Alice B. Kasakoff , John J. Bukowczyk, and John Herd Thompson on previous versions of this paper presented at conferences and from colleagues and graduate students at Western Michigan University on a version presented at a History Department research colloquium. Their suggestions and especially those of this volume's clear-sighted and generous editors, Elizabeth A. Jameson and Sheila McManus, greatly improved the essay. Thanks finally to Michael J. Schroeder for his help on the project.

NOTES

1. Anne Anderson Perry, "The American Woman in Canada," *Saturday Night*, 1 April 1922, 31.

2. Perry, "American Woman in Canada," 31.

3. See Kathleen E. Oliver, "Splendid Circles: Women's Clubs in Calgary, 1912–1939" (master's thesis, University of Calgary, 1992). See also two essays in *Standing on New Ground: Women in Alberta*, ed. Catherine A. Cavanaugh and Randi R. Warne (Edmonton: University of Alberta, 1993): Nanci Langford, "'All That Glitters': The Political Apprenticeship of Alberta Women, 1916–1930," 71–85; and Catherine C. Cole and Ann Milovic, "Education, Community Service, and Social Life: The Alberta Women's Institutes and Rural Families, 1909–1945," 19–31.

4. See the announcement of the initial meeting, which included an open invitation for membership: "Organization of a Club for American Women," *Calgary News Telegram*, 26 March 1912; and also "First American Woman's Club Organized," *Calgary News Telegram*, 1 April 1912.

5. *Western Standard Illustrated Weekly*, Souvenir Edition "Opportunity Number," (Calgary: Calgary Women's Press Club, 12 June 1913), n. p.

6. On Calgary's transformation see the *Western Standard* 1913 special issue, cited above; for more general information on the city's economy, see David Bright, *The Limits of Labour: Class Formation and the Labour Movement in Calgary, 1883–1929* (Vancouver: UBC Press, 1998). On the transformation of agriculture in the area surrounding Calgary and elsewhere in the prairies, see Cecilia Danysk, *Hired Hands: Labour and the Development of the Prairie Agriculture, 1880–1930* (Toronto: McClelland and Stewart, 1995), and more generally John Herd Thompson, *Forging the Prairie West: The Illustrated History of Canada* (Toronto: Oxford University Press, 1998), 43–104.

7. The stories of some of these immigrants and others who partook in the "opening of the West" are featured in chapter 12 of Dirk Hoerder, *Creating Societies: Immigrant Lives in Canada* (Montreal and Kingston: McGill-Queen's University Press, 1999).

8. For a general overview, see R. H. Coates and M. C. Maclean, *The American-Born in Canada: A Statistical Interpretation* (Toronto: Ryerson Press, 1943), especially pages 16–17, 24, 50, 56, 59. Estimates vary; see the discussion in John Herd Thompson and Stephen J. Randall, *Canada and the United States: Ambivalent Allies* (Athens and London: University of Georgia Press, 1994), 79–82.

9. Howard Palmer with Tamara Palmer, *Alberta: A New History* (Edmonton: Hurtig, 1990), 83. For a discussion of Americans migrating to the Canadian West before the 1890s see Simon Evans, "Tenderfoot to Rider: Learning 'Cowboying' on the Canadian Ranching Frontier," in *Cowboys, Ranchers and the Cattle Business: Cross-Border Perspectives on Ranching History*, ed. Simon Evans, Sarah Carter, and Bill Yeo (Calgary: University of Calgary Press; Boulder: University Press of Colorado, 2000), 61–80; on settlement patterns on both sides of the border see John W. Bennett and Seena B. Kohl, *Settling the Canadian-American West, 1890–1915* (Lincoln: University of Nebraska Press, 1995); and on the recruitment of Americans see Harold Martin Troper, *Only Farmers Need Apply: Canadian Government Encouragement of Immigration from the U.S., 1896–1911* (Toronto: Griffin, 1972); and also Michael B. Percy and Tamara Woroby, "American Homesteaders and the Canadian Prairies, 1899 and 1909," *Explorations in Entrepreneurial History* 24 (1987): 77–100, which offers a succinct overview of the historiography on this topic. There is a small but growing literature on migrations across the U.S.-Canada border. The classic work is Marcus L. Hansen and John Bartlett Brebner, *The Mingling of the Canadian and American Peoples* (New Haven, CT: Yale University Press, 1940). On migration from Canada to the United States see two important recent studies by Canadian scholars: Bruno Ramirez, *Crossing the 49th Parallel: Migration from Canada to the United States, 1900–1930* (Ithaca, NY: Cornell University Press, 2001) and Randy William Widdis, *With Scarcely a Ripple: Anglo-Canadian Migration into the United States and Western Canada, 1880–1920* (Montreal and Kingston: McGill-Queen's University Press, 1998). Increased scholarly interest on migration in this borderlands is attested to by special issues of two U.S. scholarly journals: John J. Bukowczyk and David R. Smith, eds., "Canadian Migration in the Great Lakes Region," Special issue, *Mid-America* 80 (Fall 1998): 208–34; and Donna R. Gabaccia, ed., "Migration and the Making of North America," Special issue, *Journal of American Ethnic History* 20 (Spring 2001): 3–132. See also Erika Lee,

"Enforcing the Borders: Chinese Exclusion along the U.S. Borders with Canada and Mexico, 1882–1924," *Journal of American History* 89 (June 2002): 54–86. For a regional approach applied to the Great Lakes Basin see Nora Faires, "Leaving the 'Land of the Second Chance': Migration from Ontario to the Great Lakes States in the Nineteenth and Early Twentieth Centuries," in *Permeable Border: The Great Lakes Basin as Transnational Region, 1650–1990*, ed. John J. Bukowczyk, Nora Faires, David R. Smith, and Randy William Widdis (Pittsburgh: University of Pittsburgh Press, 2005).

10.   Ten years later the number of Americans exceeded 5,000, remaining near this level through 1941, but dipping to 6 percent of the city's growing population. These figures calculated from Max Foran, *Calgary: An Illustrated History* (Toronto: James Lorimar, 1978), tables VII and VIII.

11.   Palmer and Palmer, *Alberta*, 125.

12.   Evans, "Tenderfoot to Rider," 70–72, 76–79; Foran, *Calgary: An Illustrated History*, 86–88; and Paul Voisey, "In Search of Wealth and Status: An Economic and Social Study of Entrepreneurs in Early Calgary," in *Frontier Calgary: Town, City, and Region, 1875–1914*, ed. Anthony W. Rasporich and Henry C. Klassen (Calgary: University of Calgary Press, McClelland and Stewart West, 1975), 221–41.

13.   The General Federation of Women's Clubs was founded in 1890; see the organization's official history, Mary B. Wood, *The History of the General Federation of Women's Clubs for the First Twenty-Two Years of Its Organization* (New York: General Federation of Women's Clubs, 1912). The Calgary Local Council of Women was established in 1896; see Marjorie Norris, *A Leaven of Ladies: A History of the Calgary Local Council of Women* (Calgary: Detselig, 1995). The period of the late nineteenth century through the 1920s was the heyday for the founding and consolidation of such women's societies, the literature on which is, of course, voluminous. For a comprehensive synthesis on U.S. societies from the nineteenth through the mid-twentieth century see Anne Firor Scott, *Natural Allies: Women's Associations in American History* (Urbana: University of Illinois, 1991). Scott's carefully researched overview is generally admiring of these associations, de-emphasizing conflicts within and among such groups. An influential examination of divisions within such organizations is Nancy Hewitt, "Beyond the Search for Sisterhood: American Women's History in the 1980s," *Social History* 10 (October 1985): 299–321. For a sense of the historiography regarding the significance of these institutions' gender separatism see two contributions by Estelle Freedman: "Separatism as Strategy: Female Institution Building and American Feminism, 1870–1930," *Feminist Studies* 5 (Fall 1979): 512–20; and "Separatism Revisited: Women's Institutions, Social Reform and the Career of Miriam Van Waters," in *U.S. History as Women's History: New Feminist Essays*, ed. Linda K. Kerber, Kathryn Kish Sklar, and Alice Kessler-Harris (Chapel Hill: University of North Carolina, 1995). A recent contribution stresses the impact of activist women and their clubs in shaping urban politics, even before suffrage; see Maureen A. Flanagan, *Seeing with Their Hearts: Chicago Women and the Vision of the Good City, 1871–1933* (Princeton and Oxford: Princeton University Press, 2002).

14.   Norris, *Leaven of Ladies*, 13, 63–72.

15.   Elise A. Corbet, "Woman's Canadian Club of Calgary," *Alberta Historical Review* 28 (1977): 29–36; Oliver, "Splendid Circles," 52–54. See also *The Calgary Club Woman's Blue Book, 1916*

(Calgary: Calgary Branch of the Canadian Woman's Press Club, 1916), 23–25 and *The Alberta Club Woman's Blue Book, 1917* (Calgary: Calgary Branch of the Canadian Women's Press Club, 1917), 67, 69. Unlike the AWC, which had no male counterpart, there was also a Men's Canadian Club, with which the women's organization regularly participated.

16. *Calgary Club Woman's Blue Book, 1916*, 25.

17. Oliver, "Splendid Circles," 49–52; Norris, *Leaven of Ladies*, 69–70. The Imperial Order of the Daughters of the Empire began in part to broaden support for the British effort during the Boer War (1899–1902); the Calgary branch began in 1909.

18. In the first half of the twentieth century, as in more recent years, tariff issues raged between the United States and Canada, with tremendous consequences for Albertans. On the "reciprocity debate" see, for example, Ross Hawthorne Bayard, "Anti-Americanism in Canada and the Abortive Reciprocity Agreement of 1911" (PhD diss., University of South Carolina, 1971); and for a good discussion of the impact of high U.S. tariffs on Albertan ranchers in the 1920s see Max Foran, "Fighting a Losing Battle: Canadian Stockmen and the American Tariffs, 1920–1930," *Alberta History* 74, no. 4 (Fall 2000): 775–98. For an overall discussion see Thompson and Randall, *Canada and the United States*, 86–92; Robert Craig Brown and Ramsay Cook, *A Nation Transformed: Canada, 1896–1921*, The Canadian Centenary Series (Toronto: McClelland and Stewart, 1974), 162–87; and L. E. Ellis, *Reciprocity 1911: A Study in Canadian-American Relations* (New Haven, CT: Yale University Press, 1939).

19. James H. Gray, *R. B. Bennett: The Calgary Years* (Toronto: University of Toronto Press, 1991), 116–19.

20. "Two Greatest Dangers," *Calgary News Telegram*, 12 March 1912. The controversy over this speech continued for several weeks, with Bennett claiming he had been misquoted, to the benefit of his Liberal opponents; see "R. B. Bennett Is Willing To Resign And Run Again If Electors Of Calgary Demand That He Do So," *Calgary News Telegram*, 25 March 1912.

21. See Gray, *Bennett*, 120–22, and P. B. Waite, *The Loner: Three Sketches of the Life and Ideas of R. B. Bennett, 1870–1947*, The 1991 Joanne Goodman Lectures (Toronto: University of Toronto Press, 1992), 42–60. Bennett's nationalist vision is discussed in Carl Berger, *The Sense of Power: Studies in the Ideas of Canadian Imperialism, 1867–1914* (Toronto: University of Toronto Press, 1970). Vociferously anti-Chinese, throughout his career Bennett regarded foreigners as subjects for assimilation. As Conservative leader Bennett launched another noisy anti-American campaign during the election of 1930; see John Herd Thompson with Allen Seager, *Decades of Discord: Canada, 1922–1939*, The Canadian Centenary Series (Toronto: McClelland and Stewart, 1985), 201–05.

22. *Glimpses of the Past*, American Woman's Club of Calgary, Golden Anniversary booklet, 1962, p. 4, American Woman's Club Records, Account Number 5979 (hereafter cited as AWC Records), Box 7, File 36, Glenbow Archives, Calgary, AB. This area featured middle- and upper-middle-class housing built in the boom decade after the turn of the century. One frequent address for AWC members was "The Devenish," located in the 900 block of 17th Ave. S. W., an elegant brick apartment building erected by investor and contractor O.G. Devenish, whose wife was an AWC member. (Occupational data from *Henderson's Calgary City Directory, 1915*). Between April 1914 and November 1918 at least ten

club members resided at The Devenish, with three sequentially occupying the same apartment. Addresses of club members are given on application forms filed between 1912 and 1942; see the alphabetical card index to applications, AWC Records, Box 6, File 27. For a description of the development of Mount Royal as a site for substantial and costly single family residences see the first-person account of an early home buyer in *Western Standard*, Special Issue, 12 June 1913.

23. General Meeting Minutes, 1934–1938, Report of the Annual May Luncheon, 1938, ledger, p. 19, AWC Records, Box 1, File 5. The clubhouse is located at 1010 14th Avenue S. W.

24. "Organization of a Club for American Women," *Calgary News Telegram*, 26 March 1912.

25. The total number is 488. The percentage married may be an underestimate. Of the twenty-five members who did not list themselves as "Mrs" only nine called themselves "Miss," the remaining sixteen using their names without a title; for the purposes of this discussion I have included them among those not married. Marital status could and did change. Some who joined as single subsequently married, and some may have been or later became widowed or divorced. These data derive from the alphabetical card index of application forms (1912–1942), AWC Records, Box 6, File 27.

26. Of the seventy-five founding members, *Henderson's Calgary City Directory, 1912*, provided information on fifty-two husbands' occupations. Of these, six held professions (one as an attorney in R. B. Bennett's firm); nineteen were executives or managers of large businesses, including oil, lumber, flour milling, and agricultural implement concerns; another twelve were bankers or entrepreneurs in real estate and allied businesses; twelve more worked in middle-level managerial and sales positions for an array of enterprises; three had craft jobs; and one was a farmer. These data confirm references in *Glimpses of the Past* and in Kate Gunn, "The American Woman's Club of Calgary, 1912–1921: 'A Home Away From Home,'" *Fort Calgary Quarterly* 4 (Winter 1983): 8–11.

27. See Thompson, *Decades of Discord*, 186–87.

28. Data on all but two of these members are from *Henderson's Calgary City Directory, 1912*; on McNeill, information derives from the obituary of Walter Floyd McNeill, undated clipping, Newspaper Clipping Files, Glenbow Library, Calgary, AB; and on McKillop from the obituary of Archie McKillop, (Calgary) *Daily Herald*, 25 April 1921, Newspaper Clipping Files, Glenbow Library.

29. These data are fragmentary and derive from an analysis of the occupations of sixty-seven members or their husbands from 1913 to 1945, as listed in volumes of *Henderson's Calgary City Directory*.

30. On Mrs E. P. (Georgina) Newhall, see Norris, *Leaven of Ladies*, 187–96, and photograph p. 128.

31. See "Women Who Make News Include Club Leader" (stamped 4 April 1942) and "Woman Appointed to Hospital Board" (stamped 24 October 1963), in Clipping File Local History Collection, Castell Central Library, Calgary Public Library, Calgary, AB (hereafter, Local History Collection, Castell, CPL).

32. "80 Years of Calgary Local Council of Women, 1912–1992—In Honor of Calgary's Centennial, 1994," Scrapbook, Local History Collection, Castell, CPL; Norris, *Leaven of Ladies*, 263.

33. Norris, *Leaven of Ladies*, 163–73, photograph p. 125; "Alberta Women We Should Know—Alice Jamieson," in *Pioneer Women of Western Canada*, ed. Margot Smith and Carol Pasternak, researched and compiled by Men and Women Unlimited, Calgary, Alberta, as part of an Opportunities for Youth Project (Toronto: Ontario Institute for Studies in Education, 1978), 50–54. Jamieson arrived in Calgary with her husband, R. R. Jamieson, in 1902; he later served as Calgary's mayor. See Jean Leslie, "Reuben R. Jamieson, Mayor 1909–1910," in *Past and Present: People and Events in Calgary—Accounts by Calgary Authors* (Calgary: Century Calgary Publications, 1975).

34. Data on place of birth rely on evidence for one hundred forty members; the information derives from the alphabetical card index of membership application forms filed between 1912 and 1942, AWC Records, Box 6, File 27.

35. The figure is 57.1 percent. Of the fourteen states extending along the international divide from Maine to Washington, only New Hampshire and, surprisingly, Idaho had no representatives among the AWC's membership.

36. *Glimpses of the Past*; Gunn, "American Woman's Club," 8.

37. General Meeting Minutes, 1925–1930, minutes for meeting of 7 January 1930, ledger pp. 171–72, AWC Records, Box 1, File 4.

38. "Beavers Tales: The Man Who Catered to Stampede Appetites," *Albertan Sunday Tab*, 8 July 1979, Clipping File—Biography, Local History Collection, Castell, CPL. Mrs Beavers' sister also lived in Calgary for more than sixty years, but seems not to have joined the AWC. See Minutes, 1951–1975, Hospital and Memorial Minutes, n. p., AWC Records, Box 6, File 23, obituary clippings.

39. Information on all these members are from obituaries pasted into Minutes, 1951–1975, Hospital and Memorial Minutes, n. p., AWC Records, Box 6, File 23, obituary clippings.

40. See General Meeting Minutes, 1930–1934, minutes of meeting of 3 September 1934 at which a report is provided of that year's Decoration Day service at Calgary's Union Cemetery for "11 departed members." AWC Records, Box 1, File 4a.

41. American Woman's Club 60th Anniversary, 1912–1972—Lake Bonavista Inn, oversize, AWC Records.

42. *The Bluebird Cookbook*, American Woman's Club of Calgary, (yellow book), c. 1960, p. 3, Cookbooks Collection, Box 2, Glenbow Library, Calgary, AB.

43. Norris, *Leaven of Ladies*, 86–89. Before the war the Local Council, in cooperation with its constituent member, the Women's Canadian Club, had been active in efforts to Canadianize southern and eastern European immigrants, singling out those from the Ukraine as in special need of acculturation; this view infused some of their war-time activities. See more generally Frances Swyripa and John Herd Thompson, eds., *Loyalties in Conflict: Ukrainians in Canada during the First World War* (Edmonton: Canadian Institute of Ukrainian Studies, University of Alberta, 1983).

44. Palmer, *Alberta*, 171–73; P. Whitney Lackenbauer, "Under Siege: The CEF Attack on the RNWMP Barracks in Calgary, October 1916," *Alberta History* 49 (Summer 2001): 3.

45. On men born in the United States who served in the Calgary-based 50th Battalion (1914–1915) and the 3rd, 12th, and 13th Regiments Canadian Mounted Rifles, Canadian Expeditionary Force, see "Alberta Family Histories Societies, Canadian Expeditionary Force, Nominal Rolls," available at http://www. afhs.ab.ca/data/rolls/index.html. For an

overview see Fred Gaffen, *Cross-Border Warriors: Canadians in American Forces, Americans in Canadian Forces from the Civil War to the Gulf* (Toronto: Dundurn Press, 1995), 13–16.

46. Of the approximately 45,000 men from Alberta who served in the war, over 6,000 perished. Palmer, *Alberta*, 167.

47. I base this view on discussions of AWC activities in the *Calgary Club Woman's Blue Book, 1915* (Calgary: Calgary Branch of the Canadian Women's Press Club, 1915), 26–27 and the *Calgary Club Woman's Blue Book, 1916*, 25–28. Unfortunately club minutes are available only beginning in August 1916, and these records are partial until December 1917; see Executive Board Minutes, 1916–1921, AWC Records, Box 3, File 14; and General Meeting Minutes, 1917–1925, AWC Records, Box 1, File 3.

48. On the speaker, see *Calgary Club Woman's Blue Book, 1915*, 27. The concert is reported on at the meeting of 28 August 1916, the first meeting for the initial extant minute book; see Executive Board Minutes, AWC Records, Box 3, File 14. Serbian relief received substantial support in Calgary, especially from the Imperial Order of the Daughters of the Empire; see *Alberta Club Woman's Blue Book, 1917*, 98–99.

49. *Glimpses of Our Past*, 8; *Alberta Club Woman's Blue Book, 1917*, 72.

50. Executive Board Minutes, minutes for meeting of 27 October 1916, AWC Records, Box 3, File 14.

51. Lackenbauer, "The CEF under Siege."

52. On the planning of the event see Executive Board Minutes, 26 January 1917, AWC Records, Box 3, File 14; see also *Alberta Club Woman's Blue Book, 1917*, 72.

53. *Alberta Club Woman's Blue Book, 1917*, 73.

54. The totals for May 1917 to May 1918 were 203 articles to the U.S. Navy League and 16,880 to the Canadian Red Cross; June 1918 to December 1918, 320 and 20,507 articles, respectively. *Glimpses of Our Past*, 8–9. On totals for each month see, for example, General Meeting Minutes, 1917–1925, minutes for meeting of 7 May 1918, ledger pp. 18–19, AWC Records, Box 1, File 3.

55. General Meeting Minutes, 1917–1925, minutes for meeting of 4 February 1919, ledger p. 34, AWC Records, Box 1, File 3.

56. *Daughters of the Allies Conservation Cook Book: A Collection of Tested Recipes Compiled by the Friday Unit* (Calgary: n.p., June 1918), 5, Cookbooks Collection, Box 2, Glenbow Library, Calgary, AB.

57. Executive Board Minutes, 1916–1926, meeting of 29 December 1916, AWC Records, Box 3, File 14.

58. General Meeting Minutes, 1917–1925, meeting of 7 November 1919, ledger p. 56, AWC Records, Box 1, File 2; Executive Board Meeting Minutes, 1916–1926, minutes for meeting of 29 March 1923, Box 3, File 14; and General Meeting Minutes, 1917–1925, meeting of 2 September 1924, ledger pp. 249–50, Box 1, File 2.

59. General Meeting Minutes, 1917–1925, meetings of 3 December 1918, ledger p. 27 and 7 January 1919, ledger p. 32, AWC Records, Box 1, File 2; General Meeting Minutes, 1930–1934, meeting of 2 January 1934, ledger p. 165, AWC Records, Box 1, File 4a.

60. Executive Board Meeting Minutes, 1916–1926, minutes for meetings of March 1920 (n. d.), 6 May 1924, and 28 August 1925, AWC Records, Box 3, File 14.

61. On economic conditions during the early 1920s see Bright, *Limits of Labor*, 120–44.

62. H.H. McKinney is listed as "agency manager for South Alberta, Northern Life Assurance Co. of Canada" in *Henderson's Calgary City Directory, 1919*.

63. General Meeting Minutes, 1917–1925, ledger pp. 128–29, AWC Records, Box 1, File 3.

64. For example, see General Meeting Minutes, 1925–1930, minutes of meetings of 6 November 1928, ledger p. 123, and 5 November 1929, ledger pp. 158–60, AWC Records, Box 1, File 4. Such talks often were held to mark Armistice Day.

65. General Meeting Minutes, 1934–1938, minutes of meeting of 3 April 1934, ledger p. 183, AWC Records, Box 1, File 5.

66. General Meeting Minutes, 1934–1938, minutes of meeting of November 1935 (n. d.), ledger pp. 67–72, quote p. 72, AWC Records, Box 1, File 5.

67. General Meeting Minutes, 1934–1938, minutes of meetings of April 1936 (n. d.), ledger p. 107; February 1937 (n. d.), ledger pp. 150–51; October 1937, ledger p. 185, AWC Records, Box 1, File 5; and General Meeting Minutes, 1938–1942, minutes of meeting of 1 April 1938, ledger p. 12, AWC Records, Box 1, File 6.

68. General Meeting Minutes, 1934–1938, minutes of meeting of 4 December 1934, ledger p. 15, AWC Records, Box 1, File 5.

69. General Meeting Minutes, 1925–1930, minutes of meeting of 4 March 1930, ledger p. 181, AWC Records, Box 1, File 4; General Meeting Minutes, 1934–1938, minutes of meetings of 2 December 1930, ledger p. 13; 7 January 1933, ledger p. 107; and 7 February 1933, ledger p. 114, AWC Records, Box 1, File 5.

70. See, for example, General Meeting Minutes, 1934–1938, minutes of meetings of 7 March 1933, ledger p. 24, and 2 January 1934, ledger p. 160, 165, AWC Records, Box 1, File 5. On the impact of the Depression see Thompson, *Decades of Discord*, 193–276, and especially on relief camps, 269–72.

71. General Meeting Minutes, 1938–1942, minutes of meeting of 6 February 1940, ledger pp. 97–98, AWC Records, Box 1, File 6.

72. General Meeting Minutes, 1938–1942, minutes of meeting of 5 September 1939, ledger p. 75, AWC Records, Box 1, File 6.

73. American Woman's Club of Calgary, Calendar, Season of 1940–1941, pp. 2–3, AWC Records, Box 7, File 35.

74. American Woman's Club of Calgary, Calendar, Season of 1940–1941, p. 5, AWC Records, Box 7, File 35. The attribution for this poem provided in the club's calendar is "Courtesy of the New York *Times*."

75. Notably the club apparently had reproduced this poem once before, in its yearbook for 1934–1935. At that point the AWC was still affiliated with the Local Council and was becoming more active in the Peace Council. See General Meeting Minutes, 1930–1934, minutes of meeting of 3 September 1934, ledger p. 191, AWC Records, Box 1, File 4a.

76. The Spitfire would become a legendary British fighter plane. General Meeting Minutes, 1938–1942, minutes of meeting of 5 November 1940, ledger pp. 124–25, AWC Records, Box 1, File 6. At the same meeting they set up twice-weekly sewing sessions of "layettes and clothing for [the] British homeless."

77. American Woman's Club of Calgary Guest Book, 1940–1964, signatures for 17 November, 11 December, and 15 December 1940 and 26 January, 9 February, 23 February, and 9 March 1941, AWC Records, Box 7, File 34.

78.   General Meeting Minutes, 1938–1942, minutes of meeting of 4 February 1941, ledger p. 138, AWC Records, Box 1, File 6.

79.   On Canadian troops and the conduct of the war, see, for example, Donald Creighton, *The Forked Road: Canada, 1939–1957*, The Canadian Centenary Series (Toronto: McClelland and Stewart, 1976), 62–109.

80.   Cochrane and Area Historical Society, *Big Hill Country: Cochrane and Area* (Cochrane, AB: Cochrane and Area Historical Society, 1977), 296.

81.   General Meeting Minutes, 1938–1942, minutes of meeting of 2 September 1941, ledger p. 160, and Annual Report, 1941/1942 (filed April 1942), ledger pp. 156, 163, AWC Records, Box 1, File 6.

82.   American Woman's Club of Calgary Guest Book, 1940–1964, 9 March 1941, AWC Records, Box 7, File 34.

83.   Laura Wexler, *Tender Violence: Domestic Visions in an Age of U.S. Imperialism* (Chapel Hill: University of North Carolina, 2000), 6.

84.   The Travel Committee reports are in General Meeting Minutes, 1942–1946, minutes of meeting of 6 April 1943, ledger p. 45, AWC Records, Box 2, File 7; and Minutes, 1941–1967, Arts and Crafts Department, minutes of meeting of 17 November 1942, ledger p. 31, AWC Records, Box 5, File 21.

85.   General Meeting Minutes, 1942–1946, minutes of meeting of 1 May 1942, ledger p. 5, AWC Records, Box 2, File 7.

86.   Minutes, 1941–1967, Arts and Crafts Department, minutes of meeting of 16 February 1941, ledger pp. 6–8, AWC Records, Box 5, File 21.

87.   General Meeting Minutes, 1942–1946, minutes of meetings of 6 September 1943, ledger p. 58, and 1 February 1944, ledger p. 75, AWC Records, Box 2, File 7. The minute taker made two errors in the notes for these meetings. The ship should be listed as the "corvette *Calgary*," referring the HMCS Calgary, K-231, launched in 1941. See http://www. marine.forces/ca/calgary/about/ship—about—e.asp?category=70. Regarding the ship, the minute taker probably meant HMCS *la Malbaie*, a Flower class corvette, K-273. See http://uboat.net.allies/warships/ship/870.html. My thanks to John Herd Thompson for calling these mistakes to my attention and providing these corrections.

88.   See "About the United Nations—History," available at the official website of the United Nations, http://www.un.org/aboutun/history/html. Roosevelt first used this phrase a month after the U.S. entry into the war, at a meeting on 1 January 1942 with representatives from twenty-five other nations, including Canada, fighting the Axis.

89.   This photograph appeared in the *Calgary Herald*, 30 September 1942; see the accompanying article "United Nations Tea Attracts More than Four Hundred."

12

EXCERPTS FROM
POURIN' DOWN RAIN[1]

CHERYL FOGGO

DURING A RECENT COMMITTEE MEETING where a group of women were working on some documents, I mentioned that I wanted to be cautious about the wordsmithing. "Published words live forever," I said. One of the women responded in genuine distress: "Surely our writing has to be taken in the context of the day. Do we have to worry about what people will think of us fifty years from now?"

The world moves on, things change, and our knowledge grows. Writers are no different from others in their experience of change, but we are set apart by the fact that our words, frozen in time, reveal our past ignorance.

When I started writing *Pourin' Down Rain* in 1985 there was no Internet and very little printed material documenting the experiences of western Canada's Black pioneers. The elders of the community weren't accustomed to thinking of their stories as interesting or of historical relevance. They feared exposure and backlash. I had to perform cartwheels and headstands to get people to talk about the past—with the exception of my Great-aunt Daisy. But even she, like the others, didn't want to talk about racism.

Those are the reasons—and there may be others—that *Pourin' Down Rain* seems incomplete to me now. But the upside to the passage of time and the long-term exploration of a topic is that we sometimes get to witness the change we work to create in the world. Elderly former residents of Alberta and Saskatchewan's Black pioneer communities now appear to feel honoured by the attention my work and the work of other historians has brought to their stories, and I've had the opportunity to witness their dignified presence at events where their lives have been celebrated. Some speak more freely about both the joys and sorrows of Black Canadian life and don't seem to fear that talking will lead to reprisals.

These pages are excerpts, dealing with my family's physical and psychological cross-border experiences spanning several generations and decades. But they were written twenty years ago, based on the knowledge I had at that time. As you peruse them, know that in the distant and recent past, many Black citizens were refused service in Canadian prairie restaurants, hotels and recreational facilities, and that a group of supremacists conducted a cross-burning in Alberta in 1990, the same year *Pourin' Down Rain* was published.

* * *

OUR STREET CONTAINED the closest thing to a Black community that one would find in Calgary in 1961. Ricky Hayes' parents were biracial, but he, his brother Randy and sister Debbie considered themselves Black. The Hayes', their grandparents across the alley, my family and the Saunders and Lawson families up the road comprised what I believe was the largest concentration of Black people in a single Calgary neighbourhood.

My parents had an attitude of kinship toward the other Black families on the street. The families knew one another, they knew each other's parents and grandparents, and probably because of that "knowing," they communicated to us our connection to other Black children. We played together. Without isolating ourselves from the other children in the neighbourhood and without any discussion of it, we sensed a link that transcended our environs.

Across the street from our house was another field which we had to cross to reach the railroad tracks leading to the twin bridges, the Bow River, and ultimately, to the paths that took us "up in the hills."

Most summer days we spent meandering along the tracks to the river, the usual goal being a picnic in the hills. The picnic, however, was not really the point. The point was the adventure we would sometimes encounter along the way.

On a very warm day, if there was no breeze, the heat from the iron rails and sharp smell of oil and metal bouncing up into our faces would drive us down from the tracks to walk through the high grasses. This meant slower going, but it was good to sniff the flowers instead of the heat and to dig around what someone would insist was a badger hole.

From the first time my brothers pronounced me old enough to go along with them, until I was sixteen and we moved from Bowness, the journey along the tracks to the river, across the bridges and up into the hills was real life. It was the meeting place, it was where we went to talk and light campfires, it was something we did that our parents did not do.

Across the alley from us lived two children, a brother and sister, who never joined the treks to the hills if we and the Hayes children were going. Their father forbade them from associating with us, and effectively ostracized his children from the rest of the neighbourhood by prohibiting them from joining any games where we Black children were present. When groups formed for kick-the-can or softball, we were often aware of these two children's eyes peering out from the cracks in their fence. They were there, we were aware of their presence, and in retrospect, their loneliness seems palpable.

When I was young, I was minimally aware that racism was a special problem. People who shared our neighbour's prejudices seemed so rare and to have so little effect on my life that I did not attribute their bigotry to a world condition.

My mother had implanted in the minds of my two older brothers, my younger sister and myself that we were special, not ordinary in any way. She would refer to our bigoted neighbour with utter contempt, as "the likes of him," implying that his ideas and his two unfortunate children were unworthy of our time or thoughts.

The diligence of our mother freed the minds of me and my siblings from the self-hatred that can cripple Black children born in ghettos.

Still, even a fiercely proud mother's constant reassurances cannot protect her Black child from learning, sooner or later, that skin is a badge you will always wear, a form of identification for those in the world who wish to brand you.

One afternoon upon returning from school I overheard my mother talking on the telephone to Mr Leavitt, the principal of my elementary school. He was calling to plead with her to try to persuade Floyd Hayes to discourage his children from fighting at school. Floyd was the brother of my mother's twin sister's husband and the father of the aforementioned friends, Randy, Ricky and Debbie.

"I'm afraid that I can't agree with you, Mr Leavitt," she was saying. "I'm not going to tell them how to handle their problems. They came from a place where they can't fight. Where they come from a Black person doesn't have a chance against racists, and if Mr Hayes has decided his children are going to fight name-calling with their fists, that's up to him."

When my mother replaced the receiver on its hook on the wall, I pestered her with questions. What did Mr Leavitt want? Why had he called her? Were Randy and Ricky in trouble? What did she mean when she said Floyd had come from somewhere else where they couldn't fight it? Fight what?

"Jim Crow. They couldn't fight Jim Crow down there, but he's determined he's going to fight it here."

"Who is Jim Crow?"

"It's not who, it's what. It's called Jim Crow when Black people aren't allowed to ride at the front of the bus, or drink from the same fountains as Whites."

"Jim Crow?" I repeated. "Jim Crow. Where is the Jim Crow?"

"Kansas. Floyd and them were all born in Kansas."

If Floyd "and them" were all born in Kansas, that meant that my Uncle Allen, Floyd's younger brother, had been born there too, and that he had lived with this Jim Crow.

"Is Kansas in Canada?" I asked nervously.

"No, oh no," my mother said. "We don't have that kind of thing here. Kansas is in the States. Allen and Floyd and them never went to the movie houses when they were kids, not because they didn't believe in it, but because nobody was going to tell them that they had to sit up in the balcony or at the back. They came to Canada to get away from that, and they figure they're not going to tell their kids to stand by while anyone calls them 'nigger' either."

My mother was clearly quite agitated by Mr Leavitt's call. I knew that she would repeat the entire conversation, with some embellishment, to her sisters Pearl and Edie on the telephone later that evening.

As for me, I was relieved to learn that Kansas was not in Canada. Here was yet another story, another horrific tale of life in "The States," fuelling my growing belief that I was lucky to have been born in Canada.

Only short days before Mr Leavitt's call I had learned that my grandparents, my mother's father and mother, had also once lived in America.

The discovery came to me when I asked my mother to explain why my grandpa was White, yet his brother, Uncle Buster, was Black.

My grandfather was something less than five feet, ten inches tall. He had grey eyes, he wore glasses over his long, narrow nose and he was light-skinned.

He had been called George Washington Smith at birth, but upon joining the Canadian Army in 1919 he revealed the full extent of his embarrassment over the name and lied to his commanding officer, saying that his middle initial stood for Willis. Thereafter, he was known as George Willis Smith and that is how I knew him.

I believe he possessed an average build, although it is difficult to be certain as he always dressed in loose clothing, in particular a pair of grey-beige pants and a yellow shirt.

He had a deep voice and a low, rolling, rumbling laugh. He began most sentences with the phrase, "Well, ya take." He called his five sons

"Son," his four daughters "Daughter" and he sometimes called me "Granddaughter."

He would say, "Well, ya take, Granddaughter, I don't yodel when big girls (referring to my grandmother, who was singing in the kitchen) are listenin'. I only yodel for special small girls."

He was born in Chandler, Oklahoma, on October 31st, 1897. When I say that he was light-skinned, I mean that his skin color was indistinguishable from that of any White person.

That is why, in 1963 when I was seven years old, I asked my mother how he could be White and his brother be Black.

She turned and stared at me. "Your Grandpa is not White."

"He is," I said.

I went to the china cabinet and took the photograph of my grandparents with their children taken on the occasion of their fortieth wedding anniversary. Carefully, I took it to my mother and placed it in her hands.

"Look."

My mother took the picture and brushed it gently, wiping away imaginary dust.

"He has very fair skin, honey, but he isn't a White man. What he would say if he knew his grandchildren thought so!" She was very amused and continued, "You see, just look at his hair."

I looked, but seeing nothing remarkable about his metallic-grey, brushed-back hair, did not speak.

"You're not going to find any White man on earth with hair like that," she said. "Daddy has him some bad hair."

"Bad" was how she described any head of hair, like my brother Richard's or my cousin Sharon's, that was very tight and nappy. She frequently caused me considerable grief by comparing my hair with my sister's, whose loose and supple hair qualified as "good hair."

I continued to gaze glumly at the photograph in my mother's hand. I was embarrassed at having been wrong about my grandfather. There he sat, beside my dark-skinned grandmother, to whom all along I thought he had been blissfully and interracially married.

"Grandma is Black." I finally said.

"Uhhm hmm, no one would ever mistake your grandmother for White. Daddy and Mama used to run into trouble when they went back to the States. If Daddy wears a hat, you see, he can't lay claim to his heritage. He used to wonder why nobody bothered him when he went into the White areas.

"Once, Mama and Daddy went to Oklahoma to see Mom's relatives. They'd been shopping and made plans to meet in a restaurant for lunch. Daddy got there first, took a table and told the waiter that he was waiting for his wife. He didn't take his hat off until he sat down. When Mama got there she joined Daddy at his table, but no one came to take their order. The waiter walked all around them, just like they weren't there. He acted like he was deaf when Daddy said 'Excuse me.'

"Finally a person came from the kitchen and whispered, 'I'm sorry, but we won't be able to serve you today.'

"Daddy was shocked. He was a young boy when they left the States and had forgotten what it was like there. He really got angry. He stood up and said, 'You sure were planning to serve me before I took my hat off.' He started to go toward the man, but Mama stopped him. 'No George, let's just get our things and go,' she said, 'We don't need for you to land up in jail down here.' Mama and Daddy got out of there and shook the dust of that place off of their feet. Daddy's never gone back again, never again."

Knowing my grandparents to be the gentle, lovely people that they were, I couldn't imagine what kind of madness would cause them to be treated in such a manner. I began to fear the very words whenever I heard someone refer to "The States." I vowed that I, like my grandfather, would not bother to darken America's doorstep.

* * *

VARIOUS MINORITIES will occasionally experience periods of trendiness in North America. An event or string of events in a foreign country will trigger the onset of a phenomenon such as the Nehru jacket. Fashions in hair and clothing will reflect the influence of the season's foreign culture of choice. Suddenly, even people who despise cooked fish will know everything there is to know about sushi. Japanese models will sprinkle the pages of *Vogue*.

In the early seventies, North American Blacks experienced our episode of modishness, or what we referred to then as being "in."

Even our neighbours in Bowness had heard that "Black is Beautiful." Comics like George Carlin and groups like the Rolling Stones were bragging about their Black connections. White bands wore afros, White students at Bowness High School followed suit and played blues on their harmonicas in the courtyard.

It was a short-lived time, but fortunately for me occurred during my adolescence. While undergoing the standard severe pain of being fourteen, I had my newly "cool" blackness to give me a sense of purpose.

I felt noble the night that I decided I would no longer straighten my hair. I was going natural. Bolstering my confidence was the shriek of delight that I elicited from Sharon when I informed her of my decision and displayed my afro to her. Her approval more than compensated for the titters that greeted me when I walked into my classroom at school the next day. My resolve to demonstrate that I was "Black and Proud" in the way that James Brown described in his song was only cemented when a classmate shouted "Cheryl, did you stick your finger in an electrical outlet?" and my fellow students burst into laughter.

My older brothers and I had begun what could not actually have been considered dating, as that word implies actually going out somewhere, but what might be considered "pre" dating. Our forays into relationships with the opposite gender consisted of eating lunch with that person in the cafeteria, going to Bowness Park or Market Mall to hold hands during spares, or perhaps meeting on weekends to play records.

The average citizen of Calgary found biracial dating to be a great curiosity and passers by in vehicles would often strain their necks to ogle us if we ventured onto public streets in physical contact with a White friend of the opposite sex.

This was such a frequent occurrence that, in all honesty, I had ceased to take note of it until the advent into my life of a fellow student of

Bowness two years older than I, named Brian. I had met Brian at a camp for elementary school students which the two of us had been selected to attend as counsellors. We had been mutually intrigued. He informed me, for some reason, in the early stages of our attraction, that his father and grandfather were bigots. I was taken aback by this pronouncement, but as Brian indicated total disagreement with their views and clearly seemed intent upon pursuing our relationship, I shrugged it off.

When our week in the foothills camp ended and we returned to the city, I noticed that Brian was very disturbed by the stares we encountered on the street, blushing and becoming fidgety. I decided after a week or two that we should discuss his discomfort.

"Doesn't it bother you?" he asked me.

"Well, I don't like it, but what am I supposed to do, run after a car shouting, 'Hey, don't look at us?'"

"I don't know," he replied. "It just gives me the creeps."

We did not return to the topic again.

A week later, Brian did not appear at our usual morning meeting place at the school. When I saw him later, between classes and walked toward him smiling, he ignored me and hurried past. I stood in the hallway, stunned.

Over the next days I retained hope that Brian would explain his actions, but gradually I had to accept that he had rejected me utterly and did not wish to tell me why.

Had his parents learned of our friendship and forbidden it? Had a friend of his chided him regarding me? Was he simply unable to continue tolerating the curiosity of strangers? I do not know the answers to these questions now, nor does Brian know of the tremendous impact that our brief encounter has had upon my life.

Had I been older, or younger, I may have been more rational about my ordeal with Brian. As it was, already crippled by the daily horror of adolescence, I felt as though Brian had pierced my life with a poison dart.

I believed that I had only myself to blame for what had happened. I had trusted when I should not have done so. I had been drifting through my life with closed eyes.

I was not Black enough, I concluded. Too many years in a White world had caused me to forget, once too often, that I was Black and that my blackness was the first thing seen and reacted to by every white person that I met and that many, many people would never see beyond my skin. Whether I liked it or not, the world was Black and White and I had been attempting to live in the middle.

I began to retreat from what I perceived to be "White culture." I immersed myself in the literature of Black authors, became fascinated by the history of Black Americans and was attracted to Black music that reflected a "revolutionary" message. I no longer believed that Canada was a refuge from racism and resented being raised in isolation from other Blacks.

* * *

ON APRIL 16TH, 1912, my great-aunt Daisy celebrated her fifth birthday at a tiny train station in a town called Delmenie, Saskatchewan.

That day, she said, it was "pourin' down rain. It was pourin' down rain when we pulled out of the station in Oklahoma and it was pourin' down rain when we pulled into Delmenie, Saskatchewan."

She had been travelling with two older sisters and two older brothers, and the five of them were greeted by their mother and eldest sisters, Maude and Mary. They walked to a house that someone in town had rented, and as Daisy dashed from beneath the protection of their umbrellas to pick flowers that she saw growing along the path, her mother despaired, calling out to the little girl that she would "catch her death."

It had been more than two years from the time that my great-grandfather Rufus had announced that the family would leave Oklahoma to live in Canada, and almost two years since the family had been together. Rufus had arrived in Saskatchewan in 1910, along with hundreds of Black American farmers, mostly Oklahomans. He, like his fellow immigrants, was given a parcel of land, 160 acres, for the filing fee of ten dollars. He built a cabin and began to make preparations for the arrival of his wife and twelve children, who would come in twos and threes until the summer of 1912. Then, they would begin to live in their new world, as Canadians.

My great-grandfather transplanted his family approximately ten times in the waning years of the nineteenth and early years of the twentieth centuries. He was restless—nervous about the welfare of his children living Black in an increasingly hostile society. Especially after his parents' deaths (Jackson Smith on December 12, 1892 and Mary Smith on March 7, 1893) he no longer felt tied to his birth state, Arkansas. He, along with multitudes of former slaves, drifted into two districts known then as "Indian Territory" and "Western Territory," lands that, although within the boundaries of the United States of America, were not states. Black people could vote in the territories.

This attempt to remain a step ahead of total denial of human rights was only a mediocre success for Rufus Smith and his peers. Blacks could vote in the territories, but they were not welcome there. Lynchings and house burnings were as common in the territories as elsewhere, but Black people, cornered, believing that they must seize their humanity in the territories or be crushed, fought their enemies with every means available to them. Black men, including my great-grandfather, joined the Socialist Party of America, which at first promised to uphold them. The Socialist option proved to be a disappointment for Blacks when the party, reluctant to alienate poor White farmers and labourers, began to renege on its early commitment to Black concerns.

Frequent armed encounters between Blacks and Whites prompted Rufus Smith to move from town to town in the Indian Territory—from Wagoner to Bristow, to Fischer and finally to Tulsa, where the Smith family settled into a white house with a fence, on Frankfurt Avenue. This is where they were living in 1910 when Blacks lost voting privileges, three years after the territories had been merged into a state called Oklahoma.

At precisely the same time the Black Oklahomans were being brutalized by southern law, the Canadian government was taking out full-page ads in southern newspapers, offering 160 acres of land in its unsettled western provinces to anyone who could produce the filing fee of ten dollars.

To the almost unanimously Christian Blacks, the juxtaposition of these two events seemed to be much more than coincidence. Many of them began to believe that the "Promised Land" for which they had been searching throughout their lives lay to the North—a country about which most of them knew nothing except that it had sheltered weary slave travellers at the end of their journey on the underground railroad.

* * *

SOME RESIDUAL INNOCENCE, or naïveté from my childhood, allowed me to achieve adulthood with my belief in Canada as a non-racist society intact. I had experienced racism of the individual variety, but I trusted that my country's history was unblemished by sweeping, legislated bigotry.

Only when curiosity about my family's place in the Canadian demography prompted me to read about the reception of Blacks into Canada, only after I dissected my own family's oral histories, did I recognize my error.

Canada has frequently practised discrimination based on color and race, and every recognizable minority that lives here today has felt it.

The prospect of "too many" brown, black or yellow people making their home in Canada has, in the past, filled many White Canadians with fear, and in some cases, loathing. The same is true today.

When my great-grandfather crossed the forty-ninth parallel, he believed, in the way that many Black people of his time drew Biblical analogies to their own lives, that he was a kind of Moses, leading his family to the promised land. He had heard the Canadian winters could be harsh, but, having nothing in his past to teach him the meaning of the word "harsh," he was unprepared. He was also unprepared for Canadian racism. He learned that Canada's message of welcome had not been intended for him, or others like him.

We, the undersigned residents of the city of Edmonton, respectfully urge upon your attention and upon that of the government of which you are the head, the serious menace to the future welfare of a large portion of Western Canada, by reason of the alarming influx of Negro settlers. This influx commenced about four years ago in a very small way, only four or five families coming in the first season, followed by thirty or forty families the next year. Last year several hundred Negroes arrived in Edmonton and settled in surrounding territory. Already this season nearly three hundred have arrived; and the statement is made, both by these arrivals and by the press dispatches, that these are but the advance guard of hosts to follow. We submit that the advent of such Negroes as are now here was most unfortunate for the country, and that further arrivals in large numbers would be disastrous. We cannot allow as any factors the argument that these people may be good farmers or good citizens. It is a matter of common knowledge that it has been proved in the United States that Negroes and Whites cannot live in proximity without the occurrence of revolting lawlessness and the development of bitter race hatred, and that the most serious question facing the United States today is the Negro problem...There is not reason to believe that we have here a higher order of civilization, or that the introduction of a Negro problem here would have different results. We therefore respectfully urge that such steps immediately be taken by the government of Canada as will prevent any further immigration of Negroes into Western Canada.

This petition, issued by the Edmonton Board of Trade and supported by the signatures of 3,000 Edmontonians, was typical of reactions to Black immigration into Calgary, Winnipeg and Saskatoon. Also typical were threats of violence (which, true to gentle Canadian nature, were mostly not acted upon) and newspaper editorials carrying headlines like, "DARK INVASION" and "NO DARK SPOTS IN ALBERTA."

Canada's Liberal government, whose intent in advertising for pioneers throughout America had not been to attract Black farmers, faced the wrath of Canadian citizens and the Conservative opposition in the House of Commons. One such Conservative member is known to have stood one day to enquire whether it would not be wiser to "...preserve for the sons of Canada the lands they propose to give to niggers."

The dilemma of the government was this: how to squelch the flow of Blacks into Western Canada without interfering with the campaign to attract White farmers?

Attempts to censor inquiries from American farmers that arrived through the mail were pointless, as no envelope gave any clue to the color of its sender. Endeavours to find Blacks unfit to enter the country were ineffective also. Most of the Blacks that possessed the courage to migrate to an unknown land were also in excellent physical and financial condition. Bribing the border doctors was futile, as too few of them were willing to accept money to falsify records.

The solution that worked in the end was simple. The Canadian government hired a few Black men to travel throughout the American Southwest, to warn Black churches and organizations about the horrors of life in Canada. These paid men convinced thousands of Black people that Canada was barren and frigid, and offered them no better opportunities than what they already had.

Black immigration into Western Canada slowed, then trickled, then stopped in 1912, four years after it had begun with its "four or five families coming in the first season."

For the approximately two thousand Blacks who had already settled in Alberta and Saskatchewan, these developments were disappointing. Their numbers would remain small. It had been their hope to build an independent community that existed peacefully alongside its neighbours. They now believed that it would be a struggle for their community just to survive, let alone to be an example of Black success and racial harmony to the rest of the world.

Worse than this was the unsettling awareness that their welcome to Canada was not what they had expected, that their quest for a racial nirvana had been naïve.

There were two benefits that my great-grandfather and his peers reaped from their lack of large numbers in Canada. One was a network of closeness and support for one another. The other was that the Ku Klux Klan seemed to be unaware of their presence.

When the original furor over their arrival had subsided, the prairies' Black settlers analyzed their circumstances and most of them concluded that they had done the best thing for themselves and their families. Canada offered Blacks the right to vote, unsegregated education for their children and a relatively peaceful existence alongside their White neighbours, whose attitudes ranged from sullen tolerance to unfettered acceptance. Their lives were unmarred by lynchings and cross burnings.

NOTE

1.　Cheryl Foggo, *Pourin' Down Rain* (Calgary, AB: Detselig Enterprises, 1990), 4–10, 51–53, 105–107, 109–112.

THE BORDERLANDS OF
WOMEN'S WORK

THE ARTICLES in this section cross a number of unmarked boundaries in western histories. Historians Laurie Mercier and Cynthia Loch-Drake cross a temporal boundary to write about the period of World War II and the decades after it, rather than the frontiers of European colonization and settlement. They also explore a marginalized borderland of western labor history as they bring women's work and gender relations to the center of western working-class communities. Focusing on women's ties to one international labor union, the articles probe women's paid and unpaid labor, as single women and wives, during a pivotal period of change in women's work.

U.S. historian Laurie Mercier's prize-winning book *Anaconda* illuminated the importance of gender in the union community of one smelter city, Anaconda, Montana. Here, Mercier explores the ways that women's auxiliaries of the International Union of Mine Mill and Smelter Workers (Mine Mill) responded to Cold War pressures on both sides of the border during the 1950s. Cynthia Loch-Drake's article, which comes from her

University of Calgary M.A. thesis, represents some of the newest Canadian scholarship on women workers. Loch-Drake chronicles some of the few women who belonged to Mine Mill as union members and labor activists during the 1947 strike at the Medalta Potteries in Medicine Hat, Alberta. The strike revealed a great deal about how gender operated in the potteries, in the union, and most of all in the Alberta justice system, which treated male strikers as dangerous brutes and jailed them, but portrayed militant women strikers as helpless victims who needed protection.

Like those Alberta officials, most labor historians before the 1970s focused on labor unions and the minority of male wage earners who organized unions and waged strikes. Historians ignored the vast majority of people who worked because those people did not work for wages or belong to organized labor. This included most women, who, until recent decades, worked outside the public wage system. Older labor histories might, at most, mention the few women wageworkers who labored in unionized industries like textiles and shoe making.

If women workers were absent from traditional labor histories, they entered most western histories only as overworked pioneer helpmates.[1] The few historians who focused on cross-border histories recognized that workers regularly crossed the 49th parallel to mine, harvest, thresh, herd cattle, and cut timber.[2] They often belonged to the same international unions, like Mine Mill, that operated in both the United States and Canada. Because so many of these industries employed only men, women became invisible, though their work was essential to western industries and communities. Not until quite recently did historians suggest that western workers, like workers throughout North America, responded with a variety of strategies to changing industrial work conditions, nor did they consider the significance of women's work in male-dominated industries.

Since the 1970s, new histories have shifted the focus from organized labor to workers, including women, and to an expanded understanding of work that includes women's domestic labor, the work involved in bearing and raising children, and unpaid service work that organizes and maintains social institutions. This enlarged understanding of work encouraged new research on the women who provisioned the fur trade, served as cultural intermediaries, tanned hides, raised chickens and made butter for market, labored on family farms and ranches, and others who sold food, lodging, or sex to the men who outnumbered women on resource frontiers. In western mining towns on both sides of the 49th parallel women provided the service work, paid and unpaid, that supported the male workforce in a key western industry. The first histories of mining town women recognized their unpaid household labor, as well as the boardinghouse keepers, laundry workers, cooks, and sex workers who provided "domestic" services for the unmarried male majority. They highlighted, too, how women supported the miners' unions through their purchasing power, by organizing working-class social life, and with crucial strike support. Most of these histories focused on fabled boomtowns of the late nineteenth and early twentieth centuries.[3]

Mercier and Loch-Drake both explore women's roles in Mine Mill (1916–1967), a union that long preoccupied labor historians who struggled to explain why western workers were weird exceptions to a moderate mainstream. Organized in 1893 as the Western Federation of Miners (1893–1916), the union endorsed the Socialist Party, helped found the Industrial Workers of the World, and waged the strikes chronicled in dramatic labor histories. Changing its name in 1916 to the International Union of Mine, Mill and Smelter Workers (1916–1967), the union emphasized its commitment to organizing all workers in the mining industry, regardless of job or skill. That commitment to industrial unionism led it, in the 1930s, to help found the Congress of Industrial Organizations (CIO). Mine Mill advocated organizing all workers regardless of skill, industry, race, or gender, but, as Mercier and Loch-Drake demonstrate, it had some difficulty at times extending that egalitarian vision of labor unity to the masculine bastions of the mines and smelters and to the women of western mining and smelter towns.

Both articles illuminate a key transitional period in women's work as increasing numbers of married women entered the paid workforce during and after World War II, first to take the places of men in military service, and then for the same reasons most people work for wages: to support themselves and their families. That historic shift was particularly stark in mining and smelting towns, where paid work in the only local industry had been restricted to men. Mercier and Loch-Drake take us far beyond older debates about organized labor to illuminate the conflicting ideologies of work and gender that women confronted as they entered the public worlds of work, organizing, and labor politics in the postwar period.

The conflicted terrain of class and gender was further complicated by the ideological contexts of the Cold War. In both Canada and the United States, anti-communism became part of the rhetoric of renewed attacks on organized labor after World War II, in which Mine Mill was a frequent target. Mercier shows how women in the Mine Mill women's auxiliaries engaged in both sides of that ideological debate, on both sides of the border. Loch-Drake shows how the complex terrain of class, gender, and Cold War reaction led to different images of men and women activists, and different rewards and sanctions for their work as union members. In concert, these articles show how focusing on one cross-border institution, in this case a union, can provide interesting comparisons of how class and gender operated in different local and national contexts. They take us far beyond the questions of older labor histories to changing postwar gender roles, and to the local, personal, and private impacts of public work and public politics. They help us link the staple industries of older western histories to contemporary labor and gender relations.

NOTES

1.   See Beverly Stoeltje, "A Helpmate for Man Indeed: The Image of the Frontier Woman," *Journal of American Folklore* 88, no. 347 (January–March 1975): 27–31; Elizabeth Jameson, "Women as Workers, Women as Civilizers: True Womanhood in the Canadian West," in *The Women's West*, ed. Susan Armitage and Elizabeth Jameson (Norman: University of Oklahoma Press, 1987), 145–64.

2.   Walter Sage, "Some Aspects of the Frontier in Canadian History," Canadian Historical Association, *Annual Report*, 1928; "Geographical and Cultural Aspects of the Five Canadas," Canadian Historical Association, *Annual Report*, 1937; Herbert Heaton, "Other Wests Than Ours," *Journal of Economic History* 6, Issue Supplement: The Tasks of Economic History (1946): 50–62; Paul F. Sharp, "When Our West Moved North," *American Historical Review* 55 (1950): 286–300.

3.   For some of the early work on mining town women, see Elizabeth Jameson, "Imperfect Unions: Class and Gender in Cripple Creek, 1894–1904," *Frontiers* 1, no. 2 (Spring 1976): 85–117; also in Milton Cantor and Bruce Laurie, eds., *Class, Sex, and the Woman Worker* (Westport, CT: Greenwood Press, 1977), 166–202; Marion Goldman, *Gold Diggers and Silver Miners: Prostitution and Society on the Comstock Lode* (Ann Arbor: University of Michigan Press, 1981); Mary Murphy, "The Private Lives of Public Women: Prostitution in Butte, Montana, 1878–1917," in *The Women's West*, ed. Armitage and Jameson (Norman: University of Oklahoma Press, 1987), 193–206; Paula Petrik, *No Step Backward: Women and Family on the Rocky Mountain Mining Frontier, Helena, Montana, 1865–1900* (Helena: Montana Historical Society Press, 1987).

13

"A UNION WITHOUT WOMEN IS ONLY HALF ORGANIZED"

Mine Mill, Women's Auxiliaries, and Cold War Politics

in the North American Wests

LAURIE MERCIER

THE "UNSETTLED PASTS" CONFERENCE helped me recon-sider the permeability of borders and regions, especially regarding the influence of ideologies on the way people think about society, culture, and politics. Just as capital, and the power structures it has erected, has freely crossed borders, the ideas and strategies of social movements have also migrated, as the "international" character of U.S./Canadian labor unions reveal. We have seldom looked closely at the cross-border rela-tionships within unions to compare how working class women and men absorbed, negotiated, and contested ideologies about gender, race, cap-italism, nation, and labor.

The International Union of Mine, Mill and Smelter Workers (IUMMSW or Mine Mill) had a profound influence on miners and mining communities in both countries, particularly in the West. The union was the successor to the Western Federation of Miners (WFM) founded in Butte, Montana, in 1893. Influenced by socialists, defeats of miners' actions in Coeur d'Alene, Idaho, and increasing mechanization and consolidation in the industry, the WFM sought to create for western miners a more democratic and militant alternative to the craft-oriented American Federation of Labor. Enduring industry and government repression and competition from the radical Industrial Workers of the World (IWW), by 1916 the WFM had diminished in strength. It reorganized as the IUMMSW, with more conservative bread-and-butter goals, and limped along with few locals through the 1920s. Then, with the revival of the American labor movement in the 1930s, the Montana locals breathed new life into Mine Mill and helped organize other western, southern, eastern, and Canadian unions. Charges of communist influence began to plague the union on both sides of the border even as it enjoyed strike and organizing successes. Responding to governmental, business, and trade union anti-communism, the Canadian Congress of Labour expelled Mine Mill in 1949; the U.S. CIO expelled it in 1950. Although this ostracism made Mine Mill vulnerable to intense raiding by the United Steel Workers of America (USWA) through the 1950s and early 1960s, it remarkably held on to most of its western Canadian and U.S. locals, although its eastern unions succumbed to Cold War and Catholic Church propaganda. In 1967, facing a more accommodating USWA leadership and a declining industry, Mine Mill members finally voted to formally merge with USWA.[1]

Mine Mill's perseverance is significant because it actively resisted the Canadian and U.S. cold wars, and its policies and organizing methods shaped local and regional politics. During the 1950s it counted 120,000 members in fifty Canadian locals and in mines, smelters, and fabricating plants in the U.S. Mine Mill pressed its members to move beyond bread-and-butter issues to pursue broader social and political concerns. It helped communities forge alliances with other unions, develop political clout, create labor-oriented cultural institutions, and obtain better housing, education, and recreation. Unlike most labor unions at mid-century, Mine Mill was often "the heart of the community."[2] Mine Mill also had one of the largest union auxiliaries, officially encouraging women's involvement in community and labor affairs.

Women's auxiliaries were quite active in connection to many male unions from the 1930s through the 1960s, especially in extractive industries that excluded women from the workforce. Yet few women's and labor historians have explored their history, perhaps discomforted by their roles as "auxiliary" or secondary to men's unions, and because their goals and interests were often at odds with wage-working women. Nonetheless, auxiliaries are important to examine because they symbolize many of the contradictions apparent in the mid-twentieth-century labor movement, especially in progressive but male-dominated unions such as IUMMSW, and they reveal how women negotiated gender restrictions, including their formal exclusion from the main industry and union, to express their political desires.[3] Through their auxiliary work, we see how women struggled to be more than loyal helpmates to union brethren, to overcome the constraints of assigned gender roles, and to assert their economic and political interests, which at times coincided with and at other times differed from men's goals.[4]

Although Mine Mill embraced a progressive internationalism, it also celebrated its roots in the Western Federation of Miners and an occupational and regional exceptionalism that codified mining as a male domain. It was explicitly anti-imperialist and officially advocated gender and racial equality, but it also embraced a masculinity that was exclusionary. The union often pursued contradictory politics on parallel tracks—publicly advocating equity for all workers while locally promoting white male privilege, and resisting Cold War anti-communism while embracing a conservative domestic ideology. This essay will explore how women in Canadian and U.S. mining communities asserted their class politics with a union that at least in principle advocated more gender inclusion than much of North American labor. It will also examine how ideological struggles and their outcomes influenced developments across gender, region, and national borders. But first, it is useful to examine the regional context that inspired the ideals of masculinity that Mine Mill adopted, which subsequently made it difficult for male unionists and women auxiliary activists to create openings for women's union engagement.

WESTERN WORK AND THE MASCULINE IDEAL

FROM THE LATE NINETEENTH through the late twentieth century, resource-based industries—logging, mining, agriculture, fishing—distinguished the gendered and racialized character of work in the U.S. and Canadian Wests. Even though women and people of color worked in these industries or the service sectors that supported them, narratives about regional work reinforce the concept of a white, male "wageworkers' frontier."[5] These occupations elicit images of tough, masculine outdoor work and independence. They have also resisted hiring women and certain ethnic groups except when labor demands have overwhelmed the exclusionary rigid boundaries they erected. The white male breadwinner ideal and the reputed toughness of the work that supposedly discouraged women from employment often disintegrated when labor markets expanded, when families required multiple breadwinners, or when these "rugged" jobs became seasonal and low-paid, which then made women and people of color "ideally suited" for the work.[6] "Fishplant reality," Jill Stainsby finds in her study of the gendered division of labor within British Columbia canneries, offered a stark contrast to the romanticized autonomy of the male fisher and exposed women workers to "noisy machinery, unpleasant (often cold and wet) surroundings, long hours of performing monotonous, repetitive labor, and inadequate rewards."[7] Industries, unions, and male workers perpetuated this social order and a regional identity that reinforced the belief that its work required rugged masculinity. Unions and workers might preserve jobs for white men, but employers could resist improving conditions or providing adequate workers' compensation by exploiting stereotypes that rendered workers "tough enough" to handle the most dangerous conditions or too rootless and family-less to warrant company-provided protections.[8]

Even during World War II, when much of Canada and the United States opened industrial jobs to women, company, government, and union officials sought to preserve men's claims to traditional western occupations. Montana's war manpower director, for example, claimed that the state needed "men for the hard, heavy and unpleasant jobs" in mines, mills, and woods "where women cannot be used." Anaconda Copper Mining Company and Mine Mill union officials agreed that mines, mills, and smelters could not employ women because the work required strength and stamina. But physical prowess evidently was not the chief requisite, because the company began recruiting retired and disabled men. When the company tried to bypass union seniority rules to give women "soft" positions, union leaders, struggling to preserve a male breadwinner workplace while maintaining labor principles, alternated between insisting that women be excluded as a weaker sex and that they be treated equally.[9]

The war years provide ample examples to illustrate the shifting ground of gendered and racialized work categories. In the northern U.S. West's one-industry towns, employers and city officials often pushed to hire local women to avoid attracting southern blacks, southwestern Mexican Americans, or immigrants to their communities. In Anaconda, Montana, the Anaconda Company manipulated perceptions of difference to convince union representatives to allow women into its smelter. Appealing to racial prejudices, management threatened to import African Americans and Mexicans to fill the labor void, emphasizing that they would prefer Anaconda women "rather than Mexican boys," but the federal government could send "colored men" any time. Management and labor then agreed that they would preserve community values that championed white male *and* female breadwinners.[10]

Wartime labor demands and subsequent relaxation of occupational barriers presented unprecedented opportunities for women of many races and ethnicities, especially in new aircraft and shipbuilding plants. Mining and logging remained off limits, however, except for a small percentage of women who found work in processing ore and timber. Why did western urban shipyards and aircraft plants actively recruit women, while mining and most logging communities resisted hiring them?[11] Well-entrenched gender ideologies, accompanying lore about the work, and past union struggles for job security in automating industries influenced practices. The industry's needs and economic position also explain the difference: the minerals industry had been declining except during the war boom, and as a new industry, shipbuilding demanded new recruits. Whereas women never constituted more than 5 percent of the smelter workforce in Anaconda, they made up 28 percent of Portland's shipyard workers.[12]

The postwar period brought a rapid resumption of restrictions, underscoring the fluidity of these ideologies and how pinned to power relations they were. Nonetheless, women in mining communities were often fundamentally changed by their wartime experiences, as represented by married women's increasing participation in the labor force. Women who worked in the Anaconda smelter during the war lost their jobs, but the independence they tasted lasted in subsequent work and family roles. Erma Bennett recalled that after the war people "tried to change it back," but it was "the beginning of the change" in women's roles as they sought greater public and economic participation.[13]

Women had better luck inserting themselves into some of the region's forest products mills. Although their work in the woods was limited to cooking and truck driving, women found some opportunities in sex-segregated production work. Unlike their counterparts in the minerals industry, who were laid off and replaced by returning servicemen at war's end, a small percentage of women remained in forest products mills. In 1942 when a plywood factory opened in Port Alberni, British Columbia, to aid the war effort, women rushed to apply for positions and soon became 80 percent of the workforce. Susanne Klausen demonstrates how the women's presence challenged "the tenacious myth that women are unsuited to forestry." Yet the single-industry community gave preferences to local women and expected them to leave their jobs after the war. Industries, male workers, and their unions appealed to stubborn ideologies about occupational segregation as well as to the women's sense of community solidarity that privileged the male family breadwinner. Port Alberni plywood women were not forced to leave after the war, but their numbers and status shifted as the mill hired more male workers. The range of "women's jobs" narrowed while "men's jobs" expanded, and tensions between male and female workers increased.[14]

In the postwar period, many western union leaders and workers seized upon a special regional masculine identity to advance their clout and resist employer and anti-communist attacks. Unions highlighted regional differences to assert an independent and often more militant course, distancing themselves from what they perceived as eastern, conservative, bureaucratic unionism. Union iconography and rhetorical traditions championed masculine workers in contrast to weak and feminized bosses. Mine Mill survived anti-communist hysteria in the 1950s partly through its embrace of a masculine regional identity to resist red-baiting attacks by the USWA-CIO, (U.S.) House Un-American Activities Committee (HUAC), the U.S. Justice Department, the Canadian Congress of Labour, minerals corporations, and the media.[15] USWA organizers, in fact, realized that they were dealing with "an entirely different unionism" in which workers and their locals valued their autonomy and tight-knit communities more than international unions. Geography, the nature of the mining industry, and a masculine, militant heritage, these organizers concluded, had made western locals more independent and less susceptible to red-baiting.[16] However, Mine Mill's association of militancy with masculinity created strains with community women it hoped to organize in support of union efforts and in resistance to Cold War attacks.

MINE MILL AUXILIARY MOVEMENT

ALTHOUGH RELATIVELY FEW WOMEN worked in mines and mills during the war, women's auxiliaries expanded, reflecting women's desires to participate in the political and economic decisions affecting their lives, even if excluded from minerals industry workplaces. Women had initiated or revived auxiliaries across the United States during the CIO organizing drives and strike waves of the 1930s. Canadian unions followed suit. Yet many international unions were ambivalent about women's potential clout and interference. For example, USWA president David McDonald laid down strict guidelines for emerging auxiliaries that explicitly excluded the women from steelworkers councils and granted them limited roles to "create a closer and more fraternal feeling between the families of union members" and assist the union.[17]

IUMMSW recognized the broader political and economic value of women's participation and actively encouraged organizing women into auxiliaries, often pronouncing, "A union without the women is only half organized." Eighteen of ninety-five organized auxiliaries sent delegates to the Mine Mill convention held in Joplin, Missouri, in August 1941. In a series of resolutions offered to the convention, the Butte-Anaconda women delegates, at the forefront of organizing efforts since the 1930s, urged male unionists to adhere to the 1940 convention pledge to organize auxiliaries for every local.[18] Auxiliaries had the right to send delegates to union conventions and to attend local union meetings and make recommendations. The 1944 constitution of the IUMMSW Ladies' Auxiliary differed significantly from other union and fraternal auxiliaries that stressed women's helping roles. The women adopted the union's preamble, which emphasized class struggle and emancipation of the working class through industrial unions.[19] Also at the 1944 convention, in what seemed to be an assertion of their independence, Ladies' Auxiliary delegates by a majority vote asked that the union's constitution be amended to convert the auxiliary into an autonomous organization. The international officers, executive board, and delegates concurred.[20]

Despite Mine Mill praise for the move, auxiliary women did not universally welcome the autonomy vote. Many auxiliary members wrote to international president Mary Orlich of Butte to complain about the changes, and some officers resigned their district posts. Many women believed they would lose their hard-won clout, since their auxiliary was the only one in the CIO to gain a voice and vote at Mine Mill conventions, and they feared financial instability. Responding to complaints, Orlich agreed that she was sorry to hear about the international election results, "but we still feel that we cannot afford to discard all the hard work that has gone into the creation of the Auxiliary movement... It may be a little difficult to start out on our own, but...there is a great deal for the women to do, so let us not become discouraged, because we are no longer with the men. I think that we all can show them that we can do the job better as women leaders."[21] A few months later, after a failed membership drive, Orlich scrambled to rally her locals at the same time she alluded to a changing world that made women less interested in joining auxiliaries: "We are going to have to

FIGURE 13.1: *Mary Orlich (seated third from right) with International Union of Mine, Mill and Smelter Workers Ladies' Auxiliary Group.* [Courtesy of Don Orlich]

adapt ourselves to [the Autonomy]....I realize how difficult it is to organize women, because in my own home local, we have a good-sized [union] membership, but we have a poor percentage of women in the Aux....I realize also that women are going on the production lines, but I say that should not break up our Auxiliaries."[22] The lack of women's interest in joining auxiliaries plagued the auxiliary movement in the postwar period. As more women entered the workforce, and as male unions stubbornly resisted expanding substantive opportunities for women's participation or championing women's issues, there was little appeal to join yet another community organization that required dues.

While end-of-the-war wage opportunities and the auxiliaries' autonomy hampered organizing in the States, District 8 (eastern Canada) and District 7 (western Canada) successfully organized new locals and expanded memberships. Part of the enthusiasm came with the revitalization of mining unions—once strong under the WFM in the late nineteenth and early twentieth centuries—when in 1944 the Canadian government relaxed union organizing regulations. The culture of Mine Mill may have shaped eastern and western mining communities more profoundly than particular regional or Canadian sensibilities, but the long history of western militancy assisted union organizing as wartime migrations put westerners in contact with eastern workers. Pearl Chytuk, who moved to Sudbury, Ontario, from Regina, Saskatchewan, in 1941, observed striking regional differences. Chytuk was able to get a job at the Inco smelter during the war, but she was surprised that people were fearful of talking about unions: "Out west we were talking unions for beauty salons and restaurant workers, but in Sudbury, people were reluctant to talk about it." While working at the smelter, Chytuk could not participate in the auxiliary, so she actively organized for Mine Mill Local 598. She remembered the hesitancy of some of her male co-workers, but many of the women activists were "from the west where we always felt more free." At the end of the war when the women at Inco were laid off, Chytuk returned to the Ladies' Auxiliary where she actively pursued working-class goals.[23]

GENDER AND THE COLD WAR

DESPITE MINE MILL'S ENTHUSIASM for auxiliaries across borders, by the late 1940s the Cold War intervened to heighten gender and ideological divisions within the international. President Mary Orlich, tireless advocate for the auxiliary movement, mounted anti-communist charges against the left-leaning union in the conservative *Saturday Evening Post*: "I want to organize all the housewives in America to fight this scourge; I want to inform the women of America how their way of living is threatened. The commies are a common enemy, and the people don't know it."[24] Through the 1940s Orlich had frequently invoked the language of class in urging others to "war on these big bosses [for] a decent living wage" and to "share the profit." Despite the hardships of the 1946 strikes, Orlich implored Mine Mill women to mobilize others to join auxiliaries and to be more than "a card carrier" and fight for a guaranteed annual wage and to "impress upon the minds of our Parent Union locals the need for women's organizations." But within a year, Orlich, like many North American labor activists, became alarmed at publicized threats of communism and quickly diverted her wrath away from corporations and onto Mine Mill. Her correspondence reveals that Montana Senator Burton K. Wheeler, New Deal populist turned anti-communist, and CIO conservatives persuaded her that domestic communists, many of whom were in the labor movement, threatened American security. Her claims that communists had overtaken Mine Mill and her calls for women's militancy created a firestorm among the union's supporters.

Women's reaction to Orlich was mixed; some called for her resignation, others offered support. The Canadian locals appeared most outraged, suggesting that anti-communist charges held less potency north of the border. Kay Carlin of Sudbury wrote to Orlich that the article "is having one hell of an effect over here.... I know that we are in this Union Movement to fight reaction and big business regardless of our race, creed or political beliefs.... I can only say it has thrown a blight over the Union when you accuse them of being dominated by Communists, when you know that is not the truth.... By doing these things you are playing right into the hands of reaction.... I may be forced to take a stand on that article by members here in Can[ada] and by my own sense of what is right." Charlotte M. Rash, recording secretary of the Copper Mountain, British Columbia, Auxiliary No. 139, signaled to Orlich that her local "voted unanimously to demand your resignation as president of our auxiliary. We no longer feel that you are worthy of our confidence." E.M. Bausquet, recording secretary of the Trail District Ladies' Auxiliary No. 131, reported to Orlich that

at our last meeting [we] unanimously endorsed all letters written by our Sister Locals demanding your resignation as Pres of the Auxiliaries.... You say it is the Commies who are disrupting the

unions, but if you want our frank opinion, it is people like your-
self, who are the stooges of Big Business by playing right along
with them in the labor splitting tactics, who are the true disrupt-
ors....We women of the Auxiliary are fighting with our brothers
of the Unions for unity of all people and security for the people,
not for disunity and unemployment. This is also what our boys in
the armed forces fought for. You are in the same category as the
Hitlerites in Germany and Mussolinis in Italy who first disunited
the unions through rotten propaganda and then were able to
build Nazism and Fascism. Do you want this to happen in
America? We believe that you have made a terrible error in
attacking a minority group in the Union and that you [must]
resign immediately as President of the IUMMSW Auxiliaries and
as Vice-President of the [Congress of Women's Auxiliaries] CIO.[25]

A few Canadian women, however, wrote to Orlich expressing their
confusion about the affair and questioned the motives of their leaders.
Referring to the Canadian auxiliaries' boycott of the special auxiliary convention called by Orlich in Salt Lake City in September, Maes Whitehead,
of Lake Penage, Ontario, asked Orlich to clarify whether "all this trouble
of Canadian delegates not attending the convention" was due to "trouble"
from the International or District 8's own Kay Carlin: "Surely we didn't
put all that work in the Auxiliary to have it torn down by gossip...a lot of
our girls in Sudbury are in an uproar over our delegates not going to Salt
Lake."[26] The evident dissension in Sudbury would simmer for the next
decade and ultimately unravel labor unity in the East.

While women may have divided ideologically over the affair or questioned the tactics of Orlich or her opponents in damaging the auxiliary
movement, male Mine Mill members widely condemned Orlich for "meddling in men's union affairs." When Orlich publicly blasted what she
viewed as communist domination of Mine Mill, male unionists dismissed
her red-baiting as a particular gender rather than political weakness and
characterized Orlich as a "simple little housewife" who foolishly contributed to "anti-union hokum." They insisted that because "women are

different" they were susceptible to disloyalty, unlike "true men" who "always feel bad when they've betrayed their friends." Moreover, men questioned the efficacy of the auxiliary movement and marginalized its potential strength. William Mason, Mine Mill executive board member for District 1, and Harry Baird, treasurer of the Montana Anti-Discrimination League, wrote in the *Saturday Evening Post* that "this sort of meddling in men's union affairs is responsible for the present situation wherein only 35 of the 1000s of Butte miners' women care to be in the auxiliary."[27] The auxiliary may have had few members, revealing its weakness in the union and community, but unlike its male counterparts who were required to join Mine Mill in closed shops, women were voluntary members, often without their men's support, and often lacked money to pay dues or fund their activities. Mine Mill may have halted this early anti-communist attack in its backyard, but its gender stereotyping eliminated an important source of potential support and ultimately impeded working-class solidarity as it faced accelerated anti-communist attacks in the Cold War period.

The controversy, which "paralyzed" auxiliary activities through 1947, led the IUMMSW executive board to investigate charges and to appoint a trial committee. Mine Mill president Maurice Travis urged local auxiliaries to keep their organizations intact despite the flap.[28] As her "trial" approached, Orlich and financial secretary Dora Young wrote to all local auxiliaries emphasizing that the "International has absolutely no authority....Ours is an autonomous organization and all Local Auxiliaries are legally and morally bound to follow our own constitution...if any local auxiliary ignores, as officers we have no choice but to follow provisions of our constitution (art 17)."[29] Orlich's absolutism indicated to many women that her tactics paralleled the undemocratic methods of the "red" union that she attacked.

A trial committee met in Chicago on 4 February 1948 and charged Mary Orlich and her associates as seeking to destroy the IUMMSW through "illegal machine control," slandering the International Union and, among other allegations, deliberately neglecting Canadian locals "for disruptive reasons." The trial committee recommended to the executive board that a new Ladies' Auxiliary be organized, that auxiliary locals "desiring to remain loyal" send per capita tax not to the former auxiliary but to the IUMMSW office until new officers could be elected, and that all auxiliary charters and documents be retrieved from Orlich.[30] Protesting to CIO secretary James Carey, Orlich provided examples of where Mine Mill refused to provide any rulings or information because the auxiliary was no longer in its jurisdiction, "yet they meddle into our business because we women will not be dominated by their Red Tactics." Mary Orlich continued her fight against communism but became marginalized after she lost her auxiliary platform. Even the Steelworkers, which initially found her useful in attacking Mine Mill, by 1955 urged their members to leave her "out" of raids planned in Butte-Anaconda, labeling her "nothing but a Company stooge."[31]

A NEW AUXILIARY

DESPITE ITS PROMISES to increase the Auxiliary's autonomy, the IUMMSW, alarmed at the destructive potential of the women's group, used its constitutional authority to dissolve it. Nonetheless, IUMMSW men chose to revive and reform, not eliminate, the auxiliary movement. After the trial the executive board appointed Marie Goforth as a full-time organizer for the new Ladies' Auxiliary. Canadian auxiliaries, under the leadership of Kay Carlin, Dorothy McDonald, and others, remained strong, but the U.S. movement was slow to reorganize after the Orlich debacle. Mercedes Steedman notes that in the shadow of Orlich's early red-baiting, "US auxiliaries moved cautiously, at the same time as the Canadian auxiliaries pushed for a stronger position within the recently autonomous Canadian Mine Mill Council."[32]

Mine Mill made a concerted effort to generate greater enthusiasm by expanding auxiliary coverage in its newspaper. For example, it featured an essay contest on "What Being a Member of a Mine-Mill Auxiliary Means to Me," and it included the essay of prize-winner Rachael Wood, financial secretary of the Trail auxiliary. A former wartime smelter worker, Wood justified wives' increased participation in union affairs as she affirmed women's loyalty to Mine Mill political goals. She reminded her sisters that women needed to join men in "upholding our International Constitution" and "preserve the democratic rights of all workers" including "freedom to choose one's own...politics."[33]

Although the Auxiliary seemed safely purged of rebellious elements, women members still pushed for a more active role in union issues, resisted men's meddling, and often pursued their own agenda that did not match men's goals. The *Mine-Mill Union* reported that at the 1951 Women's Auxiliary annual convention held in Nogales, Arizona, the women adopted an ambitious program of education and support for IUMMSW but failed to report what appeared in a banner headline in the Auxiliary's own newsletter concerning women's rights. The newsletter announced that delegates to the convention had adopted a new women's rights resolution advocating equal opportunity for women in the workplace and public life, revealing how working-class women embraced feminism long before the "second wave" women's movement became activated in the 1960s. The women also vowed to seek joint activities with local unions to discuss the role of women. Mine Mill's silence on these goals indicates reluctance by the union to share with its locals the more independent interests of its auxiliary women.[34]

The newsletters and files of the Mine Mill Auxiliary reveal local women's persistent struggles during the 1950s and early 1960s to gain acceptance in their communities and to win the respect of their union men while pushing for wider roles. Male delegates to the IUMMSW convention consistently offered support, and the executive board and organizers repeatedly plugged the potential women could offer labor. But resistance on the local level must have been firm. Recognizing the lack of follow-up to their annual resolutions supporting the Auxiliary, some male union members reminded their compatriots that "very often the winning or losing of a major labor struggle hinges upon [women's] support in the home, in the community, and even on the picket lines." But the rank-and-file's ideas of "support," except during a strike, kept women at home, and many auxiliary women pushed for broader participation in union affairs.[35]

Despite the hard work of several Auxiliary officers to win more substantial roles for women in the IUMMSW, the Auxiliary international movement limped along, severely lacking in funds to send delegates to the international convention, pay a coordinator, or print a newsletter. The international's lofty rhetoric about gender inclusion was not matched by its paltry budgetary allocations to women's efforts. Just ten women delegates—all from the western United States and western Canada— attended the 1956 Mine Mill convention, focusing their attention on community projects, political action, and the revival of the Auxiliary newsletter. The women pushed to become part of policy committees of local unions, particularly Health and Welfare, convincing men that women could watch their doctor and hospital bills more effectively. Auxiliary president Eva Pence, of Cobalt, Idaho, demanded to know why men hesitated in asking women to help in policing the health plan. "Are they afraid to take the women out of the home for an hour or two? Or," she asked, "is it that they think all women are without a mind to think with?" She noted that women "are the ones" who stay with children when they are sick, take them to the hospital, administer medicines, and speak with health professionals and were certainly capable of working on the health committees. Pence instructed auxiliary members to offer their help to the local union and, if refused, to try again until they see "that the women can do more than cook a good dinner, put on a banquet or help with that dance or picnic." Pence's irritation persisted, and in subsequent convention meetings she complained that local unions always depended on the auxiliaries in a crisis, such as strikes, election campaigns, or for "some food cooked and served...but when we need help we are forgotten and have no place in the labor movement." Ultimately she and other Auxiliary leaders decided to drop their national effort to revive auxiliaries and revert to organizing members and programs on a local level.[36]

American women envied their sisters in Canada, whom they believed wielded more influence in the labor movement through their auxiliaries. There, women could attend local union meetings and make recommendations. "We had a voice, we could always express our views," noted auxiliary member Ruth Reid, "even if we couldn't always vote." Former Mine Mill organizer Clinton Jencks recalled his efforts in New Mexico to involve more women in the union, but men resisted because they feared losing some of their power and privilege. Jencks wondered "why the Canadian women were so courageous and making the international officers so uncomfortable and demanding the right to attend international union conventions and...to say something on the floor and not just to be the auxiliary that serves the coffee and the cookies." He discovered that some Canadian male and female activists realized that Mine Mill could be so much more effective in gaining women allies by strengthening the auxiliary movement. After the Canadian auxiliary became autonomous in 1955, U.S. and Canadian sisters continued to exchange news and ideas. In a memo to auxiliary members, President Eva Pence grumbled, "The women in Canada are receiving the aid of the Mine-Mill. In the two years since the Autonomy, Canada has advanced while we are just moving along." Pence concluded that this was "due to the Local Union members" whose ambivalence or outright hostility turned away potential supporters.[37]

In some ways Canadian women may have had a greater voice in union affairs, but examples from the East reveal that gender and Cold War divisions were not restricted to the States. During the critical 1958 Inco strike in northern Ontario, Sudbury merchants and politicians organized a "back-to-work" movement of union members' wives. Auxiliary members organized counter-demonstrations in support of the strike, but the local and national media were predisposed to favor the anti-communist effort in order to weaken Mine Mill. Mercedes Steedman describes how gender tensions within the union provided fertile ground for an effective use of Cold War propaganda among the women. Women's Auxiliary No. 117 provided food for picket lines and organized outside aid for striking families, but as the strike wore on and families became more desperate, the Back-to-Work women launched a campaign to purge the local of its "red" leaders as well as end the strike. The Mine Mill Auxiliary sought to counter this effort with its own mass meeting and pledge to march on City Hall to demand support for the union in its negotiating efforts. The union bargaining team, however, was furious that the auxiliary had ventured a politically naïve act that might backfire and tried to halt the event, which then allowed Back-to-Work supporters to dominate the public arena. With Mine Mill men and women divided, anti-Mine Mill forces gained control of the union. Soon, workers and their families switched allegiances to a different union.[38]

Far to the west a similar catastrophe struck Mine Mill in Anaconda, Montana. Despite geographical differences, Sudbury and Anaconda had much in common. They had two of the largest Mine Mill locals, making them strategically important to those who wished to destroy the union and were thus specific targets of USWA raids. The communities were ethnically diverse, predominately Catholic, opened their smelter jobs to local women during WWII, limited women's economic opportunities after the war, and were dominated by large multinational minerals corporations. Both communities created alternative politics and cultures based on Mine Mill's influence, developing, for example, a summer camp, an annual smelter workers' celebration, and union halls that served as community centers. In the postwar period, both Anaconda and Sudbury were transformed from company towns into union towns. Unlike in Sudbury, where the women's auxiliary was quite strong, the Anaconda auxiliary disintegrated after the Mary Orlich scandal. Yet in both places the local unions were ambivalent at best in supporting women's auxiliary work, and gender divisions helped anti-communist arguments take root. Workers and their families came to believe anti-Mine Mill propaganda that linked the union to the strikes that created tremendous economic hardships and bargaining ineffectiveness. Many decided that they were better off to relent than to continue to endure USWA and other union raids in order to preserve what remained of community unionism. The case of Anaconda and Sudbury demonstrates that more than a western, masculine, militant heritage shaped the Cold War ideological struggle. Religion, local politics, USWA strategy, and gender divisions played greater roles in undermining Mine Mill than did regional and national influences. Most of Mine Mill's western locals in Canada and in the U.S., aside from Anaconda, remained impervious to Cold War assaults, but the capitulation of the two important locals severely damaged Mine Mill's ability to survive and ultimately led to the formal merger with USWA in 1967.[39]

AUXILIARY DECLINE

BY THE 1960S, almost all the women's auxiliaries of Mine Mill had become inactive or dissolved. The international made an effort to revive them, but its preoccupation with USWA raiders, trials of its officers, an empty treasury, a changing industry, an endless cycle of contract negotiations, and its persistent adherence to gender assumptions contributed to its lukewarm response to the auxiliary movement. Women still complained about men's meddling, and the weakened international seemed incapable of bringing gender peace to its locals. In June 1962 the Bisbee Ladies' Auxiliary of Local 551 complained to the international that Mrs Elkins was controlling the auxiliary's presidency thanks to her husband, who was president of the union. Ruth Brady wrote that Mr Elkins had said, '"As long as I'm president there will be no re-election.' We then asked him who gave him authority to decide? He then said, 'When you step out of line it is his job to stop it, we could either go on like we were, or desolve [sic] the auxiliary.' As I see the situation, we need no [Dictator]."[40]

The Bisbee situation reveals another reason why men and women were often indifferent and at times antagonistic toward auxiliaries. Although they often provided spaces for women's democratic participation in labor politics, auxiliaries, like many male unions, pursued agendas of a leadership that varied in ideological interests. Many leaders, such as Mary Orlich, had conservative political goals in adopting a rigid anticommunist position, but relied on militant strategies that asserted auxiliary autonomy from male union dictates. Her successor, Eva Pence, was not a cold warrior but continued to seek an independent, active role for the Auxiliary.[41] Both women's frustrations lay not only with the international for its insignificant financial allocations despite public claims to boost Auxiliary membership, or with men's open resistance in many union locals, but also with women who neglected their auxiliary duties. It was difficult to find volunteers to serve in elected posts or to pursue activities that advanced both unions and auxiliary.

Auxiliaries were not necessarily representative; they counted as their members a very small percentage of the eligible wives, sisters, and daughters of union members, and unlike unions that required workers to vote and fund union activities, auxiliaries were voluntary, independent, and self-sufficient. But efforts to dismiss auxiliaries as potentially detrimental rely on old myths in the labor movement (and labor history) that portray women as fundamentally conservative. These preoccupations with women's position rest on gendered assumptions that do not account for individual ideological difference or the forceful personalities who shaped (and sometimes controlled) auxiliary affairs. After all, analyses of labor unions' anti-communist or anti-Cold War positions, or their accommodation to or resistance to management's demands, do not rest on the degree of conservatism among men as a group.[42] Sometimes women's and men's goals were different, as when Mine Mill women advocated equal rights or better health care, but women were hardly less militant than men.

Other ideological differences among women surfaced in addition to perceived threats of communism. Just after the war, Mary Orlich had tried to resolve the racial tensions that haunted Alabama auxiliaries as white women refused to work with District vice-president Viola McGadney, who was African American.[43] Similar tensions arose in the American Southwest, as Mexican American women sought equal treatment and opportunities to serve as officers in their auxiliaries. In 1956 Mexican American women from Clifton-Morenci, Arizona, complained to the international that Anglo women "run the show." Women's outspokenness often challenged Mine Mill official positions against racial discrimination. For example, several women questioned the union's editorial in 1952 that called on readers to protest to the National Broadcasting Company its "use of a stereotyped, clownish Mexican character" on the Judy Canova show. Mrs Annie Petek, of East Helena, Montana, protested that "what has made America strong is that each of us can take a joke about ourselves" and suggested that the anti-racist editorial "sounds very much like something Joe Stalin would print to stir up trouble." Although Mine Mill Auxiliary members took an oath to oppose discrimination, latent racism emerged in letters to the Mine-Mill Union newspaper, and one suspects in other forums, through the 1950s, revealing how intertwined were ideologies about race, the Cold War, and the role of the labor movement.[44]

Local gender tensions conflicted with more egalitarian ideals advocated by the international, revealing that such ideologies were often contested. The left-leaning Mine Mill simultaneously advocated difference—the uniqueness of mining and smelting required rugged men—and equality. Its 1954 film *Salt of the Earth* in many ways reflects the union's enlightened gender politics—while at the same time rendering its women's auxiliary powerless. Based on the 1951 strike by predominantly Mexican American zinc miners in New Mexico, the film featured blacklisted Hollywood producers and mining community actors. Banned and boycotted at the time because of its "communist" makers, the film has become a minor cult classic in college courses because of its feminist content. Striking Mine Mill miners allowed their wives to take their place when an injunction prevented their picketing, and emboldened by their activist roles, the women began demanding that their issues, such as clean water, be considered in union negotiations, and that in the household men allow them more autonomy. Admired by mining women who saw the film, the New Mexico auxiliary members, who initially after the strike were allowed greater roles in the union, gradually lost their clout due to men's resistance. The well-publicized New Mexico story offered hopeful possibilities to auxiliary members who longed for social change, yet it also revealed how temporary those gains might be. Union members both sought women's support, especially during critical strikes, and worked to contain that support within domestic roles. Although auxiliaries appeared to reproduce the sexual division of labor, the degree to which women acted independently and asserted their own class goals reflected the changes in family structure and women's visible roles in the workplace and public arenas, which many men found threatening. Ideologies about difference often sank deeply within many rank-and-file workers who resisted their own union's rhetoric of solidarity across skill, race, region, and gender.

An analysis of women's labor auxiliaries in male-dominated industries reveals how women and men searched for, negotiated, and contested appropriate political roles for women. The story of women's auxiliary participation in strikes is well known; but although many women yearned for greater and long-term political involvement, local and international unions seemed incapable of granting them more than limited roles. In most union auxiliaries, women searched for an appropriate niche. They may have pledged to build industrial unions, but excluded from the workplace and discouraged by male unionists from participating in substantive local affairs, they often fell back on traditional auxiliary activities, sponsoring card parties, socials with the male union, and showers for brides. In the postwar period, as women entered the wage market in increasing numbers, became influenced by a revived women's movement, and found other avenues for political participation and social expression in their own unions, political parties, and clubs, auxiliaries became anachronistic for most.

By following the rise and decline of the Mine Mill auxiliary, we see that gender and political ideologies shaped union responses to the Cold War in Canada and the United States. Mine Mill's celebration of its western, masculine, and militant independence helped the union resist red-baiting and shore up support in its western locals. However, the persistence of beliefs about men's superiority in work and union affairs and the infrequent ability to embrace the potential of working class solidarity across gender lines, damaged the long-term survival of the progressive, embattled union. As women's aspirations for greater participation in union affairs rose, they became more disappointed in male resistance, especially at the local level. Unions and their auxiliaries provide a fruitful arena in which to explore how political and gender ideologies take root and spread across nation and region. These examples underscore how many women persisted in their pursuit of active political roles in the male unions that shaped their lives and communities.

NOTES

1.   Laurie Mercier, "'Instead of Fighting the Common Enemy': Mine Mill versus the Steelworkers in Montana, 1950–1967," *Labor History* 40 (Fall 1999): 459–80.

2.   Ruth Reid, quoted in "Panel Review," in *Hard Lessons: The Mine Mill Union in the Canadian Labor Movement*, ed. Mercedes Steedman, Peter Sucschnigg, Dieter K. Buse (Toronto: Dundurn Press, 1995), 151.

3.   For discussions of auxiliaries see Melinda Chateauvert, *Marching Together: Women of the Brotherhood of Sleeping Car Porters* (Urbana: University of Illinois, 1998); Paula F. Pfeffer,

"The Women Behind the Union: Halena Wilson, Rosina Tucker, and the Ladies' Auxiliary to the Brotherhood of Sleeping Car Porters," *Labor History* 36 (Fall 1995): 557–78; Susan Levine, "Workers' Wives: Gender, Class and Consumerism in the 1920s United States," *Gender and History* 3 (Spring 1991): 45–64; Marjorie Penn Lasky, "Where I Was a Person: The Ladies' Auxiliary in the 1934 Minneapolis Teamsters' Strikes," in *Women, Work, and Protest: A Century of US Women's Labor History*, ed. Ruth Milkman (Boston: Routledge Press, 1985), 181–206; Christiane Diehl-Taylor, "Partners in the Struggle: The Role of Women's Auxiliaries and Brigades in the 1934 Minneapolis Truck Drivers Strikes and the 1936/37 Flint General Motors Sit-Down Strike," unpublished research paper, University of Minnesota, 1990; Judy Aulette and Trudy Mills, "Something Old, Something New: Auxiliary Work in the 1983–1986 Copper Strike," *Feminist Studies* 14, no. 2 (Summer 1988): 251–68; Deborah Silverton Rosenfelt, ed., *Salt of the Earth* (New York: Feminist Press, 1978).

4. See, for example, Kathryn J. Oberdeck, "Not Pink Teas: The Seattle Working-Class Women's Movement, 1905–1918," *Labor History* 32 (Spring 1991): 193–230.

5. Carlos A. Schwantes has written extensively about the male worker's milieu. See, for example, *Radical Heritage: Labor, Socialism, and Reform in Washington and British Columbia, 1885–1917* (Seattle: University of Washington Press, 1979); "Protest in a Promised Land: Unemployment, Disinheritance, and the Origin of Labor Militancy in the Pacific Northwest, 1885–86," *Western Historical Quarterly* 13 (October 1982): 373–90; "Images of the Wageworkers' Frontier," *Montana: The Magazine of Western History* 38 (Autumn 1988): 38–49.

6. Ideas about domestic roles, region, race, gender, and class become so closely enmeshed that the segmentation of work around difference appears to be "natural." Feminist scholars have explored this process of segmentation, the promotion of inequalities in the workplace, and the male breadwinner wage ideal and accompanying female wage. See, for example, Alice Kessler-Harris, *A Woman's Wage: Historical Meanings and Social Consequences* (Lexington: University Press of Kentucky, 1990), 1–19; Maurine Weiner Greenwald, "Working-Class Feminism and the Family Wage Ideal: The Seattle Debate on Married Women's Right to Work, 1914–1920," *Journal of American History* 76 (June 1989): 118–49; Ruth Milkman, *Gender at Work: The Dynamics of Job Segregation by Sex During World War II* (Urbana: University of Illinois Press, 1987), 6, 124. For reviews of some of the literature that links the social construction of masculinity to work, breadwinning, gender relations, and skill monopolization, see Steven Maynard, "Rough Work and Rugged Men: The Social Construction of Masculinity in Working-Class History," *Labour/Le Travail* 23 (Spring 1989): 158–69; Karen Anderson, "Work, Gender, and Power in the American West," *Pacific Historical Review* 61, no. 4 (1992): 481–99; Jens Christiansen, Peter Philips, and Mark Prus, "Women, Technology, and Work: The Gender Division of Labor in U.S. Manufacturing, 1850–1919," *Research in Economic History* 16 (1996): 103–26.

7. Jill Stainsby, "'It's the Smell of Money': Women Shoreworkers of British Columbia," *BC Studies: The British Columbian Quarterly* 103 (Fall 1994): 59–81.

8. William G. Robbins, "Labor in the Pacific Slope Timber Industry: A Twentieth-Century Perspective," *Journal of the West* 25, no. 2 (1986): 10, 8.

9. Plant Manpower Analysis, 18 November 1943, ACM Collection, Box 62, Folder 3, Montana Historical Society Archives, Helena, MT.

10. Laurie Mercier, *Anaconda: Labor, Culture, and Community in Montana's Smelter City* (Urbana: University of Illinois Press, 2001), 67–68.

11. For a description of the specific myths, traditions, movements, and legislation that forbade women from working underground, see Angela V. John, *By the Sweat of their Brow: Women Workers at Victorian Coal Mines* (London: Croom Helm, 1980); Jane Mark-Lawson and Anne Witz, "From 'Family Labor' to 'Family Wage'? The Case of Women's Labor in Nineteenth-Century Coalmining," *Social History* 13 (1988): 151–74; Barbara Kingsolver, *Holding the Line: Women in the Great Arizona Mine Strike of 1983* (New York: ILR Press, 1989), 1–21.

12. Karen Beck Skold, "The Job He Left Behind: American Women in the Shipyards during World War II," in *Women, War, and Revolution*, ed. Carol R. Berkin and Clara M. Lovett (New York: Holmes & Meier, 1980), 57; Amy Kessleman, *Fleeting Opportunities: Women Shipyard Workers in Portland and Vancouver During World War II and Reconversion* (Albany: State University of New York Press, 1990). Karen Anderson, in her study of women war workers, concludes that labor markets, rather than community values, determined such variations. She notes, for example, that women made up just 4 percent of Baltimore shipbuilders, compared to 16 percent in Seattle, because of greater availability of black male workers in the East. Karen Anderson, *Wartime Women: Sex Roles, Family Relations, and the Status of Women during World War II* (Westport, CT: Greenwood, 1981), 31, 46.

13. Mercier, *Anaconda*, 91.

14. Susanne Klausen, "The Plywood Girls: Women and Gender Ideology at the Port Alberni Plywood Plant, 1942–1991," *Labour/Le Travail* 41 (Spring 1998): 199–235.

15. The literature on the Cold War and labor unions is extensive. See, for example, Reg Whitaker and Gary Marcuse, *Cold War Canada: The Making of a National Insecurity State, 1945–1957* (Toronto: University of Toronto Press, 1994); Harvey A. Levenstein, *Communism, Anticommunism, and the CIO* (Westport, CT: Greenwood Press, 1981); and Steve Rosswurm, ed., *The CIO's Left-Led Unions* (New Brunswick, NJ: Rutgers University Press, 1992).

16. Mercier, "'Instead of Fighting the Common Enemy,'" 472–73.

17. "Description of Method for Applying for Charters," 1938, USWA Hague collection, Box 47, folder 12, Labor Archives, Pennsylvania State University, University Park, PA.

18. International Union of Mine, Mill and Smelter Workers (IUMMSW), "Report of the Proceedings of the 38th Convention of the IUMMSW," Joplin, Missouri, August 1941, 9–10, 84–85.

19. IUMMSW, "Constitution of Ladies' Auxiliaries," 1944, Norma McLean collection, Shelf G3, Box 184, Anaconda Historical Society, Anaconda, MT.

20. IUMMSW, "Report of the Proceedings of the 41st Convention," Pittsburgh, 11–16 September 1944, 47–48.

21. Mary Orlich to Mrs G. B. Colwell, Bessemer, Alabama, 6 February 1945, Orlich collection, courtesy of Don Orlich, in possession of author (hereafter cited as Orlich collection).

22. Orlich to all auxiliary district vice-presidents, 18 February 1945, Orlich collection.

23. Orlich report to auxiliaries, 2 September 1946, Orlich collection; Mike Solski and John Smaller, *Mine Mill: The History of the IUMMSW in Canada Since 1895* (Ottawa: Steel Rail Publishing, 1985), 124; Steedman, et al., *Hard Lessons*, 162–65.

24. "Miner's Wife Fights Off Red Invasion of Union," *Saturday Evening Post*, 18 January 1947.

25. Kay Carlin, Sudbury, to Orlich, 27 January 1947; Charlotte M. Rash, rec sec, Auxiliary No. 139 Copper Mountain, BC, to Orlich, 25 March 1947; E.M. Bausquet, secretary, Trail & District Ladies' Auxiliary No. 131, Rossland, BC, to Orlich, n.d., all Olrich collection.

26. Maes Whitehead, Lake Penage, Ontario, to Mary O, 4 October 1947, Orlich collection.

27. Correspondence, Orlich collection; William Mason and Harry I. Baird, Butte, to Editors *Saturday Evening Post*, 23 January 1947.

28. M.E. Travis to all IUMMSW Ladies' Auxiliaries, 9 December 1947, WFM-IUMMSW collection, Box 126, folder "Executive Board Action re Controversy," University of Colorado, Boulder, CO (Hereafter cited as UCB.)

29. Orlich and Young to all local auxiliaries, February 1948, Orlich collection.

30. "Report of the Committee to Try International Ladies' Auxiliary Officers," 4 February 1948, Chicago, WFM-IUMMSW collection, Box 126, folder "Executive Board Action re Controversy," UCB.

31. Otto Orr to Charles J. Smith, USWA, Los Angeles, August 4, 1955, USWA District 38, Box 8, Folder 10, Labor Archives, Pennsylvania State University, University Park, PA.

32. *People's Voice*, 12 November 1948; Margaret Driggs, "A Mine-Mill Wife Looks at Miners' Con Problem in Butte," 1 April 1949; Mercedes Steedman, "Godless Communists and Faithful Wives, Gender Relations and the Cold War: Mine Mill and the Strike against the International Nickel Company, Sudbury, Canada, 1958," in *Mining Women: Gender in Development of a Global Industry, 1670–2000*, ed. Laurie Mercier and Jaclyn J. Gier (New York: Palgrave Macmillan Press, 2006). In 1955 Mine Mill became the first international union to grant autonomy to Canadians.

33. Rachael Wood, "What Being a member of an MMSW Auxiliary Means to Me," *The Union*, 24 April 1950, 6.

34. *Mine-Mill Union*, 8 October 1951; "Women's Rights—New Plank in Auxiliary Program," Ladies' Auxiliary of the IUMMSW, *Newsletter*, v. 1, n. 1, October 1951, WFM-IUMMSW collection, Box 159, folder "Auxiliary Newsletter," UCB.

35. "Substitute Resolution for Resolution 41," IUMMSW convention, n.d., WFM-IUMMSW collection, Box 9, folder 1, UCB.

36. *Mine-Mill Union*, April 1956; IUMMSW Auxiliary president Eva Pence, reports, ca. 1955 and 1956; Pence to IUMMSW and Ladies' Auxiliary, n.d., WFM-IUMMSW collection, Box 159, folder "Auxiliary," UCB.

37. Reid and Jencks quoted in Steedman, *Hard Lessons,* 8, 153, 171; Mine Mill *Auxiliary Newsletter*, 21 July 1955; and Eva Pence, to members of the International Union of Mine Mill and Ladies' Auxiliary, ca. 1957, WFM-IUMMSW collection, Box 159, folder "Auxiliary Newsletter," UCB. That the border and auxiliary separation remained fluid is represented by continued British Columbian attendance at Auxiliary meetings and conventions in Spokane, Salt Lake, and other United States western cities.

38. Solski and Smaller, *Mine Mill,* 136–67; Steedman, "Godless Communists." See Katherine G. Aiken's discussion of pro- and anti-Mine Mill women activists in Kellogg, Idaho, in

"'When I Realized How Close Communism Was to Kellogg, I Was Willing to Devote Day and Night': Anti-Communism, Women, Community Values, and the Bunker Hill Strike of 1960," *Labor History* 36 (Spring 1995): 165–86.

39.   For a full discussion of the role of gender, ideology, and regionalism in Mine Mill's decline in Anaconda, see Mercier *Anaconda* and "Instead of Fighting the Common Enemy."

40.   Ruth N. Brady, Bisbee, to IUMMSW, Denver, 15 June 1962, WFM-IUMMSW collection, Box 258, folder 16 "Ladies' Auxiliary 1962," UCB.

41.   Scholars have often overlooked the role of leadership in shaping a union or auxiliary. Julia Ruutila steered the ILWU auxiliary in Portland in a more radical direction in the 1960s, protesting police brutality, boycotting Dow Chemical, participating in Peace Walks against the Vietnam War, and supporting the Committee for a SANE Nuclear Policy. As Sandy Polishuk has noted in her oral history biography of Ruutila, these auxiliary leaders carefully strategized ways of "bringing along" other women in the auxiliary as well as in the male union. Polishuk, *Sticking to the Union: The Life and Times of Julia Ruuttila* (New York: Palgrave Macmillan Press, 2003). Explaining their broader interests beyond the workplace, ILWU auxiliary president Valerie Taylor noted in 1962 that "Waterfront workers' wives hate injustice and human exploitation…[and] know foreign policy marches through her [sic] kitchen." Joan Fox, comp., *A History of Federated Auxiliaries of the ILWU, 1934–1984* (Seattle: self-published, 1993).

42.   Where older studies of western industrial unions and communities have ignored women altogether, more recent studies have often debated whether women have had a more militant or conservative influence on labor unions. Richard Rajala contends that single male loggers supported the IWW because "work and life were not separate spheres" and "their class orientation was not mediated to the same extent as in the case of those with stronger family and community allegiances." Elizabeth Jameson and John Belshaw, for example, have found that settled families actually fostered militancy and increased demands for better wages and conditions. Richard Rajala, "Bill and the Boss: Labor Protest, Technological Change, and the Transformation of the West Coast Logging Camp, 1890–1930," *Journal of Forest History* 33 (October 1989): 176–79; Elizabeth Jameson, *All That Glitters: Class, Conflict, and Community in Cripple Creek* (Urbana: University of Illinois Press, 1998); John Belshaw, *Colonization and Community: The Vancouver Island Coalfield and the Making of the British Columbian Working Class* (Montreal: McGill-Queen's University Press, 2002).

43.   Mrs W. A. Oneal, president, Bessemer, AL (Frances Perkins Auxiliary) to Mary Orlich, February 26, 1945, Orlich collection.

44.   Dulcie M. Johnson, IUMMSW secretary, Denver, to Eva Pence, chairman IUMMSW Auxiliaries, Cobalt, Idaho, 22 June 1956, WFM-IUMMSW collection, Box 159, folder "Auxiliary," UCB; "Open Forum: the Judy Canova Show," *Mine Mill Union*, 25 February 1952.

14

JAILED HEROES AND KITCHEN HEROINES

Class, Gender, and the Medalta Potteries Strike in Postwar Alberta

CYNTHIA LOCH-DRAKE

IN OCTOBER 1947 a packed courtroom in Medicine Hat, Alberta, received "with silent shock" the sentencing of seven male workers from the local pottery factory to thirty days of hard labour in the Lethbridge "gaol" for picket line violence.[1] The men, together with eight women, had been involved in two separate picket line incidents at the Medalta Potteries factory, which was a major employer in the small Alberta city of nearly 13,000. The more serious incident, a "mauling," sent one man to hospital with minor injuries; the other resulted in a smashed load of pottery. All of the men and women had pleaded guilty to a charge of intimidation. One man also pleaded guilty to assault. The eight women, however, received only suspended sentences. Local Magistrate T. O'B. Gore-Hickman said he "hesitated to send young women to jail" where they would be fingerprinted and their criminal files started. The defence lawyer also asked for the leniency of the court "in the case of the female workers, the majority being 17 or 18 years of age."[2] Neither party expressed such solicitude on behalf of any of the men—the youngest man was eighteen.[3]

Outraged by the men's harsh sentences, the International Union of Mine, Mill, and Smelter Workers (hereafter Mine Mill), which represented Medalta workers, appealed to Medicine Hat City Council to lobby provincial and federal governments for a reduction in the men's sentence. At a regular council meeting, before the request could be debated, Mayor William Rae accused the union's international representative, who led the delegation, of being an agent of Moscow whose "sinister purpose" was "a calculated plan designed to make capital out of human misery." Calling William Longridge "an individual with a deformed brain, a misfit, who admits receiving the gold of Moscow," Rae urged council not to be deceived by "this dastardly scheme" and to intercede in the "political chicanery." Rae was careful to distinguish between the union's leader, who was the target of his attack, and rank-and-file workers, who were "misguided individuals" placed in an "unfortunate position."[4] Two days after the virulent attack the strike collapsed, ending seventy-two days of successful picketing that had kept pottery production at the factory to a minimum. Workers returned to their jobs without a contract and with no guarantee that the company would take back all striking workers.

Within the larger framework of Alberta labour history, the Medalta Potteries strike marks a crucial turning point in public attitudes toward organized labour that placed workers on the defensive in the postwar era. The strength of government responses to the Medalta strike—as measured by political rhetoric and court decisions alone—suggests there was significant grassroots support for organized labour and a fair wage among ordinary Alberta men and women in the immediate postwar years. Initial public support for worker militancy quickly evaporated in the overheated atmosphere of anti-communist hysteria fostered by the Cold War. Profoundly gendered treatment of workers by the courts, the press, politicians, and the union intensified public ambivalence toward male workers who, increasingly, were perceived as dangerous, yet naïve. Women workers' activism was largely ignored or downplayed. When women's actions pushed them onto the public stage they tended to be seen as innocent victims of either industrialists or organized labour, depending on the context. The union's masculinist culture and militant stance contributed to these perceptions, as did some of the beliefs and attitudes of rank-and-file workers, both male and female. Women workers were proud of the often heavy physical labour they performed and many resented the low wages it returned. Yet the Medalta strike demonstrates how traditional notions about respectable femininity helped put women workers back in the kitchen during the postwar years.

Differential treatment of women's labour activism stemmed largely from conflict between dominant middle-class notions of gender difference and the reality of inadequate and insecure working-class wages, which made women's role essential in the "male" domain of paid work. This conflict generated an expectation that women would not be militant, which limited the public impact of their personal strength, solidarity, and effectiveness in job actions. The emphasis on gender difference also served to reinforce, rather than challenge, women's inferior status as wage earners. Finally, an emphasis on male ignorance and female innocence made Medalta workers an easy target for allegations of insidious communist influence. These allegations cultivated a political climate hostile to organized labour, which helped make possible "draconian" revisions to Alberta's labour laws in the months following the Medalta strike.[5] For all of these reasons the Medalta strike sheds light on a crucial, formative period in Alberta labour history, an era that established the legal and ideological framework for labour relations that endures in the province today.[6]

This study examines how the interplay of class, gender, and notions about whiteness shaped the pottery workforce and the organization of work and wages, as well as the course of the Medalta Potteries strike. Viewed through the prism of class and gender, public portrayals of worker militancy are seen more clearly as a major factor in the erosion of broad-based support for worker activism. A public offended by the apparently brutish behaviour of male workers and unwilling to examine the implications of women workers' involvement more easily dismissed reasonable demands for higher wages.

Contemporary accounts of the Medalta strike, as well as the only scholarly study to date, portray it as an event manufactured primarily by union leaders from outside the community who manipulated the pottery workers.[7] The involvement of women workers is virtually ignored. This current study is based on interviews I conducted from 2000 to 2001 with eight former Medalta workers, six of whom were women, as well as my examination of photographs, company, union, court, and press records. Although it is based on a small sample of workers who are not representative of the workforce—all of them were young at the time of the strike; six were teenagers—their narratives offer insight into the class and gender politics of the strike. Collectively these sources suggest there was a substantial core of militant workers at the pottery. They also reveal that women, who constituted 42 per cent of the workforce, were well represented within this militant core and played an important role on the picket line and at union events.[8]

The Medalta strike was part of a wave of labour unrest that swept the country in 1946 and 1947.[9] Canadian workers, buoyed by a new sense of entitlement stemming from wartime sacrifices, fought to hold onto the gains made possible by wartime labour shortages and postwar economic expansion. PC1003, a federal labour law that was Canada's equivalent to the American Wagner Act, was passed during the war in response to the growing strength of the trade union movement. It gave Canadian workers the right to organize and to bargain collectively.[10] Rapidly rising inflation and fears of postwar unemployment intensified the efforts of many workers to improve their position through union membership and job action.

The determination of unions and workers to ensure that they cornered a share of Alberta's burgeoning wealth was matched by the right-wing provincial government's resolve to suppress labour unrest after the war. Premier Ernest Manning's belief in the values of individualism, self-sufficiency, and free enterprise, rooted in his faith as an evangelical Christian, made him suspicious of any form of collectivism.[11] His antipathy toward organized labour intensified after the Leduc oil strike in February 1947. The explosion of economic development triggered by this major oil discovery aggravated the existing labour shortage and threatened to strengthen the hand of organized labour in the province.[12] Eager to reassure American oil investors of its ability to maintain labour peace and keep wages low in the province, Manning's government became even less sympathetic to the concerns of workers.

A national meatpacking strike that coincided with the Medalta strike, shutting down major plants throughout the province, exacerbated Premier Manning's anxieties about worker unrest. The result was shrill government denunciations of labour that had seismic effects for the pottery workers.[13] On 18 October, five days after publicly urging all workers to cross picket lines, Manning told a large audience that industrial production in Canada was "being deliberately sabotaged by industrial and distributing combines and by those who deliberately are fomenting industrial unrest in furtherance of those philosophies which make capital of distress."[14] Alberta Public Works Minister W. A. Fallow built on the conspiracy theory by describing rank-and-file union members as "helpless men and women browbeaten by a few."[15]

It was within this climate of anti-communist hysteria and intense suspicion that Medicine Hat Mayor William Rae attacked the union leadership's appeal for support, drawing on the same kind of rhetoric. The mayor's virulent attack, which was splashed across the local newspaper, marked a crucial turning point in the strike.[16] It seems likely that union leaders recognized a sea-change in the public's perception of workers and the strike. Within two days they ended the strike and workers began returning to their jobs on the company's terms.[17] Three weeks later a slate of labour candidates, which included one of the jailed Medalta workers, was defeated in a municipal election that attracted a record voter turnout. Although not a complete rout—the labour candidate for mayor garnered 40 per cent of the votes cast—labour's lack of success in the municipal election represented a major shift in the mood of the community from the first days of the strike.[18] Nevertheless, Mine Mill's ability to maintain enough support among Medalta workers to survive the devastating 1947 strike despite this shift in public opinion demonstrates strong grassroots labour activism in the factory during the immediate postwar years. The union was still advocating on behalf of workers a year after the company went bankrupt in September 1954.[19]

Medicine Hat was a provincial hot spot for labour unrest in 1947.[20] Six of the thirteen strikes that occurred in Alberta that year erupted in and around the city, which was the fourth largest in the province.[21] The city had an extensive and diverse industrial base, and women were well represented in the city's manufacturing sector, accounting for 23 per cent of manufacturing wage earners provincially, compared to the provincial average of 12 per cent.[22] The pottery factory, which had produced sturdy, affordable crocks and everyday dishes since 1912, was a major player in the local economy.[23] Workers struck over wages while struggling to sign a first contract several months after being organized by the International Union of Mine, Mill, and Smelter Workers.[24] Mine Mill had a proud history as a militant and progressive union that dated back to the turn of the century when miners on both sides of the 49th parallel fought to improve workers' lives.[25] Mine Mill embraced industrial unionism long before this concept became popular within the mainstream labour movement in the late 1930s.[26] The union also had a history of organizing more diverse and disadvantaged workforces.[27] In the 1940s it was one of the few unions in Alberta to attempt to organize workplaces that employed women.

Medicine Hat was targeted by Mine Mill and other industrial unions because of its status as a low-wage area of the province.[28] The collapse of the region's agricultural economy in the 1920s and '30s because of intense drought had forced those families that did not abandon their farms to eke out a marginal existence by relying on wage work in Medicine Hat.[29] This generated a large pool of cheap labour for local factories. A wage freeze during World War II had kept wages low at the pottery, despite labour shortages generated by government contracts and military enlistments.[30] In 1947 it was difficult for even a skilled senior male worker to support a family on his wages. Employee lists at the time of the strike reveal that within a workforce of 250 people, thirty-eight families had more than one person working at the pottery. As former worker Christine Pocsik explained, "Families worked there. Let's [look at] the Stickels— Chris Stickel the Dad, he was the foreman, and the son and the daughter worked there so there was three of them bringing home money, bringing home their cheques, and I'm sure that was probably a good living then...There were a lot of young kids working there whose dad worked there. That's how a family survived."[31]

Average wages in Medicine Hat were lower than in any other major Alberta city. Within Medicine Hat, Medalta Potteries was notorious for its low wage levels. The average weekly wage in the Canadian clay products industry in 1947 was $34.91, and in Canadian manufacturing industries it was $35.66.[32] Information available is insufficient to determine an average wage rate at the factory in 1947; however, management figures released during the strike set the top wage rate at $33.60 per week for males and $21 per week for females paid on an hourly basis.[33] During the strike, management and the union disagreed about the proportion of workers whose earnings approached the top end of the rate schedule, but it is clear that Medalta wages were well below the industry average.[34] Medalta had a high incidence of minimum wage violations throughout its history, particularly in the case of female workers.[35]

Working conditions at the pottery were harsh. The main stages of the manufacturing process were clay preparation and jiggering or slip casting to produce the pottery shapes, then decorating, glazing, kiln firing, and finally checking and packing the finished ware for shipping. Many of these stages involved heavy lifting and constant exposure to temperature extremes, choking dust, and chemical fumes. Back injuries, respiratory problems, and one woman's sensational partial scalping by a conveyor belt pulley demonstrated the high physical price paid by many workers.[36] There was no job security, split shifts operated without a wage differential, and when sales orders were strong a regular work week was the maximum set by law—forty-eight hours in 1947. Government inspectors often found that work conditions at the factory did not meet legislated standards.[37]

Many young, unmarried daughters from farm families were among those seeking paid work in Medicine Hat because sons, rather than daughters, usually inherited the family farm. It was also assumed that women's activities on the farm were limited to domestic work and farm chores such as milking cows and feeding the chickens. As Christine Pocsik explained, it was her brother who began running the farm when her father left periodically to take paid work: "because I was a girl I wasn't mechanical wise or anything. I couldn't go out and fix things if they broke down."[38] These class-based understandings of masculinity and femininity helped re-shape attitudes toward workers during the strike. They have been traced to industrialization and the middle-class notion of the male breadwinner as someone able to support and control his family and household. Within the new industrial order, middle-class womanhood was characterized by economic dependence, fragility, passivity, and social subordination.[39]

Working-class women developed distinctive notions of femininity that departed from the middle-class ideal. Several of the women who had worked at Medalta expressed pride in their ability to perform heavy lifting and maintain a high pace of work. Yet they spoke with distaste of the dirt and dust associated with clay, and they had no desire to become a jiggerman, the most highly paid job and filled exclusively by males because it involved immersing your hands in clay all day. Engilena Kessler was relieved to move from the trimming department, where her hands were constantly dry and cracked from sponging the clay pieces, to decorating, where she painted finished product. All of the women interviewed, even those who saw it as just a job, felt proud of their ability to support themselves, even if it meant sharing a one-bedroom apartment with several women and sleeping on a couch in the kitchen.[40] What they did resent was management's lack of concern that they performed back-breaking work for such low wages. Asked how women coped during the war when they performed one of the heaviest jobs, moving pottery in and out of the kiln using cement containers, Engilena Kessler said, "those saggers, they were heavy. I don't think girls should have been lifting those. Yeah, I thought that was asking a lot of staff."[41]

Like working-class women in other historical contexts, the women workers at Medalta held a concept of working-class femininity that embraced hard physical labour and economic independence, yet they often accepted middle-class strictures for respectable behaviour.[42] As a result, women workers tended to view their interests as continuous with men's on the assumption that in the future they would marry and leave the paid workforce for the domestic sphere. Engilena Kessler, who was dating her future husband—one of the strike leaders—at the time of the strike, felt male workers were more entitled to higher wages than were women workers. She remembered feeling critical of some women workers' hostile attitude toward management during the strike: "There were some women who were very intense. Yes, very...I could relate to the men's situation more so because there was no room for advancement or for, you know, they were being underpaid...because they were trying to establish homes. Women in those days did not make up homes for themselves as they do today. Women...relied more on their husbands to be the wage earner."[43] Ironically, Kessler, like most of the women interviewed, continued to work throughout her marriage, including the years when her two children were young.[44] The influence of late twentieth-century feminism and a lifetime of experience can be seen in the distinction Kessler drew between the situation of women in 1947 and in 2000. Through the lens of time, Kessler still saw women's interests as continuous with men's in 1947, but she felt this was no longer the case.

Although Canadian working-class families had never had the luxury of a "breadwinner wage," this middle-class ideal became compelling for male workers following World War II when the right to organize and to bargain collectively brought it within reach for the first time for many male workers. The new legislation was framed by notions of rights and freedoms that implicitly excluded women workers, who were viewed as economically dependent temporary workers and were largely unorganized.[45] Yet the proportion of women in the paid labour force, particularly married women, had increased dramatically to meet first wartime production demands, then the needs of a booming postwar economy.[46] This posed a serious threat to men's privileged access to paid work, particularly the ideal of a male breadwinner. As a result the postwar era was a reactionary period during which patriarchal gender roles were reinscribed more firmly in the media and ambivalence toward women workers intensified.[47]

In the conservative postwar social climate, the traditional nuclear family with a stay-at-home wife and mother was glorified and became the template for social mores and social policy. Federal daycare nurseries were closed. Federal income tax policy that had been changed during the war to accommodate married women who worked was revised.[48] Married women were barred from civil service jobs, and the new unemployment insurance system imposed extra requirements on married women.[49] Gendered minimum wage rates persisted, reflecting the assumption that working women did not support a family while working men did.[50] Similarly, gender-specific lifting and seating regulations designed to protect women's reproductive capabilities reinforced the idea that women were more fragile than men and that their primary role was to bear children, not perform paid labour.[51]

In the Canadian West these class-based gender ideals were racialized by Anglo-Canadians as part of an effort by whites to legitimize their claim to the territory from which they had so recently displaced Aboriginal peoples.[52] Those invested in whiteness cultivated racial and ethnic stereotypes that contrasted the image of fragile, vulnerable Anglo white womanhood with images of aggressive Aboriginal and Amazonian "Galician" womanhood. Distinctions of whiteness were used to assert the superiority and dominance of the Anglo-Saxon elite over Aboriginal peoples and the multitude of diverse immigrant groups that had arrived on the Prairies in the early twentieth century.[53]

These racialized notions of gender difference, which reinforced the middle-class ideal of a male breadwinner, were fostered by ethnic dynamics at the pottery. In 1947 Medalta employed an almost exclusively white workforce of mainly second-generation Northern and East-Central European immigrants.[54] Most of the men and women interviewed were from families that had immigrated from German-speaking parts of Eastern Europe, although one person was born in Hungary and the family of another had immigrated from Norway. Former worker Engilena Kessler estimated that roughly 75 per cent of Medalta workers were from a German-speaking family in the late 1940s when she worked at the factory, and most of them spoke German.[55] Medalta management and artisans were primarily of English, Scottish, or Anglo-Canadian origin, which were still the predominant ethnicities of the elite in most Alberta communities in the 1940s.

German-speaking immigrants to Alberta, many of whom settled in the Medicine Hat area around the turn of the twentieth century, were easily assimilated because they were white, and they held similar cultural values, including a strong work ethic and patriarchal ideals rooted in notions of gender difference.[56] Public hostility toward Germans during the two world wars accelerated the assimilation process.[57] During the war Medalta workers were forbidden to speak German to the German POWs who worked at the pottery.[58] It is likely that their recent status as "enemy aliens" also intensified the conservatism of Medicine Hat's German-speaking residents and farmers, making them feel more vulnerable to anti-communist red-baiting in the immediate postwar years.

In a society that privileged people of Anglo-Saxon heritage, the increasing assimilation of German-speaking peoples by 1947 combined with profound conservatism to foster ethnic affinity between workers and management, which obscured class differences and mitigated anti-management hostility.[59] All but one of the workers I interviewed were born in the Medicine Hat area, and they tended to embrace the cultural values and traditions of the British-dominated elite. Former worker Engilena Kessler, who worked in the all-female art department, spoke glowingly of her supervisor, English immigrant Tom Hulme, "the nicest man to work for." Kessler especially appreciated the English tradition of tea, which Hulme would make and allow the women to drink at their tables while they worked.[60] Even those workers who related bad experiences with particular managers or foremen couched them in terms devoid of ethnic slurs. Sipping tea in the art department may also have reinforced in women workers the notion of inherent female difference that was prized by the middle-class Anglo elite.

Comments by several former Medalta workers demonstrate the process by which non-Anglo white workers reinforced gendered and class-based notions of whiteness. In an interview, a male former pottery worker of Russian-German descent denigrated the tall, strong build of one of the few Métis women who worked at the pottery during the strike with the comment she "was built like a big squaw." A response by another former worker who was female, that this Métis woman "would punch you right in the nose for [saying] that," implicitly contrasted images of aggressive Aboriginal women and passive, diminutive white women.

In the same way, the male worker's implied criticism of a Ukrainian farmer for not working his "hefty" daughters in the fields reinforced a code of white Anglo middle-class femininity by suggesting that their size and strength made them unfeminine. While working on a threshing crew in the 1940s for the farmer, who had six children, including four daughters, the former Medalta worker said, "The boys were out helping, the daughters stayed and helped Mom cook, milked the cows, did the chores while the men were out working. They weren't allowed to—well I off and asked my boss that, I said, 'How come you don't have any women on this crew?' and he said, 'Well they couldn't stand it,' and I said, 'Well there's some pretty big girls out there.' They were hefty farm girls, you know."[61] The Ukrainian farmer's refusal to acknowledge his daughters' physical strength can be seen as an effort to demonstrate their conformity to the Anglo elite's concept of femininity. In this context the former Medalta worker's comments suggest an attempt to stake a claim to whiteness that was still tenuous for Albertans of Ukrainian heritage in 1947. Their purchase on whiteness was not secure until the 1950s and '60s, after more than a half-century of virulent nativist attacks by pro-imperialist Anglo-Saxons on the Prairies.[62] His disparaging comments may also demonstrate the need to buttress a claim to whiteness by German-speaking peoples who had only recently been viewed as enemy aliens.

Comments by former workers about Aboriginal males centred on a perceived difference between white and Aboriginal attitudes toward work that helped justify their exclusion from the factory. As one male worker explained, when asked why no Aboriginal or Métis males worked at the pottery, "They were too damn lazy, that's why." The notion of the degenerate Indian, who was physically and morally weak, reinforced the social superiority of a white working-class masculinity for which harsh working conditions have been seen "as a challenge to masculinity, rather than as an expression of the exploitation of capitalist relations of production."[63]

These class-based gender and racial stereotypes were used to legitimize exclusive white access to more highly paid industrial jobs. During World War II, women of colour gained access to higher paid industrial work for the first time because of widespread labour shortages; however, they tended to be assigned the heaviest and dirtiest types of work.[64] A Métis woman found that her first job at the pottery as a kiln worker required that she lift the heavy cement saggers that held the pottery pieces in the kiln and were often very hot—a job usually performed by men. After the war, she attained a position in the decorating department, which was one of the most congenial areas in which to work.[65] The fact that several former workers could quickly recall one of the few Métis people who worked at Medalta, and no one could remember any other visible minority workers at the plant, suggests that workers assumed a white identity and marginalized those considered racial "others" in the community. Racial or ethnic difference appeared to play a role in shaping the workforce, and it helped obscure class lines between management and workers, but it was not a salient factor in the strike itself, likely because the workforce was almost entirely white.[66]

The pottery industry has a long tradition of employing women workers that is linked to both cultural expectations about femininity and the economic advantages of hiring women who could be paid much less than men.[67] This tradition reinforced notions of gender difference in ways that strengthened class cohesion but limited gender consciousness. At Medalta Potteries the majority of tasks were determined by gender, and most departments were either male or female, although men nearly always supervised. Jobs to which men were given exclusive access involved technical skill, the supervision of men, or were especially heavy or dirty, such as loading pottery pieces into the kiln.[68] Women performed the lighter, purportedly less skilled tasks, such as attaching handles and spouts to cups and teapots, or trimming because their "small and quick hands" were said to be more dexterous than men's.[69]

During the war women stepped into male jobs out of necessity, but by 1947 pre-war gender segregation had been re-established. In only a few jobs did men and women actually work alongside each other performing the same tasks, such as glazing pottery pieces on the conveyor belt.[70] Women in those jobs earned 68 per cent of the male wage on the eve of the strike.[71]

Women were paid lower wages based on the cultural assumption that they were temporary workers who were economically dependent on a father or husband.[72] Middle-class cultural assumptions about women's inherent domesticity also limited women's job alternatives to domestic work and waitressing, which were not as well paid as factory jobs.[73] These assumptions helped generate a steady supply of women workers and made their employment profitable for Medalta Potteries, particularly during the war when women performed "male" jobs at the female rate. A postwar construction boom combined with strong industrial and farm productivity in and around Medicine Hat to prevent employers from laying off women workers as servicemen returned from the war.[74] Gender-specific wage rates and promotional opportunities meant that there were only two wage categories for women workers at the factory: "inexperienced" and "experienced." A female worker was hired at the "inexperienced" rate and after a certain period of time, usually three to six months, was awarded the "experienced" rate. No further wage increases were structured into the rates for female employees. For males there were three wage categories differentiated by skill and age but not experience. "Juniors and apprentices" earned the lowest rate. Once a male was over twenty-one years of age he was awarded the "unskilled" rate. Only men could be awarded the "skilled" rate for particular jobs.[75] This gender-specific criteria for wage increases reflected management's assumption that male workers were committed to a career because they supported a family, while women were supported by either their father or a husband.

<FIGURE 14.1: *Men were given exclusive access to jobs that involved technical skill, such as Automatic Tunnel Kiln Operator, 1943. [Courtesy of Glenbow Archives M 5827/2]*

FIGURE 14.3: *Men and women generally sat on opposite sides of the room during union hall meetings. The average age of women in this audience is significantly lower than the average age of men. A Mine Mill union meeting of Medalta Potteries workers at the Moose Hall in Medicine Hat, after the strike, circa late 1940s. [Courtesy of Dorothy Beierbach]*

The gendered segregation of work and gendered wage rates tended to foster class solidarity and inhibit gender consciousness within the Medalta Potteries workforce by preventing most women workers from comparing themselves with their male co-workers. The women and men interviewed who worked in a single-sex department accepted with no difficulty the gender-based differential in wages and job opportunities at the time. Young, single women working in a gender-segregated department, who often married a man they met at the factory, supported the strike issue of higher wages, but they did not necessarily see their own best interests served by the ideal of equal pay. Only one woman interviewed did not work in a gender-segregated department, and she expressed the most resentment about the wage discrepancy between men and women workers. Rosetta Brosnikoff, who worked the conveyor belt in the glazing

<FIGURE 14.2: *Women worked on the conveyor belt attaching handles and spouts to cups and teapots, or trimming because their "small and quick hands" were said to be more dexterous than men's. 1943. [Courtesy of Glenbow Archives M 5827/2]*

department a few years after the strike, said "That was one of the sore points, because you worked side-by-side with a man and he got more money than you did."[76]

The combination of young, single women with a large number of middle-aged, married men at the pottery seemed to foster a father-daughter relationship that further enhanced class cohesion but undermined the equal status of women as co-workers.[77] Clarence Sailer, a strike leader, had teenage children and a niece working at the pottery. His niece, Dorothy Beierbach, was the most class-conscious person I interviewed and was one of the eight women who pleaded guilty in connection with the two most serious picket line incidents.[78] Within a conservative community that embraced patriarchal notions of authority and respect, these filial bonds likely strengthened class solidarity.

A comment by a former woman worker about use of the factory washrooms suggests that the combination of young women and men of all ages within the workforce also generated a latent sexual tension in the workplace. The woman said only the women's washroom was located upstairs, requiring that women workers climb a long flight of stairs located in the open shop: "And of course it overlooked not only the area that we worked in but it overlooked the area where they made crocks, and of course this was all men, so every time you walked up that flight of stairs you knew that the men were looking at you."[79] The men's washroom was on the main floor.

The filial tenor of relations between young women and older men did much to preserve the respectability of workers within the factory by neutralizing these sexual undertones to a large extent, but it compromised their status as equal partners in the struggle for better wages and work conditions. Several women interviewed mentioned the helpfulness and kindness of older men with whom they worked. Rosetta Brosnikoff, who was a member of the union executive while still a teenager, remembered with fondness the older men who would ensure her safety by walking her home in the evening after union meetings.[80] Another worker said she enjoyed working with her supervisor, Clarence Sailer, who took on a protective role by helping women workers whenever they needed a hand with lifting. Engilena Kessler boarded with her foreman, Chris Stickel, and recalled being annoyed by Stickel's insistence on a curfew at night when she was dating her future husband.[81] In a different way, sexual tension between young men and women workers, who often eventually married, likely fostered a perception of young single women workers as potential wives more than co-workers. Three of the six women I interviewed married a man they met at Medalta Potteries.

These complex workplace, family, community, and union dynamics coalesced to generate broad-based grass-roots support for Medalta workers when the strike broke. In a government-supervised vote only months before the strike, 200 of the 222 eligible pottery workers voted in favour of certification under Mine Mill, and no votes were cast against it.[82] In interviews, former workers reported that workers "came out in droves" for union meetings during the months leading up to the strike.[83] Two days before the walk out, in an unsupervised union vote, 98 per cent of workers voted in favour of the job action.[84] When 213 workers walked off the job on 12 August 1947, only eight workers remained on the job.

The mayor and the larger community of Medicine Hat also expressed substantial support for the job action in the belief that low industry wages were hurting local businesses. A spontaneous parade by striking workers through the city's downtown core proceeded without harassment by local police.[85] In the first weeks of the seventy-two-day strike, Mayor William Rae tried to facilitate a settlement by arranging a meeting with the two sides. City council approved a community tag day, which allowed union members to raise $475.23 by soliciting citizens on city streets.[86] A city alderman also spoke at the union's well-attended strike rally, which raised $214 in the first weeks of the labour action.[87] Only a handful of people responded to Medalta advertisements for new employees during the first month of the strike.[88]

There was a perceptible shift in attitudes toward the unionized workers, however, as strike events unfolded. An unfounded allegation that the union was not legally certified, harsh court rulings on minor picket line disturbances, and a focus on male pickets helped project an image of workers as unlawful, unreasonable, and violent, yet at the same time ignorant and naïve. In the first days of the strike Medalta launched a spurious civil action that claimed Mine Mill was not legally certified.[89] This allegation dominated headlines during the strike. When the civil claim was finally dealt with after the strike ended, the court found that the government had used the wrong certification form because of new legislation passed in the spring.[90] This legal manoeuvre put the union on the defensive throughout the remainder of the strike. In particular, Calgary Justice Clinton B. Ford's severe interpretation of an injunction, which made any picketing illegal, together with the allegation that the union was not legally certified, cast workers and their union leaders in the role of senseless outlaws.[91] Gender played an essential role in constructing this image. The middle-class assumption that working-class men are inherently aggressive and that females are passive, vulnerable, and economically dependent shaped the attitudes and actions of all parties involved in the dispute.

The difference in the behaviour of men and women workers was less significant than court charges, convictions, sentences, and press reports would suggest. Indeed, previously unpublished court evidence, oral interviews, and photographs all muddy the stark contrast conveyed in contemporary reports. The number of women workers charged was only slightly less than the number of men; however, there were significant differences in the types of charges laid and in the way they were handled by the press and the courts.[92] Male workers were charged with more numerous and more serious strike-related charges than those laid against female workers. Similarly, while the names of women charged were published in the newspaper, their actions were never described, yet men's were sometimes described in great detail.

There is a remarkable disparity between accounts of strike-related violence that occurred. The impression of lawlessness and violence conveyed by news reports and judicial remarks is at odds with what former rank-and-file workers related in oral history interviews.[93] It is difficult to assess how a filter of more than fifty years affected the memories of workers. A shift in Alberta's political culture to the right, and the community's collective memory of the strike as an "embarrassment," likely compromised the willingness of former workers to acknowledge left-wing views held

FIGURE 14.4: *Women workers were well represented in a march through the streets of downtown Medicine Hat on the first day of the Medalta Potteries strike, 12 August 1947.*
[*Courtesy of Hanna Osborne*]

during the turbulent postwar years. The context of other evidence, however, and the consistency of their respective responses gives credence to worker testimony that allegations of violence were exaggerated.[94] Engilena Kessler said workers were stunned by the jail sentences: "It was very shocking...It was like they picked six or seven or eight fellows out of this group of 200 out there and said 'These are the guys that we're going...to set an example [with].' It just blew me right out of the water and still to this day I don't know what they were trying to prove."[95] One male worker who was jailed but who refused to be interviewed stated that he was not on the picket line at the time of the incidents.[96] One of the seven women given a suspended sentence said she appeared in court but never learned what she was supposed to have done.

The fact that women were charged in numbers roughly equal to men in the crucial court case suggests that women workers were well represented during these picket line disturbances. It also suggests that management, which reported the incidents, saw women's presence as an effective force on the picket line and needed to make an example of them as well as the men. The strength and effectiveness of women's picket line presence is demonstrated in court affidavits, oral interviews, and photographs. Several women interviewed insisted that women participated "equally" on the picket line. Women were well represented in a series of picket line photographs taken by former workers who were interviewed.[97] Court questioning by the company lawyer in unpublished strike documents reveals that management suspected "girls" of using sticks in the mauling incident and that women workers actively helped obstruct individuals and vehicles, including trucks and rail cars. "A bunch of girls" surrounded the plant manager's car and lined up to form a barricade across the road during the mauling incident.[98]

The two most serious picket line incidents, which resulted in jail sentences, involved very different levels of violence, but their handling by the courts and the press conflated them in a way that exaggerated the degree of violence and implicated all of the fifteen individuals involved to a similar degree. Although they occurred about a week apart, newspaper accounts of the two incidents were published at the same time, immediately after the second incident. Despite explicit detail in the press report about the violence alleged, particular actions were not attributed to individuals, so it is impossible to determine from the news reports who did what.

The first incident was a minor case of property damage. It involved obstruction of a truck that had crossed the picket line and was stopped by strikers when it returned from the factory hauling pottery. Part of the load was dumped on the ground and broken.[99] Three men and one woman, Josie Longridge—who was married to the union's international representative, William Longridge—were charged with "watching and besetting" in connection with this incident for leading a group of workers who stopped the truck.[100] The second incident, which involved personal injury, was described by the newspaper as a "mauling." According to press reports, one male strike breaker was "kicked about the body after he was thrown to the ground," and four other male strike breakers were "pummelled by fists and sticks." One man went to hospital and was released the next day.[101] It was also reported that strikers tried unsuccessfully to "drag" several "girls" from the back of a manager's car and called them "abusive and foul names."[102] Fifteen unionists, seven of whom were women, were charged in the "mauling" incident. One man was charged with assault.[103]

The type of charges laid and press coverage implied that everyone charged was equally involved in the most serious acts of violence, even though only one man was charged with assault. The magistrate's severe words confirmed this interpretation. According to a press report, Gore-Hickman asserted that "acts of assault committed by groups of persons threw guilt on all taking part, whether they were the actual ones who committed the act or not. Should murder result every member was guilty."[104]

But the differential treatment of male and female pickets belied the magistrate's stern words about equal guilt. Josie Longridge was the only woman picket charged in both incidents.[105] Longridge was not a worker; she was married to William Longridge, the prominent communist Mine Mill leader. Significantly, her full name was never published in the newspaper nor recorded in the court ledger; instead, she was always described as "Mrs. William Longridge." It was through oral interviews that I learned her first name.[106] The authorities' refusal to use Josie's first name emphasized her identity as a married woman and made her actions the responsibility of her husband rather than a reflection of her own beliefs and political activism. Her husband's status as a prominent communist union leader in the province reinforced this emphasis.

The magistrate's decision to ignore even the actions of a mature woman also reveals the anxieties of male authorities. The magistrate was unable to take women's militancy seriously, because to do so would have risked emasculating male management and police and could have cast him as a bully in the eyes of the community. Taking a lenient stance instead made the judiciary appear chivalrous and paternalistic, and it reinforced the notion of essential gender differences and patriarchal power on which postwar Canadian society was structured. Gore-Hickman's comments that he "hesitated to send young women to jail" demonstrated his refusal to acknowledge that women workers were capable of militant behaviour. Courtroom lenience toward women that is construed in chivalric terms serves the needs of a male judiciary.[107] The distinction between male and female workers, which convinced Gore-Hickman to send the men to jail, also undermined the reality and legitimacy of committed and effective women picketers; this differential treatment also served to underscore that only men were the real workers, buttressing their privileged claim to paid work.

Significantly, defence lawyer A.Y. Spivack also asked for the lenience of the court "in the case of the female workers, the majority being 17 or 18 years of age," although he did not request lenience for any of the men, one of whom was eighteen.[108] The lawyer's request reveals a fundamental ambivalence toward women workers within the male union leadership. Mine Mill encouraged women's involvement in the union and on the picket line, and it strove to address their particular needs. Yet in this instance the union lawyer chose not to promote an image of militant women workers who stood shoulder-to-shoulder with their male co-workers in labour activism to secure fair wages and conditions. Instead, he affirmed working women's respectability according to conventional, primarily middle-class norms of passive and vulnerable femininity.

Pervasive middle-class notions of femininity helped cast women workers' militancy in a negative light, which undermined their effectiveness during the strike and eroded their claim to equal wages. Militancy jeopardized women workers' claim to respectability, which hinged on their ability to conform to middle-class gender norms held by the police, the judiciary, and journalists. This factor made some women unwilling to act militantly. Perhaps more importantly, powerful gender norms reduced the effectiveness of female militancy that did occur. As Joy Parr has demonstrated, these norms could bring "neighbourly wrath" upon women workers who were militant.[109] In Medicine Hat, gender norms prompted newspapers, employers, the state, and unions to ignore or downplay the militancy of women workers. In both cases the legitimacy and strength of the labour movement was weakened in the eyes of the public.

Organized labour's adherence to middle-class gender norms was conflicted, particularly within progressive left-wing unions like Mine Mill, which upheld democratic and egalitarian ideals. The predominant concern of all industrial unions in the 1940s was to secure unskilled male workers steady work at a wage adequate to support a family—something only skilled craftsmen had been able to attain in the past.[110] The presence of women in a bargaining unit created ambivalence and contradictions as unions tried to improve the situation of women workers within a patriarchal paradigm. Internal struggles over whether or not contractual seniority rights should give women access to male jobs, and pressure exerted by male workers on married women to give up their jobs to men, demonstrate some of the conflicts created by privileging male workers.[111]

Viewed as daughters or potential wives more than workers by their male co-workers and union leaders, women were treated as more fragile and less capable on the picket line than men. Engilena Kessler said women participated equally on the picket line, but only men took the leadership role within teams of pickets: "every group had a leader and it was always the men that were the leader of the group. Maybe it was for protection. I don't know."[112] When women workers' actions forced them into public consciousness, there was an emphasis on their vulnerability, which was clear in the crucial court case. The union also capitalized on perceptions of female vulnerability by giving young women workers a prominent role in its public appeals for support. Two young women workers were appointed to solicit donations during a whirlwind fundraising tour of mining communities in the Crowsnest Pass during the strike. An impassioned speech by a teenage woman worker at the fundraising rally held in the first weeks of the strike elicited strong support within the community. The particular appeal of "girl workers" was also implied in a letter from an official of the United Mine Workers of America based in a small town in the Crowsnest Pass and directed to the striking Medalta workers. Encouraging them to hold a tag day fundraiser in Blairmore, he wrote, "If girl workers were selected for this work I feel sure the result would be worthwhile."[113] The care with which the two women dressed for the occasion, despite their low wages, suggests that the women did not see themselves as victims but felt a pride in their appearance, grounded in their confidence and self-worth as wage-earners. The image of women workers as vulnerable and in need of male

FIGURE 14.6: *A woman picketer holds a sign saying "We Demand No Discrimination, Equal Pay for Equal Work" on the first day of the Medalta Potteries strike, 12 August 1947.*
[Courtesy of Hanna Osborne]

protection reinforced the notion that they were economic dependants, which made their needs secondary to men's. This self-image helps explain their attitude toward the issue of equal pay for equal work, which photographs and news accounts suggest was raised to some extent during the strike. None of the women or men interviewed remembered anything about the issue of equal pay, even though one woman had taken two photographs of women workers holding a picket sign stating "We Demand No Discrimination, Equal Pay for Equal Work." Given that the workers interviewed were very young at the time of the strike—most were teenagers—attempts to improve women's wages relative to men's may not

<FIGURE 14.5: *Mabel Cranmer (née Degg) (left) and Dorothy Beierbach (née Sailer) pose during their fund-raising tour of mining communities in the Crowsnest Pass, 29 September 1947. The women's careful grooming in comparison with their regular work wear (see Figure 14.6) signals a working-class respectability derived from their dignity and self-respect as self-supporting wage-earners.* [Courtesy of Dorothy Beierbach]

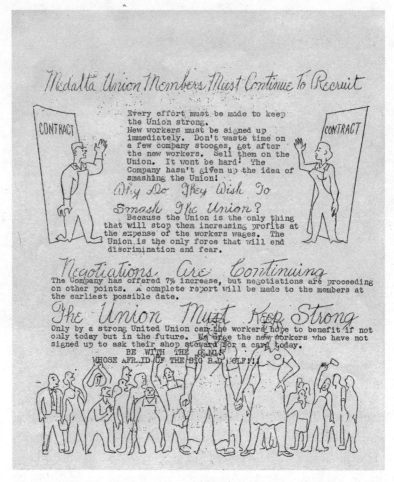

FIGURE 14.7: *This union bulletin was published during the first weeks after Mine Mill was certified at Medalta Potteries. The depiction of women workers as equals with men in the graphics appears to be linked to a recruitment drive targeting women workers.*

[*Courtesy of University of British Columbia Archives, "Union Bulletin" circa June 1947, Box 128, File 25, Mine Mill, UBC*]

have seemed relevant. Such attempts would have appealed most to older women workers, or to those who had some work experience. The union also initially demanded a wage increase of 33 per cent for women and only 21 per cent for men. In its first wage concession during the strike, however, Mine Mill reduced its wage demand to 12 per cent across the board, which effectively widened the gendered wage gap. This evidence suggests that the demand for equal pay for women may have been a

FIGURE 14.8: *Graphics in two union bulletins issued during the first weeks of the strike reinforced the notion that workers were male and women's role was primarily domestic.* [*Courtesy of University of British Columbia Archives, "Strike Bulletin" 14 August and 3 September 1947, Box 128, File 25, Mine Mill, UBC*]

recruitment strategy promoted by union leaders more than a grassroots movement grounded in an egalitarian vision of male and female workers. A union bulletin depicting women workers as the strong, capable equals of men also suggests that the issue of equal pay was primarily a strategic issue raised by the union. The high proportion of women workers at Medalta (42 per cent) would have made equal pay advantageous to men whose jobs could be threatened by lower-paid female workers.[114]

Tabling an offer that sacrificed women's wages tacitly reinforced the belief that male workers' wages were more important than women's. Notwithstanding the recruitment bulletin, an underlying view of women workers as secondary in importance to men dominates the images and rhetoric in union literature. Women were either erased by the assumption that all workers were male or, particularly in strike bulletins, they were portrayed in a domestic role. Combative union rhetoric about "fighting" the boss implicitly excluded women, whose respectability hinged on their ability to conform to conventional norms of femininity that could be jeopardized by militant female behaviour. Similarly, talk of "rights" excluded women workers who were not accorded the same entitlement to paid work and a self-supporting wage that men enjoyed in the immediate postwar years when returning war veterans and male breadwinners had priority in the job market.[115]

A "Welcome Home Reception and Supper" organized by the union for the "Seven Labour Heroes" when they returned from jail after the strike had ended confirmed the differential status of male and female workers. Being sent to jail signaled the men's status as true workers, something that was denied the women who had been charged alongside them. The event was used by the union to counter the image of male workers as lawless and dangerous by portraying them as honest, respectable breadwinners. According to press coverage of the dinner, one jailed worker said defiantly, "We are not ashamed of our crime and punishment." Another speaker commented on the irony of calling Canadians "glorious and free... when men can be confined to jail for defending their rights and their bread and butter livelihood."[116]

The role of women workers, who had been charged in equal numbers and who participated fully on the picket line, was ignored at a reception for "labour heroes" that focused exclusively on the jailed men. Oral interviews and photographs reveal that many women workers, including some of those charged, joined the wives of male workers and union officials in the kitchen to organize and prepare the banquet of home-cooked fare for the reception supper.[117] The local newspaper's extravagant detail about the banquet menu—noting everything from the "celery, olives,

FIGURE 14.9: *Back to the kitchen—Women workers, as well as the wives of male workers and union officials, prepared the banquet for the seven labour heroes during the Welcome Home Reception and Dinner held at the Moose Hall in Medicine Hat, 6 November 1947. From left to right, Selma Stickel, Josie Longridge (married to union leader William Longridge), Dorothy Beierbach, and Ruth Sandau. The other two women have not been identified.*
[Courtesy of Dorothy Beierbach]

relishes, sliced tomatoes, hot rolls, baked ham, mashed potatoes, gravy, peas and carrots mixed" to the "ice cream, assorted cake, tea and coffee"—was the only record of public acknowledgement the women workers received.[118]

Placing women workers at the labour heroes' table was not an option in 1947—it would have risked casting them as harlots, the most widely understood role for working-class women in public at the time. Their retreat to the kitchen placed them in the conventional and respectable role of dutiful daughters and helpmates. Although theirs was the first generation of working-class women in Canada to remain employed in significant numbers after marriage, it was not until the 1960s and '70s, when their daughters came of age, that women began to claim a legitimate place as equals in the paid labour force.

The court sentences and the labour heroes' dinner demonstrate a profound ambivalence toward women workers that influenced the outcome of the Medalta strike and the strength of the labour movement in the postwar era. Gendered understandings of male and female workers fostered exaggeration of male workers' behaviour, which compromised their respectability. These understandings also undercut the public impact of women workers' solidarity and militancy. The legitimacy of Medalta workers' reasonable demands for higher wages was more easily dismissed by a public offended at the apparently brutish behaviour of male workers and alarmed by communist allegations. Gendered interpretations of workers' actions helped deal a devastating blow to initially broad-based public support for Medalta workers and created an eerie silence about the activism of women workers, which helped put them back in the kitchen figuratively and, to some extent, literally for two decades.

AUTHOR'S NOTE

This article was strengthened immeasurably by discussions with Elizabeth Jameson, Sarah Carter, and Kathryn McPherson. I also benefited greatly from helpful comments offered by members of the Women's History Reading Group at York University. Many thanks to Bettina Bradbury, Kristin Burnett, Laila Haidarali, Janice Kim, Liz Millwood, Anne Rubenstein, and Shannon Stettner.

NOTES

1. Engilena Kessler (née Stappler), interview by author, 1 February 2001, Edmonton, AB.
2. *Medicine Hat Daily News*, 11 October 1947 (hereafter cited as MHDN).
3. Medicine Hat Police Arrest Records, 11 October 1947, M93.1.5, Medicine Hat Museum and Art Gallery (hereafter cited as MHM).
4. Medicine Hat City Council Minutes, 20 October 1947, M96.6, MHM.
5. The new laws penalized unions for striking illegally and prohibited recruitment on company property without permission. Warren Caragata, *Alberta Labour: A Heritage Untold* (Toronto: James Lorimer & Company, 1979), 140–41; Alvin Finkel, "The Cold War, Alberta Labour, and the Social Credit Regime," *Labour/Le Travail* 21 (Spring 1988): 123–52.

6. Judy Fudge and Eric Tucker, *Labour Before the Law: The Regulation of Workers' Collective Action in Canada, 1900–1948* (Don Mills, ON: Oxford University Press, 2001).

7. Anne Hayward, *The Alberta Pottery Industry, 1912–1990: A Social and Economic History* (Hull, QC: The Canadian Museum of Civilization, 2001); MHDN, 21 October 1947; *Calgary Herald*, 28 August 1947. Warren Caragata's brief account of the strike is an exception in that he identifies wage demands as the main cause of the walk out. See Caragata, *Alberta Labour*, 140–41.

8. Despite communist leadership within Mine Mill, these workers were not radical. They continued to support the existing political and economic system but felt entitled to a greater share in its rewards. The word *militant* is used here to indicate assertiveness, aggression, or combativeness; it signals workers' rejection of paternalistic relations with their employer. See Bryan D. Palmer, *Working-Class Experience: Rethinking the History of Canadian Labour 1800–1991* (Toronto: McClelland & Stewart, 1992), 41–48.

9. See Gregory S. Kealey with Douglas Cruikshank, "Strikes in Canada, 1891–1950," in *Workers and Canadian History* (Montreal and Kingston: McGill-Queen's University Press, 1995), 407 for a graph that traces the strike wave.

10. PC 1003, passed by the federal government in February 1944, established procedures to certify unions, forced employers to recognize trade unions, defined unfair labour practices, and created an administrative apparatus to enforce the legislation. One peculiarly Canadian aspect of the legislation is that neither the union nor the employer was allowed to hold a strike or lockout during the term of an agreement or before submitting to compulsory conciliation. This feature tended to benefit employers by creating delays. The American Wagner Act, which was passed nearly a decade earlier and influenced PC 1003 significantly, did not contain this provision. Bryan Palmer, *Working-Class Experience*, 279–80.

11. Alvin Finkel, *The Social Credit Phenomenon in Alberta* (Toronto: University of Toronto Press, 1989), 86, 136–37.

12. John Richards and Larry Pratt, *Prairie Capitalism: Power and Influence in the New West* (Toronto: McClelland and Stewart, 1979), 160.

13. Alvin Finkel notes the connection between the meatpacking strike and the government's determination to reassure oil investors. *The Social Credit Phenomenon*, 110.

14. *People's Weekly*, 18 October 1947.

15. *People's Weekly*, 18 October 1947.

16. MHDN, 21 October 1947.

17. MHDN, 24 October 1947. Medalta allowed all striking workers to return, even those who had been jailed. This worker "victory" likely resulted from the company's desperate need for workers because of a labour shortage rather than the union's negotiating strength.

18. MHDN, 9 December 1947. Medalta jiggerman Clarence Sailer placed last in the campaign for councillor.

19. After the factory closed, the union continued to negotiate with the local federal unemployment insurance officer to gain benefits for former workers. Letter to J.W. McLane, U.I.C. office, Medicine Hat, from Charles J. Barber, Secretary, and M. Dillon, Business Agent, 5 April 1954, Local 895, Box 128, File 25, International Union of Mine Mill and

Smelter Workers (hereafter Mine Mill), University of British Columbia Library, Rare Books and Special Collections (hereafter cited as Mine Mill, UBC).

20. The city's industries included flour mills, a porcelain plant, brick yards, a glass factory, Canadian Pacific Railway workers (who were among the first organized workers in the province), and green houses, among others. "Medicine Hat Becomes Unionized," undated Canadian Congress of Labour circular, circa June 1947, Box 127, File 1–1a, Mine Mill, UBC.

21. Strikes and Lockouts in Canada During 1947, Department of Labour Research and Statistics Branch, Canada, supplement to *The Labour Gazette*, April 1948. According to the 1946 census, the four largest cities in Alberta were Edmonton (population 113,116), Calgary (100,044), Lethbridge (16,522), and Medicine Hat (12,859). *Census of the Prairie Provinces*, 1946, vol. 2.

22. *Census of the Prairie Provinces*, 1946, vol. 2, Table 15, Gainfully occupied, 14 years of age and over, by industry and sex, for the cities of Lethbridge and Medicine Hat, and Table 19, Gainfully occupied, 14 years of age and over, by industry and sex, showing birthplace and mother tongue, for the province of Alberta.

23. Jack Forbes, "Manufacturing Process History of the Medalta Potteries National and Provincial Historic Site 1912–1954," Parks Canada, 2000.

24. The union was demanding a 33 per cent wage increase for women and a 21 per cent increase for men. The company offered 7 per cent across the board. MHDN, 12 August 1947.

25. Mine Mill was first named the Western Federation of Miners. See Jeremy Mouat, "The Genesis of Western Exceptionalism: British Columbia's Hard-Rock Miners, 1895–1903," *Canadian Historical Review* 71, no. 3 (1990): 317–45; John Hinde, *When Coal was King: Ladysmith and the Coal-Mining Industry on Vancouver Island* (Vancouver: UBC Press, 2003); Mercedes Steedman, Peter Suschnigg, and Dieter K. Buse, *Hard Lessons: The Mine Mill Union in the Canadian Labour Movement* (Toronto & Oxford: Dundurn Press, 1995); Elizabeth Jameson, *All That Glitters: Class, Conflict and Community in Cripple Creek* (Urbana: University of Illinois Press, 1998); and Melvyn Dubofsky, *We Shall Be All* (New York: Quadrangle, 1969).

26. Industrial unionism is the organization of all workers in an industry, including the unskilled, into a single union. It became successful in the late 1930s, first in the United States and then in Canada, in response to technological changes that created mass production and thus eroded the power of skilled workers who had previously dominated organized labour's craft unions. Palmer, *Working-Class Experience*, 250–54.

27. James J. Lorence, *The Suppression of Salt of the Earth: How Hollywood, Big Labor, and Politicians Blacklisted a Movie in Cold War America* (Albuquerque: University of New Mexico Press, 1999), 20. The movie documents Mine Mill's policy of racial equality and the crucial role workers' wives played in a key strike in New Mexico.

28. "Present working conditions and wages in this area, stand as a threat to organized workers in other parts of this province and elsewhere. Thus making an intensive organizing campaign a necessity," from "Medicine Hat Becomes Unionized," undated union bulletin, circa 1947, Box 128, File 25, Mine Mill, UBC.

29. David C. Jones, *Empire of Dust: Settling and Abandoning the Prairie Dry Belt* (Edmonton: University of Alberta Press, 1987).

30. Government war contracts forced the company into twenty-four-hour production during the war. Ed Gould, *All Hell for a Basement* (Medicine Hat, AB: City of Medicine Hat, 1983).

31. Christine Pocsik (née Steigel), interview by author, 23 September 2000, Medicine Hat, AB.

32. *The Clay Products News and Ceramic Record*, August 1948, 1; *Historical Statistics of Canada* (Ottawa: Canadian Government Publishing Centre, 1983), E41–48.

33. These figures do not include piecework rates that allowed some women and men to earn a top rate of $35 and $43, respectively. Unemployment Insurance Commission: Report on Industrial Dispute, 13 September 1947. Completed by company manager Jack Cunliffe, RG 27, vol. 456, Strike 154, Department of Labour, Library and Archives Canada (hereafter cited as LAC).

34. A statement by each party in the dispute concerning wage rates was published in MHDN during the strike. See "Medalta Facts," 9 October 1947, and "Further Facts Re: Medalta," 11 October 1947.

35. This fact is particularly striking given that women represented only about 10 per cent of the workforce in the 1920s and appear to have maintained a similar proportion during the 1930s, although few figures are available for those years. Workmen's Compensation Act (Accident Fund) Alberta, 1925, Medalta Potteries Ltd. Fonds (hereafter cited as MPF), PR69.00235, File 65; government wage summary form, 1927, MPF PR69.00235 File 272, Provincial Archives of Alberta (hereafter cited as PAA).

36. In June 1941 a woman worker was half scalped when her hair caught in a rotating shaft. A Workman's Compensation Board directive had been issued five months earlier ordering the company to place guards on the moving machinery. Letters between Medalta Potteries and the WCB, May 1941, MPF PR69.00235, File 438, PAA.

37. The factory did not have a lunchroom or the proper number of toilets, and its sanitary conditions were described as "fair." H.M. Bishop's Inspector's Report on Medalta Potteries factory, 15 June 1926, MPF PR69.00235, File 69, PAA.

38. Christine and Alex Pocsik, interview by author, 23 September 2000, Medicine Hat, AB.

39. Joy Parr, *The Gender of Breadwinners: Women, Men, and Change in Two Industrial Towns, 1880–1950* (Toronto: University of Toronto Press, 1990).

40. Hanna Osborne, interview by author, 23 September 2000, Medicine Hat, AB.

41. Engilena Kessler, interview by author, 16 September 2000, Edmonton, AB.

42. See Pamela Sugiman, *Labour's Dilemma: The Gender Politics of Auto Workers in Canada, 1937–1979* (Toronto: University of Toronto Press, 1994); Julie Guard, "Womanly Innocence and Manly Self-Respect: Gendered Challenges to Labour's Postwar Compromise," in *Labour Gains, Labour Pains: Fifty Years of PC 1003*, ed. Cy Gonick, Paul Phillips, and Jesse Vorst (Winnipeg, MB/Halifax, NS: Fernwood Publishing, 1995): 119–38; Joan Sangster, *Earning Respect: The Lives of Working Women in Small-Town Ontario, 1920–1960* (Toronto: University of Toronto Press, 1995).

43. Kessler interview, 1 February 2001.

44. Kessler interview, 1 February 2001.

45. Anne Forrest, "Securing the Male Breadwinner: A Feminist Interpretation of PC 1003," in *Labour Gains*, 139–62.

46. In Canada the number of married women working for wages more than doubled between 1941 and 1951, rising to 11.2 per cent. Veronica Strong-Boag, "Home Dreams: Women and the Suburban Experiment in Canada, 1945–60," in *Rethinking Canada: The Promise of Women's History*, 3rd ed., ed. Veronica Strong-Boag and Anita Clair Fellman (Toronto: Oxford University Press, 1997), 380.

47. Scholars generally agree that there was a concerted effort to reinscribe traditional gender roles, but there is debate about the extent to which that goal was achieved. See Ruth Roach Pierson, *"They're Still Women After All": The Second World War and Canadian Womanhood* (Toronto: McClelland and Stewart, 1986); and Jeff Keshen, "Revisiting Canada's Civilian Women During World War II," *Histoire sociale/Social History* 30 (1997): 239–66. For studies of the United States see Elaine Tyler May, *Homeward Bound: American Families in the Cold War Era* (New York: Basic Books, Inc., 1988); and Joanne Meyerowitz, ed., *Not June Cleaver: Women and Gender in Postwar America, 1945–1960* (Philadelphia: Temple University Press, 1994).

48. During the war a wife could earn any amount and still be treated as a full dependant. Ruth Roach Pierson, "Gender and the Unemployment Insurance Debates in Canada, 1934–1940," *Labour/Le Travail* 25 (Spring 1990): 77–103.

49. Ann Porter, "Women and Income Security in the Postwar Period: The Case of Unemployment Insurance, 1945–1962," in *Canadian Women: A Reader*, ed. Alison Prentice et al. (Toronto: Harcourt Brace & Co, 1996), 324–25.

50. In August 1947 the minimum wage for women workers in Alberta was $18 per week (37.5¢ per hour) and the minimum wage for men was $25 per week (52¢ per hour) based on a forty-eight hour week. *Alberta Employment Standards Policy Manual*, circa 2000, Alberta Human Resources and Employment, Employment Standards Department.

51. Women were to be provided with seating to rest when not working and were prohibited from heavy lifting. *Alberta Labour and Social Legislation History*, Unpublished report, Alberta Department of Labour, 1970.

52. Sarah Carter, *Capturing Women: The Manipulation of Cultural Imagery in Canada's Prairie West* (Montreal & Kingston: McGill-Queen's University Press, 1997). See "Introduction: Defining and Redefining Women," 3–47.

53. Howard Palmer, "Strangers and Stereotypes: The Rise of Nativism, 1880–1920," in *The Prairie West: Historical Readings*, 2nd ed., ed. R. Douglas Francis and Howard Palmer (Edmonton: University of Alberta Press, 1995), 308–34.

54. English was not the first language for 17 per cent of Medicine Hat's population in 1946. Of those individuals, 49 per cent were German-speaking. The next three most common languages in the community were Russian (21 per cent), Polish (4 per cent), and Chinese (3 per cent). *Census of the Prairie Provinces*, 1946, vol. 1, 546–47.

55. Kessler interview, 16 September 2000.

56. Howard Palmer, *Land of the Second Chance: A History of Ethnic Groups in Southern Alberta* (Lethbridge, AB: *The Lethbridge Herald*, 1972), 193, 235, 246.

57. Palmer, "Strangers & Stereotypes," 312–14.

58. Kessler interview, 16 September 2000.

59. In her study of nursing students in Medicine Hat, Florence Melchior found that middle-class women of British origin had the greatest access to placements in the local nursing school. German-speaking and Scandinavian women worked at the potteries doing less prestigious work for lower wages. Florence Melchior, "Nursing Students at Medicine Hat General Hospital, 1894–1920," Unpublished paper, "Unsettled Pasts" Conference, University of Calgary, 2002.

60. Kessler interview, 16 September 2000.

61. I elected not to identify several quotations out of consideration for individuals still living. Although all of the people interviewed were offered anonymity, no one chose to remain anonymous, so the names provided in the study are actual names.

62. Helen Potrebenko, *No Streets of Gold: A Social History of Ukrainians in Alberta* (Vancouver: New Star Books, 1977), 26.

63. Thomas Dunk, *It's a Working Man's Town: Male Working-Class Culture* (Montreal: McGill-Queen's University Press, 1991), 97, 114.

64. Alison Prentice et al., eds., *Canadian Women: A History*, 2d ed. (Toronto: Harcourt Brace Canada, 1996), 346. Women of colour had previously been limited to domestic work.

65. Kessler interview, 16 September 2000; Union Minutes, Box 128, File 26, Mine Mill, UBC.

66. Race was never raised as an issue in news reports, union bulletins, company or government records, or by those interviewed.

67. Marc Jeffrey Stern, *The Pottery Industry of Trenton: A Skilled Trade in Transition 1850–1929* (New Brunswick, NJ: Rutgers University Press, 1994); Jacqueline Sarsby, "Sexual Segregation in the Pottery Industry," *Feminist Review* 21 (November 1985): 67–93.

68. Only men could hold the job of jiggerman. This was the most skilled position in the factory and involved the use of a jiggering wheel to shape the soft clay into various products. Hayward, *The Alberta Pottery Industry*, 75.

69. In a 1940 letter from Medalta's chief rival, Medicine Hat Potteries, to the government justifying its need to exceed minimum wage regulations by employing more females at the low "apprenticeship" rate, G. B. Armstrong explained: "Our work for these girls is not hard but requires the small and quick hands that are not found in male employees." This claim was common throughout the industry. Letter 8 February 1940, Board of Industrial Relations, GR69.0131, PAA.

70. Rosetta Brosnikoff (née Worrall), interview by author, 23 September 2000, Medicine Hat, AB.

71. See "Medalta Facts," MHDN, 9 October 1947, and "Further Facts Re: Medalta," MHDN, 11 October 1947.

72. The female minimum wage rate was 72 per cent of the male rate in August 1947, but the actual difference between male and female wages in the province was much larger because, according to a 1946 government wage survey, a far greater proportion of women workers than men earned an amount equal to or near the minimum wage. "Survey of Wage Rates Current in Alberta During the Last Half Year 1946" by H. P. Rocke, Chief Inspector, Board of Industrial Relations, 26 December 1946, GR1967.0071, File 470.N, PAA.

73. After years of doing domestic work and child care on the farm, or for neighbouring families on a barter basis, Hanna Osborne said when she finally got a steady paying job

in the pottery at the age of twenty-three, paying 25 cents an hour, "*that* was a good job, uhuh." Osborne interview.

74. A number of women interviewed worked at the pottery after they got married. Each reported that few married women worked at the factory in 1947, but married women were not pressured to leave. Dorothy Beierbach, interview by author, 14 December 2000, Medicine Hat, AB; Brosnikoff interview, 23 September 2000; Kessler interview, 16 September 2000.

75. "Medalta Facts" by Medalta Potteries management, MHDN, 9 October 1947.

76. Rosetta Brosnikoff, interview by author, 23 September 2000 and 20 May 2001, Medicine Hat, AB.

77. The age difference is evident in photographs of workers, and in the average age of men and women workers compiled by the union in a 1952 chart through a random sampling to determine average earnings. The average age of women workers was 25, and the average age of men was 32. The oldest woman employed at the pottery was 37, and the oldest man was 67. "Individual Average Earnings, Picked at Random, Over Six-Month Period, January–June, 1952, Inclusive," 18 October 1952, Box 128, File 125, Mine Mill, UBC.

78. MHDN, 11 October 47; Beierbach interview.

79. The worker wished to remain anonymous.

80. Brosnikoff interview, 20 May 2001.

81. Kessler interview, 16 September 2000.

82. It was the first 100 per cent certification vote to be achieved in the province. *Mine Mill Organizer*, May 1947, Local 881, Box 127, File 1, Mine Mill, UBC.

83. Kessler interview, 1 February 2001.

84. Jack Cunliffe Examination for Discovery, 3 October 1947, Medalta Potteries Statement of Claim filed 19 August 1947, GR1985.0289, Box S.C. 1318, File S/C44436, PAA. Union leaders probably chose to hold an unsupervised vote to circumvent delays created by new provincial labour legislation modeled on PC 1003 that made conciliation/arbitration mandatory and allowed the employer to prepare for a strike.

85. The local newspaper emphasized the "illegality" of a parade held without a permit. MHDN was owned by city industrialist, J. H. (Hop) Yuill. His ownership of several local businesses, including Medalta's main competitor, Medicine Hat Potteries, gave him a vested interest in a strike that threatened to raise local labour rates. Autobiography of Joseph Harlan Yuill, researched and compiled by Kathleen Dirk, "Living in Medicine Hat: The Yuill History 1883–1985." Unpublished Manuscript, 1985, MHM.

86. MHDN, 10 September 1947.

87. MHDN, 29 August 1947.

88. In a letter to his superiors in Ottawa on 11 September 1947, J.W. McLane, manager of the local National Employment office, wrote: "Less than 1% of the workers of this plant have applied at this office for employment and only a few have made inquiries regarding drawing Unemployment Benefits and on the opposite side of the picture we have made very few referrals on the order placed by the company [for replacement workers]." A labour shortage also kept the number of Unemployment Benefits applications low. It is difficult to determine the extent to which the low number of applicants for pottery jobs

during the strike reflects strike support. Letter from J.W. McLane to Director of Industrial Relations, Department of Labour, RG 27, vol. 456, Strike 154, PAC.

89. Medalta used this pretext to fire all 213 striking employees less than a week after the strike began and to solicit new job applicants. MHDN, 16 August 1947.

90. A letter from government officials stated "the majority of the employees had elected the Union as their Bargaining Agent, and...the fault was only a minor one and in most cases would not even be questioned." Judgement by Justice Hugh John Macdonald, 19 November 1947, Medalta Potteries Statement of Claim filed 19 August 1947, GR1985.0289, Box S.C. 1318, File S/C44436, PAA. Letter from the Department of Trade and Industry to Mine Mill, 1 December 1947, Box 127, File 1, Mine Mill, UBC.

91. MHDN, 22 August 1947.

92. Fifty union members were charged in connection with the strike and eighteen of them were women. Women represented 36 per cent of those charged; they comprised 42 per cent of striking workers, based on court reports published throughout the strike in MHDN, August through October 1947. Actual court records for strike-related charges could not be located.

93. For more strike detail see Cindy Loch-Drake, "Jailed Heroes and Kitchen Heroines: Class, Gender and the Medalta Potteries Strike in Postwar Alberta" (master's thesis, University of Calgary, 2001).

94. Some of the workers interviewed did not know each other at the time of the interviews.

95. Kessler interview, 1 February 2001.

96. Letter 16 February 2001 in the author's possession. The worker asked to remain anonymous.

97. Dorothy Beierbach and Hanna Osborne kindly allowed me to examine and reproduce a number of personal strike photographs they had taken during the strike.

98. Alex Pocsik Examination for Discovery, 3 October 1947, Medalta Potteries Statement of Claim filed 19 August 1947, GR1985.0289, Box S.C. 1318, File S/C44436, PAA.

99. The union made restitution for the damaged goods, Alex Pocsik Examination for Discovery, 11 October 1947.

100. Alex Pocsik Examination for Discovery, 1 October 1947.

101. Alex Pocsik Examination for Discovery, 29 September 1947.

102. Alex Pocsik Examination for Discovery, 29 September 1947.

103. The man charged with assault was Ralph Lattery. Individuals charged with watching and besetting were Matthew Wolfer, Mrs William Longridge, Valentine Stach, Olga Bierbach, Laura Rife, Ralph Lattery, Bertha Heller, Annette Heller, Clarence Sailer, Selma Stickel, Irene Entzminger, Ruby Kessler, Arthur Reiger, Les Bogie, and Albert Pawlawski. Alex Pocsik Examination for Discovery, 29 September 1947.

104. Alex Pocsik Examination for Discovery, 11 October 1947.

105. Only one conviction was obtained against Josie Longridge, although two convictions were obtained against Matthew Wolfer, the one man charged in both incidents. 4 October 1947, Ledger of Convictions and Dismissals by Magistrates Under Section 793 of Criminal Code Part XVI, Medicine Hat Courthouse.

106. I initially speculated that the *s* in *Mrs* was a typo and that newspaper accounts were actually referring to William Longridge.

107. Chivalry is rooted in the notion that women must be protected by men because they are weak and defenceless and are therefore less responsible than men. In her assessment of two Canadian murder cases in which women were acquitted, Carolyn Strange has made explicit the ways in which judicial chivalry has served to obscure and perpetuate injustice outside the courtroom stage. Carolyn Strange, "Wounded Womanhood and Dead Men," in *Gender Conflicts: New Essays in Women's History*, ed. Franca Iacovetta and Mariana Valverde (Toronto: University of Toronto Press, 1992), 176. See also Joan Sangster, *Regulating Girls and Women: Sexuality, Family, and the Law in Ontario, 1920–1960* (Don Mills, ON: Oxford University Press, 2001).

108. The ages of the men were more evenly distributed across the age spectrum compared to those of the women: one man was twenty-three, two were twenty-four, and two were thirty-five. Medicine Hat Police Arrest Records, 11 October 1947, M93.1.5, MHM.

109. Joy Parr, *Gender of Breadwinners*; see esp. chap. 5, "Womanly Militance, Neighbourly Wrath," 96–119. Parr's analysis of a bitter strike at the Penmans factory in Paris, Ontario, in 1949 reveals an effort by the United Textile Workers of America to minimize the militancy of women workers. The Penmans workforce had more women workers (56 per cent) and included a larger proportion of older, married women when compared to Medalta. This may in part account for the Penmans workers' greater militancy. Another similarity to the Medalta strike is the attempt by Penmans and the state to discredit the workers' union with allegations of communist influence.

110. Guard, "Womanly Innocence"; and Forrest, "Securing the Male Breadwinner," 119–38.

111. Sugiman, *Labour's Dilemma*, 51–57.

112. Kessler interview, 16 September 2000.

113. "Strike Donations," Box 127, Mine Mill, UBC.

114. Postwar U.S. workplaces that employed a large proportion of women tended to garner more male support for equal pay as a way of ensuring that cheaper women workers did not threaten male jobs. Ruth Milkman, *Gender at Work: The Dynamics of Job Segregation by Sex During World War II* (Urbana and Chicago: University of Illinois Press, 1987).

115. Alice Kessler-Harris, *Out To Work: A History of Wage-Earning Women in the United States* (New York: Oxford University Press, 1982), 295–99.

116. MHDN, 7 November 1947.

117. Beierbach interview.

118. MHDN, 7 November 1947.

TEACHING BEYOND BORDERS

THE CHALLENGES of *writing* comparative and borderlands histories of the North American West that include women are, if anything, even tougher when it comes to *teaching* those histories. Anyone who teaches western history must confront the ongoing male-centredness of the region's narratives. Trying to incorporate a comparative approach involves having to confront the nation-centredness of the narratives and historiography. Adding gender into the mix can seem almost impossible. These two articles show how two experienced teachers, one based in England and one in Montana, have risen to these and other challenges.

Margaret Walsh, who teaches at the University of Nottingham in England, highlights the obstacles and opportunities of teaching the history of women in the Canadian and U.S. Wests outside of North America to non-North American students. Her students have little exposure to comparative history, little knowledge of the North American West, and whatever knowledge they might bring into the classroom is likely to have been informed by American popular images of its West. This may sound daunting to many, but Walsh sees it as an advantage in that a more "symmetrical template is possible" when the whole class is approaching a topic as outsiders.

It may be fortunate to have this advantage, as Walsh describes the daunting questions such a course poses. On what grounds can the two Wests be compared, and how can gender be incorporated at a fundamental level? How can one bring together two very different historiographical and theoretical trajectories? Walsh offers useful strategies and themes to frame the course and the questions it must address about the two Wests and about how gender has operated, historically, in both.

Mary Murphy teaches at Montana State University in Bozeman and, therefore, faces a different challenge, because she and her students are "insiders" to at least one part of the course content. This is an advantage in her classroom because her students can bring their own relevant family histories into the room, even if the downside is that "the myths of the West as created in the late 19th and early 20th centuries are alive and well and wreaking havoc every day." Unlike Walsh, Murphy must begin by tackling persistent male-centred and jingoistic myths about both Wests before students can imagine women at the centres of western histories and probe the similarities and differences of women's lives on both sides of the border. Murphy offers a conceptual structure of organizing the course around two axes: the apt and useful metaphors of longitude and latitude. The "longitudes" of her course focus on the economic, legal, and political "commonalities of women's experiences across the border." The "latitudes" focus on "how, despite the commonalities of geography, of women's biology, and of a dominant Anglo culture, women's lives in the American and Canadian Wests differed because of the structure and policies of the two nation states," including crucial legal differences in access to land, definitions of race, and treatment of racial ethnic minorities.

Both Walsh and Murphy offer strategies to teach critical thinking. The comparisons of two national histories, two Wests, and of how being male or female mattered, combine to invite new insights into the significance of nations and the significance of gender.

Walsh and Murphy teach through the border in two key ways: they use the border as a teaching tool while highlighting its permeability.

The challenges of teaching a gendered and comparative history of the North American West thus have a significant payoff, deconstructing Western myths, making it easier to incorporate non-traditional elements into the familiar narratives, and demonstrating simultaneously how much and how little a border can matter.

Walsh's and Murphy's classrooms are an apt metaphor, too, with which to conclude this volume, posing as they do the challenges of teaching simultaneously the boundaries of difference that must be respected and the borders of social inequalities that remain to be bridged. The histories of women in all our Wests clarify the dual meanings of borders—those that protect, and those that exclude. This volume, we hope, takes us one step over the lines that have erected the borders of privilege and exclusion in our histories, our classrooms, in our Wests.

15

GENDERED STEPS ACROSS THE BORDER

Teaching the History of Women in the American and Canadian Wests

MARGARET WALSH

THE HISTORY of the American and Canadian Wests has a long but rather thin and piecemeal pedigree. Occasional articles and books borrowing each other's theories or ideas trickle through the publications of both countries' western history. Similarly, case studies sometimes cross the border in a specific location or focus on a particular trans-border theme.[1] But the comparative mode, or combined Canadian-American approach, has been and remains elusive, unlike that of its counterpart in the Southwest.[2] There is a growing interest in the Mexican-American border and the impact of both countries on each other's past development. That contested area has frequently been viewed and discussed as a difference between whites and non-whites and between Anglos and Hispanics, whether in terms of language, politics, or culture. The Canadian-American boundary offers less visible and less threatening dimensions. Americans do not seem to be concerned about a foreign presence to their north, perhaps because it has been predominantly white and English-speaking, perhaps because there has not been a major migration south into their heartland, and perhaps because they dominate their northern neighbour economically. Canadians, most of whom live near the lengthy international boundary, have tended to view the overwhelming force of the American presence from a position of economic inequality and have preferred to be perceived as a separate cultural entity rather than as an inferior or Americanized adjunct.[3]

Teaching the comparative history of two neighbours who have a considerable amount in common physically and share some cultural affiliations, but few institutional links, has proved difficult as much because of their different historical traditions as for the unavailability of source materials. In fashioning a course that facilitates an understanding of two societies at the same time as being educationally fulfilling, the main challenge has been to find reasoned grounds on which to compare the societies. Initially some framework was needed to enable individual stories and themes to add up to a unit that was accessible to students. Perhaps the edge of the picture need not be rigid, but it must be functional and be capable of taking on some recognizable identity. A handful of historians have already pioneered the comparative approach, and their work offers some potential models, but their dialogues are in part dependent on selections of two sets of texts that have not been directed toward comparative history and thus leave much to the imagination.[4]

Incorporating gender into, or, better still, engendering such a comparative unit has been much more demanding because the newer historical materials on women must be integrated with the older materials that claimed to be history but were actually HIS story. In the past quarter century women have certainly been portrayed on their own account as dynamic persons and are no longer ignored or marginalized. Yet they need to be placed in a symmetrical relationship with men. So far few books and articles on comparative western history are written with reference to both women and men.[5] Only for a few themes, like fur trading and farming, has gendering teaching become more viable as outstanding research has been accomplished and has changed the face of western history. Other themes have proved to be so demanding or lacking in new research that traditional trajectories must be used because of practical difficulties finding evidence. Though the infamous counterfactual approach can offer some interesting speculative insights into the history that might be produced when gendered theoretical approaches have been worked out and research undertaken, the practical offerings and suggestions that can be made remain limited. It is thus important to retain clearly defined concepts of masculinity and femininity throughout a module. By persistently asking what was important for women and for men, and what difference did it make to experience western endeavours as a female or a male, module participants can be prompted to consider the existing written, visual, and oral evidence from two perspectives and then to come to a human viewpoint.

If teaching a comparative Canadian-American module in North America is unusual, then it is extraordinary in the United Kingdom.[6] Such a module, however, offers great potential for creating frameworks and discussing themes and ideas. Undergraduates start with little background and with access to limited resources, even given easy access to relevant websites. They may well know about the myths and images of the West from the media and literature, but this romantic West is much more likely to be American than Canadian. They are unlikely to have a solid factual grounding in western history. Furthermore, because all participants are outsiders "looking in," they are detached from and are unrestrained by the academic cultures of either American or Canadian historians. Indeed they are likely to be critical of both traditions. So a new or a symmetrical template is possible.

Such a template must address the traditional male-focussed and romantic picture that has been spread in both the media and in the older western histories. Comparative analysis is an effective tool for deconstructing such legends. Both countries have created myths from historical events, but the heroes and images are different in subject matter and in method of treatment. By putting together such heroes as American cowboys and Canadian Northwest Mounted Police, or George Armstrong Custer and Louis David Riel, or by comparing American literary notions of the Great American Desert with Canadian literary views of the northern wilderness, students learn to analyse how, why, and for whom history has been constructed.[7] As the majority of North American romantic heroes are male, a greater awareness of masculinity is immediately visible. Such constructions of raw masculinity increasingly appear naïve because of the absence of any female presence let alone any female contribution.[8] Asking students to examine existing romantic and male-dominant visions, aided by some of the tools of literary criticism and by cultural approaches to history, has proved to be a valuable device for making history both more realistic and gender aware. Students then not only have the opportunity to question how history is written, but also why recognizing femininity as a social construct or discussing the female absence/presence is needed to make western history realistic.

Before considering any imagery, it is essential to establish the parameters and nature of the North American West. There may well be a geographical entity that is separated behaviourally and nationally by the 49th parallel, but for historians in both countries there are many Wests. In Canada the West can be considered to be that part of the nation west of Ontario that was accumulated after the British established the Dominion of Canada in 1867. This consisted of Rupert's Land or the Hudson's Bay Company Territory, comprising the Hudson's Bay drainage basin, and the North Western Territory, comprising the unappropriated crown lands of the Arctic drainage basin, lands that the British formally handed to the new Canadian federation in 1869. It also included British Columbia, which came into the Confederation in 1871. Even from its early years this West has been separated into what became the Prairie provinces and British Columbia. Both of these Canadian regions have in turn had little to do with the North. That area, consisting of the Northwest Territories and, more recently, Nunavut, are located above the Prairie provinces of [Manitoba], Saskatchewan, and Alberta, while Yukon Territory "tops" British Columbia. From an international perspective, the Territories are as "western" as the provinces, but Canadian historians frequently write about a tripartite division and separate identities.[9]

Yet this geographical division of the Canadian West has not proved to be as problematic for comparative purposes as have the strident confrontations of American historians discussing their West or their Wests. For some seventy-five years the Frontier Thesis of Frederick Jackson Turner dominated teaching and research, pointing to the West as a national experience. At one time in its history the entire nation had been part of the West. For Turner the West was also a character-forming experience and a positive achievement. Europeans or Euro-Americans migrated across the continent from the Atlantic to the Pacific coast, building a modern democracy from wild nature.[10] More recently, New Western historians have claimed that the West is a region with a long and continuous history. It is that part of the United States that lies west of the Mississippi River, but for some historians it may be west of the Missouri River or perhaps the hundredth meridian. Usually the region stretches to the Pacific Ocean, but on occasions it also includes the geographically discrete states of Alaska to the north and Hawai'i in the Pacific Ocean. Yet for other western American historians, the Rocky Mountains more clearly divide the western prairies and plains from the coastal areas into two regions.[11] When outsiders examine the disputes on both sides of the border, it makes more sense to recognize the diverse methodological and geographical debates about the location of the various Wests and then to superimpose a much larger map that facilitates discussions of a West with flexible boundaries. Thereafter these boundaries or concepts can be determined by the thematic topics being examined.

Students, however, need some existing framework with which to start organizing and interpreting the larger and more flexible area. Taking the United States as a starting point, Europeans have the choice of Turner's Frontier Thesis, which has been applied, albeit erratically, north across the border. Or they can adopt one of the various approaches of the New Western historians. Practitioners like Patricia Limerick, Richard White, and Donald Worster have fragmented and rejected any canon for the lands below the 49th parallel. Within the New West as region, neo-imperialists sit side by side with environmentalists, who contest with social historians and those who prefer to consider a capitalistic exploitation of a boom and slump nature. More recently still, a newer meaning for American western history involving the common story of the frontier-to-region process has been suggested in what might be called a greater West.[12]

In Canada students can also select from differing frameworks for examining their West. The staples thesis of political economist Harold Innis examines Canadian development and the expansion of finance and capital in a westward direction in terms of mercantile ties with Europe. His work offered an approach that was popular for many years in the early and mid-twentieth century. It was replaced by historian Maurice Careless's interpretation of metropolitanism that also connects the links between cores and peripheries, but which incorporates major cities with their class and ethnic patterns. Careless went beyond the pure environmental factors to add values. The literary critic Northrop Frye has challenged both of these interpretations, however, by raising issues of Canadian cultural identity. For Frye, every part of Canada is a separation with communities isolated from one another in a "garrison mentality." Historical geographer Cole Harris has also talked about islands of settlement from different parts of Europe and eastern Canada. These are discontinuous islands forming a fragmented human structure that is bound together economically by transport and communications and politically by provincial status. More recently, western historian Gerald Freisen has suggested that the Canadian West has a changing complexion. It has in the past been the two region vision of the Prairies and the Coast, but this has been replaced by a single economic and social experience. Yet within this single West are four provinces, each with distinctive political life and identity. Overall, however, these Canadian templates have had a much smaller impact on traditional or recent western Canadian scholarship than the assorted American templates have had on western American scholarship.[13] There is a welter of diverse options from which students can choose to adopt or adapt in order to construct a comparative western approach. Provided that students are aware of the origins and assumptions of these views, they can apply them across the border and then use a gendered lens emphasizing femininity and masculinity.

With the historical contexts discussed and a blank map to fill, the themes to be considered should raise questions about similarities and differences between the two Wests and the distinctive characteristics of western Canadians and Americans. The themes must also be gendered, even within topics that are supposedly neutral. Focusing on the nineteenth and early twentieth centuries, when the North American West was occupied, settled, or invaded by European or Euro-American/Euro-Canadian migrants, the range of themes or topics is extensive. Possibilities include environment, land and its availability; peoples of the West, which needs to be subdivided between pre-Euro contact and in-migrants; western mobility, or transport and travel; making a living, which can be subdivided between exploiting and protecting natural resources and farming; and creating western communities, which include social networks like church and school, and institutional arrangements like law enforcement and government. Clearly behavioural patterns are connected to prior habits. There is a cultural continuity with family or ethnic arrangements. Yet there is also a response to a new geographical setting. Government actions further shape western identities. Women and men were frequently present together in the West, but they saw life from different viewpoints. Even when women were absent from some western spaces, their very absence shaped a masculine character that requires specific analysis.

To illustrate the potential of such a gendered North American module, three themes will be used as case studies. Farming is examined first, because is it accessible to comparative analysis through both women's and gendered history. The fur trade, though earlier in chronology, needs to be discussed second, because the research input has been very different on either side of the border. Fur trading has been studied in more sophisticated gendered ways in Canada than in the United States. The example set by Canadian historians has suggested gendered paths that Americans have recently started to follow. Thirdly, law, order, and violence offers much scope for comparative discussion, but the historian needs to understand and interpret myths as well as historical evidence. In romantic stories and media visions, the heroes and villains are rarely analyzed explicitly from gendered perspectives. The contrasts between the three themes suggest what is currently possible and what might be accomplished.

The North American West was settled primarily by farmers. There were relatively more of these in the Canadian prairies and the American plains, though farming was also a significant occupation in the coastal valleys across the mountains. The Pacific Coast states and the province of British Columbia may well have urbanized because of port functions and the extractive economy of minerals and lumber, but they still contained farming communities. So too did the northern areas of Alaska and the Canadian territories, though they were far fewer in number and importance. For traditional historians farming meant going west, whether from eastern parts of Canada or the United States or from Europe, squatting on land, buying it from governments or speculators, or homesteading it for free or very cheaply. Having acquired land, male farmers then worked hard to make a living, struggling against the elements, the machinery manufacturers, financial intermediaries, and transport companies. If they succeeded, theirs was a triumph of democratic capitalism in the United States or imperial development in Canada. If they failed, they became hired labourers either on farms or in urban enterprises to which they migrated. This traditional narrative of farming, often told at the macro-level in terms of the growth of wheat, dairy, or cattle belts rarely mentioned the contributions of women. Development, whether at the farm unit size or at the regional level, was assumed to be a product of male decision-making and male endeavours. Women did not feature as partners and workers. They were non-persons in that they did not vote and were subordinate to males, functioning as wife, mother, and housewife. Women infrequently owned farms, and when they did they were constrained to work within a male-dominated environment. The farmer's West was masculine territory.[14]

Women's history insisted on changing this perspective into one in which women were not only important but were central to survival and success. The female interpretation of pioneer farming in the North American West frequently used the lens of personal experiences. Recovering an abundance of information from personal letters, diaries, and farm accounts, women have become an essential part of any historical account of farm operation. They fulfilled the triple function of domestic labour, barnyard work, and unpaid fieldwork. Rarely could a farm enterprise be successful without female input. Both the productive and reproductive functions of women in the home as wife, mother, and housewife were essential for health, well-being, and future labour supply. The barnyard work of raising and storing vegetables and looking after farm animals not only provided food year round, it contributed "butter and egg" money. The cash sales of this and other household produce could support a farm during difficult times or, in more prosperous years, were considered as female perks available to purchase store goods. Women further contributed directly to farm output in cereals and cattle raising by doing outdoor work, frequently at planting or harvesting times.[15] They were also significant in the undervalued social processes of farming activities: as central agents in cultivating reciprocal relationships both on the farm and within the rural community, farmwomen brokered both survival and success with a form of moral capital and a process of neighbouring.[16]

There are two sets of lenses: the male (and possibly the macro view) and the female (and possibly the micro view), and these need to intersect. Occasionally they have been placed together within the same framework when historians have discussed family ventures.[17] Then it has been possible to raise gendered issues in a social history setting. Women's domestic roles and men's outdoor labour were similar across the border. Indeed, when specifically discussing American women, Glenda Riley has suggested that the female farming frontier was more a repetitive experience focused on domesticity than a question of different responses to geographical circumstances, as with men.[18] But taking the generic problems of acquiring capital, altering the landscape, finding machinery, and getting crops to market, then men, too, faced similar problems. The differences between many Americans and Canadians lay in particular geographies and whether land was suitable to raise wheat, corn, livestock, or other cereal and animal products. Other patterns become complicated by institutional arrangements and ethnic cultures. The most visible of these differences has been the Canadian imperial and the American democratic agendas. Though some historians would argue that both governments had an affinity with the United Kingdom, one remained within the

British Empire while the other rejected the British authority. But the time-space matrix was also important in terms of technology. The availability of improving farm machinery and access to different modes of transport influenced the potential for both family survival and success. There are many ingredients that need a new gendered dimension.

So which fruitful comparative questions can be posed? Moving across the political boundary between the Canadian prairies and the American plains, it might be useful to consider how pioneer farming families migrating to Alberta in the early twentieth century found that their experiences differed from families who moved to Montana some quarter century earlier. How did families acquire their farms? If they bought them rather than homesteaded them, how did they raise the capital or acquire the credit? What difference did it make to Canadians to have benefited from the experience of their American counterparts? Did all farmers combine subsistence with market approaches? How was the farm technology different in both countries? Did those living in Alberta have better and cheaper access to rail transport than those living in Montana, and how did they market their crops? Did ethnic affiliation make a significant difference either to farming patterns or the social lives of families and especially women? Or were Mennonites, for example, on both sides of the border likely to run their farms in similar ways?[19]

Certainly there were institutional differences in legislation that affected women. In the United States single women over the age of twenty-one who were citizens or intending citizens could homestead or file for up to 160 acres of surveyed land in the public domain. In Canada the vast majority of women were excluded by regulations from access to homesteads available to any man over the age of eighteen. Only if she was the head of a household could a woman earn title to 160 acres provided she farmed this quarter section. Furthermore, married women in the West had no claim to a share in their husband's property. It was not until the second decade of the twentieth century that individual Prairie provinces passed laws to ensure that women were neither left homeless nor penniless.[20] Does such a difference mean that farmwomen north of the border were more likely to be involved in political activism than their American counterparts? Or does it mean that they were acquiescent about their status and considered that they were part of a farming unit that was subject to impersonal market systems rather than being a woman without a formal stake in the family enterprise? Many more questions could be raised, but the answers may provide suggestions rather than a working template for gendered comparative history.

Looking at an earlier example of western development in the shape of the fur trade, two different historical traditions have developed on either side of the border even though the border itself was not a hindrance to business for many years. French merchants and trappers may have entered the fur trade using the St Lawrence waterway, but they spread across the Canadian prairies, down the Mississippi River to the Gulf Coast and up the Missouri River long before separate political identities were established. The British, in the shape of the Hudson's Bay Company, also crossed boundaries with impunity, and American fur companies were not averse to trapping and trading north of the border, whether in the Great Lakes region, the Rocky Mountains, or on the Pacific Coast. Though the companies retained their national identities, they did not worry whether their workers in the field were European or Native Americans; they were more concerned with profits. But while traders crossed boundaries, fur-trade historians have not often done so. If they had they would have benefited from cross-cultural approaches and methodologies.

Early studies of the fur trade tended to be company histories or biographies, using whatever archival materials were available. Historians of the Canadian trade were able to take advantage of the massive records kept by the Hudson's Bay Company to examine the cautious behaviour of the London-based operation. They also had access to the records of the more flamboyant North West Company, whose French and Scottish merchants worked from Montreal. American historians also wrote business histories of major companies or their owners, like John Jacob Astor and the American Fur Company, and Manuel Lisa and the Missouri Fur Company.[21] Such histories were male capitalistic enterprises and were viewed as such. But they also became the seat of adventurers, especially in the United States. Romance flourished when the Euro-American trappers in the Rocky Mountains in the second and third decades of the nineteenth century became "mountain men." These trappers, who wintered in the mountains and exchanged their beaver catch for several days' worth of drink, gambling, and sex, became the heroic figures of many a "tall tale" and many traditional narratives. Masculinity oozed. The picture of the bearded trapper in buckskin leggings and fringed leather jacket contributed to the stereotypical male-dominated west.[22] There was no place for women in this triumphal wilderness where men were able to commune with nature. Certainly there was the occasional mention of a "squaw," but the contributions of aboriginal women were apparently irrelevant to the triumphal masculine romp.

Such women were anything but irrelevant in Canadian fur-trade history. When female historians, educated by feminist studies and equipped with an awareness of multiculturalism, examined the archival records, native women became a central and essential part of the long chain of activities that constituted the fur business. They were intermediaries economically, socially, and politically. As workers in the business, they processed furs and supplied provisions; as sexual partners they provided family and kin for white traders and helped to create a society of mixed bloods, or Métis, who have handed down a distinctive legacy of cultural blending; as diplomats they negotiated trade relations with First Nations and acted as interpreters. Such revisionist history changed the face of the Canadian fur trade by moving it away from the leadership of the company elite or the visions of popular heroes to the previously unknown workers. It undermined the masculinity of fur trading by making women central. Furthermore it examined the relationships between the women who married "according to the custom of the country" and the incoming white wives of the traders in terms of race and community hierarchy. Social tensions at fur-trading posts were an important part of life affecting a range of activities. Though this centring of women has in turn been criticized, it is now impossible to consider the Canadian fur trade without recognizing gendered partnerships and integrating gender considerations of femininity and masculinity into any discussion.[23]

Historians of the American fur trade have been slow to follow the gendered and multicultural example set by the Canadians some twenty years ago.[24] Such a delay may stem from a variety of reasons. The American fur trade was smaller and shorter than its Canadian counterpart, and there has not been as much interest in or distinct identification of the descendants of native-European unions in the United States. Very few historians of American fur trading have been fully cognizant of the recent trends in women's and social history. Furthermore, New Western historians have set a different agenda for western history. It has remained for historians of the Middle West and the Great Lakes region to rise to the challenge. Here in the *pays d'en haut,* the French as well as the English were involved in fur trading, and they retained similar patterns of behaviour to those developed north of the Great Lakes. But American historians contemplating following the role model set by Canadian historians found that they could draw on a different historical tradition. For the New Indian History had already recognized the extensive cultural contact that took place between Euro-American incomers and Native Peoples. There was a trade and cultural exchange process that allowed different ethnic groups to negotiate a relatively peaceful existence. Fur trade historians recognized this exchange but placed much more emphasis on the role of women as cultural mediators and economic partners. As in Canada, native women were central to fur-trading enterprises, and further research on other American fur regions might be more inclusive and question the dominant masculinity so prevalent in traditional histories.[25]

Canadian and American historians have both paid much attention to issues of law and order and violence on both sides of and across their border, and they have had to negotiate with myths, media, and popular culture. The frequently used general concept, turned into a question rather than a description for the comparative course taught at the University of Calgary, is that of Wild West/Mild West? The wildness of the American west is an abstract ideal associated with a rugged freedom and masculine strength. The mildness of the Canadian west takes on some aspects of womanliness in being more orderly and relatively peaceful; it is often featured as having little or no bloodshed between incoming whites and resident natives, unlike its neighbour to the south. The Canadian government negotiated seven numbered treaties with native peoples between 1871 and 1877 in which the aim was to compensate them for land cessions and to assign them to reserves. Furthermore, disputes among Anglo-Canadian settlers, and later between Euro-Canadian settlers or migrants, were resolved less aggressively because of the presence of the North West Mounted Police as agents of the Ottawa government. Formed in 1873 to keep the peace and to regulate prairie society, the Mounted Police were a disciplined and centralized organization with a flexible law enforcing function. They were able to ensure stable community development in the Prairies by being present prior to the settlement of the region and by becoming an authority in many aspects of society. They were also able maintain order during the Yukon gold rush, thereby offering a marked contrast to the chaos and violence of gold and silver rushes south of the border.[26] The Canadian West was perceived to be a safe place in large part because of the heroic role of the men in red coats.

American interpreters of the West traditionally viewed their heritage as one that was violent and bloody and often focused on land occupation, resource exploitation, and multiracial issues. Settlers moving west stimulated regular guerrilla warfare between newcomers and natives, interrupted by more formal or military warfare, usually undertaken by the American army. The federal army and state militias often managed relations with the natives, moving them westwards or onto reservations either with considerable bloodshed or subdued by passive despair.[27] This was masculine territory, and men were in charge. In disputes between competing white settlers and between white settlers and "others," like Hispanics, Chinese, and African Americans, the quality of law and justice frequently depended on the local agents of enforcement, whether sheriffs, marshals, judges, vigilantes, or particular mediators, like Texas Rangers or Wells Fargo employees. But racism did not make for peaceful relations. Even when white settlers argued among themselves, individualism, malleable law officers, the constitutional right to bear arms, and the masculine code of "no duty to retreat" encouraged both violent confrontations and physical protests. The thousands of western movies produced in Hollywood and elsewhere, and the numerous dime and pulp novels, have only served to confirm a wild image and one that was most definitely male-dominant and masculine in character.[28]

Recent interpretations of western law and order in Canada and the United States have suggested moderating these long-standing interpretations of mild and wild. From the Canadian viewpoint, some analysts suggest that the order was not always as even-handed or as systematic as earlier portrayed. Native peoples faced major difficulties under the Treaty provisions, suffering from a policy of domination, malnutrition, and starvation. While the Mounted Police served as military, police, and civil officials for a generation after early settlement, they were unable to systematically patrol, let alone manage, such a vast area as the entire Canadian Northwest in the late nineteenth century. They certainly could provide an effective force in specific areas at specific times; for example, when their numbers were increased in the Yukon at the time of the gold rush. Yet their presence was often thin on the ground when local disputes emerged in the Prairies. Furthermore, they tended to use their discretion when intervening or not intervening in disputes and taking action against law-breakers. It would seem that the Mounted Police were not as reliable and impartial as traditionally suggested. Nevertheless, they did operate in a society in which respect for authority was more ingrained and in which the use of firearms was less flagrant.[29] There was both law and disorder in the Canadian West.

American historians might decide to come to a similar conclusion. Some of these are already suggesting that the western legal system offered protection to settlers and produced no more violence than existed in other parts of the United States. They argue that in newly settling communities, whether urban or rural, misdemeanours were more prevalent than serious crimes and that institutions providing order soon followed the arrival of families. Certainly there remains a view that law did not provide justice as seen within the well-established framework of "the western war of incorporation," and that injustice for the "others," whether sheep farmers, homesteaders, Mexican miners, or Chinese workers, led both to vigilantism and rapid punishment.[30] But what is emerging from a new school of western legal historians is a call to ascertain more information about the mechanics of the western legal systems rather than continuing to deconstruct images of wildness. There are numerous layers of western legal history that have not yet been explored, and only careful examination of specifics within issues, like the law of cattle drives and the open range, law for Native Americans, water law, and mining law, can bring better understanding of the ways in which the legal order worked.[31] The relationship of violence to this order has complicated interpretations of all American society because of the question of firearms. As Americans claim the constitutional right to bear arms, the gun culture argument will neither go away nor be easily resolved, either in the American West of the nineteenth and early twentieth centuries or in American society in general in the twenty-first century.

For all the long and sometimes acrimonious discussions of mild and wild Wests, very little progress has been made with raising gendered concerns. It seems to matter little where the West is or when it is analyzed. The relative scarcity of women in non-agricultural settlements has given law and order a masculine dominance, often in connection with alcohol, gambling, and brawling. Some women were featured in this masculine interpretation because they were prostitutes who broke the law and flouted the conventions of respectable femininity. Yet often these workers were tolerated, suggesting that masculine interpretation of the law was flexible. Though tolerated, little is yet known about the sexual harassment of or violent behaviour suffered by such sex-industry workers on either side of the border. In farming settlements where there was less likely to be a sexual imbalance there is little discussion about women's personal safety and their legal rights. Certainly there have been some idealistic notions about codes of male chivalry implying protection, and women themselves have been viewed as civilizers because of their domestic functions, but very little work has been done to ascertain the veracity of such prescriptions. Furthermore, little is known about domestic violence and the incarceration of women in mental asylums. It would seem that women were treated differently from men, and this treatment may have left them vulnerable as much as protected.[32] The traditional clarion call of "missing from history" still applies to most attempts to give women a place in legal issues, let alone an equal treatment. As such, the framework for any gendered class discussion continues to be masculine. But such a discussion should not remain unchallenged. It may take much more work on gender, law, and justice on both sides of the border to answer specific questions, but at least the questions can be raised.

Some of the ideas advanced and the problems raised in connection with these three themes of farming, fur trading, and law and order may suggest that speculation sits side by side with historical research. Teaching a comparative module is sufficiently complex without insisting that gender relations and gendered issues be raised and discussed for each analytical theme.[33] But without at least attempting the framework and choosing the ingredients, both students and historians will not know which questions to ask and what kind of evidence must be recovered to advance an understanding of the gendered past. It may be necessary to wait for much more local research to be undertaken in the western American states and western Canadian provinces before viable syntheses will be accepted. But teaching is about provoking ideas and new strands of thought as well as about giving factual information and discussing cultural values. Working with what is available in a variety of sources and raising questions can provide an understanding of what gendered comparative history should be.

AUTHOR'S NOTE

The original version of this paper was given at the conference "Unsettled Pasts: Reconceiving the West through Women's History," University of Calgary, 13–16 June 2002. I was able to attend this conference thanks to a travel award from the British Academy and financial support from the University of Nottingham. The paper has been revised in the light of comments made at the conference, from listening to and reading the paper of my co-presenter, Mary Murphy, "Latitudes and Longitudes: Teaching the History of Women in the United States and Canadian Wests," and from editorial suggestions. My original ideas have been greatly improved through teaching my final year module, The North American West: Comparative American and Canadian Histories, in subsequent years. I have learned more about comparative history, its strengths and its pitfalls, from preparing the module and from interacting with students than I could have imagined. The insistence that all classes, coursework, and the examination paper be as fully comparative as sources would allow has facilitated profitable insights. Though all involved were challenged, the end results were rewarding both in terms of the comparative method and gendered possibilities.

NOTES

1. Three early and local trans-border studies, namely, Paul F. Sharp, *Whoop-Up Country: The Canadian and American West, 1865–85*, 2nd ed. (Helena: Historical Society of Montana, 1960); Alvin C. Gluek, *Minnesota and the Manifest Destiny of the Canadian Northwest: A Study in Canadian-American Relations* (Toronto: University of Toronto Press, 1965); and Karel D. Bicha, *The American Farmer and the Canadian West, 1896–1914* (Lawrence, KS: Coronado Press, 1968), offer some insights into the central parts of the continent.

2. A useful source for ideas about comparative frameworks between the United States and Canada is Seymour R. Lipset, *Continental Divide: The Values and Institutions of the United States and Canada* (New York: Routledge, 1990). For southwestern history and the Spanish impact see David J. Weber, *The Spanish Frontier in North America* (New Haven, CT: Yale University Press, 1992). For Canadian borders see W. H. New, "The Edge of Everything: Canadian Culture and the Border Field," in *Borderlands: How We Talk about Canada*, ed. W. H. New (Vancouver: UBC Press, 1998), 35–68. Two recent volumes have facilitated the teaching of the comparative Canadian and American Wests: C. L. Higham and Robert Thacker, eds., *One West, Two Myths: A Comparative Reader* (Calgary: University of Calgary Press, 2004) and Carol Higham and Robert Thacker eds., *One West, Two Myths II: Essays on Comparison* (first published as a special issue of *The American Review of Canadian Studies*) (Calgary: University of Calgary Press, 2006).

3. See Lipset, *Continental Divide*. See also Jack Bumsted, "Visions of Canada: A Brief History of Writing on the Canadian Character and the Canadian Identity," in *A Passion for Identity: Canadian Studies for the Twenty-First Century*, ed. David Taras and Beverley Raspovich, 4th ed., (Toronto: Nelson Thompson Learning, 2001), 17–35.

4. See for example courses taught by Sarah Carter and Elizabeth Jameson, Wild West/Mild West? Comparative History of the U.S. and Canadian Wests, at University of Calgary; Mary Murphy, Women in the U.S. and Canadian West, at Montana State University; Royden Loewen, Imagined Communities: Ethnicity and Nationalism in Canada and the United States, at University of Winnipeg; Frances W. Kaye, Intellectual History of the Great Plains, at University of Nebraska-Lincoln; and John Herd Thompson, The U.S. and Canadian Wests, at Duke University.

5. The best examples are Sheila McManus, *The Line Which Separates: Race, Gender and the Making of the Alberta-Montana Borderlands* (Lincoln: University of Nebraska Press, 2005); Simon Evans, Sarah Carter, and W. B. Yeo, eds., *Cowboys, Ranchers and the Cattle Business: Cross Border Perspectives in Ranching History* (Calgary: University of Calgary Press, 2000); Carol L. Higham, *Noble, Wretched and Redeemable: Protestant Missionaries to the Indians in Canada and the United States, 1820–1900* (Albuquerque: University of New Mexico Press, 2000); and Theodore Binnema, *Common and Contested Ground: A Human and Environmental History of the Northwestern Plains* (Norman: University of Oklahoma Press, 2001).

6. Canadian history is infrequently taught in the United Kingdom. It has been and continues to feature as part of imperial or commonwealth history, but as an entity in its own right it is a rare commodity. Since the Canadian High Commission has helped to support Canadian Studies in British universities, academics teaching Canadian materials have been added to existing American Studies departments or have become part of Centres for Canadian Studies. Further support has been given to stimulate the teaching of and research in Canadian Studies in the form of grants for the purchase of library resources and for encouraging other academics to enhance the teaching of Canadian materials. Modules featuring Canadian topics have become more visible, but often with a literary or cultural emphasis. Add to this paucity the declining interest in the academic study of American western history in recent years and a comparative western history course becomes a rare offering. My early knowledge of Canadian history was considerably deepened and widened by a Teaching Enhancement Award from the Canadian High Commission in the summer of 2001.

7. The classic volume of the American West as dream and image remains Henry Nash Smith, *Virgin Land: The American West as Symbol and Myth* (Cambridge, MA: Harvard University Press, 1950). For general approaches to American myth and images see Robert V. Hine and John M. Faragher, "The Myth of the West," in *The American West: A New Interpretive History,* ed. Hine and Faragher (New Haven, CT: Yale University Press, 2000), 472–511; Anne M. Butler, "Selling the Popular Myth," in *The Oxford History of the American West,* ed. Clyde A. Milner, Carol A. O'Connor, and Martha A. Sandiweiss (New York: Oxford University Press, 1994), 771–801. For Canada see Sherrill E. Grace, "Comparing Mythologies: Ideas of West and North," in *Borderlands: Essays in Canadian-American Relations,* ed. Robert Leckler (Toronto: ECW Press, 1991), 243–62; Daniel Francis, *National Dreams: Myth, Memory and Canadian History* (Vancouver: Arsenal Pulp Press, 1997); R. Douglas Francis, *Images of the West: Changing Perceptions of the Prairies, 1690–1960* (Saskatoon, SK: Western Producer Prairie Books, 1989); and Gerald Friesen, "The Imagined West: Introducing Cultural History," in *From Rupert's Land to Canada,* ed. Theodore Binnema, Gerhard J. Ens, and R.C. Macleod (Edmonton: University of Alberta Press, 2001), 195–200. There is an abundance of material on Custer and less, though still adequate information, on Riel. See, for example, Paul A. Hutton, ed., *The Custer Reader* (Lincoln: University of Nebraska Press, 1992); Robert W. Utley, *Custer and the Great Controversy: The Origins and Development of a Legend* (Lincoln: University of Nebraska Press, 1998); Roberta E. Pearson, "The Twelve Custers or Video History," in *Back in the Saddle Again: New Essays on the Western,* ed. Roberta E. Pearson and Edward Buscombe (London: BFI Press, 1998), 197–213; Douglas Owram, "The Myth of Louis Riel," 11–29, Donald Swainson, "Rielana and the Structure of Canadian History," 30–41, and George F.G. Stanley, "The Last Word on Louis Riel: The Man of Several Faces," 42–60, all in *Louis Riel: Selected Readings,* ed. Hartwell Bowsfield (Toronto: Copp Clark Pitman Ltd., 1988); and Maggie Siggins, *Riel: A Life of Revolution* (Toronto: Harper Collins, 1994).

8. The discussion of manhood and masculinity in either the American or Canadian West has yet to be developed fully. Some interesting concepts have been put forward in articles, but as in history in general, men's history is thin on the ground. For thought-provoking ideas see Matthew Basso, Laura McCall, and Dee Garceau, eds., *Across the Great*

Divide: Cultures of Manhood in the American West (New York: Routledge, 2001); Adele Perry, *On the Edge of Empire: Gender, Race, and the Making of British Columbia, 1849–1871* (Toronto: University of Toronto Press, 2001); Catherine Cavanaugh, "'No Place for a Woman': Engendering Western Canadian Settlement," *Western Historical Quarterly* 28, no. 4 (1997): 493–518; Cecelia Danysk, "A Batchelor's Paradise: Homesteaders, Hired Hands and the Construction of Masculinity, 1880–1930," in *Making Western Canada: Essays on European Colonization and Settlement*, ed. Catherine Cavanaugh and Jeremy Mouat (Toronto: Garamond Press, 1996), 154–85; Katherine Morrissey, "Engendering the West," in *Under an Open Sky: Rethinking America's Western Past*, ed. William Cronon, George Miles and Jay Gitlin (New York: W.W. Norton, 1992), 132–44; and Antonia I. Castañeda, "Engendering the History of Alta California, 1769–1848," in *Contested Eden: California Before the Gold Rush*, ed. R. Gutierez and Richard J. Orsi (Berkeley: University of California Press, 1998), 230–59.

9. For different treatments of what might be called the Canadian West see Gerald Friesen, *The Canadian Prairies: A History* (Toronto: University of Toronto Press, 1987); Jean Barman, *The West Beyond the West: A History of British Columbia* (Toronto: University of Toronto Press, 1991); William R. Morrison, *True North: The Yukon and Northwest Territories* (Toronto: Oxford University Press, 1998); and Gerald Friesen, *The West: Regional Ambitions, National Debates, Global Age* (Toronto: Penguin Books, 1999).

10. Frederick Jackson Turner, "The Significance of the Frontier in American History," in *The Frontier in American History* (New York: Henry Holt, 1920), 1–38.

11. Walter Nugent, "Where is the American West? Report on a Survey," *Montana: The Magazine of Western History* 42, no. 3 (Fall 1992): 2–23; Margaret Walsh, *The American West: Visions and Revisions* (Cambridge: Cambridge University Press, 2005), 1–18.

12. The recent debate on what is western history has become unproductive. For those who want to follow the gyrations of the discussions see Alan G. Bogue, "The Significance of the History of the American West: Postscripts and Prospects," *Western Historical Quarterly* 24 (February 1993): 195–221; William Cronon, George Miles, and Jay Gitlin, "Becoming West: Towards a New Meaning for Western History," in *Under an Open Sky*, ed. Cronon, Miles, and Gitlin, 3–17; Patricia N. Limerick, "What on Earth is the New Western History," in *Trails: Towards a New Western History*, ed. Patricia N. Limerick, Clyde A. Milner, II, and Charles E. Rankin (Lawrence: University Press of Kansas, 1991), 83–88; and Gerald Thompson, "The New Western History: A Critical Analysis," 49–72 and Malcolm J. Rohrbough, "The Continuing Search for the American West: Historians Past, Present, and Future," 123–46, both in *Old West/New West: Quo Vadis?*, ed. Gene Gressley (Worland, WY: High Plains Publishing Company, 1994).

13. Harold A. Innis, *The Fur Trade in Canada*, rev. ed. (New Haven, CT: Yale University Press, 1930; Toronto: University of Toronto Press, 1956), especially the conclusion, 383–402; J.M.S. Careless, "Frontierism, Metropolitanism and Canadian History," *Canadian Historical Review* 35 (March 1954): 1–21; Northrop Frye, *The Bush Garden: Essays on the Canadian Imagination* (Toronto: Anansi, 1971), 213–51; R. Cole Harris, "The Emotional Structure of Canadian Regionalism," in *The Challenges of Canada's Regional Diversity*, The Walter L. Gordon Lecture Series, 1980–1981, vol. 5 (Toronto: Omnigraphics Inc., 1981), 9–30; Friesen, *The West: Regional Ambitions*; Gerald Friesen, "The Evolving Meaning of

Regions in Canada," *The Canadian Historical Review* 82, no. 3 (2001): 530–45; R. Douglas Francis, "Turner versus Innis: Bridging the Gap," 473–85, and Frances W. Kaye, "An Innis, Not a Turner," 597–610, both in *American Review of Canadian Studies 33*, no. 4 (Winter 2003); and Lorry W. Felske and Beverly Rasporich, "Challenging Frontiers," in *Challenging Frontiers: The Canadian West*, ed. Felske and Rasporich (Calgary: University of Calgary Press, 2004).

14. For traditional interpretations of agriculture see Gilbert C. Fite, *The Farmer's Frontier, 1865–1900* (New York: Holt, Rinehart and Winston, 1966); Fred A. Shannon, *The Farmers' Last Frontier: Agriculture, 1860–1897* (New York: Holt, Rinehart and Winston, 1945); Vernon C. Fowke, *Canadian Agricultural Policy: The Historical Pattern* (1946; repr., Toronto: University of Toronto Press, 1978); Arthur S. Morton, *History of Prairie Settlement* (Toronto: Macmillan, 1938).

15. There is an abundant and growing literature about women's lives on western farms. For the United States see Glenda Riley, *The Female Frontier: A Comparative View of Women on the Prairie and the Plains* (Lawrence: University Press of Kansas, 1988); Dee Garceau, *The Important Things in Life: Women, Work, and Family in Sweetwater County, Wyoming, 1880–1929* (Lincoln: University of Nebraska Press, 1997); Julie R. Jeffrey, *Frontier Women: "Civilizing" the West? 1840–1880*, rev. ed. (New York: Hill and Wang, 1998); Margaret Walsh, "From the Periphery to the Centre: Changing Perspectives on American Farm Women," in *Working Out Gender: Perspectives from Labour History*, ed. Margaret Walsh (Aldershot: Ashgate Publishing Limited, 1999), 135–50. For Canada see Eliane L. Silverman, *The Last Best West: Women on the Alberta Frontier, 1880–1930*, rev. ed. (Calgary: Fifth House Ltd., 1998); Mary Kinnear, *A Female Economy: Women's Work in a Prairie Province, 1870–1970* (Montreal and Kingston: McGill-Queen's University Press, 1998), 85–99; Eliane L. Silverman "Women and the Victorian Work Ethic on the Alberta Frontier: Prescription and Description," 91–99 and Ann Leger-Anderson, "Saskatchewan Women, 1880–1920: A Field for Study," 65–90, both in *The New Provinces: Alberta and Saskatchewan*, ed. Howard Palmer and Donald B. Smith (Vancouver: Tantalus Research Limited, 1980); Sara B. Sundberg, "Farm Women on the Canadian Prairie Frontier: The Helpmate Image," in *Rethinking Canada: The Promise of Women's History*, ed. Victoria Strong-Boag and Anita C. Fellman (Toronto: Copp Clark Pitman , 1986), 95–106; and Sheila McManus, "Gender(ed) Tensions in the Work and Politics of Alberta Farm Women, 1905–1929," in *Telling Tales: Essays in Western Women's History*, ed. Catherine A. Cavanaugh and Randi R. Warne (Vancouver: UBC Press, 2000), 123–47.

16. Women's roles in the social processes of farming are best discussed in American sources. See, for example, Deborah Fink, "Sidelines and Moral Capital: Women on Nebraska Farms in the 1930s," in *Women and Farming: Changing Roles, Changing Structures*, ed. Wava Haney and Jane Knowles (Boulder, CO: Westview Press, 1988), 55–70; Hal. S. Barron, "Staying Down on the Farm: The Social Processes of Settled Rural Life in the Nineteenth Century North," in *The Countryside in the Age of Capitalist Transformation: Essays in the Social History of Rural America*, ed. Steven Hahn and Jonathan Prude (Chapel Hill: University of North Carolina Press, 1985), 327–43; and Mary Neth, *Preserving the Family Farm: Women, Community, and the Foundations of Agribusiness in the Midwest, 1900–1940* (Baltimore, MD: Johns Hopkins University Press, 1995).

17. For family histories of American farming see John F. Faragher, *Sugar Creek: Life on the Illinois Prairie* (New Haven, CT: Yale University Press, 1986); Lee A. Craig, *To Sow One Acre More: Childbearing and Farm Productivity in the Antebellum North* (Baltimore, MD: Johns Hopkins University, 1993). For a less detailed study of farming communities see Dean L. May, *Three Frontiers: Family Land and Society in the American West, 1850–1900* (New York: Cambridge University Press, 1994). A different view on gendered family farming can be located in Elliott West, *Growing Up with the Country: Childhood on the Far Western Frontier* (Albuquerque: University of New Mexico Press, 1989), 147–76. For Canadian western history see Kenneth M. Sylvester, *The Limits of Rural Capitalism: Family, Culture, and Markets in Montcalm, Manitoba, 1870–1940* (Toronto: University of Toronto Press, 2001). For some comparative insights see John W. Bennett and Seena B. Kohl, *Settling the Canadian-American West, 1890–1915* (Lincoln: University of Nebraska Press, 1995).

18. Riley, *The Female Frontier*, 1–13.

19. Royden Loewen, "Ethnic Farmers and the Outside World: Mennonites in Manitoba and Nebraska," *Journal of the Canadian Historical Association* 1 (1990): 195–214; Royden Loewen, "The Children, the Cows, My Dear Man and My Sister: The Transplanted Lives of Mennonite Farm Women in Manitoba and Nebraska," *Canadian Historical Review* 73 (1992): 344–73; Royden Loewen, "Steinbach and Jansen: A Tale of Two Mennonite Towns, 1880–1900," in *European Immigrants in the American West: Community Histories*, ed. Frederick Luebke, (Albuquerque: University of New Mexico Press, 1998), 161–78; Randy W. Widdis, *With Scarcely A Ripple: Anglo-Canadian Migration into the United States and Canada, 1880–1920* (Montreal and Kingston: McGill-Queen's University Press, 1998), 255–336; McManus, *The Line Which Separates*, 142–78.

20. For information on the Canadian Homestead legislation see Linda Rasmussen et al., *A Harvest Yet to Reap: A History of Prairie Women* (Toronto: The Women's Press, 1979), 148–49. For discussion of the dower campaign or the rights of a wife to have a share in her husband's estate, see Catherine A. Cavanaugh, "The Limitations of the Pioneering Partnership: The Alberta Campaign for Homestead Dower, 1909–1925," *Canadian Historical Review* 74, no. 2 (1993): 198–225; and Margaret McCallum, "Prairie Women and the Struggle for a Dower Law, 1905–1920," *Prairie Forum* 18, no. 1 (1993): 19–34.

21. Marjorie W. Campbell, *The North West Company* (Toronto: Macmillan Company of Canada, 1957); John S. Galbraith, *The Hudson's Bay Company as an Imperial Factor* (Berkeley: University of California Press, 1957); Kenneth W. Porter, *John Jacob Astor Business Man*, 2 vols. (Cambridge, MA: Harvard University Press, 1931); Richard E. Oglesby, *Manuel Lisa and the Opening of the Missouri Fur Trade* (Norman: University of Oklahoma Press, 1963).

22. There are many written accounts and pictorial images of "mountain men." For a romantic appreciation of these workers see Ray A. Billington, *The Far Western Frontier, 1830–1860* (New York: Harper & Row Publishers Inc., 1956), 41–68 and John A. Hawgood, *The American West* (London: Eyre and Spottiswoode, 1967), 103–30. Paintings and sketches of "mountain men" were reproduced and popularized by such firms as Currier and Ives. See Bryan F. Le Beau, *Currier & Ives: America Imagined* (Washington, D.C.: Smithsonian Institution Press, 2001), 131–40.

23. Sylvia Van Kirk, *Many Tender Ties: Women in Fur Trade Society in Western Canada, 1670–1870* (Winnipeg: Watson & Dwyer; Norman: University of Oklahoma Press, 1980); Jennifer

S.H. Brown, *Strangers in Blood: Fur Trade Company Family Marriages in Indian Country* (Vancouver: UBC Press, 1980); Michael Payne, "Fur Trade Historiography: Past Conditions, Present Circumstances and a Hint of Future Prospects," 3–22; Jennifer S.H. Brown, "Partial Truths: A Closer Look at Fur Trade Marriage," 59–80; and Heather R. Driscoll, "'A Most Important Connection': Marriage in the Hudson's Bay Company," 81–107, all in *From Rupert's Land*, ed. Binnema, Ens, and Macleod; Arthur J. Ray, *I Have Lived Here Since the World Began: An Illustrated History of Canada's Native People* (Toronto: Lester Publishing Limited and Key Porter Books, 1996), 160–77; Sarah Carter, *Aboriginal People and Colonizers of Western Canada to 1900* (Toronto: University of Toronto Press, 1999), 47–61; Sylvia Van Kirk, "The Role of Native Women in the Creation of Fur Trade Society in Western Canada, 1670–1830," in *The Women's West*, ed. Susan Armitage and Elizabeth Jameson (Norman: University of Oklahoma Press, 1987), 53–75; Sylvia Van Kirk, "'What If Mama Is an Indian?': The Cultural Ambivalence of the Alexander Ross Family," in *The Developing West: Essays in Canadian History in Honour of Lewis H. Thomas*, ed. John E. Foster (Edmonton: University of Alberta Press, 1983), 123–36; Jacqueline Peterson, "Prelude to Red River: A Social Portrait of the Great Lakes Métis," *Ethnohistory* 25, no. 1 (1978): 41–67; and Elizabeth Vibert, "Real Men Hunt Buffalo: Masculinity, Race and Class in British Fur Traders' Narratives," *Gender & History* 8, no. 1 (1996), 4–21.

24. There are some examples of women's participation in a few articles on the Mountain West. See, for example, William R. Swaggerty, "Marriage and Settlement Patterns of the Rocky Mountain Traders and Trappers," *Western Historical Quarterly* 11 (April 1980): 159–80; John M. Faragher, "Custom of the Country: Cross Cultural Marriage in the Far Western Fur Trade," in *Western Women: Their Land, Their Lives*, ed. Lillian Schlissel, Vicki L. Ruiz, and Janice Monk (Albuquerque: University of New Mexico Press, 1988), 199–215, and Michael Lansing, "Plains Indian Women and Interracial Marriage in the Upper Missouri Trade, 1804–1868," *Western Historical Quarterly* 31 (Winter 2000), 413–33. See also Barton H. Barbour, *Fort Union and the Upper Missouri Fur Trade* (Norman: University of Oklahoma Press, 2001), 127–31.

25. For the new gendered American fur trade history see Susan Sleeper-Smith, "Women, Kin and Catholicism: New Perspectives on the Fur Trade," *Ethnohistory* 47, no. 2 (2000): 432–52; Susan Sleeper-Smith, *Indian Women and French Men: Rethinking Cultural Encounter in the Western Great Lakes* (Amherst: University of Massachusetts Press, 2001). See also Tanis C. Thorne, *The Many Hands of My Relations: French and Indians on the Lower Missouri* (Columbia: University of Missouri Press, 1996). For other gendered developments of cultural and economic exchange in this region see Lucy E. Murphy, *A Gathering of Rivers: Indians, Métis and Mining in the Western Great Lakes, 1737–1832* (Lincoln: University of Nebraska Press, 2000). For discussions of Métis see Jennifer Brown and Theresa Schenck, "Métis, Mestizo and Mixed Blood," in *A Companion to American Indian History*, ed. Philip J. Deloria and Neal Salisbury (Oxford: Blackwell Publishers Ltd., 2002), 321–38. The most useful source on this subject in the New Indian History in this region and in this period is Richard White, *The Middle Ground: Indians, Empires and Republics in the Great Lakes Region, 1659–1815* (New York: Cambridge University Press, 1991).

26. Keith Walden, "The Great March of the Mounted Police in Popular Literature, 1873–1973," *Historical Papers* of the Canadian Historical Association, (1980), 33–56; R.C.

Macleod, "Canadianizing the West: The North-West Mounted Police as Agents of the National Policy, 1873–1905," in *Essays on Western History: Essays in Honour of Lewis Gwynne Thomas*, ed. Lewis H. Thomas (Edmonton: University of Alberta Press, 1976), 101–10; Robert C. Macleod, "Law and Order on the Western-Canadian Frontier," in *Law for the Elephant, Law for the Beaver*, ed. John McLaren, Hamar Foster, and Chet Orloff (Pasadena, CA: The Ninth Judicial Circuit Historical Society, 1992), 90–105; Daniel Francis, "The Mild West: The Myth of the RCMP," in *National Dreams*, 29–51.

27. Violent encounters with the native population or problems of law enforcement connected to native peoples are usually discussed as part of either military history or the history of native peoples. For example, see Robert M. Utley, *Frontier Regulars: the United States Army and the Indian, 1866–1891* (New York: Macmillan, 1973), and Robert M. Utley, *Frontiersmen in Blue: The United States Army and the Indian, 1848–1865* (Lincoln: University of Nebraska Press, 1981).

28. Roundtable, "How the West Got Wild: American Media and Frontier Violence," *Western Historical Quarterly* 34 (Autumn 2000): 277–95; Philip D. Jordon, *Frontier Law and Order* (Lincoln: University of Nebraska Press, 1970); Wayne Gard, *Frontier Justice* (Norman: University of Oklahoma Press, 1949); W. E. Hollon, *Frontier Violence: Another Look* (New York: Oxford University Press, 1974); Richard M. Brown, *No Duty to Retreat: Violence and Values in American History and Society* (Norman: University of Oklahoma Press, 1994).

29. For interpretations of Canadian policy to Native peoples see J. R. Miller, ed., *Sweet Promises: A Reader on Indian-White Relations in Canada* (Toronto: University of Toronto Press, 1991). William A. Baker, ed., *The Mountain Police and Prairie Society, 1873–1919* (Regina, SK: Canadian Plains Research Center, 1998) offers a collection of essays that demonstrate revisionist interpretations of the Mounted Police. His introductory essay, "Twenty-five Years After: Mounted Police Historiography Since the 1973–74 Centennial of the Force," (vii–xvi), provides a useful survey of changing views. See also William R. Morrison, *Showing the Flag: The Mounted Police and Canadian Sovereignty in the North, 1894–1925* (Vancouver: UBC Press, 1985).

30. Brown, *No Duty to Retreat*; Richard M. Brown, "Violence," in *Oxford History*, ed. Milner, O'Connor, and Sandweiss, 393–425; Richard M. Brown, "Western Violence: Structure, Values, Myth," *Western Historical Quarterly* 24 (February 1993): 5–20; Richard White, *"It's Your Misfortune and None of My Own": A New History of the American West* (Norman: University of Oklahoma Press, 1991), 328–52; Patricia N. Limerick, *The Legacy of Conquest: The Unbroken Past of the American West* (New York: W.W. Norton, 1987), 222–92; Clare V. McKanna Jr., *Homicide, Race and Justice in the American West, 1880–1920* (Tucson: University of Arizona Press, 1997).

31. Gordon M. Bakken, ed., *Law in the Western United States* (Norman: University of Oklahoma Press, 2000); Sarah Barringer Gordon, "Law and the Contact of Cultures," 130–42, and Michael A. Bellesiles, "Western Violence," 162–78, both in *A Companion to the American West*, ed. William Deverell (Oxford: Blackwell Publishing Ltd., 2004).

32. There is an abundance of women's history on American prostitutes in western mining communities that offers insights into lives of prostitutes as workers. Their legal entanglements have infrequently found their way into general interpretations of law and order. See, for example, Anne Butler, *Daughters of Joy, Sisters of Misery: Prostitutes in the*

American West, 1865–90 (Urbana: University of Illinois Press, 1985); Paula Petrik, *No Step Backwards: Women and Family on the Rocky Mountain Mining Frontier, Helena, Montana, 1856–1900* (Helena: Montana Historical Society Press, 1987), 25–58; Elizabeth Jameson, "Women as Workers, Women as Civilizers: True Womanhood in the American West," 145–64, and Mary Murphy, "The Private Lives of Public Women: Prostitution in Butte, Montana, 1878–1917," 192–206, both in *The Women's West*, ed. Armitage and Jameson. There is less information on prostitution in western Canada. See S.W. Horall, "The (Royal) North-West Mounted Police and Prostitution on the Canadian Prairies," *Prairie Forum* 10, no. 1 (1985): 1–16; Char Smith, this volume; Charlene Porsild, *Gamblers and Dreamers: Women, Men and Community in the Klondike* (Vancouver: UBC Press, 1998), 99–136. One of the few volumes on domestic violence in the American West remains David Del Mar, *What Trouble I Have Seen: A History of Violence against Wives* (Cambridge, MA: Harvard University Press, 1996). For insights into the Canadian West see Terry L. Chapman, "'Til Death do us Part': Wife Beating in Alberta, 1905–1920," *Alberta History* 26, no. 4 (1988): 13–22.

33. My module, The North American West: Comparative American and Canadian Histories, is not specifically gendered. The difficulties of obtaining sources is problematic, but so too is the perception of students who often do not wish to take a gendered module. Gender issues are raised in lectures and seminars and students are allowed to select their own essay titles. I have read several excellent essays that demonstrated understanding of gender issues in terms of female and male relationships, and some intriguing essays on myths that took up issues of masculinity.

16

LATITUDES AND LONGITUDES

Teaching the History of Women in the U.S. and Canadian Wests

MARY MURPHY

TEACHING THE HISTORY of women in the North American Wests is a dual proposition. The persistence of myths about the West in the popular culture of the United States and Canada means that some dismantling of those myths needs to take place before we can locate women in the past of both countries and chart their histories. In the United States one "national" myth of the West was spawned by Frederick Jackson Turner, who portrayed the frontier as the womb in which American democracy gestated, a place that nurtured individualism, materialism, and cowboys, and that was integrated into the United States through war, conquest, and the heroic actions of individual men. Canada does not figure into this American story, but the United States figures into the Canadian myth in the role of foil. One of the important components of the Canadian story of western settlement is how un-American it was. Where conquest of the U.S. West was violent, messy, chaotic, and individualistic, by contrast—so the myth goes—the settlement of western Canada was orderly, peaceful, corporate, and much less traumatic for aboriginal peoples.[1]

Despite the differences in these myths, their one common denominator is that they are stories by, about, and for European, Euro-Canadian, and Euro-American men. The myths of the West as created in the late nineteenth and early twentieth centuries are alive and well and wreaking havoc every day. Here I speak from the experience of living in Montana, and I cannot speak for the Canadian West. But in Montana and the rest of the United States, state and personal politics bear the weight of the legacy of conquest, racism, and patriarchy, exemplified in the cowboy politics for which America is notorious. As long as these myths continue to circulate in popular culture and inform, on deep-seated cultural levels, the policy making of states, then two consequences result: first, women continue to be erased from the popular history of the North American West, and second, all women and all non-white men are denied full and equal places in their respective nations. Our myths and stories tell us who we are and serve as the basis for who we believe we should be. These so-called "national" myths are not my stories. They are not what inspires in me any affection for or allegiance to this region or nation. They give me no place in the politics of the West. Retelling these stories as "national" presumes nations of white men.

While it is true that at the genesis of these stories white men were the only fully enfranchised citizens of western Canada and the United States, happily that situation has changed. It is incumbent upon us, then, to stop recounting these myths in such uncritical ways. And, more importantly, to teach alternative stories that from a scholarly point of view are more complicated, multi-vocal, and multi-cultural, and that from a political point of view allow people other than white men to see themselves as westerners, people who have a past and a future in a region and nation in which they have a right and duty to act.

In teaching a course on Women in the U.S. and Canadian West, my goal is to provide those alternative stories of the region that secure women a place in the past and the future. The metaphor of latitudes and longitudes refers to the two axes about which this upper-division course is structured. One axis is drawn from the commonalities of women's experiences across the border. That meridian intersects the parallels of the different political, economic, and legal conditions imposed upon women by the two nation states. By the end of the semester, ideally, we will first have come to some understanding of how the geographic and economic continuities of the western part of the continent shape women's work and family lives in similar ways. Second, we will have explored how, despite the commonalities of geography, of women's biology, and of a dominant Anglo culture, women's lives in the U.S. and Canadian Wests differed because of the structure and policies of the two nation states.

LONGITUDES

THE LIVES OF WOMEN in both the Canadian and American Wests have been shaped by a natural resource economy. In the United States this is usually referred to as an extractive economy, in Canada as the staples economy. Furs, fish, and timber; metals, such as gold, silver, and copper; fuels, like coal, oil, and natural gas; and a bounty of agricultural products, chiefly cattle and grains, have flowed out of the region by river, rail, and road. North and south of the 49th parallel, the West is a vast expanse of forests, fields, and grazing districts punctuated by clear cuts, oil wells, strip mines, and the skeletons of old metal mining gallus frames.[2] For a women's history course, the questions are these: what are the consequences of this kind of economy for women? How has the growth of this economy affected indigenous women? What kind of paid work becomes available to women? What is family life like? What kinds of communities are built in mining, logging, ranching and farming areas, and what role do women play in those communities?

I approach this section of the course through the frameworks of commercialized and non-commercialized domesticity. In other words, women's traditional work has been the maintenance and reproduction of the family, an unpaid task that most often takes place in the home. But once the West was conquered, it became a region in which single men were often the majority of the population well into the twentieth century. Demography and the staples economy, which provided few manufacturing jobs for women, dictated that women's paid work in the West was often some aspect of domestic work. Whether paid or unpaid, women's work, how it was organized, shared, rewarded, or suffered through, constitutes a main focus of the class.[3]

A related longitude is tied to the skewed sex ratio generated by the presence of many more white men than white women in the region. What have been the implications of that demographic profile for native and white women, and for men? One of the classic "myths" of the white women's West has been that scarcity conferred special value. For example, there are many stories from the history of mining towns of men paying exorbitant amounts of gold dust in exchange for a biscuit made by a white woman's hand or some other seemingly trivial interaction with a white woman. Typically the presence of white women, even in small doses, has been seen as a "civilizing" influence.[4] Adele Perry, in her essay "'Oh, I'm Just Sick of the Faces of Men': Gender Imbalance, Race, Sexuality, and Sociability in Nineteenth-Century British Columbia," notes that white women were seen as "necessary participants in the process of colony-building in three ways: they would raise the moral tone of the white, male-dominated society, quell the rapid development of a mixed-blood community, and ensure that British law, mores, and economic development flourished."[5] The same sentiment held true south of the border. Perry offers an anecdote that indicates some national rivalry in the competition for white women. A Canadian in 1865 noted that many respectable single men wanted to make British Columbia home, but "the scope for selecting wives is so limited that they feel compelled to go to California in search of their interesting object, and not infrequently are they tempted to remain on American soil—their industry as producers and expenditure as consumers being lost to the colonies."[6] Perry argues that the issue of gender imbalance should prompt us to look critically into the actual relationships between men and women, and between native and non-native women in this demographically tilted terrain. Closely reading some of the nineteenth-century accounts of western travelers is a good exercise through which to pursue this topic in class.[7]

A third commonality between the women's Wests, also related to demography, is the high percentage of immigrants in both regions during the late nineteenth and early twentieth centuries. For example, by 1940 half of the residents of the Prairie provinces identified themselves as other than British in origin.[8] In the United States, between 1870 and 1910 the percentage of European-born people who lived in the mountain states was the highest in the nation.[9] This made for an interesting and sometimes contentious mix of ethnic and racial cultures in western cities and countrysides. It also led to the formation of various ethnic associations in which women often played key roles; these were part of the plethora of voluntary associations that women organized on both sides of the border and that have been well-documented by historians. This material allows students to study the parts women played in the formation of communities and to see how different ethnic groups defined women's roles.

A fourth point of comparison is the role of women in the imperial agendas of both nations. This is a tricky issue to study and a tricky issue to teach. As Catherine Cavanaugh and Randi Warne point out in the introduction to *Telling Tales: Essays in Western Women's History*, "integrating women into Western colonization and settlement is complicated by Anglo women's status as both colonizer (members of the dominant culture) and colonized (by patriarchy) within a country that was both colony and colonizer."[10] There are several routes into this topic that are effective in the classroom. A fairly direct path is found by examining the activities of female missionaries and teachers charged with the "civilizing" of indigenous peoples. The ironies involved in their teaching Euro-Canadian or Euro-American culture and appropriate domestic skills to native women, while simultaneously escaping from marriage and domesticity themselves, is always intriguing to students. Yet missionary women's chafing under the male authorities of the church, Indian agents, or boarding school superintendents is a powerful lesson about the limits of Euro-American and Euro-Canadian women's "liberation." Fortunately, there is a great deal of good literature on this topic, especially in the works of Peggy Pascoe, Margaret Jacobs, Myra Rutherdale, David Wallace Adams, and Carol Higham.[11]

A more circuitous route into issues of colonialism, but one that offers the advantage of visual aids, is a discussion of the role of women artists and patrons of native arts. Joan Jensen, Margaret Jacobs, Laura Moore, Douglas Cole, and Lisa MacFarlane, among others, have written about the role that non-native women collectors and patrons of the arts played in "reviving," shaping, and developing markets for "traditional" native arts in the United States and Canada.[12] This is a more subtle part of the colonial project but speaks to the topic of indigenous peoples' self-representation and cultural production and its appropriation by non-native consumers. Another facet of this is the way in which non-native women artists chose to represent native people, their cultures, and their landscapes in photography and paint. There is now considerable literature about non-native women who photographed aboriginal peoples, much of it appropriate for class discussion, with images all over the Web for easy access. After studying some of these images, a good exercise is to have students hunt for contemporary native women painters and photographers and analyze how their work addresses issues of conquest and colonialism.[13]

It is also telling that North America's three most prominent women artists, Emily Carr, Georgia O'Keeffe, and Frida Kahlo, were all intimately engaged with painting cultural artifacts and landscapes associated with indigenous North America. I end the class with a week examining the work of these three women, drawing upon Sharyn Rohlfsen Udall's book, *Carr, O'Keeffe, Kahlo: Places of Their Own*. There are many websites that have digital images of all three women's paintings, providing students access to a wide array of their work.[14]

LATITUDES

I COME NOW to the latitudes of this project—that is, how the policies and practices of Canada and the United States cut through the meridians of women's lives north and south of the border. Despite the shared Anglo culture of the majority of peoples in Canada and the United States, political structures, property laws, and foreign policy developed quite differently. To illustrate how the state affects women's lives, we need to focus on some particular issues, and among those possibilities are homesteading and women's property rights, the situation of women in the relocation of Japanese Americans and Japanese Canadians during World War II, and the legal status of aboriginal women.

Women homesteaders and farmers are a favorite topic of western women's historians, and accounts by rural women form some of the classic texts of the field. Among these are Elinore Pruitt Stewart's *Letters of a Woman Homesteader*, published in the United States in 1913, and Georgina Binnie-Clark's *Wheat and Woman*, published in Canada in 1914.[15] The stories of farm women's lives echo across the border. Isolation, loneliness, hard physical labor, high birth rates and a dearth of competent medical care, as well as love of the plains and prairies, satisfaction found in gardens and raising poultry, pleasure in dances, pie socials, and club meetings are common experiences of women in the Prairie provinces and the plains and mountain states. But American and Canadian stories diverge when it comes to access to land ownership. Women on both sides of the border could buy land, but many more women in the United States could claim free land under a variety of homestead laws. This forms a basic difference between the experiences of Stewart and Binnie-Clark. Elinore Stewart filed on a homestead and used her prose to advertise the happiness and independence western homesteads could provide women. Georgina Binnie-Clark was barred from homesteading and had to buy her farm. She used her pen to agitate for women's right to homestead.

In Canada the only women who could file on homestead land were widows, divorced women, and—if well documented—separated or deserted wives who had children under eighteen years of age for whom they were the sole support.[16] Rural Canadian women's lives were made even more precarious by the abolition of dower laws in the Prairie provinces, which eliminated women's control over the disposal of family property and negated widows' legal guarantee of inheritance. Both issues prompted long political struggles for women's property rights. In the United States controversy revolved around married women's rights to homestead, but the original Homestead Act of 1862 held that single women could claim free land. And while dower rights steadily eroded in the nineteenth-century United States, Married Women's Property Acts, passed in a variety of states beginning in the 1850s, predated those laws in Canada, and gave women south of the border economic protection that women north of the border did not have.[17]

Another example of state policy shaping women's lives is the story of the Issei and Nisei in the North American West. Both the United States and Canada practiced institutional racism in their treatment of residents of Japanese descent during World War II. Both declared defense or security zones along the West coast and implemented policies to remove the roughly 23,000 Japanese Canadians and 100,000 Japanese Americans from that zone. But the two countries did not carry out their policies in precisely the same fashion, and the differences particularly affected family life. In the United States, although male leaders of the Japanese American community were interned immediately following Pearl Harbor, many were united with their families when moved to relocation camps and, in general, families remained together. In Canada, able-bodied men were initially sent to work in road camps in British Columbia and sugar beet projects on the Prairies, or to internment in a POW camp in Ontario. The remaining Japanese Canadian population, including women and children separated from their husbands and fathers, were moved to former mining towns where they lived in poorly renovated ramshackle buildings or newly built small cabins. There they had to support themselves using their savings, through subsistence, and with the proceeds of state-run property sales, which garnered them a pittance of the value of their belongings. While the majority of Japanese Americans also lost property, it was not taken through government process and in some cases, as in the community of Cortez, California, studied by Valerie Matsumoto, residents were able to arrange custodial management of their property during the war so that they could return to their homes when the government released them from the camps. Perhaps the most significant difference between the two countries is that the United States rescinded exclusion orders in 1944 and 1945, and Japanese Americans were permitted to return to the West coast. In Canada, Japanese Canadians were forced to choose between deportation and relocation east of the Rockies *after* the war, and they were not permitted back into British Columbia until 1949.[18]

There are many powerful works that portray the relocation experience. For class discussion, I have juxtaposed the reading of Joy Kogawa's
novel *Obasan,* about her family's Canadian travails, with the film *A Family
Gathering,* produced by Lise Yasui and Ann Tegnell, about Yasui's family,
which was removed from the Hood River region of Oregon.[19] Both these
texts provide good historical background about the government policies that devastated the lives of Japanese Canadian and Japanese American
families during the war. They are both told from a female's point of view,
and they are excellent means of exploring the impact of state policy on
women's lives and the nature of history as a social and familial construct.
Kogawa's protagonist and Yasui must break through years of silence and
sort through multiple tales in each family's past to uncover pivotal events
that took place during the war. The mystery of both texts, as well as the
women's engagement in the reconstruction of their families' histories,
helps draw students to the immediacy of the past and the personal consequences of state policies.

The "politics of identity" is at the core of the internment experience
and is an issue that has become an integral part of many women's studies classes. How do race, class, and gender interact to form women's
identities? How do the political identities of women of different races
and classes intersect with feminism? How do we acknowledge and respect
the multiplicity of women's identities and yet find commonalities that
affect all women? There are many approaches to these questions, and
frequently the investigation seeks answers in the realm of culture, ethnicity, and sexuality. But the state also shapes identity politics, and another
way to examine that is through the laws and regulations by which Canada
and the United States legislated the identity of aboriginal women who
married non-Indian men. The following examples point only to the
legal differences in the fate of Indian women who chose to marry white
men. In the course of a class they can be put in the context of the long
history of intermarriage during the fur-trade era and the social and cultural effects that new legal structures had on family formation and on
the status of men and women who stepped outside their cultures to
marry.[20]

In both countries, state practice had its roots in complicated beliefs about race, assimilation, miscegenation, and patriarchy. Both countries started with the premises of English common law, yet the law as implemented in the two nations established different legal, political, and economic conditions for native women. Beginning with the 1869 Enfranchisement Act and continuing through a series of Indian Acts, the Canadian government decreed that "an Indian woman who married a non-Indian man lost her status as a registered Indian, as did her children."[21] This meant that she lost her eligibility to live on reserve land. Subsequent Indian Acts deprived her of additional rights and privileges of registered Indians. If widowed, she did not regain her status unless she married another Indian man. If she married an Indian from another band, she was transferred to that band regardless of her own wishes. The law stripped from her many of the structures that supported her Indian identity. Conversely, if a white woman married an Indian man, she obtained legal status as an Indian, as did her children, and they could all live on a reserve. Women and children's "racial identity" followed that of father and husband, at least in a legal sense.[22]

In the United States, no single federal law addressed the status of men and women of mixed marriages. Instead, states enacted a web of laws to prohibit such marriages from taking place at all. Washington Territory passed a law banning marriage between whites and persons of "more than one-half Indian blood" in 1855. Oregon adopted a similar measure eleven years later.[23] As greater numbers of Asian immigrants and African-Americans arrived in the West after the Civil War, the laws were enforced more stringently to prevent marriage between whites and Chinese, Japanese, Filipinos, Hawai'ians, and blacks, but provisions against marriage between whites and Native Americans remained in place in many states.[24]

Another significant difference in the attitudes toward mixed marriages and mixed-blood children in the United States was how the state quantified Indians. In 1910, during the height of Jim Crow segregation in the U.S., the Census for the first time enumerated the children of Indian and white marriages as "mixed-bloods," defined as "all persons of mixed white and Indian blood who have any appreciable amount of Indian blood." They were to be counted as Indians "even though the proportion of white blood may exceed that of Indian blood."[25] Because most mixed marriages occurred between white men and Indian women, children's "racial identity" followed that of their mothers.

In addition, a legal twist shaped different experiences across the border for native women who married white men in the United States. Murray Wickett's study of Oklahoma in the late nineteenth century turned up hundreds of men who took advantage of the provision that "if a white citizen of the United States intermarried with a tribal citizen of one of the independent Indian nations, that person received full citizenship rights in the tribe, including the right to share in tribal lands."[26] Texans seeking grazing lands after the Civil War were assiduous and blunt suitors. One Chickasaw woman declined a Texan's unflattering proposal that they get married because "you have the land. I have the cattle."[27] When the Indian nations realized how exploitative such marriages could be, they took measures to rectify the situation; in some cases they required that whites provide proof of "good moral character" before receiving a marriage license, in other instances marriage license fees were set so high that indigent whites would be prohibited from marrying natives.[28] In these examples, federal and tribal laws, north and south of the border, shaped the identity of indigenous women, their economic welfare, and the communities in which they could raise their children.

Shortly after I began working at Montana State University, I decided that it only made sense to include Canada in my western women's history class, because the two Wests shared so much in terms of environment and economy. As I have taught this course, I have come to see a reason for teaching a comparative class that did not occur to me when I was simply thinking about being more geographically inclusive. All of us who teach women's history take as a given that race, class, and ethnicity are part of the constructions of gender and of identity. But I confess that the role of the state in the construction of gender had been something of a sleeping monster in my teaching. Organizing a class that deals with women in different nations makes clear how integral the state is in that process, and further, it allows students to see more clearly how gender is constructed in different times, places, and societies.

Teaching western women's history in a public western university is enormously fun. Practically all the students have family stories relevant to the course material. In some semesters we have "show-and-tell" days during which students bring in artifacts and photographs that relate to their family's connection to the region. Students often discover hidden women's histories in their own families. All the rewards that come from teaching women's history—acquainting students with a past that, for most, was unknown or shadowy at best, witnessing their outrage at oppression and their admiration for women who defied constraints to achieve personal or social goals—are augmented in this class because using a comparative approach nudges students to see that history's "unfolding" is not a "natural" process, but is one of struggle and choice that can develop quite differently depending upon the country in which one lives. Introducing students to new women's voices, telling different stories, allows them to see their ancestors as the actors who engendered this region's past and to see themselves as contemporary creators of the North American Wests.

AUTHOR'S NOTE

My thanks to Susan Kollin and Sheila McManus for their careful reading of this essay.

NOTES

1.　C.L. Higham and Robert Thacker, eds., *One West, Two Myths: A Comparative Reader* (Calgary: University of Calgary Press, 2004).

2.　General texts that describe the economy of the U.S. West include Richard White, "*It's Your Misfortune and None of My Own": A New History of the American West* (Norman: University of Oklahoma Press, 1991), and Robert V. Hine and John Mack Faragher, *The American West: A New Interpretive History* (New Haven, CT: Yale University Press, 2000). On the Canadian West see Jean Barman, *The West Beyond the West: A History of British Columbia* (Toronto: University of Toronto Press, 1991), and R. Douglas Francis and Howard Palmer, ed., *The Prairie West: Historical Readings*, 2d. ed. (Edmonton: University of Alberta Press, 1992).

3.　There are many monographs and collections of essays on women in the U.S. and Canadian Wests that analyze domesticity and work among other topics. For example, see Gillian Creese and Veronica Strong-Boag, eds., *British Columbia Reconsidered* (Vancouver: Press Gang Publishers, 1992); Mary Kinnear, *A Female Economy: Women's Work in a Prairie Province, 1870–1970* (Montreal: McGill-Queen's University Press, 1998); Catherine A. Cavanaugh and Randi R. Warne, eds., *Telling Tales: Essays in Western Women's History* (Vancouver: UBC Press, 2000); Susan Armitage and Elizabeth Jameson, eds., *The Women's West* (Norman: University of Oklahoma Press, 1987); and Elizabeth Jameson and Susan Armitage, eds., *Writing the Range: Race, Class, and Culture in the Women's West* (Norman: University of Oklahoma Press, 1997).

4.   See Susan Lee Johnson, *Roaring Camp: The Social World of the California Gold Rush* (New York: W.W. Norton, 2000) for a wonderfully insightful analysis of gender in the gold rush.

5.   Adele Perry, "'Oh, I'm Just Sick of the Faces of Men': Gender Imbalance, Race, Sexuality, and Sociability in Nineteenth-Century British Columbia," *BC Studies: The British Columbian Quarterly* 105–106 (1995): 34.

6.   Perry, "Oh, I'm Just Sick," 33.

7.   To help frame the discussion of race and colonization, see Ann Laura Stoler, *Carnal Knowledge and Imperial Power: Race and the Intimate in Colonial Rule* (Berkeley: University of California Press, 2002); and Anne McClintock, Aamir Mufti, Ella Shohat, eds., *Dangerous Liaisons: Gender, Nation, and Postcolonial Perspectives* (Minneapolis: University of Minnesota Press, 1997). On western women's travel narratives, see Brigitte Georgi-Findlay, *The Frontiers of Women's Writing: Women's Narratives and the Rhetoric of Westward Expansion* (Tucson: University of Arizona Press, 1996).

8.   Cavanaugh and Warne, *Telling Tales*, 9.

9.   Mary Murphy, *Mining Cultures: Men, Women and Leisure in Butte, 1914–1941* (Urbana: University of Illinois Press, 1997), 8.

10. Cavanaugh and Warne, *Telling Tales*, 12.

11. Peggy Pascoe, *Relations of Rescue: The Search for Female Moral Authority in the American West, 1874–1939* (New York: Oxford University Press, 1990); Margaret Jacobs, *Engendered Encounters: Feminism and Pueblo Cultures, 1879–1934* (Lincoln: University of Nebraska Press, 1999); Myra Rutherdale, *Women and the White Man's God: Gender and Race in the Canadian Mission Field* (Vancouver: UBC Press, 2002); David Wallace Adams, *Education for Extinction: American Indians and the Boarding School Experience, 1875–1928* (Lawrence: University Press of Kansas, 1995); and Carol L. Higham, *Noble, Wretched & Redeemable: Protestant Missionaries to the Indians in Canada and the United States, 1820–1900* (Albuquerque: University of New Mexico Press, 2000).

12. Joan M. Jensen, *One Foot on the Rockies: Women and Creativity in the Modern American West* (Albuquerque: University of New Mexico Press, 1995); Laura Jane Moore, "Elle Meets the President: Weaving Navajo Culture and Commerce in the Southwestern Tourist Industry," *Frontiers: A Journal of Women's Studies* 22, no.1 (2001): 21–44; Douglas Cole, *Captured Heritage: The Scramble for Northwest Coast Artifacts* (Seattle: University of Washington Press, 1985); Lisa MacFarlane, "Mary Schäffer's 'Comprehending Equal Eyes,'" in *Trading Gazes: Euro-American Women Photographers and Native North Americans, 1880–1940*, ed. Susan Bernadin et al. (New Brunswick, NJ: Rutgers University Press, 2003).

13. Bernadin, et al., *Trading Gazes*; Laura Wexler, *Tender Violence: Domestic Visions in an Age of U.S. Imperialism* (Chapel Hill: University of North Carolina Press, 2000); Judith Fryer Davidov, *Women's Camera Work: Self/Body/Other in American Visual Culture* (Durham, NC: Duke University Press, 1998); Anne Maxwell, *Colonial Photography and Exhibitions: Representations of the "Native" and the Making of European Identities* (London: Leicester University Press, 1999); Carol J. Williams, *Framing the West: Race, Gender, and the Photographic Frontier in the Pacific Northwest* (New York: Oxford University Press, 2003). On contemporary native photographers, see Jane Alison, ed., *Native Nations: Journeys in American Photography* (London: Barbican Art Gallery, 1998); and Diane Newmaier, ed., *Reframings: New American Feminist Photographies* (Philadelphia: Temple University Press, 1995).

14. Sharyn Rohlfsen Udall, *Carr, O'Keeffe, Kahlo: Places of Their Own* (New Haven, CT: Yale University Press, 2000).

15. Elinore Pruitt Stewart, *Letters of a Woman Homesteader* (Boston: Houghton Mifflin, 1913); Georgina Binnie-Clark, *Wheat and Woman* (Toronto: Bell & Cockburn, 1914).

16. Binnie-Clark, *Wheat and Woman*, xxi.

17. For an overview of western Canadian women's legal battles, see Alison Prentice, et al., *Canadian Women: A History* (Toronto: Harcourt Brace Jovanovich, 1988). For a discussion of the homestead dower, see Catherine Cavanaugh, "The Limitations of the Pioneering Partnership: The Alberta Campaign for Homestead Dower, 1909–1925," in *Making Western Canada: Essays on European Colonization and Settlement,* ed. Catherine Cavanaugh and Jeremy Mouat (Toronto: Garamond Press, 1996). On U.S. women's legal status, see Joan Hoff, *Law, Gender & Injustice: A Legal History of U.S. Women* (New York: New York University Press, 1991).

18. On the experience of Japanese Canadians, see Patricia E. Roy, *Mutual Hostages: Canadians and Japanese during the Second World War* (Toronto: University of Toronto Press, 1990); Roy, "Lessons in Citizenship, 1945–1949: The Delayed Return of the Japanese to Canada's Pacific Coast," *Pacific Northwest Quarterly* 93 (Spring 2002): 69–80; and Midge Ayukawa, "From Japs to Japanese Canadians to Canadians," *Journal of the West* 38, no. 3 (July 1999): 41–48. On the U.S. experience, see Valerie Matsumoto, *Farming the Home Place: a Japanese Community in California, 1919–1982* (Ithaca, NY: Cornell University Press, 1993).

19. Joy Kogawa, *Obasan* (New York: Godine, 1982; New York: Anchor Books, 1994); Lise Yasui and Ann Tegnell, producers, *A Family Gathering* (PBS video, 1989).

20. For the broad context of these issues see Sylvia Van Kirk, *Many Tender Ties: Women in Fur Trade Society in Western Canada, 1670–1870* (Winnipeg: Watson & Dwyer; Norman: University of Oklahoma Press, 1980); David Smits, "'Squaw Men,' 'Half-Breeds,' and Amalgamators: Late Nineteenth-Century Anglo-American Attitudes Toward Indian-White Race-Mixing," *American Indian Culture and Research Journal* 15, no. 3 (1991): 29–61; Martha Hodes, ed., *Sex, Love, Race: Crossing Boundaries in North American History* (New York: New York University Press, 1999).

21. Sarah Carter, *Aboriginal People and Colonizers of Western Canada to 1900* (Toronto: University of Toronto Press, 1999), 117.

22. For a fuller discussion, see Kathleen Jamieson, *Indian Women and the Law in Canada: Citizens Minus* (Ottawa: Advisory Council on the Status of Women, 1978), and Jamieson's

update on the law in "Sex Discrimination and the Indian Act," in *Arduous Journey: Canadian Indians and Decolonization*, ed. J. Rick Pointing (Toronto: McClelland & Stewart, 1986), 112–36. Also see Jean Barman, "What a Difference a Border Makes: Aboriginal Racial Intermixture in the Pacific Northwest," *Journal of the West* 38, no. 3 (July 1999): 14–20.

23. Barman, "What a Difference a Border Makes," 18.

24. Peggy Pascoe, "Race, Gender and Intercultural Relations: The Case of Interracial Marriage," in *Writing the Range*, ed. Jameson and Armitage, 71; Margaret Jacobs, "The Eastmans and the Luhans: Interracial Marriage between White Women and Native American Men, 1875–1935," *Frontiers: A Journal of Women's Studies* 23, no. 3 (2002): 32; and Roger D. Hardaway, "Unlawful Love: A History of Arizona's Miscegenation Law," *Journal of Arizona History* 27, no. 4 (Winter 1986): 377–90.

25. Barman, "What a Difference a Border Makes," 19.

26. Murray R. Wickett, *Contested Territory: Whites, Native Americans, and African Americans in Oklahoma, 1865–1907* (Baton Rouge: Louisiana State University Press, 2000), 37. Ironically, many of the same Indian nations passed strict laws against intermarriage with African Americans.

27. Wendy St Jean, "'You Have the Land. I Have the Cattle': Intermarried Whites and the Chickasaw Range Lands," *Chronicles of Oklahoma* 78, no. 2 (2000): 187.

28. Wickett, *Contested Territory*, 38.

CONTRIBUTORS

SUSAN ARMITAGE is Claudius O. and Mary W. Johnson Distinguished
Professor of History at Washington State University and Director
of the Center for Columbia River History. She is the co-editor (with
Elizabeth Jameson) of *The Women's West* (1987) and *Writing the Range:
Race, Class, and Culture in the Women's West* (1997) and a co-author of a
widely-used U.S. history textbook, *Out of Many*. She is currently at
work on a history of women in the greater Pacific Northwest.
Professor Emeritus at the University of British Columbia, **JEAN BARMAN**
has taught Canadian educational history at the University of
British Columbia. Her *Sojourning Sisters: The Lives and Letters of Jessie
and Annie McQueen* (Toronto: University of Toronto Press, 2003)
won the Canadian Historical Association's Clio Award and the
Governor General's Medal presented by the British Columbia
Historical Association, both for best book in British Columbia
history published in 2003.
NORA FAIRES teaches history and women's studies at Western Michigan
University. A scholar of migration, she is co-author of *Jewish Life in
the Industrial Promised Land, 1855–2005* and *Permeable Border: The Great*

Lakes Basin as Transnational Region, 1650–1990. She plans to expand her research on gendered imperialism by investigating chapters of the American Woman's Club established in Canada and in other nations.

CHERYL FOGGO has been published and has produced extensively as a journalist, screenwriter, poet, playwright, writer of fiction and non-fiction, and as a young adult novelist. Her books have received many provincial and national award nominations, including the Governor General, the Blue Heron, the Silver Birch, and the R. Ross Annett. Her most recent play, *Heaven*, received a national playwriting nomination as well as a Betty Mitchell best new play nomination and aired on CBC's national *Sunday Showcase* in 2004. Also an award-winning screenwriter and director, her documentary film *The Journey of Lesra Martin* won a bronze award at the Columbus International Film and Video Festival. Her journalism has been published in *Canadian, The Globe and Mail, Canadian Consumer, Western Living, Legacy, AlbertaViews, Alberta Venture, Calgary Magazine*, and *The Calgary Herald*. Ms Foggo was invited in 2006 by the Canadian High Commissions of Jamaica and Barbados to participate in those countries' Black History Month celebrations.

MARGARET D. JACOBS is an associate professor of history at the University of Nebraska, Lincoln, and the author of *Engendered Encounters: Feminism and Pueblo Cultures, 1879–1934* (1999). She is currently working on a manuscript, "White Mother to a Dark Race," regarding white women's roles in the United States and Australia in the removal of indigenous children from their families to institutions between 1880 and 1940.

ELIZABETH JAMESON holds the Imperial Oil-Lincoln McKay Chair in American Studies at the University of Calgary. She was Co-Chair of the "Unsettled Pasts" conference organizing committee, and served on the Steering Committee of the 1983, 1984, 1987, and 2000 Women's West Conferences. She has published on the histories of western women, western labor, mining, and the Canada–United States borderlands. Her books include two co-edited anthologies (with Susan Armitage), *The Women's West* and *Writing the Range: Race, Class, and Culture in the Women's West*, and *All That Glitters: Class, Conflict, and Community in Cripple Creek*.

JOAN M. JENSEN is a Professor Emeritus of history at New Mexico State University. A senior scholar of rural women's histories, her many books include *With These Hands: Women Working on the Land*, and *Promise to the Land*. In 2006, the Minnesota Historical Society Press published her *Calling This Place Home: Women on the Wisconsin Frontier, 1850–1925*, which received "Honorable Mention" for social/cultural history from the Merle Curti Award Committee of the Organization of American Historians. She is the co-author, with Darlis Miller, of a formative essay in western women's history, "The Gentle Tamers Revisited."

CYNTHIA LOCH-DRAKE is completing a doctorate in history at York University in Toronto, Ontario. She developed an interest in women and work in Alberta while living in Fort McMurray during the 1980s and working at the Syncrude oil sands plant, and at the local newspaper.

SHEILA McMANUS is Associate Professor of History at the University of Lethbridge in southern Alberta. Her book *The Line Which Separates: Race, Gender, and the Making of the Alberta-Montana Borderlands* was published by the University of Nebraska Press in 2005.

LAURIE MERCIER is Professor of History at Washington State University Vancouver (the other Vancouver). She is author of *Anaconda: Labor, Community and Culture in Montana's Smelter City* (University of Illinois, 2001) and co-editor of *Mining Women: Gender in the Development of a Global Industry, 1670–2005* (Palgrave/MacMillan, 2005)

MARY MURPHY is Michael P. Malone Professor of History at Montana State University, Bozeman. She is the author of *Hope in Hard Times: New Deal Photographs of Montana, 1936–1942* (Montana Historical Society Press, 2003), *Mining Cultures: Men, Women, and Leisure in Butte, 1914–1941* (University of Illinois, 1997), and numerous articles in gender history.

HELEN RAPTIS is an assistant professor in the Education Faculty at the University of Victoria. Her areas of study include educational history, sociology, and policy studies.

MOLLY P. ROZUM is an assistant professor of U.S. history at Doane College in Crete, Nebraska. She earned her PhD at the University of North Carolina at Chapel Hill and is a native of South Dakota. Her research focuses on sense of place and regional identity on North America's northern grasslands.

CHAR SMITH completed a Master's degree at the University of Calgary with a focus on women's legal history. This article stems from her thesis research on prostitution in British Columbia. She is currently co-owner of a historical research consulting firm focussing on women's and First Nations research and litigation management.

Professor Emeritus **SYLVIA VAN KIRK** has recently taken early retirement from the University of Toronto where she taught Canadian History for almost 30 years. She pioneered courses in women's history and aboriginal/non-aboriginal relations and has written widely on aspects of early western Canadian social history. Her book *Many Tender Ties: The Role of Women in Fur Trade Society in Western Canada 1670–1870* has become a classic in its field. Van Kirk is now living in Victoria, and her current research projects focus on the experience of HBC/native families as they settled in colonial Victoria in the mid-19th century. She is also branching out into "living" history projects and is helping to develop heritage programming for the Church of Our Lord, Victoria's oldest church building, opened in 1876.

MARGARET WALSH is Professor of American Economic & Social History in the School of American & Canadian Studies at the University of Nottingham, UK. Her recent publications include *Making Connections: The Long Distance Bus Industry in the United States* (2000) and *The American West: Visions and Revision* (2005).

INDEX

American Society of Equity (ASE),
183–84
American Women's Club of Calgary
activities, 263, 270, 272–73,
274–76
membership, 265–66, 267–70, 275
origins, 238, 262–63, 264, 265
purpose, 261–64, 270, 282–84
response to World wars, 271–72,
273, 276–82
Anaconda, MT, 332
Anaconda Copper Mining Company,
319
Anaconda (Mercier), 309
Ancestors in the Americas (PBS program),
176
Anderson, Benedict, 32
Anzaldúa, Gloria, 32, 33
Armitage, Susan, 9
art, Native, 416
Asher, Julia Short, 38–40

Baird, Harry, 327
Baker, Conrad, 40
Baker, George, 36
Barron, Hal, 130
Battles, Mrs., 40
Bausquet, E. M., 325
beauty, 39–40, 137, 143, 146, 157
Beavers, Mrs. Roy, 269
Beierbach, Dorothy, 358, **366, 371**
Benfield, Dorothy, 281
Bennett, Erma, 320
Bennett, R. B., 266–67
Binnie-Clark, Georgina, 417
Blackfoot
and Annora Brown, 130, 131, 136,
138, 139
fear of, in U.S., 37–38

mobility across Canada–U.S.
border, 34–35
and Nez Perce, 59
and North-West Rebellion, 38, 39
Blatchford, Mrs. William H., 270
Bly, Carol, 170
Boag, Peter, 66–67
Booth, Cleo, 225
border crossing
and economic opportunity, xxii–
xxiii, 166–67, 242–43
to escape trouble, xxii, 247–48
by ethnic groups, xxii–xxiii
for family ties, 167
and gold rush fever, 71–72
by Natives, 173
by prostitutes, 237–38, 239,
241–43, 247–49
and questions of identity, xix,
239–40
and transnational histories, 18
white women's experience of, 4,
13, 40–41, 118
borderlands
Annie McQueen's experience of,
116
effect of, on BC prostitution, 244,
245–46, 253–54
grasslands women's experience
of, 156
historians' interpretations of,
31–32, 42–43, 50
Icelander immigrant view of,
147–48, 150
in Jensen family history, 167
Mary Dodge Woodward's
experience of, 8
and Métis, 173
as portrayed in *Lone Star*, 7–8

Cold War, 312, 317, 321, 324–27, 331–32, 334

Collins, Patricia Hill, 204

colonialism
on Alberta's grasslands, 138–39
in BC, 73–74, 122, 123–24
and disappearing cultures, 175
and racist assumptions, 101
and removal of Native children from families, 192, 193, 196–99, 206
by white women, 415–16. *See also* race and racism

communism, 316, 321, 324–27, 342, 345

communities, 40, 68, 245–47, 252, 294–95, 316

comparative history, xiv–xv, 385–86, 392–401

Congress of Industrial Organizations (CIO), 311, 316, 321, 325

Cosgrove, Mrs. Clarence, 270

Coultis, Mrs. S.G., **281**

Cowaret, Kathleen, 228–29

Cowdrey, Mary, 12

Cranmer, Mabel, **366**

Cridge, Edward, 88

Critchley, Mrs. E.T., 270, **282**

Crosby, Emma Douse, 103–07, **104,** 112

Crosby, Thomas, 103, 105

Daughters of the Allies, 272, 276

democracy, 152

Densmore, Frances, 172

deportation, 238, 250, 253–54

Depression of 1930s, 273–74, 275–76

disease, 59–60, 65–66

Dissette, Mary, 200

distance education, 228–29

Divet, Edith L., 13

Dodge, Daniel, 9–10

Dodge, Walter (Walter Woodward), 9, 12

Donation Land Law, 68–69

Douglas, Abel, 109

Douglas, Amelia, 62, 84

Douglas, James, 62, 65, 70, 72, 86

Dream Dance, 172

Drew, Sadye Wolfe, 40–41

DuBois, Constance Goddard, 206–07

ecological consciousness, 132, 138–39, 143–44, 146, 154–57, 159n9

Edmonton, AB, 304–5

education
BC government role in, 111, 215–16, 218, 221, 222–26, 227, 231
in Calgary, 266
by correspondence course in BC, 218, 222, 223, 224–26
distance education in BC, 228–29
industrial schools, 34–35
and industrial training for Natives, 203–04
of interned Japanese-Canadian students, 222–26
language intstruction for immigrants, 227–28
Native boarding schools, 191–95, 198, 203
and racism in BC, 189–90

Elkins, Mr. and Mrs., 333

Emmerton, Caroline, 184

environmentalism. *See* ecological consciousness

ethics and writing history, 177–81, 255n8

ethnicity, xxii–xxiii, 19, 244–46,
350–51, 350–52, 352, 415. *See
also* immigration
exceptionalism, 43

Fallow, W.A., 345
farming
in Alberta, 133, 134
in BC, 116, 117
industrial, 130, 138
male domination of, 10, 11, 392
in Oregon Country, 66–67
as theme in western history
teaching, 392–95, 417–18
on U.S. grasslands, 130, 141, 148,
154–55
in Wisconsin, 167
women's role in, 183–84, 185. *See
also* homesteading
Farnham, Thomas, 62
First Nations. *See* Native peoples
Fisher, George, 109–10
Flanagan, May, 35
Fleming, Tom, 216
Fletcher, Alice, 197, 198, 199, 203, 205
Foggo, Cheryl, 238–39, 293–307
Folsom, Cora, 199
Forcade, Mrs. V.V., **282**
Ford, Clinton B., 360
forest industry, 320
Fort MacLeod, AB, 134, 135
Foucault, Michel, 32
Fraser River gold rush, 71–72
Freisen, Gerald, 390
frontier framework of western
history, 15–16, 19, 150–51, 389,
411–12
Frye, Northrup, 390

fur trade, 17, 56, 60–63, 70–71, 391,
395–97. *See also* Hudson's Bay
Company

Geddes family, 40
gender conflict
assumptions about historical role
of, 99, 101
in union auxiliaries, 328–31, 333
and division of labour, xx, 10,
57–58, 310–11, 318, 353–55
in industrial work, 317–20
in Medalta strike, 343, 360,
363–64, 370–72
in Mine Mill, 317, 319, 326–27, 329,
331–32, 335
over access to wage work, 349–50
over anti-communist attacks on
unions, 326–27, 331–32
over wage rates, 347, 350, 355–58
in unions, 311, 335–36
German immigration, 166, 167,
171–72, 174, 175, 180–81, 350,
351
Gibson, James, 62
Gibson, Mary Douglas, 38
Gilpin, Eunice, 13
Gjerde, Jon, 19
Goforth, Marie, 328
Goldman, Marion, 246
gold mining, 71–72, 105, 176
Gordon, Annie McQueen, 110–17, **114**
Gordon, James, 115–16
Gore-Hickman, T. O'B., 341, 363
Grahame, William, 37
Great Britain, Government of, xviii,
72–73, 74, 266, 393–94, 395
"great man" history, 95
Green, Harry, 11
Griswold, Helen Tyler, 200

history, 311, 315–16, 346
legacy, 316–17
and Medalta Potteries strike, 342, 345, 359
racial tensions in, 334
and women's auxiliaries, 322–24, 328–35
mining, 18, 71–72, 242–44, 311–12, 316–24, 413–14
missionaries, 64, 71, 73, 83, 103, 105–06, 200–02, 415
Mitchell, Rose, 193, 194
Montana, 33, 35, 316, 319, 412
motherhood, 196–99, 201–02, 203–04, 247
Motter, Mrs. F. M., 281
multiculturalism, 17–18, 84, 142–43, 171–72
mythologized West
African-Americans' roles in, 146–47
Annora Brown's rejection of, 133–34
and Canadian v. U.S. level of violence, 16–17, 29, 116, 137–38, 145–46, 150, 249, 397–400, 411–12
deconstruction of, in history courses, 387–88, 391
Era Bell Thompson on, 141–42, 144–45
and fur trade, 396
and marginalization of women, xix–xx, 15–16, 19, 411–12
Natives' role in, 15–16, 17, 20, 46n27, 141–42
and practice of good history, 43, 381–83
prostitutes' role in, 242, 243, 253

role of men and women in western settlement, 15–16, 19, 29–30, 56, 131–32, 411–12, 414
Thorstina Jackson Walters' experience of, 150, 151

National Council of Women, 265
national histories, xvi, 3–4, 14, 19–20
nationalism, 265–66, 267, 277
nation states, 32, 41–42
Native peoples
and art, 416
assimilation policy, 192–93, 195–97
under British control in BC, 72–74
in Constance Lindsay Skinner's writing, 118, 120–21
and Canadian Government, 33, 398, 420
child removal to boarding schools, 191–95, 199–208
and colonialism, 415–16
and disease, 65–66
in Era Bell Thompson's writing, 141–42, 147
education of, 189–90, 203–04
effect of Canada–U.S. border on, 7, 18, 34–35
fear of, 12, 37–39, 152, 153
feelings of victimization, 174
and fur trade, 61, 62, 396, 397
and gold mining, 71
Indian Acts, 34, 36, 92, 420
Isabella W. St German's story, 177–78
legal status in Canada and U.S., 33–34, 419–21
life of Maria Fisher, 107–10
and missionaries, 103, 105, 106

increased policing of, 249–54
in mining towns, 72, 311
mobility of, 245–46, 249
and Native women, 34, 73
violence in, 400

Quinton, Amelia S., 195–96, 197,
200–01

race and racism
and Asian immigration to
Canada, 167, 251
in BC education, 189–90
and British immigration schemes,
74
in Constance Lindsay Skinner's
writing, 120–21
in Era Bell Thompson's story, 142,
146, 147
on the frontier, 17, 18
in fur trade, 60, 63, 70–71
and industrial schools, 34–35
and inter-racial relationships,
300–02
and Japanese relocation camps,
190
of McQueen sisters, 115, 116
at Medalta Potteries, 351–52, 353
and Native child removal policy,
199–208
Native concept of, xx–xxi, 59, 110
racist assumptions about people
of colour, 101, 123, 156, 248,
279, 350, 352–53
in resource-based industries, 318,
319, 334
social concept of, xx–xxi
and status of African-American
women, 35–36

Thorstina Jackson Walters' view
of, 152, 154
towards African-Americans, 142,
296–97, 299, 303
towards African-Canadians,
239–40, 294, 295–96, 304–07
towards mixed race couples, 109,
110
towards Native wives of
Europeans, 83, 84
towards Ross family, 83, 84, 85,
86, 88
in U.S.–Mexico relationship, 30
Rae, William, 342, 345, 359
railroad, 110–11, 112
Rash, Charlotte M., 325
RCMP (Royal Canadian Mounted
Police), 16, 17, 163n51
Reat, S.C., 268
Red Cloud Woman, 172
Red Feather Woman, 172
Reel, Estelle, 196, 198–99, 203,
204–05
Reginbal, Alfred, 279
regional history, 49–50, 51–52, 56
regional identity, 69–70, 75, 130,
146–47, 157
Reid, Ruth, 330
religion, 105–06, 111, 196, 199, 200–02,
253. See also missionaries
Rember, John, 65
Riel, Louis, 11, 12
Riel Rebellion, 11, 12, 13, 34, 38–39, 150
Riley, Glenda, 393
Robbins, Martin, 17
Rocky Mountains, 39–40
Roosevelt, Theodore, 160n20
Ross, Charles, 51–52, 82–83
Ross, Flora, 84, 85, 88–89, 91
Ross, Isabella, 51–52, 82–87, 88, 91